The Best of Writers & Company

The Best of
Writers & Company

Eleanor Wachtel

BIBLIOASIS
WINDSOR, ONTARIO

FIRST EDITION

Library and Archives Canada Cataloguing in Publication

Wachtel, Eleanor, author
    The best of writers & company / Eleanor Wachtel.

Issued in print and electronic formats.
ISBN 978-1-77196-074-8 (paperback).--ISBN 978-1-77196-075-5 (ebook)

    1. Authors, English--20th century--Interviews. 2. Authors, English--21st century--Interviews. 3. Authors, Canadian--20th century--Interviews. 4. Authors, American--20th century--Interviews. I. Title. II. Title: Best of writers and company.

PN453.W2485 2016   820.9'00914   C2015-907388-X
                                              C2015-907389-8

Readied for the press by Dan Wells
Edited by Carroll Klein
Copy-edited by Allana Amlin
Typeset by Chris Andrechek
Cover designed by Gordon Robertson

 Canada Council for the Arts   Conseil des Arts du Canada    ONTARIO ARTS COUNCIL / CONSEIL DES ARTS DE L'ONTARIO

 Canadian Heritage   Patrimoine canadien

Published with the generous assistance of the Canada Council for the Arts and the Ontario Arts Council. Biblioasis also acknowledges the support of the Government of Canada through the Canada Book Fund and the Government of Ontario through the Ontario Book Publishing Tax Credit.

PRINTED AND BOUND IN CANADA

To
Sandra Rabinovitch
&
Mary Stinson

CONTENTS

Notes Towards an Introduction   ix

Jonathan Franzen   1

Edwidge Danticat   19

Orhan Pamuk   45

Aleksandar Hemon   79

Anne Carson   113

Doris Lessing   135

Hilary Mantel   161

W.G. Sebald   185

Alice Munro   205

J.M. Coetzee   223

Yiyun Li   239

Seamus Heaney   265

Toni Morrison   281

Mavis Gallant   307

Zadie Smith   323

Acknowledgments   355

NOTES TOWARDS AN INTRODUCTION
by Eleanor Wachtel

In late 1975, when I moved to Vancouver, I heard about a job on the local morning show at CBC Radio. It was behind the scenes, as a producer, but once I met with the executive producer, it turned out that the position was already filled. I could freelance, he said. But I had to do something that the regular studio host could not do, something a little unusual—quirky was probably the word.

I brought in a list of ideas and he checked off half a dozen. I set out with a home portable tape recorder and tried to interview a Mexican mime who was performing at the Art Gallery. Next, I talked to a sociologist at UBC who was studying sign language in sawmills. Because of the excessive noise, the workers had developed a sophisticated system of communicating with each other, even telling jokes in sign language.

Clearly, I had not grasped the medium of radio.

My third attempt was more successful: an interview with Frances Adaskin, who had accompanied her violinist husband, Harry, all her professional life and was making her solo piano debut at age seventy-two. She was gracious, charming, articulate. The result was my own debut on live radio, with a carefully crafted script; I would be interviewed by the show's host and introduce my tape clips. I learned to write the way I speak, so I could have the reassurance of my own words in front of me. I did many of these 'tape-talks' as they were called, as well as short documentaries, and for six years as theatre critic for the morning show, I would be on the air the morning after the night before. After a play, I'd go home, eat something to stay awake, and sit at the typewriter, creating a tiny play—a dialogue between the hosts and me. I'd bring in the script: an introduction and questions for them, answers for me. I remember one host who would read the newspaper while I delivered my lines; she'd look up when I finished and pitch the next question.

Probably the height of this freelance radio work was the opportunity in 1980 to interview Tennessee Williams for the network CBC show *Sunday Morning*, when his play *The Red Devil Battery Sign* was produced by the Vancouver Playhouse. He wore a white suit and for most of our hour together his eyes were closed. Later, I read that he'd close his eyes when he was bored. Twice he became animated: when I asked if he was rich and when I misquoted Blanche's famous line from *A Streetcar Named Desire*, "I've always depended on the kindness of strangers." I said "relied" but of course "depended" has the right weight. Williams had a tic of punctuating his speech with "y'know," and for weeks afterwards I'd imitate it because I had spent so much time editing our conversation down to clips for the *Sunday Morning* mini-doc.

Another aspect of my West Coast literary career was writing lengthy profiles of BC authors—from bill bissett and Audrey Thomas to Phyllis Webb and Jack Hodgins—for *Books in Canada*. I even slipped in a couple of non-BC writers like Elizabeth Smart and Carol Shields. I'd take my own photographs and could write in a more personal style than my magazine work for more commercial outlets such as *The Financial Post Magazine, Homemaker's* or *City Woman*.

But by the mid-'80s I came to realize that geography—not biology—is destiny if you're a CBC freelancer. Not only would you be paid less if you worked for local as opposed to national radio shows (something that has since changed) but opportunities for meaningful work in the arts were drying up 'in the regions.' In late 1987, I accepted a one-year contract to be 'literary commentator' for a three-hour weekend omnibus CBC arts program in Toronto called *State of the Arts*. A year later it morphed into a daily arts show, *The Arts Tonight*, and I was invited to stay on as writer-broadcaster, contributing tape-talks and also one-minute-twenty-second pieces (including forty-second clips) for the morning segments known as *The Arts Report*—the haiku of arts journalism.

I would still write the odd magazine feature, but I found the rhythm of radio, its immediacy, appealing. Occasionally, I'd be invited to fill in for *The Arts Tonight* host, Shelagh Rogers. When interviewing for print or tape clips, I'd aim the mic at the guest and fade into the wallpaper; although I was encouraging and engaged, I lacked presence. Now as a host, I had to learn to make audible responses.

One day, over lunch with the department head, I was asked what my ideal job would be. I said to host a weekly show, since it would allow for greater depth than a daily. He smiled: not likely. At this point, I'd been offered a tenure-track position teaching creative non-fiction at a university in BC and a job as a literary bureaucrat in Ontario, but he didn't know that. Still, I opted to continue with the insecurity of radio because it was more fun. Hard to believe that was more than a quarter century ago. A few months later, a weekly book show lost its host and I was invited to take over and create a new one.

Twenty-five years ago, the world looked a little different. In 1990, Germany was newly reunified. Yugoslavia's communist regime collapsed. In South Africa, the dismantling of Apartheid began, with Nelson Mandela finally released from prison. A crisis building in the Persian Gulf would soon lead to war. And the first Internet server was created—the foundation for the World Wide Web.

Twenty-five years ago, I sat behind a microphone at CBC Radio and welcomed listeners to a new program called *Writers & Company*. The format wasn't exactly the same then, but what hasn't changed, from the very beginning, was the desire to delve into the work and lives of the best writers—new and established—from around the world.

I have to admit that when I looked back to see who was on the show that very first season, I was amazed. To give you just a sample: from Canada, Alice Munro, Mordecai Richler, Rohinton Mistry, Margaret Atwood, Carol Shields. From England, Penelope Lively, Angela Carter, William Boyd, Peter Ackroyd, Victoria Glendinning, A.S. Byatt, Fay Weldon. From the US, Mark Helprin, Amy Hempel, George Plimpton, Calvin Trillin, Gordon Lish. From St. Lucia, Derek Walcott. From Israel, Amos Oz. From India, Vikram Seth. From Kenya, Ngugi Wa Thiongo. From South Africa, J.M. Coetzee and Nadine Gordimer. Among others.

Some of these writers went on to win the Nobel Prize in Literature. Many came back on the show with new work. A span of twenty-five years has given me the opportunity to follow a career from the inside, so to speak. Through the years, every interview has provided its own particular and memorable pleasure.

I've interviewed many writers but Michael Ondaatje is the only writer to have interviewed me. Right from the start, he was a great friend to *Writers & Company* and to me. When I first moved to Toronto, he invited me to parties and made me feel welcome. After the program was on the air for only a couple of years, he suggested that I publish a selection of interviews, recommending Louise Dennys at Knopf Canada. The result was *Writers & Company* (1993) and *More Writers & Company* (1996). When the show approached its tenth anniversary in 2000, Michael agreed to participate in a celebratory event. His name on the panel helped us entice other international writers. Then for the program's twentieth anniversary, when a colleague proposed that *I* be interviewed on stage, I balked, saying only if Michael Ondaatje were the interviewer. I figured I was safe, but he's such a good sport that before I knew it, I landed in front of a sold-out audience of more than 450 at the Bluma Appel Salon at the Toronto Reference Library.

Michael began like this:

ONDAATJE You've become these last years a very essential tradition in radio, not just for writers, but for readers in Canada. And you've been grilling writers for over twenty years, so it's a great pleasure to turn the tables on you. Let's go back to the beginning, the way you usually do.

What's your earliest memory?

WACHTEL My earliest memory: I grew up in Montreal and my first couple of years were spent in the area of the city that Mordecai Richler describes as St. Urbain Street. It wasn't actually St. Urbain Street—that's where he grew up—but it was in that neighbourhood. And I remember crawling down a very long hallway. I never really knew how to describe that environment, but when I interviewed contralto Maureen Forrester, who also grew up in Montreal, she called it a "railway apartment," and I realized that's what it was. There was this long hallway, with rooms off the side like on an old-fashioned train. And the end of the hall, probably the kitchen, seemed very far away as I was crawling along there. My goal was to pull out the pots and pans from the bottom cupboards so I could play with them, creating a certain percussion. We didn't have a lot of toys. But all this had to be before I was two and a half, because then we moved to a different, aspiring middle-class neighbourhood.

Michael asked me about all sorts of things—from childhood reading and the literary life in Montreal to special influences and how I got into radio. Then we came to *Writers & Company*.

ONDAATJE When the first *Writers & Company* was being hatched, what was the idea behind it, and how did that change? Did you imagine it to be what it in fact became?

WACHTEL When it started, the idea was to have more than one interview per program, with some performance element—a dramatic feature or reading—so it would have more of a magazine format. I think the first interview that became a whole show was with Nadine Gordimer, because I remember introducing it, saying, "Today a special program with Nadine Gordimer." It was special because I was a huge admirer of hers, but also because we devoted a whole program to one person. I remember being most nervous before I interviewed her. It wasn't face to face: she was in Johannesburg, I was in Toronto. And I had read somewhere that she had a tongue like a carving knife, so my stomach was just flipping as I sat alone in the studio. But once I asked her the first question, I could tell from the generosity of her answer that it was going to be okay.

ONDAATJE I know you've come up against some writers who have quite strict rules.

WACHTEL There was one. The first time I interviewed J.M. Coetzee, he came to Toronto for the International Festival of Authors with a wonderful novel, *Age of Iron*, which I thought was terrific. He agreed to do two interviews, one for radio and one for *The Globe and Mail*, and I was the radio. It wasn't that he knew me or anything, just that it was, I think, public radio.

So he came into the studio and just before we began, he pulled out a little notebook. It had a pencil in the spine and very thin paper, and he started rustling through it, so I thought, he's checking my name in his appointment book to see who he's talking to. But he said, "Do you mind if I write down the questions?" I said that I didn't mind. Luckily, it wasn't live radio. I'd ask a question, he would write down the question, there would be a long silence, and then without making eye contact, he would answer the question. He would take apart the question a little bit, but would then definitely address it. And this went on, back and forth: question, silence, answer, question, silence, answer. And then after about twenty minutes, he said, "I've lost my voice," but he said it just like I did now, in a normal voice. So I said, "Have some water." He drank and then we continued. By the time the interview was over, he was completely relaxed, and he sat in the studio and just chatted away. That was back in 1991.

Then in 2000, I did a special series in South Africa. One of the advantages of these series is that I get to talk to a lot of people who are well known in their own country but not necessarily outside. But also in going to South Africa, I wanted to see Nadine Gordimer and J.M. Coetzee. He had just won the Booker Prize—his second—for *Disgrace*, though he didn't go to London to accept and didn't give any interviews associated with it. So my producer got in touch—I work with Sandra Rabinovitch on all my special series—saying that I would be coming to Cape Town and would really like to see him. He said, "I really don't like to do interviews, but I remember our last occasion fondly, so I will consider it. But I want to see the questions ahead of time, and I won't talk about myself, about my work, or about South Africa." Such a request is totally exceptional, yet as you know, I'm very tenacious, so we sent in a series of questions, and I guess they somehow came a little bit too close to one of those three forbidden subjects. He sent them back, and he said he didn't really think it was going to work. But I was so determined. And also, he's a beautiful reader, and he had agreed to read from *Disgrace*. Then I remembered that he had written a lot of critical work about Beckett and Dostoevsky, and if we just focussed on those writers and people he had written about, that maybe we could get away with it, and he agreed. So it was a very strange interview. I actually was able to work in a little bit about his background because he had written several memoirs. I knew I couldn't ask directly, but I talked about language and growing up speaking Afrikaans and speaking English and the culture and that sort of thing. And he also—very charming of him—when I asked the questions, he'd respond as if he had never heard them before. He wouldn't go so far as to say, "Oh, that's a good question!" but he responded with apparent interest. I also did allow myself a little bit of follow-up to his answers.

ONDAATJE In fact, it's a great interview. It's really interesting and true.
WACHTEL You published it—
ONDAATJE We published it in *Brick*, yes. Just a wonderful interview because he really is talking about very specific things, and he's so careful. "You mean the New Testament or the Old Testament?" when you asked him about the Bible.
WACHTEL One of my friends tuned into the program late. In my introduction to the broadcast, I said what had happened, what subjects were verboten. But she missed the beginning, and she's listening, she's listening, she's listening, and there's no discussion of his life, his work, *Disgrace*, or South Africa. She called me up and said, "What happened? Did you get hit by a brick or something?"
ONDAATJE I think one of the really wonderful things *Writers & Company* has been doing lately—well, not just lately—is when you've travelled to another country and interviewed writers there. You've gone to India, China, Russia, Turkey, the Middle East, New Zealand, Chile. What made you do that kind of programming, and what stands out for you among these series?
WACHTEL I can't remember where the idea first came from to go to a country and interview its writers. I know that I had wanted to do it even before I was able to, before there was funding. In the early and mid-'90s, I did a series on African writers in exile, but through studios and not actually getting to go anywhere. I remember doing the same thing with writers from Ireland, and it was terrible at the end of one of these conversations to hear a writer say, "It's too bad you're not here; we could go out and sink a pint."

But finally, in 1998, I went to India to produce the first major series on the occasion of the fiftieth anniversary of independence, which was actually 1997, but the Indian celebration of that anniversary was held a little bit late. And, as I mentioned, the tremendous advantage of going to a place is to talk to writers who aren't that well known outside the country. I had already interviewed Salman

Rushdie and Arundhati Roy and Anita Desai. But using an occasion like the fiftieth anniversary, you get a hinge moment in a way, to bring in social and political issues to the conversation and to interview writers in their homes. I remember in India, for instance, interviewing Nayantara Sahgal, who is Nehru's niece and Indira Gandhi's cousin. She lives in Dehradun, in the foothills of the Himalayas. My delight was in going to her house and seeing family photographs on the walls, and just talking to her about growing up through that whole period of the fight for Indian independence.

Another writer in that series was Shashi Deshpande, who lives in Bangalore, in the south, and I remember that in particular because it was so hot. At that time, I used a little minidisc player and one microphone. Before I arrived, she closed all the windows because it was very noisy; there was construction outside on the street. Then I made her turn off the ceiling fan because it would have created too much noise during the interview. And we were both sitting there, sweat pouring down, and we started taking various garments off, and the microphone was sliding through my fingers during the interview. You wouldn't know if you weren't there, but it was memorable.

ONDAATJE Have there been writers who were particularly elusive?

WACHTEL There were a number who were on my wish list for a very, very long time. One of them was Philip Roth, and in fact, he had actually agreed to be interviewed and then cancelled; that was eighteen years ago. And then a few years ago, he agreed again and then cancelled again. Finally last year, I actually got to interview him so I think the show needed to be around for twenty years just so I could get to interview Philip Roth, among other people, like Joan Didion. I'd admired his work for a long time, and it was a great opportunity. I was able to interview him at his apartment on the Upper West Side of New York and it was great. The thing that surprised me was that I had read some interviews—I hadn't read about a razor-sharp tongue or anything like that—but I had read some interviews with him, and he seemed quite truculent in an interview setting, even when he knew the interviewer. So I was a bit worried about going to see him, but he was remarkably gracious and patient. I asked him a question that I hadn't really planned to ask. And it went like this...

WACHTEL What would you like to be if you could live your life again?
ROTH I don't think I would want to be a writer. There are many hard occupations, to be sure. This is one of them. It's very gruelling because you're always an amateur whenever you begin a new book. Yes, you've written before, but you didn't write that book before. So you start off with scraps, and the first six months of a book are usually extremely frustrating and wearying. Everything goes to pot. Your writing goes to pot. Your imagination is insufficient. You don't know what the hell you're doing. You don't know where you're going. And then when you finish a book, you have to start again and come up with another idea, which is also gruelling. So I don't think I'd choose to be a writer again.
WACHTEL Despite the various gratifications—
ROTH Yes, despite the gratifications.
WACHTEL And the successes which you've had?
ROTH Yes, I have had considerable success. No, I don't think I would want a child of mine to do it either. It's too demanding. You are alone. You're the only person who can make it happen. Nobody can help you. And you have to drag this thing out of you. I find it very difficult. I'm sure there are writers who are fluent and who write the way birds sing.
WACHTEL I haven't met them.
ROTH No? Maybe Chekhov did, but I don't.

Although I've often thought that I would have been a good doctor, that I would have enjoyed contact with my patients and that I would have gotten gratification from the work itself. And the problem is that I don't even think in the next life I'm going to be able to do the pre-med course. I'm going to be stuck.

ONDAATJE He's a much more likeable person in his radio interviews than he is in his books. You're right. In the few interviews I've read with him in print journals, he is an unlikeable character.
WACHTEL But what do you think of what he said?
ONDAATJE I don't believe it for a second. Do you believe it?
WACHTEL About whether he'd want to be a writer? You don't believe he wouldn't want to be a writer in his next life?
ONDAATJE He seems to be a compulsive writer. He's not exactly retiring at the age of sixty and playing golf.

WACHTEL Well, he's seventy-six, seventy-seven, now. That's right. He's publishing a book every two years. [Roth actually declared his retirement two years later, in 2012, at age seventy-nine.]

ONDAATJE I'll tell you, what I love about your interview with him is its quietness and its intimacy. There's actually a point where he's talking about his father. You ask him something about his father, and he goes "Hmm," as if he'd never been asked this question before, and it's very, very beautiful. There's something in your interviews with the writers, a link you find between an aspect of their lives and how that influences their work. So you're not really asking them details about biography, but you talk about some emotional state that is important to them and, therefore, important to their work. And that's also why it's very good when you're talking about, with writers like Roth or Mavis Gallant, a book that's thirty years old. So in fact when he's talking about *Goodbye, Columbus* or *Portnoy's Complaint*, he's wonderful and very honest and direct. He has sort of figured out now where it lies in the context of his life. Whereas the new book, he's still not sure. You really do have to wait twenty years to interview everybody from now on.

§

Mavis Gallant was quite different from Roth. When I first interviewed her in 1992, she was full of wit and observation but somewhat daunting, challenging my questions.

On another occasion, when I asked her about love—one of her characters had compared it to practising scales on the piano—she said, "Eleanor, are you asking me if *I* think that? I'm ashamed of you." This was in front a TV crew that flinched en masse, and yet I knew even then that she would continue and elaborate on the question and the story (from *Across the Bridge*, 1993).

Talking to Mavis was not exactly ask, then duck and cover, but rather ask, back it up, and wait. She was ready with a response. When I went to Paris in 2008 to interview her, aged eighty-five, she was not only as quick and engaged as ever, but even enthusiastic. Her memory, like her writing, boasted a remarkable precision, an attention to detail that went back to her days as a journalist for the now defunct *Montreal Standard*.

Gallant had been keeping journals from the time of her arrival in France more than fifty years earlier. She'd been going through them, with an eye to publishing excerpts. I was asking about what it was like for her to look back on some of this material. And she launched into a long account of Christmas Day 1962.

It wasn't a happy time. She'd been invited to Germany by a close friend, a journalist, who had recently married. She and her new husband had bought a house and she wanted Mavis to meet the husband and see the new house. Mavis described how she'd been ill but had recovered. So what would be better than to buy some new clothes and go to a place she hadn't seen before? The trip was a disaster: her friend's mother took an instant dislike to her. The husband's family wouldn't receive foreigners. Mavis was left on her own on Christmas Eve while the friend went to her husband's family and the mother went to Midnight Mass without her.

So there she was, alone in a strange house with huge picture windows and the blackness outside. "I couldn't draw the drapes," she said, "and I saw every ghost. I was frightened, I was scared to death. There were two huge sheep dogs growling." (She growls.) The parrots' cage was open and two parrots hopped and flapped about (their wings had been clipped). "I was terrified. I kept seeing headlines in *The Globe & Mail*: 'Canadian writer mauled to death by dogs, parrots, and man with a knife!'"

Finally, she got to her room, locked the door, and called the airport to book the next flight out, only to get an answering machine saying everything was shut down for the holidays. At the end of the tale, Mavis said to me, Of course you can't use this. This happened repeatedly—during another story she added, You know, I'm just talking. Later, which is why you're getting to read this, she revised her view, concluding that her friend and her mother were likely dead and she didn't care about the husband anyway.

When I was doing research about Mavis Gallant, I started to feel that there are two camps or perspectives on Canada's two master storytellers, Mavis Gallant and Alice Munro, as if you needed to champion one over the other, like favouring the Rolling Stones over the Beatles, or Jean-Luc Godard over François Truffaut. I don't know why that should be, but the absurdity of it hit me as I reflected on how lucky we are to live in a place that produced and has been the beneficiary of such extraordinary talent.

I've always loved stories—the more digressions the better—the stories I read but also the stories writers tell me about themselves and how they see their lives, how those lives intersect with their writing, but mostly I admire their particular combination of candour and imagination.

I remember Carol Shields saying that she never read novels to escape—not even when she was very ill—but reading for her was a necessary enlargement of her life. Carol quoted St. Augustine who equated reading a book with having a conversation with the absent. In a sense, my work is double happiness, as the Chinese saying goes: having a conversation with the absent through their writing and then having a conversation with the present, with the author.

So then... Here I am, sitting with my headphones on, in a studio in Toronto, waiting for the hook-up to a studio in London or New York or Berlin; or on stage at a festival, or at a writer's home in another country, full of anticipation. I've done the research, I've read the books. I feel like I've crammed for an exam; I have it all in the front of my head. Who this writer is. Dozens of questions have been prepared; it's like a road map, though neither the route nor the destination is a sure thing. In fact, the best part is when the writer pauses to think, when something unexpected happens, surprising. Now it begins.

JONATHAN FRANZEN

Dubbed "The Great American Novelist," Jonathan Franzen's breakthrough novel, *The Corrections,* won the 2001 National Book Award and sold over three million copies worldwide. Even before it was published, *The Corrections* was a hit, with magazines vying for a first interview with Franzen. With foreign sales and movie rights, Franzen made more than a million dollars before it hit the stands.

His next novel, *Freedom* (2010), was greeted with even more hoopla. Franzen became the first writer in a decade to make the cover of *Time* magazine, and reviews compared his book to *War and Peace,* calling it "a work of total genius" and "the novel of the century." *Freedom* was not only a bestseller, with *The New York Times* declaring it "a masterpiece," it received so much attention that it triggered a backlash, with some journalists eager to take potshots at its author. The irony is that Jonathan Franzen is the guy who famously wrote an essay in *Harper's Magazine* lamenting the death of the social novel in America, the decline in the status of the novelist, and his own despair because of—as he put it—"the failure of my culturally engaged novel to engage with the culture I'd intended to provoke."

Franzen had started out full of hope and enthusiasm for the literary life. Growing up in the Midwest, he graduated from a good eastern school, Swarthmore College, in 1981. Then he devoted himself to his writing, publishing his first novel, *The Twenty-Seventh City* (1988), when he was twenty-nine. Four years later, he produced another ambitious book, *Strong Motion* (1992). It didn't do as well as his first, and by the mid '90s, when he wrote the *Harper's* piece, "Perchance to Dream," he was stalled in the middle of his third novel. That book, through many rewrites and jettisoning of huge chunks, became *The Corrections*, the social novel par excellence, followed by *Freedom*, which was even more politically engaged with twenty-first-century America, but again through the lives of a Midwestern family. Between the two novels, Jonathan Franzen published two books of non-fiction, *How to Be Alone* (2002) and a memoir, *The Discomfort Zone: A Personal History* (2006).

I met Franzen with each of his blockbuster books, including his 2015 novel, *Purity*—in that case, travelling to Santa Cruz, California, to his house that backs onto a small ravine—a good source of birds to feed his relatively recent passion. Birds and the environment are at the centre of *Freedom* and it's that conversation from 2010 that is published here.

WACHTEL You call yourself a "twitcher"—a British term for passionate bird-spotters. Can you tell me a bit about the culture? Is there a twitcher personality?

FRANZEN I'm not really a twitcher. "Twitcher" is what the Brits call people who start twitching when they learn that a rare bird has been seen, and they become literally, physically, agitated with eagerness to see that bird. So it's a term of derision in the British Isles. It extends more broadly to birdwatchers. And I am indeed a birdwatcher, and I'm excited to see a bird that's rare, but I don't chase them, and that's actually a key distinction. I do list them, however, so I guess I'm pretty far down the road.

WACHTEL Is it cool to be a birdwatcher? You said, when you started out, that you felt a "creeping sense of shame" about what you were doing. What was that about?

FRANZEN Oh, it's totally uncool to be a birdwatcher. People warned me when I was getting into it, "Don't do this. This is very uncool." Partly it's because it tends to be older, no longer well-dressed white people who do it. In other words, it's an uncool demographic. But it's also uncool because... well, what is "cool"? Cool is not caring about stuff, right? You're cool. You're not hot. And to be out there eagerly looking for something with binoculars puts you in a position of actively seeking and advertising the fact that you're passionate about something, so it is really almost definitionally uncool.

WACHTEL In an essay called "My Bird Problem," which appears in your book *The Discomfort Zone: A Personal History*, you describe how you went birdwatching for the first time after your mother died. What made you want to do that?

FRANZEN My mom died in Seattle, and I had gone out there and was staying in my brother's little house in Puget Sound. I was going to be spelling off my brother and sister-and-law, taking care of my mom on the weekends, but she didn't last long enough for that to work more than one weekend. But there I was, right after she died on this island in July, and the place was full of birds. And it was not like I was going to just start working three days after she died, so there was a lot of sitting around. And here was this life that was ongoing, these beautiful things, these beautiful and hard-to-see creatures. I could become absorbed for hours looking at them, trying to find them, trying to figure out what they were. And those were hours I wasn't grieving, thinking about all the hard stuff that I needed to be thinking about after she died. So it was an escape in some fashion, but it was an escape driven by the beauty of the birds themselves, and it was the very first intimation of what it might be like to really love something in nature, to love other living things as I never really had before.

WACHTEL To develop that awareness—I remember my experience was almost like there was another dimension of reality to be aware of, birds in the environment, in nature.

FRANZEN Yeah. The first time I really went out was in Central Park. I had gotten involved with a woman whose sister and brother-in-law were really intense birders, and they came to see us in New York, which is where birders come in May and September because it's one of the great places in North America to see lots and lots of kinds of birds. They get trapped in the park while on migration.

WACHTEL Trapped?

FRANZEN Trapped. Well, they need trees and grass. They've been flying all night, and if you're flying over the south Bronx, you look for green, and Central Park is where they see it. So they spend the day there, and you don't have to go to them. They have come to you. That was the really revelatory moment, when I realized this park that I thought I knew so well, was in fact just as you say, this whole other dimension that I had been missing.

WACHTEL Birdwatching has taken you out of your own natural habitat to other parts of the US: Arizona, Minnesota, Florida. And it was on these solitary trips, you say, that your affair with birds began to compound the very grief you were seeking refuge from. Tell me about that. What did you experience?

FRANZEN It's a problem when you start caring about something. You then risk the loss of that thing. If you live long enough, you realize that the deeper you go into loving somebody, the greater the grief, potentially, you're setting up if you lose that person. And the same was true when I began to care about wild birds. When I was in my late twenties and early thirties, I'd been very environmentally conscious. I'd been angry at what mankind was doing to the world, but that was actually pretty easy to walk away from. I reached a point where I was so sick of being angry, I was so sick of trying to escape people in the wild and then being enraged when people would disturb my solitary idyll that I just walked away from it and became a city person and felt okay about myself because I lived in New York City. It's actually a pretty environmentally efficient way to live.

But once you start having this positive feeling for something in nature, you become aware of how much these animals are dependent on certain kinds of habitats, certain kinds of arrangements of open space. You set yourself up for this terrible sadness when you go out and see their homes being destroyed, and you find yourself in the very uncool position of feeling like you actually need to devote your time and attention to trying to help them, and that was something I had never experienced before. I had been very content to stand satirically or polemically on the sidelines and criticize what was wrong in other people and in our social and political arrangements. To put my heart on the line and try to do something positive for these birds, was a very new thing for me. It is very sad.

I spent this last spring reporting a story for *The New Yorker* on the mass killing of migratory songbirds in the Mediterranean. I knew about the problem. I thought it was under-publicized and I really wanted to raise awareness of it. But I also knew, going into it, that I was going to see wild creatures being killed and in terrible pain and in torture. None of that would have bothered me before. So there is sort of "no gain, no pain" in the world of the heart.

WACHTEL I know the numbers are astronomical. In your piece about that, you say something like a billion songbirds are killed deliberately by humans each year.

FRANZEN I think a billion migratory birds between Africa and Eurasia in the course of spring and fall migrations—that was an estimate that I'd found in many sources and was a little worried was not going to make it past the *New Yorker* fact checker. But it sailed through. You can cut that number in half if you want to be safe, but 500 million out of a total migration of five billion, and you're talking about at least 10 per cent of all migratory birds deliberately killed along the way.

WACHTEL And in many instances, in countries where it's illegal.

FRANZEN Oh, yes. It's illegal throughout the European Union in most instances. And we're talking about continents and countries where all of these populations are in pretty calamitous decline. The main problem, of course, is habitat loss and intensive agriculture, but to also be doing this is just a terrible insult to the injury.

WACHTEL Yet in many countries, it's part of their cultural tradition. You noticed that in Cyprus one of the most common warblers is a national delicacy, which you tasted.

FRANZEN I did, I did, as a journalist. It was probably the saddest evening of the year for me. I don't want to do straight-up advocacy in my reporting because I don't know what you really accomplish with that. The only people who read to the end of a piece of environmental advocacy are people who don't need it. So I try to write for readers who see the world in complicated terms, and one of the things I owe them therefore is to try to understand both sides of the issue. And that, for me, in the Mediterranean article, meant talking with lots and lots of poachers, hearing their stories, trying to understand where they were coming from and also, in one instance, yes, tasting the national delicacy of Cyprus. It had to be done because you need to establish a certain amount of credibility as a journalist, or people are just going to say, "Oh, he's writing about the environment again. I'll flip the page to something else."

WACHTEL I suppose it's not surprising that someone who's such a sharp observer of people, with a self-confessed attraction to solitude, should find pleasure and purpose in observing birds. But at one point in your essay "My Bird Problem," you remember watching some common shore birds in Florida and, you write, "Camped out amid high-rise condos and hotels, surveying the beach in postures of sleepy disgruntlement, with their heads scrunched down and their eyes half shut, they looked like a little band of misfits." You go on to say, "what I felt for them went beyond love. I felt outright identification." Tell me about that identification. Why and how?

FRANZEN I think an undeniable element of my attraction to birds is my attraction to literary fiction and my sense of community and team spirit with readers and writers of a certain kind of book. I'm the kind of person who, turning on any sport on TV at random, first tries to figure out who's favoured and root for the other side. And if I can't figure that out, I'll just pick whoever is trailing in the game and then root for that side because I have an almost perverse attraction to lost causes and hopeless cases. And I find such beauty in literature and such intense comradeship in the books and also in the kind of people who read those books that I've dedicated my whole professional life to trying to advance our cause, trying to keep the thing going, trying to save this somewhat threatened variety of artistic expression.

So that all mapped really easily onto caring about threatened and endangered bird species, which are being pushed to the margins by this ever-increasing sprawl of modernity.

WACHTEL And seeing them as misfits too? I know you acknowledge it's dangerous to anthropomorphize but—

FRANZEN Right. I do go on to talk about all the ways in which I see birds in myself, and that's not anthropomorphizing.

WACHTEL That's reverse-anthropomorphizing.

FRANZEN Yes. That's zoomorphizing or something. I don't even know the word for it.

In Florida, there are birds that do very well with people. I love a pelican, and yet in Florida the pelicans are so tame, you can practically feed them French toast from your back porch. Same thing with the cormorants and some of the ducks, a lot of the seagulls. They just fit in so well with humanity. And the people I spend most time with are the ones who don't fit in so well, for whom daily life can be something of a trial. They might be a bit depressive. They might be eccentric. So to see all of these collaborator birds and then to find, on the least charming stretch of beach, a place nobody else wants to be, this little motley band of sandpipers and plovers—yes, I just thought, Hey, those are my peeps, as it were.

WACHTEL I'd like to talk about your own misfit self, as captured in your memoir *The Discomfort Zone*, your happy and, in many ways, also difficult childhood growing up in the Midwest in the sixties and seventies in Webster Groves, a suburb of St. Louis, Missouri. Can you sketch in a bit of the background, the time and place that shaped you?

FRANZEN Yes. My parents were Depression children, and although my father had not served in the Second World War, my two much older brothers were part of the Baby Boom, and I was born in late 1959, in the last four months of the official Baby Boom. I was a little kid when the sixties and all of that rebellious youth culture broke over the country; it came right into the house through my brothers and caused an enormous amount of conflict and distress. The generation gap was enormous between my parents and my brothers, but I was this kind of weirdly neutral third party in all that. My brothers had conflicts with each other. Really, any line you drew between any people in the family besides me, there was a lot of conflict in that connection. I was too young, really, to participate in that, and everybody seemed to like me, so I was exposed to all of these adult conflicts while being allowed to remain a child.

And then as the sixties turned to the seventies, I was in a Christian fellowship back when it meant something a little different to be in a Christian fellowship. There were a lot of people from druggie backgrounds and troubled families in that group, and everything kind of bled together. The counterculture. People were experimenting with a sort of sincerity that was never seen again in American culture. And I was part of this Christian youth fellowship and had a prolonged childhood, even as a lot of really harsh stuff was happening, not only in my home, but in the homes of lots and lots of kids I was in the fellowship with. So it was a time of ferment coupled with this weird, prolonged innocence. That's how I would describe it. The seventies were a very middle-class time. It was the time when income disparity between the wealthy and the not wealthy was at an all-time low in the history of the country. I'm not nostalgic for that time, and yet there was something very centred about it. I wanted to go back and tell the story of those times and secondarily of myself.

WACHTEL Your essay "House for Sale" opens with you clearing out and preparing to sell your old family home in St. Louis following the death of your mother, and it's a terrific essay. In it you say that the house had been your mother's novel, "the concrete story she told about herself," and the task of depersonalizing the house becomes quite a painful journey back into the life of your family, with your mother very much at the centre. You've described her as a very dominant personality. In what way?

FRANZEN She had strong opinions, and like many people whose lives were something of a disappointment to them, she took refuge in a fairly strict morality. That's what you do when life is not working out quite the way you want it to. She was steadily, but I don't think terribly happily, married. She had a lot of health problems. And so she invested probably too much attention in her kids and then brought this really severe sense of moral judgment to bear on us and a kind of oppressive, ethical sense of responsibility to society.

WACHTEL Too heavy because you were a kid?

FRANZEN Yes, exactly. It's a lot to have to deal with. When my second brother went off to college, I was still only in fourth grade, and there I was alone for the next eight years at home with her, having to bear the brunt of all of that frustrated emotion. She was a handful. She was an old-fashioned person, and part of the frustration for her was that she didn't have a suitable outlet for her great talent and her great energy. She had not enough to do and, I think, overdid it with her kids because that was the project she had.

WACHTEL And you describe yourself as over-identifying with her.

FRANZEN How can you help it? Yes. Part of it was that she really was not well. She had health problems, and a certain kind of guilt came along with that for me. When I would lash back at her or even when I would think snarky thoughts about her, I would be brought up by this feeling of, yes, but she's got a hard life, she's not doing well, how can I be doing that to her?

WACHTEL That was when you were younger. Did you get to a better place later?

FRANZEN I did. Alas, it was really only towards the end of her life that I started getting anywhere with her. It was really only after she was gone that I came to a full appreciation of what a rather good parent she was and was able to access the love that had been there all along. I hadn't been able to find my way to that love because I couldn't stand to be with her for more than a few days at a time. She really did drive me crazy. I was not the kind of son she expected to have. I was different. I was eccentric. I was trying to do something in art. And I didn't dress the way she wanted me to dress. I didn't marry the way she wanted me to marry. I didn't feel that I was a disappointment, and I had some strong backup from my dad and my brothers. But it meant that time with her was often stressful. And now I'm getting to have the rest of my life thinking about her and reaching the age she was when I was first getting to know her and coming to have a proper appreciation for who she was and the complexity of who she was and getting in touch with the love that had been there all along.

WACHTEL You've also written very movingly about your father and his struggle with Alzheimer's in your essay "My Father's Brain," then drawing on some of that experience in your portrait of the father Alfred Lambert in your novel *The Corrections*. When you were growing up, he was, as you put it, "allergic to any kind of fun. There wasn't a silly bone in his body." He never told a joke. That couldn't have been easy for you as a kid. What was your relationship with him like?

FRANZEN It was actually reassuring because I was just a kid. He was very, very powerfully and seriously a grown-up. He had his own compromised sense of self. He was very shy. He was rarely able to demand what he deserved professionally. He had a crucial shortage of self-confidence. But he was physically very powerful. He had a huge temper. And he was just dead serious. He was a real adult and there was no question about that. In a way, that's very liberating to a child. You don't have to be Dad's pal, Dad's best friend or something. I could be the son. I'm eternally grateful to him for that.

My mom had that too. There was no question. She was overly disclosive, but not because we were pals; it's just that she couldn't help expressing her opinions and venting some of her feelings. But she too was a scarily adult person, and I appreciated the sharpness of that division. The kind of person who becomes a writer tends to have a rather watery, ill-defined sense of self. You flow into various possible personalities. You're not quite sure whether you're even male or female sometimes. And having parents for whom the categories were clear was a great blessing.

WACHTEL Although you said at a young age you became secretive to save your identity.

FRANZEN Yes, oh, absolutely. They had no category for me and, to some extent, my brother who had pursued art himself for a while. They had no category for us because they had come through the Depression poor and believed in hard work and financial security. All of this art stuff was frivolous, but I knew it was important to me and I had to keep it secret. That's silence, cunning, and exile, and the cunning is all about knowing what to do when your personality is not fully formed yet. To keep it safe, you basically hide it so that it can grow on its own schedule and not get crushed before it has a chance to defend itself.

WACHTEL You have this odd line in an essay called "Two Ponies" where you say it took you half your life to achieve seeing your parents as cartoons. What do you mean by that?

FRANZEN I think it's akin to what I was saying about adults being adults and children being children. There's a comfort in clear, dark lines, and that's what cartoonists draw with. They simplify. But I think particularly what I meant in the line in that chapter of *The Discomfort Zone* was that we're all neurotic, and it's very hard to live over long periods with members of your family who are expressing these neurotic conflicts within themselves in unpleasant, angry, trying ways. And one way you come to forgive that and make it okay is to turn it into a cartoon of itself. The more extreme expressions you exaggerate further until suddenly, instead of being emotionally ruled by them, you're laughing at them and, in that, really forgiving them. Paradoxically, people become more human when you render them in cartoon form.

WACHTEL You even go on to say, "To become more perfectly a cartoon myself, what a victory that would be."

FRANZEN The program with *The Discomfort Zone* was to do a cartoon version of myself. I'm harder on myself than on the rest of the people in that book put together. Really, I'm just murderously hard on myself, making myself the butt of as many jokes as possible; the point of all that is I didn't want to be blaming somebody for who I was, and I didn't really have a problem with who I turned out to be, so it seemed safest to put the blame on me, and yet that begins to seem cruel or self-hating if you don't do it in a cartoon form.

WACHTEL *The Corrections* was set in the late 1990s, and in your novel *Freedom* you go back to the period of your own youth in the 1970s, but then into the twenty-first century, with a focus on 2004. Why this year in particular?

FRANZEN The chronology demanded it, basically. I had chosen people just about my age as the central couple of the book, and I wanted them to have had children young and for the children to be reaching the age where stuff was really starting to happen. This was all quite consciously an echo of the things that were happening in my family in the sixties, when my brothers reached a certain age, but I wanted to translate all of that into the language and political situation of a generation later. It basically required that the kids be born in the early eighties and that they be reaching that crucial sixteen, eighteen, twenty mark right around the time when interesting things were happening in the country. The United States went into Iraq in 2003. In 2004 we re-elected George Bush, in spite of knowing better. Those were crucial years in many ways, and I was happy to draw some energy from that time. But it was essentially set by the chronological project of trying to imagine what my parents would have been like if they had been my age.

WACHTEL Why your parents?

FRANZEN Why my parents? Because even though I had drawn certain cartoonish versions of my mother and my father in *The Corrections*, I hadn't really told anything like the story of my family, the story of the two of them, the story of our deep Minnesotan past and maybe particularly the story of my own marriage and my own relationship to my parents. That had all been avoided. *The Discomfort Zone* is mostly about me sneaking out of the house and having my real life somewhere else, and occasionally we get these little glimpses of the emotional intensity of my home life. But by and large, even in the memoir, I'm running away from that. I'm not getting into it. And I wanted to get into that here, but I didn't want to get into it in a direct way, as I wasn't really interested in writing about the seventies anymore and totally uninterested in writing about the thirties because it's just too far back to be interesting to me.

WACHTEL Although inevitably your own preoccupations find their way into the novel *Freedom*, themes of war and political corruption and overpopulation and global warming, this is nonetheless a big, absorbing family story, smart and funny and sad all at once. You talked about having a very contrarian streak, that you like to mix the tragic with the comic or offer some light in very dark times and the reverse. What kinds of impulses drove this novel? How do you see it as a novel of our time?

FRANZEN Accidentally, really. Like I said, I'm trying to throw as much energy into a book as possible. I don't write them very often, and I'd like them to be as alive as possible. That's one reason I keep going back to families as one of the organizing principles for these books:

there's so much automatic emotional charge in the mere existence of two siblings close together in age, competing with each other, dividing up the turf. I'm ready to read more about that right there. There's just energy coming off that. Or a mom who is maybe not quite as happy as she should be in the marriage, unburdening herself to her son. To me, there's just life there. And so I'll put that in the "to use" pile. And the same is true for me with all of the anxieties and the anger and the confusion and uncertainty I feel living in the present moment, trying to figure out how to be a good citizen now, knowing what I do about the environmental situation in the world and watching political discourse decay ever more grievously year after year in the United States. What should I be doing? Again, there's something about the present world that feeds the dreams and the stresses of day-to-day life. And again, I want to draw on that and let the characters draw on those energies in a book. But it's not because I have some pronouncement to make about the time we live in. I'm not even that interested in analyzing what's going on. It's there to feed into the characters. The characters are not there to illustrate some social reality.

WACHTEL At the same time, you have written these two big novels that have clearly touched a chord and that have a social dimension. I mention that in the context of your old essay about the death of the social novel. How do you feel about the role of fiction in our time, or perhaps rather about the responsibility of the novelist?

FRANZEN The only responsibility I feel as a novelist is to people who like to read the same kind of books I do. If anything has changed since the mid-nineties, when I was despairing about the future of serious fiction, it's my sense of who would be in that audience, my sense that the variety and number of people who care about good books has been greatly expanded.

But I wouldn't even call it a responsibility. It's more like I have a sense of gratitude for what I've been given directly in my life, and also I have a sense of gratitude to the writers in the past who gave me the books that changed my life. Is it a responsibility to wish to give back, to wish to pass the gift along? I don't know. I think if you care about the novel as an important part of the culture, you do have a responsibility to try to make it really, really compelling as an alternative to the other forms of entertainment that are out there. So one thing that means to me is that I don't want to publish a half-baked book. I respect that the reader is busy and doesn't have time to read very many books in a year. I don't want to put something out there until I have something new to say, and I also want to do the reader the favour of making the book really fun to read so that it's not a chore to stay in it, it's the thing you want to do, because that's the only real alternative to the world of Twitter and email and Facebook.

WACHTEL I'd like to talk a little about one of the novel's most surprisingly complicated characters, Patty Berglund. To begin with, she's a misfit in her own family, a jock rather than a creative personality, which would be funny if it weren't also tragic. You said that the novel began with Patty's voice as a third-person narrator, and it's the voice that we hear in the autobiographical section called "Mistakes Were Made."

FRANZEN There are a lot of mistakes. Some of them are hers. I think she does actually 'fess up to them. There are so many to go around.

WACHTEL What about Patty? What did you want to explore in this quirky and troubled character?

FRANZEN Patty was always a jock, but I happened upon her voice while struggling with a very different kind of novel that I eventually didn't write many years ago, and almost the first thing that came out of that voice—and it was only a couple of pages, which I then put in a drawer for literally five years—was a recollection of being the jock in her family.

So the corrosive, but lifesaving, nature of competition and the lifesaving nature of teamwork and team spirit—these were things that mattered a lot to me. I am a competitive person; I came from a fairly competitive household, it was pretty much out in the open. I don't think it was terribly unhealthy in our household. But I knew a lot about it, and I felt very strongly motivated, not by direct competition with my brothers, but always in competition with somebody. I love playing games. I like the competitive aspect of games. I like winning. And yet that's a suite of feelings that Americans are quite uncomfortable with once we get outside the arena of sports. There are emotional costs to this.

And then the team aspect: I've come to have such a strong sense of team spirit about the novel, about my fellow readers and writers and then, in the last ten years, about the team of birds. Birds and people who care about birds—they're also my team. All of these characters are versions of myself in some way.

And what Patty was doing for me was connecting with that deep sense of loyalty to the team. Part of the problem for her is that she loses her team because she is no longer an athlete, so she makes her family her team, but families don't quite work as teams the way teams do.

WACHTEL And she loses that team too, in a sense.

FRANZEN Yes. And I guess the third thing there would be the concept and problem of loyalty, which is such an organizing principle for me, but it never really means anything until it's tested. At a number of points in my life, I've had excruciating conflicts of loyalty, certainly in my long-time marriage. When I was working on *The Corrections*, I also had some issues of loyalty to myself as a writer and to myself as a person trying to survive and needing to take care of my parents, trying to figure out how little time I could spend in St. Louis so that I could keep working on the book. Excruciating conflicts of loyalty. So all of these concerns were on the table with this character.

WACHTEL Depression figures in this novel. A number of the characters experience depression to different degrees, and Patty, for all her bouncy, athletic determination, is struck by it for a long time. What interests you in depression in particular?

FRANZEN The Germans have a nice distinction in their adjectives. They have *depressive* or *deprimiert*, and *depressive* is actually a pretty good word in English, too. There is a depressive personality. There is a depressive caste of mind. I think I would describe my own as depressive. A somewhat random observation is that depressive people are generally the funniest people you'll ever meet because to not be clinically depressed and hospitalized and heavily medicated or electroshocked, but merely to cope with chronic, mid-levels of depression, makes you a depressive person. And one of the primary coping mechanisms is to laugh at stuff. So I find it a very attractive personality type. Most of the interesting people I know are depressive in some sense. We live in times when depression is widely diagnosed, so if you're writing about fairly well-off people in a time much like our own, chances are one or two of them are going to have a run-in with some sort of depression.

WACHTEL How has your own outlook been changed by those episodes in your life?

FRANZEN Again, I don't mean to ever make light of, or discount, major depression. That's a whole different animal, when you become so depressed that you become suicidal or you need major, major inter-vention. I've been very fortunate in never reaching that point. I've peered down into the dark well, but have not gone over the edge—thankfully—yet, ever. And not having gone over the edge, I have some familiarity with the cycles of moderate depression and then not being depressed or not being so depressed, and then able, after many years of living with myself, to see the ways in which depression is actually quite an adaptive feature of our psychological life. When I start to become depressed in a way that reminds me of the most serious times when I have been depressed, it alerts me that something is going on, and it raises a flag, and I have to figure out why I am falling into this state. So for me, actually, it's associated with periodic crises that can actually be worked through, and it serves a useful function in telling me that something really serious is going on, that it's time to put everything aside, shut down, figure out what's really going on. So I bring my own Patty-ish chipper optimism to the problem of depression, obviously.

WACHTEL And it's addressable in that way? It's something that you can get yourself out of?

FRANZEN Yes. There's a conversation in my head between my father, who was, I think, more unipolar depressive, and my mother, who would occasionally get low, but who always had this kind of determination to get on with life. I feel the side of me that comes with my mother kicking in just at the point when things might be getting dangerous. It's as if I say to myself, no, I'm not going to do that, I'm going to try to figure things out.

WACHTEL Walter, Patty's husband, is the definitive good man: steady, conscientious, responsible, reliable. He also cracks spectacularly in the course of the story, and depression and rage become two sides of the same coin for him. Walter's background is quite different from yours, but he shares your Minnesota roots and some of your moral outrage and sense of mission. What do you relate to most in him?

FRANZEN The title of the first Walter chapter was one of the working subtitles for this book, "The Nice Man's Anger." I wanted to write about the nicest man in Minnesota, but I actually was not born in Minnesota. The rest of my family was, and I definitely come from a Minnesotan family, but even if I had been born in Minnesota, no one would ever describe me as the "nicest man in Minnesota." They might say, "He's actually nicer than you might think." But "nicest"—I don't think anyone would accuse me of being that. I'm not doing nice work. Sorry. This part of me that Walter corresponds to is the part of me that tends to get walked on, and that I associate with my very nice Midwestern upbringing: No, you don't push back. No, you just swallow and smile. And we also share the recognition that, if you behave like this for enough decades, you build up an enormous pool of rage. And yet because you're nice, you don't know what to do with that. This is not Travis Bickle or somebody—

WACHTEL As in *Taxi Driver*. Or even Peter Finch in, "I'm mad as hell," et cetera.

FRANZEN Exactly. It's really just the torment of being so full of rage and yet still having a kind of ineluctable niceness, with all its frustrations. That interested me in Walter. And also all of these characters have to be very unlike me in order to be writable, and the fact that he is so nice was one of the key differences that made it possible.

WACHTEL Walter becomes involved in a project to preserve a single bird species, the Cerulean Warbler. Do you know this bird yourself? Have you seen it in the wild?

FRANZEN I have seen a few females. I have never seen the beautiful, blue male Cerulean Warbler, and one reason I have not is that it is one of the fastest, if not the fastest declining songbird in North America. It has, unfortunately, rather specific habitat needs. It needs mature hardwood mixed forest that has not been fragmented by development or logged over and prevented from regenerating itself properly. It also happens to be a bird that breeds especially in Appalachia, which is at the centre of a lot of interesting storylines having to do with coal and natural gas extraction and that connects directly into the administration we had for eight years in this country. So a lot of stuff just got pulled right in with that one little bird.

WACHTEL *Freedom* is an ironic motif in the novel on many levels. As Walter says, "The one thing nobody can take away from you is the freedom to screw up your life." Freedom versus responsibility is the kind of tension we alluded to earlier. But how do these two impulses or imperatives play out in your own life?

FRANZEN In my own life—oh, well! I see the conversation about health care in the United States as being emblematic—and this has a personal connection for me in a way—one side saying, "We ought to be free to have insurance or not have insurance. Nobody is going to tell me who

I can insure with. I don't want government meddling in my life." And on the other side, you have people who are saying, "What I don't want is to be worried every minute of my life about whether I'm covered or whether my child is covered, whether my insurance is going to get cut off. I don't want to have to read eight 300-page prospectuses to try to sift through the fine print to figure out what insurance is best for me. This is insane. What I want to be free of is that crushing responsibility for something that doesn't even matter that much to me. I want to be free of that anxiety." And those are the terms, I think, for all of us. You want to keep your options open. And yet you have your options open, and you can become consumed with trying to choose among those options or consumed with anxiety that you're making the wrong choice. Oddly, sometimes when you have an opportunity to restrict your choice, when you actually settle on something—and I would say, going back to our conversation about birds—when I realized, wow, I really care about this stuff, I'm going to have to do something about it, it was oddly liberating, precisely because it was constraining. Now I know what I want to do. I don't have to worry about what I'm going to do because now I know, and now I can just get on with it. To be doing something that you feel some passion for, even though it involves giving up all these choices, I think that's a liberating choice in itself.

October 2010
Original interview produced by Sandra Rabinovitch

EDWIDGE DANTICAT

At an astonishingly young age, Haitian-born Edwidge Danticat became one of the US's most celebrated new novelists. When she was scarcely twenty-five, she published her first novel, *Breath, Eyes, Memory* (1994). It was chosen for Oprah's Book Club and sold more than 600,000 copies. Danticat's next book, *Krik? Krak!* (1996), a collection of stories, came out a year later and was nominated for a National Book Award. As America's first Haitian woman to write in English, Danticat was taken up by the media in a remarkable way. Britain's prestigious literary magazine, *Granta*, selected her as one of the twenty "Best Young American Novelists," *Harper's Bazaar* included her as one of twenty people in their twenties who will make a difference. *The New York Times* chose her for their "Thirty under 30" creative people to watch. *Jane* magazine named her as one of the "15 Gutsiest Women of the Year." And *Ms. Magazine* featured her as one of their "21 (feminists) for the 21st Century." You get the idea...

It was at this point, at the cusp of a new century, in 1999, that I first interviewed Edwidge Danticat. She'd just turned thirty and had published her second novel, an ambitious book, *The Farming of Bones* (1998), which goes back to a pivotal moment in Haitian history: the 1937 massacre of some 15,000 Haitians who were working in the neighbouring Dominican Republic. I found her as impressive as her reputation and spoke to her again about her subsequent books. We met face to face only once—at the Blue Metropolis Literary Festival in

Montreal—which she attended with her husband, also from Haiti, a radio broadcaster in Miami to where she'd recently moved.

Danticat was born in 1969 in Port-au-Prince, the capital of Haiti, the poorest country in the Americas, with the highest infant mortality rate, the lowest life expectancy, and about sixty per cent literacy. Her parents became economic refugees: when Edwidge was two years old, her father left for New York City. Her mother joined him two years later, leaving Edwidge and a younger brother with their uncle, a minister, and his wife and grandson, among other relatives.

When Edwidge was twelve, she joined her parents (and two American-born younger brothers) in Brooklyn. Fluent in French and Creole, she had to learn English and endure epithets from classmates who labelled her a "boat person." "My primary feeling the whole first year was one of loss," she has said. "Loss of my childhood, and of the people I'd left behind—and also of *being* lost. It was like being a baby—learning everything for the first time."

She recovered the past—of her own life and her country—through her fiction. *Breath, Eyes, Memory* evokes elements of her childhood and traumatic uprooting. *Krik? Krak!* is about storytelling, life under dictatorship, escape to America. Her third novel, *The Dew Breaker* (2004), is a subtle, intricately woven fiction, exploring the world of a torturer and its legacy on his family and his victims. Danticat's writing is a potent mix of the personal and the political. Nowhere is this more in evidence than in her memoir of her family and especially of her father and his brother, the uncle who raised her in Haiti. *Brother, I'm Dying* (2007) starts in her own childhood and goes right up to the birth of her first daughter, recounting the impact of Homeland Security policy on her family, and especially the death of her uncle in custody. It's one of the most powerful, anguished stories I've come across. It won the National Book Critics Circle Award. In 2009, Edwidge Danticat received the MacArthur "genius" award—a half million dollars, no strings—and the following year she published a book of essays, *Create Dangerously: The Immigrant Artist at Work* (2010).

Danticat's most recent fiction is a lyrical and moving novel, *Claire of the Sea Light* (2013). Set in a Haitian fishing village before the devastating 2010 earthquake, it's a complex interweaving of stories that subtly captures Haiti's turbulent history, its extreme poverty, loss, and hope.

WACHTEL You often write about characters who live between cultures, and much of your novel *The Farming of Bones* takes place, literally, on a border:

the river separating Haiti from the Dominican Republic. This is a place with a tragic history. Can you talk about what happened there in 1937?

DANTICAT In 1937 in the Dominican Republic, Rafael Trujillo was running things, and he ordered a massacre of cane workers that was aimed at Haitians and carried out by his soldiers. It was feared, at that time, perhaps because Haiti had once occupied the Dominican Republic for twenty-two years, that this was about to happen again. When the sugar-cane industry shifted from Cuba to the Dominican Republic, and a large number of people went to work there, there was a sense of cultural invasion. And so General Trujillo ordered this massacre, in which anywhere from fifteen to forty thousand people were killed.

WACHTEL Was he fearing a kind of Fifth Column, that these Haitians would somehow take over the country?

DANTICAT It was more a fear that people would quickly intermarry; he was afraid that, within three generations, the Dominican Republic would become much more like Haiti than its own self.

WACHTEL You've said that it was your own visit to the Massacre River that inspired you to write fictionally about that genocide. What did you find there?

DANTICAT I think it was what I *didn't* find there that most moved me. I had read so much about the Massacre River, going from the first massacre of the colonists in the nineteenth century to this twentieth-century massacre. I think I had built up in my mind this angry, raging river, this body of water that just did not forget. And I felt that, when I did get there, I would sense the history, that I would see it as though unfolding on a screen. But when I got there, it amazed me that there were people washing clothes, there were children bathing, there were animals drinking. The ordinariness of life was striking to me. There's a line in the book that says "Nature has no memory," and it struck me in a great sense that it's both sad and comforting that nature has no memory, that things go on in spite of what's happened before. The title comes from the line, the verse: "It is, at this stage, too late for a beginning, but this is my feeling, that nothing can silence me but death and its plows for the farming of bones."

WACHTEL Language and identity are central to your fiction as, in a way, they have been in your life. You live in the United States but you grew up in Haiti until you were twelve. Can you tell me about the place where you lived?

DANTICAT My parents went to the States when I was young and left me with my aunt and uncle. We spent our time between the city where they lived and the provinces in summer for vacation. So I spent almost the same amount of time every year in a very remote rural setting up in the mountains, and also in the city. I grew up between those two spaces, knowing people who, like my uncle, had travelled, who had been to the United States, and other people who had never left the place on the hill where they were born. It is a combination of both things which make up the reality of Haiti.

WACHTEL How were you affected by the fact that your parents had already gone to America and you were left with relatives?

DANTICAT It was hard to feel bad about it. I missed my parents, but I was pretty young when they left and I had this very large surrogate family that was doting and took care of me and my brother. It was very hard to feel terrible: people would always tell us how lucky we were because we were surrounded by people even poorer than we were. We were told, "Your mother is in New York, your father is in New York, you get to go to school." We got to go to school. We never missed school because our parents were working to send money for it every month, and there was always that hope that they were going to send for us. So, there was a sense that we were special. I think later, when you get older, you deal with the absences and you realize that there are things that you missed that you're trying to catch up on.

WACHTEL In your first novel, *Breath, Eyes, Memory,* your Haitian narrator, Sophie, has a mother who emigrates to the United States and leaves her behind with an aunt. I'm not suggesting that it's autobiographical, but you describe the moment that Sophie has to leave Haiti to join her mother so movingly that I wondered if you remember how you felt when you were twelve.

DANTICAT Oh, absolutely. I think Sophie's leaving is fraught with more politics, but I definitely remember the emotional pull and tug, the feeling of being steeped in loyalties between the family that had taken care of me and the family that was truly my blood family, my mother and father, whom I was now going to rejoin. I definitely felt that tug and the fear of, Where would I fit in to this? I had an established space, at least, in my surrogate family, but where would I fit in in this new family? I had two brothers who were born in America; I'd only seen them once when they were babies, when my parents brought them to Haiti, and so there was a lot of discomfort about starting a new life, not as you would when you go to a new place as an adult, but really surrendering because there's nothing that you can do for yourself at this stage. So all of those feelings I knew and still remembered very vividly, and I used them to tell Sophie's story.

WACHTEL Surrendering. That's an interesting word.

DANTICAT Well, I think adults do it, too. I think it's probably more tragically painful to people who were independent linguistically, independent in other ways, to come to a new country and suddenly have to be led places. It's scary all around. People say that immigration infantilizes people. The older you get, the more you appreciate how brave people are to just leave home without any knowledge of what it's going to be like, just knowing that it might be a little better than what you're leaving, and to then *arrive* and not speak the language. It's an enormous leap of faith, and I have a great deal of respect for people who do it.

WACHTEL The idea of infantilizing people sounds accurate, and I wonder whether children are slightly more resilient because they're not that far from being in that state of helplessness.

DANTICAT And thus the surrender. I think, when you're a child, you're more used to surrendering.

WACHTEL You also write very movingly in *Breath, Eyes, Memory* about Sophie's love for the aunt who raises her. Did you experience that kind of bond with your surrogate family?

DANTICAT I think that that kind of bond is inevitable because there is a deep void that exists when suddenly you're without your mother and your father. It's even deeper than not ever having had parents because, if you are adopted at birth, you've not known anything else, and so this is your family. Later you ask questions. But I think that if suddenly you feel like your parents are plucked from you, there's a void, and you look for people to fill it. I had very close relationships with my aunt and my uncle because I was looking for them to be the parents, to be a kind of emotional source of parenting for me, to love me like my mother would have. So I think there's a really strong bond. My mother still says, "You have your other sets of parents who are in Haiti."

WACHTEL Did the sense of community among Haitians in New York help you out?

DANTICAT It helped a lot in the transition, and I think, even with the adults, that helps—having a transition, having a bridge, people who carry you while you're adjusting to the new place. So that was very important to me, having the church that we went to on Sunday and the people who lived in our building. It was like a little village. We looked after other people's children and they looked after our children. There was a sense of community. You didn't feel so anonymous, you didn't feel so stranded. I know this was a big concern to my parents; if something happened to you, there was somebody you could call who could come within seconds, who lived next door, who lived down the street. It was very important.

WACHTEL You grew up in Haiti during the regime of Baby Doc Duvalier. You were very young, but do you remember the ways it affected life in Haiti during the 1970s?

DANTICAT A lot of us *must* remember. I remember a great deal of silence, people being afraid to say anything. You didn't trust your neighbour because you didn't know who might turn you in for whatever reason. I remember Baby Doc and his men driving by in a limousine and throwing money out on the street and people just climbing on top of each other to get it. They would do it on holidays, especially at the first of the year, which is a traditional time to get money or presents from your godparents. And so, things like throwing people a bone—right now there's a very strange nostalgia for that, I think. There's a proverb that says "Yesterday is always better," but it was a really difficult time. A lot of people would just vanish overnight or they would go into exile or would run. It was a difficult time then, and it's a difficult time right now, but it's difficult for other reasons.

WACHTEL But back then, were you aware it was a bone, were you aware that it was a dangerous place?

DANTICAT I don't think I was aware. It's funny because, when we had visitors from Haiti in the last years of the dictatorship, there were things my parents could tell them that had happened in Haiti—demonstrations and so on—that they hadn't heard about in Haiti because the media was so controlled. So I don't think I was aware either. I think I just thought that's how everybody lived, it was just a normal state. But there were precautions you took. You never spoke politics to anybody, you tried to stay out of things. I think that people developed survival mechanisms and, whether you were young or old, you developed certain codes, you just picked up what you should do and what you shouldn't do.

WACHTEL You spoke Creole at home with your family, but French was the official language at school. Did that seem odd?

DANTICAT It didn't seem odd. Again, you know, that was just how it was, and that's how it is still in a lot of places. I mean, we spoke Creole at home, but the teacher, if you spoke Creole, would say, "Rephrase that." That's changing somewhat now. They have Creole schools where they teach Creole and French together; French remains a language of access for a lot of people, so it's not completely dismissed. I never felt as comfortable in French as I did in Creole, but there were things you just accepted—Okay, this is how it is—and we tried to make the best of it in the situation.

WACHTEL Did that mean that Creole had a certain context or certain associations for you because it wasn't the official language?

DANTICAT It felt, and it still feels sometimes, more intimate. For me, it just felt like this is what we speak when we're together and then, when you're at the bank or at the hospital, this is the public language, this is what shows your schooling. It's very much the same, for example, in Jamaica, with the Jamaican patois or the King's English and all the social associations that people make with the different ways that people speak.

WACHTEL And then you came to New York at twelve and they spoke English.

DANTICAT Yes, exactly. But a lot of the people who were around us, who were mostly working class, didn't speak much French, so we would just speak Creole in our space. But we knew that if we wanted to participate in the dialogue of the world and understand what was going on, we had to do our best to speak English.

WACHTEL In *Breath, Eyes, Memory*, Sophie, unlike you, arrives in New York to find a mother who is really suffering, who is well-intentioned but having a very hard time. What did you want to explore, or why did you want to explore, this kind of imperilled mother-daughter relationship?

DANTICAT I wanted to explore the ways that a young girl would become a woman on her own, without much modelling, without perfect modelling. I wanted to explore how we become women in the absence of our mothers, and the rites of passage to womanhood. I wanted to experience the whole range of womanhood. From a woman whose family has an obsession with virginity, to being raped, to all the relationships between women in the family and women outside the family, and to its traditions and legacies. I wanted to look at these things and how they're affected by migration. I think when we come to a new country, we all come with fragments. When you leave, you take what you can—you take some pictures, you take your stories, you take your memories, and the rest you feel like you can get better, and more of, in the other place. You can get better apples, you can get better bananas. But your memories—you can't get better memories. They just stay. And so, I wanted to explore how a young woman would put all those fragments together on her own because her mother's rite of passage was this violent act, which was true for a lot of women who lived in the dictatorship.

WACHTEL Sophie's mother was raped and, in fact, Sophie is the result of that rape.

DANTICAT Yes. And so, as she says in the story, she has to put all these different fragments together to create a face for herself, imagining what her father would look like, taking what's already there of her mother. So everything is a puzzle. It's almost as if, when she's taken out of where she was and put in a new place, she has to reform herself, she has to recreate a self that can survive in this place. The mother never learns that, and that's what she succumbs to.

WACHTEL There is this darker side. You say you not only wanted to explore the obsession with virginity but also the violence of rape. Tell me about the obsession with virginity, because you talk about it being a rural Haitian tradition, to physically test a daughter's virginity.

DANTICAT It's true for some Haitian women; it's not true for *all* Haitian women. You find often in stratified societies that poor women are encouraged to be marriageable. Especially in this rural setting, in this family without a father, the mother would have to be all the more forceful, all the more strict with her daughter so that people would respect them. The grandmother as well wants them to remain virgins so they can be respected and marry well, but I don't think that's a tradition that's unique to Haitian culture. A lot of women from different cultures who read the book say their mothers had taken them to doctors, for instance. There's this sense of honour, and as the mother says, "If you die, you die alone, but if you dishonour yourself, you dishonour all of us." In these very small, close communities, marriage is not between two people, it's between two families. And so, just working with all that and how those things transform, the grandmother, then, has this conversation with a daughter who lives in a new world and is trying to shape a new identity for herself.

WACHTEL You got some criticism from Haitian Americans for writing about that.

DANTICAT Yes, but I think it is important to not condemn anything, but to really have a dialogue about how we are transformed by migration and how much of what was useful to us, say, where my parents were born, is useful here. A lot of things are useful, a lot of them are part of me, but some of them aren't useful anymore. What I try to do is get closer to the experiences, not really offer answers. But I think sometimes, when you're writing about a community, some people from that community may feel you are betraying them, that you're putting on a show for the mainstream and not being a good compatriot in some way.

WACHTEL You've had to bear a lot of responsibility because you're the first woman from Haiti to write in English in America. This has been loaded on you, whether you like it or not.

DANTICAT There have been some others and there are more coming up, and I can't wait, because it's a very uncomfortable space between both communities. Some people think that you're a native informant, that what you say must be true even though it's fiction.

WACHTEL You called your short story collection *Krik? Krak!*. Can you talk about what that expression means?

DANTICAT "Krik krak" is a call-and-response that we do before telling riddles or stories. It's an introduction to the storytelling if you have an audience in front of you, and it's usually an exchange between an elder and some children, but it ranges. So the old man or woman will say "krik" and the children will say "krak," with much enthusiasm. There are a lot of different combinations that we use to warm up the listener. I wanted to name my short story collection for that tradition because I was told stories by my grandmothers and my aunts when I was young, and I felt like that was my first lesson in narrative. The storyteller's very attuned to the audience, and if the children are yawning then they'll sing a song. There's a lot of interaction. So I called it that to honour this tradition of storytelling in my past and in my life.

WACHTEL In your fiction, you'll have dreams or symbols or even visitations from the dead or the world of the spirit bump into the harshest realities. Is this something that was in the folktales and stories that you heard in childhood?

DANTICAT One of the things about the folktale is that so much is possible. Fish can fly and butterflies can sing and I think that's very liberating to the imagination of a child, the fact that another world exists. But also, not to make it sound too mystical, that there are more possibilities, the world is more than what we see. For example, if you're sitting in a room and there's a big draft, then you might think, Ah, someone's come to visit. That would be the first thing that would pop in my mind; not everyone who is Haitian would think that, but that was part of my reality.

WACHTEL In one of the stories in *Krik? Krak!,* a story called "1937," a woman's mother is accused of being a witch. She's supposed to have flown to safety from the Dominican Republic across the river into Haiti, and for this she's imprisoned as a witch. Can you talk about the spiritual dimension in that story, because there's also a Madonna, a Catholic element.

DANTICAT I grew up hearing stories about these women who fly and, if you were a child, you were supposed to avoid them. You don't go out at night because there are women with wings of flames who fly and are not good to children. I remember hearing that when I was young and I thought, God, I'd just love to see one, but if you see one, you don't live. There were women who were arrested for sorcery; people could accuse them if something happened to their child—that still happens in some cases. During the dictatorship for example, François Duvalier, Papa Doc, used some of that. He called his personal security force the Volunteers for National Security, *les Tontons Macoutes.* When you were growing up you were told that, if you were bad, the *macoute* would come for you, like a bogeyman in the night. Papa Doc had taken that and brought it to life, like a nation's nightmare. There were so many places where the scary story worked into your life. I wanted to play with some of that in the way that I had experienced it, both with African religion and with Catholicism. Ultimately, if there are women who truly fly, of course, their wings will be clipped. I wanted to play with the very narrow space where the reality and the fantasy clash against each other in real life.

WACHTEL Even though it was your grandmother and aunts who told stories, you once said, "In Haitian culture, women are taught to be silent. But I must write." Was it that very silence that made the need so urgent?

DANTICAT I don't know. And now I'm thinking, "Did I say that?" I must have been brazen at some point of my life. I just wrote a foreword for a book of testimony of women who were victims under the coup in 1993, and a lot of the women are giving testimonies about what happened to them—many of them were raped, and they go through all this struggle, some of them were beaten and went to prison—and now they're telling their stories, and there's a sense that you must tell even when it might be better for you to be silent or, if you're raped, your husband might leave you. And that's not specific to Haitian culture, you know, that whole worry about stirring things up. But, I think, in the face of the silence that came before, that if you have a voice, you must speak.

WACHTEL Women in particular?

DANTICAT Women in particular, because our society is like other societies where women, especially poor women, are not often given the opportunity to speak. Other people speak for them, which is why I always say that I don't want to be called anybody's voice: if you are somebody's voice, you render them voiceless. I want everybody to have the opportunity to speak. I think here particularly about poor women—they're always there, but other people are speaking for them, their men speak for them, other women who are better educated or better off speak for them.

WACHTEL You have a piece in *Krik? Krak!* in which a mother is disappointed and worried that her daughter has chosen writing. Did your own mother have problems with your deciding to be a writer?

DANTICAT Well, my mother was, and I think still is, nervous for me about my being a writer, and part of it comes from our legacy, in that most of the people who were writing in my mother's youth in Haiti ended up in prison or exiled. And even in my time, if anybody wrote anything contrary to the official line, they were put in prison or they were sent away or they were killed. So it wasn't the best career choice, you know. With the immigration experience—so much is given up for you, so much is sacrificed—it's expected that you will do something sane and predictably stable. So I wasn't encouraged to pursue this life.

WACHTEL And even now?

DANTICAT Now, for me, I'm thinking I need a back-up. There's a proverb that says you don't step in the river with both feet, you test it with one foot, so you're always testing. But I think there's this sense that you have to make good, you have to do well, you can't blow the life that was sacrificed for you or the things that were done for you. But my mother's hesitation about me being a writer is primarily political, the personal risk and the political risk, and all the things that a young woman, as she would put it, risks in just being out there and saying things that might offend people. The confrontational element of doing this work echoes, for her, with many of our writers who were martyred, and so that comes into play.

WACHTEL You visit Haiti quite often. In fact, you were there quite recently. What is it like for you now?

DANTICAT I have come to terms with the fact that my relationship with Haiti is different than someone who lives there, than it is for my uncle and aunt and others who live there. But I love being there. There's a kind of peace about it that I can't explain. I realize also that I'm not living there, I'm staying for a certain period of time, at the end of which I travel back home. And so, it's a relationship of insider/outsider. Being in, my soul feels a kind of unrest and I wish that things were better. There will be a point in my life when I will go back to live, I feel, but it's still a developing relationship. There are so many people who, even with the way things are, plan to go back. People in my parents' generation always planned to go back, and then the dictatorship went on for thirty years and they couldn't. But there is that pull for me, a sense that there are many times when I feel that this is where I belong, but I don't want to go back and be part of the problem. I have to find a way that I can serve first, and be there in a way that's healing for me and healing for the place at the same time. So I'm still processing my returns every time I go. It stirs a lot of emotions, and gets me thinking about a lot of things when I'm there.

WACHTEL Haiti is a country with such a history of poverty and violence. Do Haitians see their country as a tragic place?

DANTICAT I don't think people see it as a tragic place. I think if things were better, if things were, say, 30 per cent better, most people would not leave. And you can judge from the number of people who, after forty years in the United States, are still dreaming of going back. People are forced to leave, and it's heartbreaking for them to have to leave, young people especially, who, after trying and trying, feel like they have to emigrate to make it. That I find tragic, and a lot of people inside find it tragic that the people who could be building the country have to leave in order to survive. I don't think Haitians see the *place* as tragic; I think they see the circumstances, the destiny we've had, the mismanagement, the bad leadership at times, as tragic.

WACHTEL There's an old Haitian song that you quote in a story in *Krik? Krak!* where the lyrics say, "Beloved Haiti, there's no place like you. I had to leave you before I could understand you." Do you relate to that sentiment?

DANTICAT It's ironic because when you get off the plane in Port-au-Prince, usually there's a band playing that song, so everybody who goes back hears that song, and it really is true. Probably, if I moved from the United States and went to live somewhere else, I would see America differently, too. I think there's a kind of stepping out of the self, and I thank God that things are a little better now, that people can go back, and that you can have that relationship of stepping back. It's a restructuring and reclaiming of home, but reclaiming in a different way, humbly, just going as an insider/outsider, stepping into the river, one foot at a time.

April 1999

§

WACHTEL There's a deeply felt appreciation for the landscape of Haiti in your latest novel *Claire of the Sea Light*: the mountains, the sea, the flowers, even fish. It's sensual, almost tangible at times. Can you describe your own attachment to the physical landscape of Haiti?

DANTICAT It's a deep attachment that I think has grown with distance, because my visits to Haiti are often short and intense, sometimes days, sometimes weeks, but they're often moments of soaking up just how much things have changed. There are some staple places that I visit. I go to the place where my mother grew up and to where my grandmother's house still is. I go to Jacmel, where I have a lot of friends now, and I go to the south, where my mother-in-law is. So it's always this continued searching to see what's different than the last time. I think what I've started to notice most as I've gotten older is the environment: the sea, the trees, the physical landscape and how people adjust to it, how people live within it. That's become more and more striking to me as time has gone on.

WACHTEL This natural environment in your novel is at risk both on land and sea, and we're not talking about hurricanes or earthquakes. Poverty is driving the Haitians in your novel to exploit the environment. What are your own concerns for Haiti in that regard?

DANTICAT I think it's everybody's concern in Haiti. As the environment is eroded, it becomes more and more urgent for people to cut down trees to make charcoal or to live or to build. But I think it's also important to look at the history of environmental decline because it's often blamed solely on Haitians themselves, whereas it started in the previous century, during the US occupation. Entire forests were cut down and this wood sent abroad for sale. And then in the 1940s the Catholic Church started an anti-superstition campaign, by cutting down the biggest trees, which are the holiest: the silk-cotton trees called Mapou. To prevent invasions during the dictatorship, Papa Doc Duvalier would cut down entire parts of the country to create what he'd call the *cordons sanitaires* so that any invaders would have nowhere to hide. So at the beginning it was not necessarily the fault of the poor. Then you have an increasingly depleted environment that is further reduced by the fact that it has to be worked harder and is producing less.

WACHTEL With the US occupation, you're referring to the one early in the twentieth century, 1915 to 1934, and then again from 1994 to 1996.

DANTICAT Absolutely.

WACHTEL The belief systems of some of your characters include a connection to the land. Vodou seems to incorporate elements of animism, mysticism, and even Catholicism. How strong is that in the lives of Haitians?

DANTICAT Vodou is a religion as well as a worldview, and it stands in Haiti next to other religions: Protestant, Catholic. Often the practitioners of vodou are persecuted. For example, after the cholera epidemic, which was introduced to Haiti by United Nations peacekeepers, there were lynchings of vodou priests. It's a religion that's often very much under assault, so practitioners are discreet in their practice. But it encompasses a respectful life, a building of community so that in a community like the one in my book, there would be these different religions side by side, but vodou as practised by some of the characters—and in the book, some of them very distinctly—reflected more in their worldview and how they interpret certain realities.

WACHTEL Your uncle was a Protestant minister and a leader in his community. How much was religion part of your life when you were a girl?

DANTICAT My uncle was a Baptist minister so religion was a huge part of my life. We also lived next to a *péristyle*, a vodou temple. So we were in church most days, but we were also getting this other vibe. From the roof of our house, we could look down into the *péristyle* when there were ceremonies happening. And at school, we would be taken to the Catholic mass on Friday, whatever religion we were. So I was exposed to all the primary religions of the country at the time.

WACHTEL Did you understand why everyone would go to Catholic mass?

DANTICAT It's just how it was. We would go to the mass on Friday, and I would do the sign of the cross. You just did it. I didn't do communion or any of that, but I actually loved the whole ritual—the smoke, the incense—and I grew to really love stained-glass figures. I think I understood—even my uncle understood—that at the core of all of it was a strong spiritual presence. God was at the centre of all things. My family didn't want me to leave the Baptist church and join the others, but I was allowed to participate.

WACHTEL And did you feel that spiritual element in your own life?

DANTICAT I did before I understood what it was. For example, I think I grasped that there was a kind of continuum, because sometimes my uncle would have to do a wedding and a funeral and a child's christening on the same weekend, and as the family of the minister, we were expected to go to all of the ceremonies. I always wore a little white dress that my mother had sent me from the States. I realized that there was a kind of ritual to life that involves something bigger than ourselves, and whether we were saying hello to a newborn child or goodbye to a dead person, young or old, there was a continuum to it, a journey that we all travel and that eventually would all pass through. This was always repeated at funerals, that the only guarantee is that we're all going to pass through this door. Of course, I would think not me, not me.

WACHTEL I still think that.

DANTICAT I think that's the essential core of humanity. That's how we survive, because it would be so futile if we came into life knowing that and accepting it fully.

WACHTEL That proximity between the forces of life and death manifests itself in the novel *Claire of the Sea Light*. Do you think there's something about Haiti in particular that emphasizes that particular connection?

DANTICAT I don't think it's unique to Haiti. In any society where we don't split these spaces totally, as we do, say, in the United States, where it's very neat and separated… When you die, you're buried a certain way. And that is true in Haiti too, but, for example, when my Aunt Denise, who had raised me, died, we were asked if we wanted to dress her in the funeral home. Some of the family members, of course, wanted the separation. They said, "Oh, I don't want to do that." But some of us said, "Sure. It would be an honour," because she had dressed us when we were little and had taken care of us. So I think there are many places, certainly in the developing world, where that connection is felt from birth, where there is no guarantee, for example, that there will be a child after the birth, that the mother will make it, and where survival every day demands a kind of faith and effort that makes people aware that death is very much in proximity to life. Life is something that's not taken for granted; it's something that people have to work hard to maintain. There's a proverb that my mother always says: "We're all walking with our coffins under our arms." Some of us know it, and some of us don't. So I think there's a hyper-awareness of people in vulnerable populations that there is a possibility of death at all times, but miraculously it doesn't keep people from living their lives. I always find this incredibly amazing, especially if you've been living in an environment where people feel like they have so much more control over what happens to them, and they're still so careful, clinging so hard to certain things. Or you see people who are hyper-vulnerable, but live at full volume, if you will.

WACHTEL How would you describe your own faith now, having been exposed to those different beliefs when you were growing up?

DANTICAT I'm very open to all kinds of faiths. I still attend a Baptist church in Miami whenever I'm here, and when I need it. For example, after the earthquake in Haiti, I just needed to be around people of faith, and the only thing that was going on at that time was a Catholic mass. I went to seek solace there. I have tried to continue in the faith of my childhood—the songs that I sang growing up, I like singing them in church. But I don't want to tell people, *Your* faith is bad. I don't want to be part of that aspect of faith. I feel like the essential has remained for me, in that, at the core of it, is God. I still believe, in spite, sometimes, of great evidence to the contrary, that there is compassion at the core of religion, and that we are all supposed to show one another as much compassion as we can.

WACHTEL The title character of your novel, Claire, is seven. Her mother died in childbirth, and her father, Nozias, gave the baby to relatives. Nozias clearly has an emotional attachment to Claire, and he takes her back when she's three. How unusual would it be for a single, poor fisherman to want to raise his own daughter?

DANTICAT It wouldn't be unusual at all if the poor fisherman had more support. I think what's important to emphasize in a situation like this, where you write a book about something that could be very easily generalized and judged, is that the choice in this book is as singular as it might be for any individual parent. Let's say this fisherman had a lot of family around. Let's say he had remarried. He might have attempted to keep his daughter. But in this particular situation, he is a man alone, and he senses that there is another person with more means who, because of her own circumstances, might want a child. He makes a very difficult decision to give Claire to this woman. My parents had to make a similar choice for a time when they decided to move to the United States and left me and my brother with my aunt and uncle. In our case, there was the possibility of reunion. In this case, Claire's father is giving her away, at least so it appears, for good. But as a parent now, I realize it's a heart-wrenching choice. You would have to look at every single case to see what it would be like for that individual parent.

WACHTEL Your parents left you and your brother in the care of your aunt and uncle when they immigrated to the US; you were two when your father left, four when your mother joined him. How did you feel about it at the time?

DANTICAT I was too young to feel anything but that ache of the moment. I don't remember my father leaving. I remember the day my mother left. We went to the airport, and I thought I was leaving, too. When someone had to take me out of her arms, I remember a kind of scream that I would imagine now, when I think about it, and I implant the memory with the voice of one of my daughters screaming. My youngest is now four. I don't sit around doing that mostly, but every time she screams a really devastating scream, I think, Oh, this must have been what mine was like. One of my first memories is that moment of being taken out of my mother's arms, but I don't remember the rest of the day. I don't ever remember thinking in terms of, I feel bad. Obviously, I felt bad because a part of my life was disrupted, but it's something that I grew to understand later. Certainly now as a parent, the level of heartache that that must have caused, that plane ride for my mother… if I were writing this in a story, you would have to go to the mother on the plane and imagine the heartache of walking or flying into your new life and leaving this screaming child behind.

WACHTEL You and your brother were reunited with your parents in Brooklyn eight years later. Why so long?

DANTICAT It took so long because of the immigration red tape. My parents, when they moved to the US, were undocumented, and so they had to legalize their status. They started that process by returning to Haiti when I was seven, when they came with my two little brothers who were born in the States. My brothers got sick during that trip. I remember the trip was cut short, and they went back. Then it was five years before we could join them in New York because, after they had filed papers at the consulate in Haiti, they had to go back and work to prove that they could support two more children. My brother and I were finally able to join them in 1981, when I was twelve and my brother was ten.

WACHTEL What was that reunion like for you?

DANTICAT It was extraordinarily complicated because, first of all, of the shock of New York City, just getting adjusted to a whole new place, as well as getting adjusted to my new family, to my brothers, and their getting used to us. When they got older, they told us they were never told anything about us. Our parents had never told them that they had siblings, or maybe they told them, but they didn't remember because they were young. We were a shock to them, and the whole place was a shock to us. And 1981 was a very difficult time for Haitians in the United States. You had a first wave of people coming by boat to Miami, fleeing the latter end of the dictatorship. Bodies were washing up on the beaches in Miami; that was on the news every night. And you had the AIDS epidemic just starting, with Haitians as one of four groups of people who were high risk. It was Haitians, homosexuals, haemophiliacs, heroin addicts—we were the only ones identified by nationality. It was really not the easiest entry into American life.

WACHTEL Throughout *Claire of the Sea Light*, the theme of abandoned children or children in danger is present. Why did you want to tell their stories?

DANTICAT I think it was something that has always intrigued me. When I was with my aunt and uncle, we were in a house full of children like us, cousins whose families were in the United States, in the Dominican

Republic, in Canada. But also we had cousins who came from the countryside, and sometimes they came with very urgent problems and my uncle had to find care for them. One of them got TB and had to be put in the sanatorium and eventually died. We had these sorts of Victorian issues all around us. I've discovered that when you have a little child, even minor problems are just so extraordinary; you would trade your life for your child to feel better immediately. And so I think it was a way of reconciling some of the things that I watched people experience when I was younger with the fears that you develop when you become a parent and the lengths you feel you would go to protect your child. Perhaps it's a way of exposing my fears about my past and then dealing with all the things that one worries about as a parent.

WACHTEL The main town in *Claire of the Sea Light* is based on the place where your mother grew up. Can you describe it?

DANTICAT Ville Rose is a composite of many different coastal towns in Haiti, but it's primarily based on Léogâne. My parents are both from Léogâne, my mother from the district called Cité Napoléon, named after, I suppose, members of her family. She is a Napoléon. It's the place where we used to visit my maternal grandmother in the summer, but that grandmother was not my storytelling grandmother. She was more formal and formidable, a distant grandmother. I remember we would visit her, and then we would have a meal, and then we'd go to the beach, and someone would almost always nearly drown during that visit.

Léogâne was almost completely devastated by the 2010 earthquake. I remember going back then to look for my cousins who had settled there on the side of a stream. They survived and had built a little makeshift house until they could get their other house repaired.

WACHTEL You mentioned this wasn't your storytelling grandmother, although you did have a storytelling grandmother and aunts. Was it always women who told the stories?

DANTICAT In my case, yes, it was always women. The men would sometimes chime in, but in my family—I don't want to generalize—the men would tell the jokes, and then the women would tell the more folkloric stories.

WACHTEL How do you think those stories affected your own development as a writer? Not that you, at that point in your life, were collecting material, but how do you think you took them in?

DANTICAT It's funny because when people ask me who my best writing teachers were, I always think of those women because they told stories in such an audience-connected way. They could tell the same story all the time, but if it was told differently, you felt like it was new. And there were songs in the stories. And if it was late at night and you were falling asleep, they would make it suspenseful, and there was something about the dark and that connection that even then… I wasn't collecting material, but I would think how wonderful that structure was when I looked back on it. Each time you were told a story, it felt like you were being given a story that you could then pass on to somebody else. I was always too shy to tell stories in the way that they told them, but when I started reading books, I thought, Oh, this is like what they do, except you can just be one-on-one with this storyteller; there's no performance, and the movie's in your head.

WACHTEL Gang violence is a troubling element in *Claire of the Sea Light*. How serious is the problem in Haiti?

DANTICAT I can't speak for right this moment, but when I wrote this novel, I was thinking about the neighbourhood where my uncle lived, the neighbourhood where I grew up, where quite a few of the young men, some of whom we had known since they were very little, have joined gangs. My uncle had a school in the neighbourhood, and sometimes he would have some of these gang members who had been deported from the United States come into the school to teach the children English. He would really try to be a good neighbour. I remember a few of them being at my aunt's funeral, for example, and one of them came to the house and said to my uncle, "If anybody messes with you,"—that kind of thing. There was a kind of cohabitation in the neighbourhood. People lived there and they knew these young men differently than the rest of the world did, but the UN would come in and try to obliterate the neighbourhood to get one or two of them. And so it was, at least in this particular case—I can't speak for other areas—a sometimes uneasy cohabitation. Eventually, when there was an operation in which the UN shot at many of them from my uncle's rooftop, things turned ugly. My uncle had to flee the neighbourhood, and he died in the custody of US Immigration. This is a long story, which we talked about in connection with my book, *Brother, I'm Dying*.

I think gang violence is always going to be a problem, just as it would be elsewhere, when you have young men with little or nothing to do, and some of them have gone to school and been promised the possibility of a job, and then suddenly they have nothing. They are in an urban centre. They see glaring inequalities in front of them. Violence springs out of that, especially when they create gangs, and there's nothing being offered to them. Certainly, we've been very deeply touched by it in my family. I'm not excusing it, but you can understand how that can come about.

WACHTEL You recreate the complexities of that cohabitation in your novel. There's a couple whose business relies on the local gang as their clientele because they need the money to get their son out of the neighbourhood that's been destroyed by gang violence. It's such a moral bind that they're in. One young man thinks he might be able to help with the problem of violence in his town with a radio show. What's the idea behind that?

DANTICAT When I started the book it was going to be about the radio because I've always been intrigued by the whole idea of radio in Haiti. Ever since I was a little girl, especially in the neighbourhood where I grew up and in Bel Air, there was always a radio on somewhere. Even if your radio wasn't on, someone's radio was, and sometimes it was several radios on different stations, so you had a kind of chorus.

But in recent years during my visits, I've become very intrigued by talk radio, or what we would call the equivalent of talk radio here, where people since the 1990s, after the dictatorship ended, have developed a very strong form of expression. They'll speak on politics very openly, and sometimes the radio makes news because a senator or even the president comes on. But there's also these late-night radio shows where people call in with their love questions and things of that nature.

So radio was supposed to be at the centre of the book. But what we have left is Louise George, who is the hostess of a radio show called "Di Mwen" or "Tell Me"—*Claire of the Sea Light* was originally called *Dismoi*, and the centre was going to be the town through the radio. Louise is what's left of the radio, and she uses it as a tool for justice. She's also a kind of aspiring novelist who's supposedly writing a book that's like this book. She sees herself in a way that is very different from how the town sees her, but what she understands, and what another character in the book, Bernard, understands, is that the power of the radio is the power of shedding light on certain truths by sharing stories.

WACHTEL Bernard wants to bring together the criminals, the gangs, and have them talk to business people and others. He thinks he can really change things.

DANTICAT Yes. And he thinks, if there's a public conversation between, say, the gang leaders and the business owners, that will change something, and he really believes in the airing of our problems. This is where he believes the rich and the poor can meet on equal ground. He really believes in the radio as a completely democratic forum, and on some level, I think Louise George does too. And they both see that, in a place like their town where there's so little justice, this could be the court of public opinion, where people come together and decide on an outcome that allows the town to continue to exist with all of them in it.

WACHTEL But do you hold that hope for the power of radio?

DANTICAT I hold hope for the power of conversation and the power of transparency and the power of trying to cross the line and seeing what the "other" is like because I saw it in action with my uncle. I saw that, when he talked to these young men in the gangs like they were people, they were able to communicate with one another, that when he was able to see their humanity and they were able to see their own, that there was a possibility at least. And maybe it was a naive possibility, but he was a minister and he fully believed in redemption. That when they were able to be in the same space and have a conversation, there was at least a possibility that there could be a turnaround for that young man teaching English at the school or coming to the clinic my uncle ran. If you have a public conversation, as Bernard proposed, then others are listening. And his hope was that maybe this conversation could be replicated elsewhere because someone had heard it on the radio, and they could tell themselves, "If those two people can get in a room and talk, then maybe I can talk to my neighbour as well."

WACHTEL In your recent essay collection *Create Dangerously*, you investigate, among other things, the part artists can play in their communities and in politics.

DANTICAT It's something that has always fascinated me. From the time when I used to tell people, including people in my family, that I wanted to be a writer, they would always immediately tell me about writers who had been exiled or killed, even before I was born. So most often they would bring up Jacques Stephen Alexis, who's an extraordinary writer, who had been on a trip abroad and came back and was ambushed and killed by the *Tonton Macoutes*, by Duvalier's henchmen. And there was a story of two young men who were executed after they came back from Queens, New York; they were two of a group of thirteen called *Gens Haïti*. So all those stories just made me interested in how people in those circumstances came to their art.

There was also, on the opposite end of that, the extraordinary story of a poet, Félix Morisseau-Leroy, who lived during the bloody dictatorship. He decided to stage *Antigone* at the National Theatre. He rewrote it in Creole, and because people, I guess, were wearing togas, the dictatorship missed the whole point. What a lot of mothers were doing when they were picking up—or when they were too afraid to even go and pick up their children's or their husbands' or their brothers' dead bodies on the street—was very similar to Antigone's dilemma. That was his point. That was what he was thinking. But these writers were trying to find ways around censorship and repression, so they would read and stage *Caligula*. I was interested in how people functioned as artists within that space, and that's what I decided to investigate in this book.

WACHTEL How do you see the idea of "creating dangerously" in your own work?

DANTICAT I wrote that book, I think, to inspire myself to be bolder because sometimes, with the moral ambiguity of art, you try to see even the bad guys' side, you try to step into another perspective. And also the anger of really wanting to be the kind of person that wants to set things right. The idea of "creating dangerously" is borrowed from Albert Camus in one of his last lectures, given in the 1950s, called "L'Artiste et Son Temps." It was translated into English as "Create Dangerously." He said, "To create today is to create dangerously." He was wrestling at that time with the issue of his stand on Algerian independence. He had what I have come to think of as the ambivalence of the novelist, where you want to see everybody's side.

So in my own work, it's something that I'm still coming to terms with, and I try to seek inspiration from all these bold people. I am less shy perhaps in my work than, say, in my person; I am trying to speak more truth to power, if you will.

WACHTEL How much pressure is there on Haitian expats to return to Haiti? Something like 80 per cent of the country's professionals live outside the country.

DANTICAT I think a lot of people, even without necessarily returning, do help. Something close to a billion dollars a year in remittances are sent from people who live outside of Haiti. And people do return through neighbourhood or association groups that are affiliated with groups of people here: nurses' associations, lawyers' associations, doctors' associations. They go back, and while there isn't a central base where people register and help, a lot of us still have families in Haiti, and we do things like start schools. It's an aspect of Haitian life that, from the outside, we don't see, but it's ongoing. With all these issues we've talked about, with all the environmental challenges, with all the economic challenges, if people didn't have a sense of community, of being able to count on one another, and if a lot of people didn't have the outside resources of the family diaspora, then things might be a whole lot worse.

WACHTEL Your daughters are still young. How well do they know Haiti?

DANTICAT They know Haiti quite well for their young age. My husband's mother still lives there, so they go back quite a bit, at least twice a year. My oldest recently announced to me that she wants us to adopt fifteen kids from Haiti.

WACHTEL Is that all?

DANTICAT Yes. One of the things that I love about their involvement in Haiti is that it has become just another ordinary place for them. We travel quite a bit. We go to different places, and for them it's like any other place. That might sound really odd, but for a lot of us who grew up in the diaspora, we grew up with this merged feeling from our parents that Haiti was simultaneously both this exceptional paradise and this horrible, scary place where you shouldn't go. I really want them to just think of it as another place, a place where you go and see your cousins, and you go to the stream if you're in the countryside and all of that. It's something that I hope will always be part of their lives.

WACHTEL In your essay "Create Dangerously," you quote Albert Camus, who said that a person's creative work is nothing but a slow trek to rediscover "those two or three images in whose presence his or her heart first opened." What are those images for you?

DANTICAT One of them is certainly the day my mother left Haiti, that image of being peeled off her body. That's one. The second one was landing in the United States. And the third, up until recently, was the year that included the death of my father, the death of my uncle, and the birth of my daughter, that year when all those experiences converged.

But it's always changing, ever-shifting. I wouldn't want to feel as if these are the three things that I will be writing about for the rest of my life, but they are, certainly, at the core.

October 2013
Original interviews produced by Lisa Godfrey and Mary Stinson

ORHAN PAMUK

When I first interviewed Orhan Pamuk in 2002, he was already Turkey's most successful writer, both at home and abroad. *The New York Times* called him "The Best Seller of Byzantium." He deftly combined Islamic themes and traditions with western modernism—for instance, at that time, in *My Name Is Red* (1998, trans. 2001), an ambitious novel about sixteenth-century Ottoman miniaturists. Illustrators in the court of the Sultan experience the pressures and seductions of Renaissance art coming out of Venice, so completely at odds with their faith. It's a book of fable, philosophy, mystery. Pamuk had won major Turkish and international awards and *My Name Is Red* went on to win the 2003 International IMPAC Dublin Literary Award, the largest cash prize for a single novel. Pamuk is that unusual creature—a postmodernist who's popular, but that's because he's such a good storyteller.

In 2006, he won the Nobel Prize for Literature—especially for his sensitive and atmospheric memoir of both his family and his city, a book called *Istanbul* (2003, trans. 2005). In announcing the award, the Swedish Academy said that "In the quest for the melancholic soul of his native city, Pamuk has discovered new symbols for the clash and interlacing of cultures."

Pamuk's attachment to the city is profound—in fact, for much of his life he's inhabited the same building in the same neighbourhood, gazing at the same view of the Bosphorus. Pamuk was the second youngest person to win the Nobel and Turkey's first Nobel Prize winner—in any category.

But he had also become famous because he was charged with the "public denigration of Turkish identity"—under a law that's since been repealed. In speaking to a journalist, Pamuk pointed out that early in the twentieth century "one million Armenians and 30,000 Kurds were killed in Turkey." There were threats against his life, and after the assassination of the Turkish-Armenian journalist Hrant Dink in January 2007, Pamuk was assigned police protection.

Through it all, Orhan Pamuk was writing—and, it turns out, collecting. He was engaged in an extraordinary project: a novel, *The Museum of Innocence* (2008, trans. 2009), and at the same time, he was creating an actual museum to house the objects that figured in his fiction. A character's cigarette butts, ticket stubs, ephemera, arranged in vitrines that correspond to chapters in the novel. It's an amazing enterprise, drawing on Pamuk's own memories. In 2014, it won the European Museum of the Year Award.

Born in 1952, Pamuk grew up in a secular, Western-oriented environment in Istanbul. It was an upper-middle-class household, downwardly mobile. His grandfather was a very successful engineer, his father and uncles were also engineers. The assumption was that Orhan Pamuk would also be an engineer or an architect. His early interest was in painting: from the age of six or seven, he would copy reproductions of French impressionists and later he worked on Ottoman and Persian miniatures. But then, in his early twenties, he switched to writing. He dropped out of university and stayed at home until he was thirty, when his first book was published.

Orhan Pamuk's ninth novel, *A Strangeness in My Mind* (2014, trans. 2015) also reflects his love of Istanbul, but from a very different perspective. Focussing on an Istanbul street vendor, it chronicles the life of migrants from rural Anatolia to the city, resulting in its exponential growth over the past forty-plus years. He spoke to me about it from New York, where he was lecturing at Columbia University.

WACHTEL *My Name Is Red* is set in the world of art, the world of miniature painting and illumination that flourished in the Ottoman Empire. You yourself grew up wanting to be a painter. Why was that?
PAMUK I come from a family of engineers. My grandfather was a civil engineer who made lots of money building railroads; my uncles and my father were also engineers. So it was very natural in my family to

be an engineer and that was what was expected of me—of us, me and my cousins. But then I was—you don't know why this happens—the black sheep in the family. I was what was called "the artsy fellow." When I was seven, I began to draw and paint. And everyone—you know this is a cliché—remarked on what a talented boy I was. It continued like that 'til the age of twenty-one—at that time I'd committed myself seriously to painting, I even had a studio—when I switched from painting to writing.

WACHTEL When you were young, as I understand it, you used to copy reproductions of Ottoman and Persian miniatures. What was that like for you?

PAMUK When I was doing all these paintings between the ages of seven and twenty-one, I was, of course, like all aspiring painters, imitating, copying Western artists. French Impressionists like Pissarro, Vuillard, Cezanne, then Picasso. I would try to draw like them. But I remember, at the age of thirteen, picking up a little paperback volume on Islamic painting. This was the early sixties, when there were very few books on Islamic painting. But, perhaps because of a nationalistic urge, or a problem of identity, I also wanted to copy—not copy actually, but enlarge—reproductions of Islamic miniatures. This is how I, at the age of twelve or thirteen, began to get in touch with them. Of course, compared to the Impressionists, or classical Dutch painting, they were a bit different, a bit awkward. But that simplicity was closer to the Western comic books that I used to enjoy at that time, than, say, to seventeenth-century Dutch painting.

WACHTEL More like comic books because of the flatness?

PAMUK Because there were few shadows. For instance, there would be a scene in which two heroes talked and that was the essential part of the picture, the interaction of two persons. They were in front, and in the back was the landscape or street, but that was not important. And then the simplicity of the lines. The comics were in black and white at the time and that also made them look more like miniatures.

WACHTEL Working in such detail, did you ever imagine yourself in the workshops of the great miniaturists?

PAMUK No. That was later, when I switched from painting to fiction, to writing novels, at the age of twenty-three. After I published my first novel, I decided that one day I would like to write about a painter—of course a Turkish painter. But I didn't want to write about modern

Turkish painters, about whom I had a low opinion because I thought they were all imitating Western examples badly. I wanted to write about the real thing, the essential thing: the pure painting, the Ottoman painter. I also had this romantic idea of writing historical novels.

WACHTEL What was it about these Islamic miniatures and the stories that they illustrated that made such an impression on you?

PAMUK When I was writing *The Black Book*—and this is how I truly found my voice—after *The White Castle*, I decided I wanted to represent Istanbul in a new way. The previous generation of authors wrote about the city like Steinbeck would write about California—very simplistic, flat, simplified, nineteenth-century realism. I didn't want to do fiction like that, I wanted to do something more complicated, baroque, with layers and layers of history in it. With this kind of agenda in mind, I began to read thoroughly: Islamic classics, Sufi classics, romantic Islamic allegories, romances, for example, the works of Rumi and others, from which I derived lots of stories. I rewrote those stories and put them in *The Black Book*. As for *My Name Is Red,* once I had access to, and began to really, genuinely enjoy classical Persian literature, I thought that when I did this book on painting, I also wanted to go not only to the pictures but to the classical stories they illustrated. These stories, by the way, were to the people of thirteenth-century Persia, which today includes Afghanistan, Iran, Iraq, Egypt, Turkey, and some Balkan countries, what Shakespeare or Victor Hugo are for the English or American or French reader. They were classics, but no one looked at them as classics because the concept of time was different. Nothing was changing and they did not have a cult of change or an idea of modernity and originality. These books were eternal and they were eternally reillustrating the same scenes. If you were an intellectual or if you wanted to be a member of the ruling class—and in that of course you had to belong to the palace or be a protegé of one of the sultans—then you would have to be educated in one of these books. So they were the classic stories, I would say even the archetypes, that all these people, between the thirteenth and the seventeenth centuries, carried around in their heads. There were so many reproductions of these books in Turkish libraries that when they decided to produce luxuries, sumptuous goods, they illustrated no more than ten or twenty classical scenes that everyone knew. And the way they illustrated the positions of the figures was almost identical. The scenes and the placement of figures, the manner in which they were drawn, were all very limited—which almost implies that Islamic painting really covers available space.

WACHTEL Did you have a favourite image or miniature?

PAMUK No, because as a child, from that heritage, the books that were produced were limited. They would always contain ten or twelve pictures that would cover centuries. It's like looking at the sea and tasting a spoonful of the sea. You might say the sea tastes the same all the time. So I began to pick up and enjoy some of these pictures, years later. As a child I was mystified by the—I wouldn't say grotesqueness—the simplicity, naïveté, primitiveness of these pictures and the people in them, the clothes, the way they related to each other more than the beauty of the picture. I tell this to everyone, including the Turks, that in order to enjoy these pictures you have to be very patient because they don't reveal themselves in the first moment. And in fact, at the beginning, they are not very interesting to look at. First you have to know the stories, then why that scene is so important. Then you have to be patient and continue looking at them. Let me give you an example of my experience of that.

When I began writing *My Name Is Red* in the early 1990s, I did research on Persian and Islamic painting in New York, at the Metropolitan Museum, where there is a good display of classical Turkish miniatures. I would constantly go and look at and try to understand five or six of these little paintings, which were no bigger than the cover of a regular hardcover book. There was glass between them and me. I would bring my face as close as one could bring it to the picture, then stare at it for quite a long time, until my back hurt. When I did that, I was not "understanding," or even enjoying anything. But in fact I was committed to these surfaces, these colours, and I was of course reading about them, and I would think: How am I going to write a novel about these people? What did they think? What is in this picture? You would see a tree, you would see a horse, you would see a person on a horse, a girl weeping, you would see classical scenes, for example, Shirin swimming in a pond at midnight and Ferhat coming on a horse and noticing her beauty. All those little stories you can identify and relate to if you know the story and the scene.

So I spent a lot of time and in fact got a bit desperate and discouraged. After a while I would leave the room and—my feet knew the way— walk quickly to a little maze on the second floor of the Metropolitan, to a room where there would be these huge Impressionist paintings, like

Renoir's. And each time I did that, I would be—my soul would be—filled with song, with the strength and depth of the art. I was trying to dedicate my mental and spiritual energies to the Ottoman miniatures, trying to express and identify with those people who made them, but after a while I would be tired. Of course, the meaning of Renoir, or any Impressionist painting, is *there*. Your eyes are enjoying the painting, so full of song and movement and reality. On the other hand, it was for me a challenge to find depth in those miniatures. I had read all the scholarly books about those subjects. Most of what they did was what they call taxonomy: weighing, measuring, placing in history. But the relation of those colours and the pictures and the spirit was never the subject of their research. So I also wanted to do that for the first time.

WACHTEL Stories are as much at the centre of your novel as the artwork that illustrates them. In the opening chapter of *My Name Is Red,* titled "I Am a Corpse," the narrator, a dead man, says that, "if the situation into which we've fallen were described in a book, even the most expert of miniaturists could never hope to illustrate it. As with the Koran… the staggering power of such a book arises from the impossibility of its being depicted." Can you talk about the kinds of stories that *were* featured in the work of the great miniaturists?

PAMUK There are so many of them, but one story I like, and in fact that I retell in the book, is falling in love through pictures, "Hüsrev and Shirin." Hüsrev is a prince and Shirin is an Armenian princess and fate decides they fall in love with each other. Her servant gives her a picture of the boy; they go out for a picnic and she hangs the image on a tree and falls in love with him by looking at his picture. I like this theme of falling in love through pictures because in fact it is not realistic—Islamic painting never managed to produce proper portraits. In paintings you would never see a picture you could use like today's passport photos. In this story, it implies they have managed to produce this kind of picture which, after looking at it, you might fall in love with.

WACHTEL *My Name Is Red* is a murder mystery, it's a philosophical adventure, a love story. Its heroine, Shekure, says, "Perhaps one day someone from a distant land will listen to this story of mine. Isn't this what lives behind the desire to be inscribed in the pages of a book?" There's a kind of playfulness, a deliberate self-consciousness that could be described as postmodern. Why is that important to you? To make us aware of the craft of storytelling?

PAMUK First I think it's impossible to write historical fiction today as Tolstoy wrote *War and Peace,* saying that my writing is giving you the story, that I have researched the details and it's true to life and this is what happened in the past. Not only is that not convincing but I also find it a bit boring. I prefer to write a historical novel and while I do Tolstoyan research (I'm that kind of person, I enjoy doing lots of research, reading books), on the other hand, tongue-in-cheek, I prefer to tell the reader that, although this is a historical novel, I'm putting in things that you know are artificial. Although it purports to document the past, it also plays around with ideas, figures, personages from today. I myself am in the book, with my mother, my brother—

WACHTEL But you as a little kid—

PAMUK Yes, a little kid, because of how I depict the situation. My father had just left us, as it was in the book. We were two boys, one eight, one six, with a mother trying to protect us. There were other men around her and this was very autobiographical, the things I carried to sixteenth-century Istanbul. But essentially this simplicity of a mother protecting two boys who fight with each other all the time could, I thought, be carried from the twentieth century.

WACHTEL You even gave the same names to yourself, your mother, and your brother.

PAMUK Yes. My readers in Turkey ask me, So, you have a problematic relationship with your brother?

WACHTEL You describe yourself as a book fetishist. What does that mean?

PAMUK In Turkey, you are criticized for things all the time. I have made it a policy that if I am criticized, then I accept it and in fact exaggerate it. Compared to the previous generation of authors, I am more bookish, more intellectual. I allude to other authors, other texts, in a more playful, more, in fact, as you said, postmodern way. For readers and critics who are immersed in realist fiction, this is being bookish, so I exaggerate it.

WACHTEL Your novel *The New Life* opens with the line: "I read a book one day and my whole life was changed." The narrator falls in love with a book and he's transfigured by it. The book remains unidentified. The power of books: why is this such an important theme?

PAMUK Really, it's a very personal thing. My friends, people of my generation, were going out into the streets, involved in politics, or falling in love, or doing this or that. I was a shy, bookish person from the upper middle class who preferred to stay at home, amongst the books. Once you have this experience, books never leave you. You cannot change yourself. In all of my novels, at the centre, there is a book, there is a text, there is the production of a book, or the impact of a book, or someone is writing a book or we may be following the pages of that book. Not only because I like Calvino or Borges or *A Thousand and One Nights,* but also because I am simply a bookish person.

WACHTEL In terms of the playfulness in *The New Life,* the central character adopts the pseudonym Orphan Panic.

PAMUK Yes.

WACHTEL Tell me more about this household that *you* grew up in, this upper-middle-class family.

PAMUK Some of it I described in *The Black Book.* I grew up in a family that used to live in a three-storey mansion. In the early fifties, they moved to an apartment building in which, on each floor, one of my uncles, my aunt, my grandfather, my grandmother, we, used to live. So it was moving from a traditional Ottoman family mansion in which three generations lived with lots of rooms to an apartment building in which, on each floor, one uncle, with his now little family, lived. Like the mansion, the main door of the apartment building would be closed to the street but the apartment doors would be open. When I was a kid, I would go up to my grandmother's flat and play with her, then go down to my uncle's. Or my mother would forbid us, after having our lunch, to go up to our grandmother's and eat there again. So I always felt I lived in a crowded, traditional family, but in fact it was disintegrating, falling apart, over family property. My family fought constantly with each other and sued each other for property. Finally everyone moved to another place, so we had gone from a huge mansion to an apartment building, and from there to separate little apartments. That was the kind of family I lived with.

WACHTEL You say somewhere that your grandmother read atheistic poetry. What did she read to you?

PAMUK That was Turkish atheistic poetry. She was well-educated. Before she married my grandfather, she was about to be sent to France for university. She was positivistic, and she had her generation's enthusiasms—pro-European, republican, secular. There was a poet called Tevfik Fikret, whose atheistic poems she used to recite to me.

WACHTEL Was growing up in a secular household common at that time?

PAMUK Yes, it was a normal thing. The founders of the ruling class, the Turkish Republic, were very secular, Western-oriented. At the time they thought that the failure of the Ottoman Empire was perhaps due to the failure of Islam—an idea that my generation is very critical of, but that's what they thought. They were very positivistic.

WACHTEL What was your exposure to Islam when you were a child?

PAMUK The problem with my parents' generation was that they wanted to Europeanize Turkey, which was a good idea, with which I still agree, but they decided to do that by forgetting the past. They suppressed the glories of the culture of the Ottoman Empire and thought they would put in its place humanistic, liberal Western values, but they could not manage to do that. I grew up with their ideas, and then, with this secular outlook, I went back to the suppressed Ottoman past. I sometimes jokingly say that if Freud tells you that when something is suppressed it comes back in disguise, then my novels are, in fact, that disguise.

WACHTEL As a kid, though, you went to the mosque with your neighbours.

PAMUK Yes, but I was never religious. Servants of the house used to go to the mosque to meet other people, not to pray but to gossip, and sometimes they took us too.

WACHTEL When you say you're returning to this repressed Islamic past, do you experience it intellectually or spiritually?

PAMUK Intellectually. My interest in Islamic culture is not religious but secular. Compared to other generations of authors, I am among the first to show that interest. One can have a look at the glorious Islamic allegories in a very secular fashion and perhaps just like Borges, pick up stories, play around with them geometrically, find their logic, rewrite them, and then reposition them in modern Turkey. This is what I did with *The Black Book*.

WACHTEL You were saying that your grandfather was a civil engineer who made a fortune in the railway. Your mother's family were textile manufacturers. You were expected to become an engineer or an architect, and in fact, you started out studying architecture. But then, as you describe it, you locked yourself in your bedroom for eight years, to write. Was it as dramatic as that?

PAMUK I never thought I would be writing and not published for eight years, but that's how it turned out. I was twenty-two, studying architecture. I realized I didn't want to be an architect in Istanbul. The rules, the clients, the quality of architecture would depress me. I realized essentially that I am not a social person. In order to be an architect you have to know how to get along with all your clients, and I'm not that sort of person. So I decided I would be a writer, but I'm not the kind of person who would go to a writers' workshop. I simply began to write my first novel. It took me four years and I couldn't get it published. I began to write my second novel. It took me two and a half years to write three-fifths of it, but then there was a military coup and I couldn't get it published. I began to write my third novel. I was halfway through, eight years had passed and nothing had happened. I was at the end of my tether. I lived, at the age of thirty, with my now-divorced mother; my father gave me pocket money. I worked like a clerk, ten hours a day, writing, seriously. Taking myself very seriously. And suddenly, after eight years of working, the first book was published and then the third. They were successful. A month after I published my first book, I got married.

WACHTEL How did you do that? You were in your bedroom the whole time! Did you have somebody ready, waiting, right next to the publisher?

PAMUK The situation was not that awful. I had a girlfriend and we wanted to marry. The problem was that I had no income. Once I published my first book, I got some money from my family and then got married. I said I was an author, but of course I wasn't making any money. I began to make money after four or five years. I depended on my family. I was lucky in that. I was unlucky in terms of how hard it is to get published in Turkey, but it's easy for me now to find publishers outside Turkey.

WACHTEL You were soaking up all kinds of influences because you were not only writing for eight years, you were reading for eight years, and among the authors you read was Dostoevsky. I understand you're currently editing Dostoevsky's complete works in Turkish.

PAMUK In my teenage years, I admired Dostoevsky a lot, especially from sixteen to nineteen, when I read all of his novels. Their impact on my spirit was immense. He is the only novelist whose spiritual intensity was so high you're practically afraid of the things that you learn about life when you're reading. He was a great author, but I went on from there to read other authors. I learned a more polished, sophisticated Proust-Nabokov line, a highbrow descriptive sophistication. The nuances of writing seemed for a time more important for me than the immense presence and raw strength of Dostoevsky. For some time, he was on my mind and in my spirit, but not self-consciously. When I was writing *Snow* (2002, trans. 2004), which was a deliberately political novel, I wanted to have a look at *The Possessed*. I went to a bookshop and realized there is not a single, decent Turkish translation. Right after that, I told my publisher I wanted to edit the complete works of Dostoevsky, all of them of course translated. I don't speak Russian, but I would write introductions, edit, make them accessible, revitalize the author.

WACHTEL You once said he's an author whose demons you share.

PAMUK I share, first of all, his spiritual intensity, of saying something but not living in it. Not being sure of the boundaries of one's characters, and especially not being very sure of what you want. These are the spiritual things I like about Dostoevsky, but there are two things I like in particular that make it easy for me to identify with him. Dostoevsky was a Russian nationalist and he thought, and I agree, that Russia was different from Europe. All the liberals, all the occidentalists of his time, were looking to Europe. In his youth, he was one of them. He was a strong occidentalist and a liberal or a leftist. He was closely involved with a conspiratorial anarchist group. Then in his later years, perhaps because the Czar had pardoned him, he became an anti-Western Russian sentimentalist. But the problem is not with his being liberal or anti-Russian. The problem with him is his simplistic love-hate relationship with the West, the way his mind always approaches the problem: Easterners, Westerners; us, them—a sort of rhetoric of anger.

WACHTEL Do you share that?

PAMUK No, of course not. My position is that I know that this view is naive. And, in my tongue-in-cheek way, I understand I may have the same sentiments, but I am, on the other hand, beyond that. I may have the same energy, the same concerns—and don't forget the naive anti-Western sentiments, from anti-Semitism to anti-Americanism—I understand these things. I can even identify myself. I think it's an author's capacity to be able to identify himself or herself with all these strange, primitive, angry, nationalist, politically *most* incorrect voices. It is the duty of the writer, I believe, if there is any duty, to be able to identify with the most politically incorrect motivations, rhetoric. Go and try to impersonate those things. Put them together, all these strange voices, in a Bakhtinian manner, in a book. This is actually what I did with my political book, *Snow*.

WACHTEL What prompted you to write an overtly political book?

PAMUK When I began writing books in the mid-seventies, and publishing them in the early eighties, the previous generation of authors—socialist authors, ethically and morally motivated authors—had a very strong presence. I was also coming from the middle class, whose authors were perhaps too dedicated to the cause, which damaged the quality of their fiction. I decided I didn't need to be a political writer, when there were so many brave people in Turkey. I wanted instead to be like Proust or Virginia Woolf (and I could afford to do that, also). I was not political. In fact, my generation criticized me for being upper middle class and apolitical. But after ten years, I was so popular that people began to ask me things. My ideas were liberal, I was for democracy and the Kurdish question bothered me, so I wanted to do things, sign petitions. More and more I found myself involved in politics. This was not my intention at the beginning, but I turned out to be a person who made political comments and criticized the government for its violations of human rights and the essential lack of democracy, with soldiers intervening in Turkey's politics. I was doing all of these things *outside* of my books. Then I thought I would try my hand at a political novel, an outmoded form. No one's writing political novels anymore, but I will do it my way: pore over all the problems of Turkey, its anxieties about its identity, the rise of political Islam, Kurdish nationalism, Turkish nationalism, this paranoid relationship with Western Europe, all the nationalist sentiments, feelings of inferiority, anger, the anger of the damned, being poor, miserable, and being aware of what's happening in the rest of the world. I wanted to write very political fiction about these things. My characters include politically motivated, brave Islamists, Kurds, liberals—the sort of people who instigate military coups. I try to understand and narrate my story with equal distance from all of them.

WACHTEL In an essay on the September 11 attacks, you describe modern Islamic fundamentalism as the revenge of the poor against educated, Westernized Turks and their consumer society. Can you talk about the atmosphere in Turkey today and in the Islamic world around you? I see that it obviously does affect you both personally and as an artist in your book *Snow*.

PAMUK I read somewhere that Russian people after September 11 did not in fact identify with the people of the United States. I can say the same thing about the Turks. Most Turks did not identify with the sorrows of the American people, but on the other hand, they did not identify with the fundamentalists either. They also became more afraid of the Islamic fundamentalists. But then they are also poor, angry that the per capita income in Turkey is around $2,200 while in the Western world it is about $25,000. They're watching movies; the presence of the West is everywhere, running the world, while in terms of population they are the minority. There is a hidden anger which their government, Russian or Turkish, does not even represent. When September 11 was written about in Turkish newspapers, you could feel, between the lines, that they were not very sorry.

WACHTEL You talk about "the anger of the damned." Why the damned?

PAMUK It's very clear that nations like Turkey or Russia are not enjoying life as the Western world is. Maybe you cannot calculate or measure the enjoyment of life; the only thing you may have is worldly goods. Put it this way: the Russians, the Turks, and the Chinese are not consuming or enjoying worldly goods as much as Americans or Europeans do. I feel that there is a resentment. And the fact that the government of the United States, in corners of the world like Israel and Palestine, is not being just, *also* helps fuel this anger, unfortunately at the hands of Islamic fundamentalists.

WACHTEL Do you find yourself caught in the middle somehow?

PAMUK No. I have very clear ideas about the fate of Turkey. Turkey should be a secular democratic country. Everyone is caught in the middle of something. I think the people of the United States are also caught between the American government, big industrial corporations, and Osama bin Laden. So I don't see myself caught in the middle more than others.

WACHTEL To go back to your novel *My Name Is Red*, it's a tale told through a variety of perspectives, a technique you've used before. Each of the central characters has a voice: the lovers, Black and Shekure; Shekure's father; the various miniaturists; Esther the Jewish peddler who acts as a kind of go-between. But there are some surprising voices as well: a dog, a tree, a gold coin, even the colour red. Can you talk about these perspectives and why you included them?

PAMUK There is a bit of a philosophical background that the book also discusses. This wonderful Western innovation—how to see things, how to picture the depth of things with the help of perspective. My painters discuss rumours of this new Western invention, which they call perspective, that makes you paint the picture through the eyes of a certain person, not through the viewpoint of someone who sees everything, like God.

In that manner, the story is also narrated deliberately from the points of view of major characters in the story, minor characters, and some objects. But this is related to the central figure in the story who, like Scheherazade, tells a story in a coffeehouse in Istanbul. This guy hangs a picture of a dog and then impersonates the dog, both retelling an old story and commenting and making polemical statements with the audience in the coffeeshop. He puts up a picture of death; he impersonates death, the colour red, a horse, everything. Every month he tells a story. So the book has the form of everyone enthusiastically introducing himself as if looking into a camera and telling a story, and right in the middle each turns back and lives the things he tells. So it also has a Brechtian side to it. It is as if a character in a play suddenly turns to the audience and says, "You know I'm angry at this guy because of this" and "I'm now going to fall in love with this," or "If you would turn three pages back you would understand my motivations." That's the kind of thing I would do. I find it very interesting.

WACHTEL You're having fun with this because they make insightful observations about perception. The dog points out that "Dogs do speak, but only to those who know how to listen." What were you doing with that?

PAMUK Of course, there is a problem with readers, not only Turkish readers but also international readers. They always feel a bit awkward with experimentation. I have come across this so many times. Can a dog speak? What is this? I don't understand this novel. I have to play around with these kinds of objections, maybe tongue-in-cheek, exaggerating the objection a little bit.

WACHTEL Perhaps the most unusual or unexpected voice in the book is the colour red. There's this line: "Colour is the touch of the eye, music to the deaf, a word out of the darkness... I know men take notice of me and that I cannot be resisted." Red announces itself here, even in the title of the book. Why do you give it such prominence?

PAMUK I don't know, really. At the heart of each book of mine, and this is also related to the title, there is an instinct to play with something I know about, but something I know unselfconsciously. For example, I've been asked so many times, why the title *The White Castle,* because it doesn't have a prominent place in the book although they all go towards it. And then the title of this book, *My Name Is Red*: why is red given so much prominence but still not explained? I sometimes think it *is* explained. My strategy for giving a title is not to sum up a book, like *War and Peace* is a summary, not to symbolize the book as *The Red and the Black,* or not to just plainly give a name like *Anna Karenina,* but to add another twist to the layers of mystery. Sometimes my readers tell me that my books are full of mysteries. I don't think my books are obscure or full of mysteries, but I think that the novels I write—in fact, all literary novels in their fashion—are so rich that the human mind, compared to them, is limited. One reads a novel. We do not, after reading it, represent the whole of it in our mind's eye, but only some parts. If we read a novel such as *My Name Is Red* or *The Black Book,* deliberately highly textured, dense novels, we only see at the first reading some twenty-five per cent of the meaning. Not that we gloss over all the words, but our attention and memory are limited. We come out of the book with a certain vision of it. Then, at the second reading, or when someone points them out to us, we realize there are other things as well, other stories.

WACHTEL It's interesting that you talk of mystery. There's a very evocative line from the voice of a dead man, the uncle, after he's been killed. He's questioning what it is all about, what does it all mean? He says, "'Mystery,' ... or perhaps 'mercy,' but I wasn't certain of either."

PAMUK He's faced with the problem of the meaning of life. These kinds of word plays, which just come to the tip of my pen as I write, some of them well plotted and organized ahead of time, are in the textures of my books and it is so much fun to write a book when you are organizing and driving along. These little surprises constitute the texture but not the whole meaning of the book. A book is perhaps a galaxy of nerve endings through which the reader should continue to walk, each time seeing something surprising or something he may have seen before.

WACHTEL Do you know why colours engage you as they do? It's almost an instinctive thing: *The Black Book, The White Castle, My Name Is Red.* Why do colours affect you so strongly?

PAMUK Essentially I wanted to be a painter, but other things, other strong images from visual work are very important for me. That's why I want to identify myself and my characters and my imagery with colours, but I don't want to overdo it and explain it.

WACHTEL I'm interested in what the tree says. He says, "I was supposed to be part of a story, but I fell from there like a leaf in autumn." But later: "I don't want to be a tree, I want to be its meaning," which gets at the essence of the conflict in the story between traditional and Western approaches to art. What does it mean to be the meaning of a tree?

PAMUK Before, he says that a Western artist wants to draw a tree; if we impersonate that tree, the picture of the tree desires to be a tree. The desire behind that is: Draw a picture of a tree in such detail that you can't miss it as one single tree, that it *is* almost a tree. The Islamic version of the tree says he doesn't have this aspiration to be a real thing. He's quite well aware of the fact that he is an artifact. He is not a tree and doesn't aspire to be a tree but is an artifact made of a tree. What he aspires to be is not the tree itself, but its meaning.

WACHTEL The debate in the novel focuses on the book that the miniaturists have been illustrating, which uses revolutionary European approaches. There are a number of elements here: the use of perspective, individual style and character, a new kind of portraiture, even shadows—all of these are seen by the traditionalists as blasphemous, as the devil's work. Can you explain why?

PAMUK It's not blasphemy, it's a new technique. Today it's the so-called fundamentalists who would call them blasphemous. In a limited fashion, Islam permitted painting, but at the core lies the fact that Islamic tradition forbids painting. Some years later, they began to paint, but not human figures, especially not portraits. They began to paint but not with the intention of creating icons to hang on the wall. To hang a portrait on the wall, *that* was the real blasphemy. There are, of course, reinterpretations. Ottoman sultans and Arab caliphs in fact had paintings done inside the books that only they and their harem women looked at, but they were mostly not figurative. If they were figures they were seen as illustration and *part* of the illumination. Sumptuous book production and illumination were seen as an art, as an extension of calligraphy. The first thing was calligraphy, the Koran, the world of God's word and writing it beautifully. To have more beauty, they illustrated—Islamic painting was allowed ten pages per book. That is the whole history of Islamic painting. But on the other hand, it was essentially forbidden in the sense that you would not hang a picture on the wall and pray to it, that figures would not represent God, that making drawn figures was considered to be competing with God's creation, et cetera.

WACHTEL But it was more than that. It wasn't just that you wouldn't put a picture on the wall to pray to, you wouldn't even put a picture on the wall to look at. You wouldn't have a picture detached from a text.

PAMUK Yes, I need to underline this. Producing pictures was seen to be competing with God because pictures were seen as things in themselves, so it was competing with God to create them.

WACHTEL But why would shadow, perspective be—?

PAMUK Because they were the invention of Western painters and made figurative painting more realistic, which made it hard to distinguish between what is picture and what is reality. If you draw a picture of a tree with shadows, with perspective, with depth, then that tree really looks like a tree, and that is competing with God. That is Islam's essential reaction to painting.

WACHTEL The traditional Eastern approach is a deeply spiritual one. "To paint is to remember," says the head of the miniaturists. "The duty of illustrators and of those who, loving art, gaze upon the world, is to remember the magnificence that Allah beheld and left to us." As a modern secular artist, what meaning does that approach have for you?

PAMUK Most of this art theory in fact is non-existent.

WACHTEL You made it up?

PAMUK I have elaborated in the book. Islamic art theory, or art history, is very limited. It was an extension of commentaries on calligraphers. Between the thirteenth century and sixteenth century, there was a period of extensive Islamic painting. When I say extensive, it was all limited to the courts of shahs and kings and sultans. But all through that time there was little commentary on its meaning. Most things I elaborated for the first time as a sort of idea behind all these paintings. When I write about the most glorious Islamic paintings—forget the Islamic part—*the* most glorious paintings were things so pure, so out of this world, so timeless that they may be memories of God. I am in fact inventing all this rhetoric.

WACHTEL It's very persuasive.

PAMUK Thank you.

WACHTEL There are very interesting ideas that emerge. In the painting of Islamic miniatures, the height of mastery and achievement is, paradoxically, blindness. One of your epigraphs is from the Koran: "The blind and the seeing are not equal." It's a startling idea that blindness is the ultimate goal or the ultimate reward of the artist. Does this make sense to you?

PAMUK Yes, of course. When I make these comments, most of the ideas are mine. Art historians have asked me about texts concerning the virtue of blindness. What I was trying to visualize and make clear in the reader's mind was the idea of repetition, of the same scenes for hundreds of years, from which comes a kind of purity. Once you begin to redraw the same scenes, the same horses, the same weeping ladies from the same point of view, hundreds of times, then you begin to memorize them. You begin to reach what they call essential, ideal beauty. But there is a paradox here. If you devote forty years of life to drawing the same figures, the same trees, the same beauties all the time, you begin to lose your eyesight because these miniatures are so little. Once your hand really learns the craft, even memorizes it, your eyes don't see. Once you reach the level of drawing in a very subtle manner, drawing the world as God might see it, you may have lost some, or all, of your eyesight.

As I began to see this paradox, I realized that perhaps if I go to the limits, then the best artists would be the ones who would lose their eyesight because their hands, not their minds, have memorized what should be drawn. I like these kinds of paradoxes. I also like the line in the Koran that those who see and the blind are not the same. This, of course, refers to the fact that Mohammad is always trying to convince non-believers that there is a God—look, these are the signs—but some people deny it and he's very angry. Then he says that those who see and those who don't are not the same, although he doesn't actually refer to painting. This is a legitimate thing that I found in the Koran: seeing is better than not seeing, which means that pictures are better than words.

WACHTEL You have this intriguing distinction. *We* look (meaning Westerners), and *they* see.

PAMUK Another rhetorical distinction. To see, you need a perspective, you have to deliberately attempt to make a clear picture in order to reproduce another thing. Looking is enjoying with the eyes, without having your mind in it. But seeing includes the mind with what the eye sees. So I make this distinction: when you include, with the act of looking, the will of the mind to grasp what is there, then you begin to *see* things rather than look at things. Most of the time children look. When you tell children to draw a picture, then they begin to see. And because the mind is involved, there is this whole problem of organization: How do I do this? Where is the beginning? Where is the frame, where is the centre? Who's in front, and then, which one is big, which one is small? That's how we begin to see. Perhaps the whole heritage of painting—Western painting, Eastern painting—is first looking. But that's nothing. Looking deliberately—that is seeing. Then organizing what you see—that is painting. It continues like that.

WACHTEL The narrator of *The New Life* describes himself as an "unfortunate and foolish hero... trying to discover the meaning of life in this land suffering from amnesia." Why amnesia?

PAMUK I was, of course, referring to the attempts of the Turkish Republic to westernize. They thought—and I think this was the major mistake of the founders of the Turkish Republic—that they could westernize this country if they forgot the past. They forgot the past, but did not replace it with the critical humanistic values of the West. They were afraid of putting these in place. So in the country there was a huge sense of amnesia, but nothing new to fill the void. That is what I'm critical of.

WACHTEL This land suffering from amnesia, Turkey, and the city of Istanbul, where you've lived for most of your life, is not only your fictional turf but is in many ways your subject, whether historical or modern. What makes it so fascinating for you?

PAMUK It's fascinating because it's so full. Istanbul is a city of ten million. There is so much history, layers and layers of history. It's crowded. And it's fascinating because I've been living here for fifty years. There are people, like V.S. Naipaul, who move from one country to another, for generations, from continent to continent and end up being a British citizen with a conservative outlook. I admire them because they cover all these distances and identify with all these cultures and continents and change. I am not that kind of person. I have been living in Istanbul for fifty years, almost in the same neighbourhood. And now in fact I have returned to the apartment building I was born in.

WACHTEL Really? Who won the lawsuit?

PAMUK I won the lawsuit. This city, at the centre of which I live, in its European quarter, is my life. Saying I am fascinated with it is an exaggeration. You live with it, it's like your body. You're not fascinated with your body, you know it. I am not a tourist. Tourists are fascinated, I am used to it. I like it. I know how to tolerate it. I enjoy it. I sleepwalk in it because I don't notice it anymore. Then as a writer I notice it. So I get inside and outside of it. I tell its stories. And since previous generations of writers always went to Anatolia, to rural Turkey, I felt that I was king of the city, telling its stories, which are endless, like the streets of Istanbul.

WACHTEL There's a character in *The Black Book* who says that "Istanbul is a grand place, an incomprehensible place," and I think you yourself have said that the city has no symmetry, no sense of geometry, no two lines in parallel. In a sense, you draw on the off-centredness that you experience there. How does that work?

PAMUK My image of the city is not of a geographical place. It's a sort of arabesque maze that represents Istanbul in my mind's eye, rather than a geometrical space that has a Cartesian beginning and is organized and categorized. That complexity gives it a sort of mystery for me and also refers to its layers and layers of history, behind it, beneath it. I look at a city in that fashion, as I do in *The Black Book*. I replace the detective, searching for clues. He does not look for geometric clues or the Cartesian clues that he would look for in a Western novel, but more instinctive, more esoteric, more personal clues to reach a solution.

WACHTEL There's a sense that hybridity is a good thing, with modernity and history fundamentally at odds. But is this notion at odds with what we were talking about earlier, in terms of your having a character who says at the end of *The New Life* that "Today we are altogether defeated... The West has swallowed us up, trampled on us... But someday, someday perhaps a thousand years from now, we'll avenge ourselves." Even there you're playful with the names of products and goods—he has a candy called Bliss. But is hybridity a good thing?

PAMUK Hybridity is a good thing if it is done deliberately. It should not be an excuse for the loss of your culture. Hybridity is a good thing if it is a sign of democracy, wealth, and if it indicates that you can express your culture, your past, in any condition. But hybridity can sometimes turn out to be an excuse for erasing the local culture, or the resistance of the local cultures to so-called globalization. Then you have to question hybridity. In itself, hybridity is a concept that can be used to aid understanding but it is not absolutely a good thing or absolutely a bad thing. For example, when essentially Eastern art is confronted with the new methods of the West, those who are going to survive are those who are in favour of hybridity. Those artists who manage to adapt the techniques of the West are going to produce new things, while the purists, the conservatives, those who don't want to change the tradition, will come to a dead end. All of my novels are perfect productions of hybridity. I have put together Western postmodernists, or whatever fashionable secular things I have learned from Western literature, with traditional Islamic texts, with Sufi allegories, and have produced a sort of hybrid texture, on which all of my plots and novels are based.

WACHTEL *My Name Is Red* is about the making of art in an Islamic city. It's set more than four centuries ago, but your story has an inescapable resonance today. One of your characters says, "I know too well how submission to the endless attacks of hojas, preachers, judges and mystics who accuse us of blasphemy, how the endless guilt both deadens and nourishes the artist's imagination." Why both deadens and nourishes?

PAMUK When I was writing the book, in the mid-nineties, political Islam was getting stronger and stronger in Turkey, so I was deliberately and directly referring to that. The pressures of You will not do that, you will not say this, you will not write this were getting strong, so I was referring to them. But it not only diminishes, it also nourishes you, in the sense that once there are things that they do not allow you to write, of course all the good artists want to write about those subjects. All the genuine artists I know about, as soon as there is a taboo, or especially a ban that comes from the government or from certain circles, immediately want to approach that forbidden subject because that is a very human urge. Sometimes, not most of the time, there are people who come from human rights organizations, freedom of speech organizations, who ask me, "Mr. Pamuk, are there stories you cannot write in this country?" I tell them that theirs is a very romantic notion of looking at human rights. It is not that you have some story but unfortunately the government won't let you write it. It's the other way around: the government doesn't want you to tell the story, and you immediately want to do so. That's what I mean by nourishes.

WACHTEL In *My Name Is Red,* the character Enishte says: "A great painter does not content himself by affecting us with his masterpieces; ultimately, he succeeds in changing the landscapes of our minds." How do you want to change our mental landscapes?

PAMUK We were just referring to classical texts, archetypal stories. They are to today's university graduates what Shakespeare meant to earlier generations. Like Shakespeare, there are also archetypal pictures, especially in a culture where there is a very limited number of pictures. Now we are immersed in pictures, but think of sixteenth-century Istanbul.

You can't find pictures: there are no photographs, there are no newspapers, there are very few books, you are not allowed to draw pictures on the walls. The whole history of Islam is a history without pictures. But once you begin to see pictures in books, they stay with you; they are very powerful. Now we are so surrounded with pictures from television, movies, and advertisements that for us a picture doesn't have that same strength. But occasionally we have access to a picture, especially in our childhood, that stays with us, and it forms our memory. That's what I refer to as the landscape of our minds. Our minds are not made with words, but, more importantly, with pictures. There are things that we see that we will keep in our minds, but there are pictures, especially if we see very few of them, that stay with us and then become the standard for our representations of the world.

WACHTEL But how do *you* want to change our mental landscape?

PAMUK A good question. Essentially, this is the ambition of the poet: if I manage to write a few stories that, after reading, will stay in people's minds for quite a long time, that is enough for me. Maybe the only thing that I want to teach my audiences, both my Turkish audience and my international audience, is that this distinction between East and West is a very artificial thing. And even if it is not, artificial things from East and West can easily combine and make a new thing. If I can illustrate that in my reader's mind, make the reader visualize this new unique thing, then I have done my job as a novelist. If I narrate a story which is the materialization of this new thing, it is enough for me.

May 2002

§

WACHTEL You have spoken about walking the nighttime streets of Istanbul. How did that fuel your imagination?

PAMUK Until 1991, when my daughter was born, I would work 'til 4 a.m. in my studio and then take a long walk before going home. These long, solitary walks at night, when the whole of Istanbul was sleeping, left their mark on my imagination. I like the mystery of the streets, the way shadows move, the way leaves on the trees shiver even if there is no wind, things that are written on the walls—political slogans or advertisements—the chemistry and texture of old buildings, old walls.

So I landed my imagination on the character of Mevlut Karataş in order to make him a distinct individual, perhaps challenging the idea that the lower classes do not have too much life in the art of the novel. In fact, it's one of the important points about writing this novel [*A Strangeness in My Mind*]. The art of the novel is really about the middle class, the upper middle class, or, as in Tolstoy or Nabokov or Proust, about aristocrats. My challenge was to invent a character whose individuality I could explore and who is also from a lower class.

WACHTEL Do you still take long walks at night in the city?

PAMUK I do, but not at night. Now the city is a much different place: it's more dangerous, more crowded, and it's growing so fast. Its chemistry is changing in so many ways that it's hard to keep up with the differences. When I was born in Istanbul sixty-three years ago, it was a city of a million. Now they say it's sixteen or seventeen million, all in sixty-three years. The change in the last thirteen years is bigger than the change in the first fifty years of my life. Yes, I'm still walking, but now, because of my political problems, I have a bodyguard. That actually helps, because I can go to any private place, any courtyard, any dead end, any mysterious street that I sense is a bit dangerous. Now that I have bodyguards, I walk, I look. I love being a city writer. I like walking in the streets, morning and night—at any time.

WACHTEL As you say: your political problems. You had threats because of your comments about Turkey's treatment of its minorities. But where are the threats coming from now?

PAMUK I had trouble, especially in the early 2000s, when I was propagating the idea of European Union with Turkey and talking about what happened to Armenians in the early days of the First World War. I had trouble communicating these ideas. Now I'm famous because I gently criticized the government. It's in the government tabloids. It's not only me. Anyone who is radical—and I'm not even radical—or who is critical of the government, needs someone to protect them.

WACHTEL Is the city more beautiful at night?

PAMUK I like to see the town at night. I don't know why. Perhaps it assumes a more mysterious character. Also, mass touristic crowds disappear at night. Then there's a feeling that the city has been exhausted, so much having happened during the day, and now there is whatever is left over. Cats and dogs and a few people in the streets—I like that.

WACHTEL Dogs seem to play an important role in this novel, and even make appearances in other novels of yours. But here, Mevlut, the central character in *A Strangeness in My Mind*, is extremely afraid of the packs of dogs that roam the streets of Istanbul at night. Do they worry you also?

PAMUK Traditionally, Istanbul was left to dogs at night. Western observers thought that packs of dogs were dominant at night, and so strong during the day that you could feel their domination, lying in the middle of the street, barking at anyone who passed by, begging for food from the shopkeepers, et cetera. Gérard de Nerval, the French writer—a man of immense, poetic, and melancholic imagination—came to Istanbul in the 1850s and wrote about it in his *Journey to the Orient*. He observed that packs of dogs survived in Istanbul because they had a municipal function—they ate the trash—and that's why the people of Istanbul like their dogs. Dogs in Istanbul also have a symbolic value, especially from the beginning of the eighteenth century. The Ottoman rulers, the sultans and elites, wanted to slaughter all the dogs because they thought the streets of Europe, their aspirational standard, were free of dogs. This they considered modernization. There were many attempts to kill the dogs, including sending them to a nearby island so they would eat each other—very brutal, modernist attempts to get rid of the dogs. Conservative, old-fashioned residents of Istanbul wrote petitions to the bureaucracy, to the sultans: Please give us our dogs back. We'll keep our dogs. So while dogs were sometimes just pets, the desire to extinguish them, to kill them, was also part of the East-West arguments in Turkey.

WACHTEL By covering such a big canvas, the sweeping changes in the country are woven into the fabric of the story. You have three military coups, the opening of the first bridge over the Bosphorus, the political violence, the invasion of Cyprus, the 1999 earthquake, the formation of the PKK, the Kurdistan Workers Party. It's a tumultuous period, and all of these events have had an ongoing impact on this migrant community. What was it like for you to approach Turkey's history during your own lifetime through the experience of these marginal characters?

PAMUK My character Mevlut has friends who are secular leftists or radical socialists, but he's also friendly with his ultra-right-wing cousins who have very nationalistic ideas. He attends the lodge of an Islamist sect. He can do all of these things, my character Mevlut the street vendor, because he himself does not have strong ideas, political or moral. So one day he can write leftist slogans on the walls. Next day he can write ultra-right-wing slogans on the walls. For him, these events in Turkish history or the history of Istanbul do not, in the end, define his life. Yes, we see from his point of view: right after the military coups, street vendors are pressured a bit, or political slogans are cleaned off the streets and so forth. But on the other hand, my character Mevlut's life is not dramatically intertwined with big historical events. Perhaps the point the novel is making is that, in the midst of this history of the nation, or of the world, my Everyman is navigating between groups, politics, shops, historical corners, parks, buildings. And also as he walks, especially at night and in a poetic mood, he remembers all the little changes, all the memories, all the stories and gossip about things. Mevlut is lost in this history as he is also lost in the causes of the city. His enjoyment and appreciation and vision of the city is more poetic than rational. Yes, the novel has also an ethical or historical side, but then it's not very close to my character, who has a strange mind, like me.

WACHTEL Mevlut suffers throughout his life from what he thinks of as a "strangeness in my mind." That phrase, which is the title of the book, comes from the epigraph, from Wordsworth's poem "The Prelude": "I had melancholy thoughts… / a strangeness in my mind / A feeling that I was not for that hour, / Nor for that place." You say like you. How so?

PAMUK I lent my street vendor some of the strangeness of my own mind. All during my childhood and even later in my teenage years and early twenties, my friends used to say to me, "Orhan, you have a strange mind," and that stayed with me. And one day, as I was reading William Wordsworth's "Prelude," I read these lines and thought, Hmm. One day I will make "a strangeness in my mind" the title of a novel. That's why I gave Mevlut some of my imagination, some of the things that I have seen and experienced as I walked in the dark streets of Istanbul, especially between the sixties and nineties. I gave this imagination to Mevlut. I am, in a way, Mevlut, but then he is totally different from me too, as his life story testifies.

WACHTEL And when your friends observed your strange mind, what were they reacting or responding to?

PAMUK I don't know. Perhaps one can never pin down the strangeness of one's own mind. But probably if there is any strangeness in my mind, like Mevlut, it's in connecting things that one regularly doesn't connect. Connecting some shadow with an image. Connecting some past memory with something that is entirely unrelated to it. That our mind does things by itself is a wonder. And Mevlut, as he walks in the streets—and his mind works better as he walks—enjoys the products of his imagination. In fact, his imagination, like mine and perhaps like all of ours, works on its own. And he is amazed, like a painter watching his hand create a painting, as his mind suggests things that he is not in control of. Mevlut's imagination also, like my imagination, is visual. In the novel, we don't see the city directly, but we see it filtered through Mevlut's eyes and mine. His eyes pick up strange details. His mind puts them into interesting words.

WACHTEL Mevlut also has a strong spiritual bent, and while selling boza, he meets and frequently visits a man described as a Holy Guide, a teacher of calligraphy in the Ottoman tradition. Who is this Holy Guide?

PAMUK The Holy Guide is really a typical sheikh of a small sect. Let us underline the fact that it is still forbidden to found a sect and practise its religious tenets in Turkey. This was Kemal Ataturk's law, presented in the 1920s. Although we have a political Islamist government, they did not change it. We have little parish lodges, and most of them are not *very* political—they operate like shrinks, people you go to, to talk about the worries in your life. There will be also other men who are troubled, who are looking for a community. Most of these religious sects address the solitary person who is lost in the modernity and chaotic atmosphere of the city, who needs someone who would listen to his problems, who would relate to these people both by community and ideas, with the help of sacred religious words, most of which are rhetorical. These sects help a person relate to higher ideas, comfort him with friendship, and offer the existence of a community that shares some values—conservative values, religious values, or values about justice and humanity.

WACHTEL You studied calligraphy yourself when you were in your twenties. Was it at a centre anything like this one?

PAMUK Many, many things in *A Strangeness in My Mind* come from my little experiences in life. When I was studying architecture at the age of twenty-three, as I wrote in my autobiographical book, *Istanbul*, suddenly I dropped out, with the intention of quitting painting. I had thought I would be a painter until the age of twenty-three, and then I started writing my novels. My family—my aunts, my cousins, my mother—was quite astonished and shocked. One of my aunts' husbands, who was also a collector of old calligraphy, suggested that I study Ottoman calligraphy. I have an interest in old Ottoman things, and he sent me to one of the most famous calligraphers in Istanbul at that time. This was a craft that was disappearing; now it's only taught at art schools in Turkey. But I had the privilege of taking calligraphy lessons from a seventy-five-year-old master. In the novel, I used this experience, also making him the head, or sheikh, of a lodge. But most of the lodges in the '70s and '80s, since they were illegal, were posing as something else. Because of the restrictions of the secular, military governments, the lodges claimed to be old Ottoman music clubs or calligraphy institutions or something associated with the past. Actually, the cultural thing was real, but it was also just a facet of the organization. Behind it, there would be forbidden religious—most of them really—artistic, not political, activities.

WACHTEL Has your own interest in mysticism grown?

PAMUK When I was in New York in 1985, I was a young, ambitious, postmodernist writer, and I wanted to find my voice. I was deeply secular, as I am now, but I began to ask myself questions, seeing American libraries, museums, the vast international culture that existed. I began to ask questions about my Turkish identity. That's how I began to read old Sufi stories, texts. That helped me write *My Name Is Red*, which is about old Sufi texts, illustrated books, and *The Black Book*, which again is set in Istanbul, based on old, classical Sufi stories. But then also around that time, I'd been reading Borges, Calvino, and my interest in old, classical Sufi texts were more literary, nothing to do with religion. From Borges, I learned to treat old, classical texts as almost postmodern texts. So my interest in classical Ottoman, Arabic, and especially Persian Sufism was literary. Sufism in Islam is a different way of doing music and art. There is very little art and music in Islamic culture that is not related to a Sufi sect or lodge.

My attempt after my postmodernist infatuation was to reread these texts and appropriate them—that was the word that was used in the '80s—appropriate them in a very secular, modernist, or postmodernist way, and use them in my books. *My Name Is Red* and *The Black Book* were written with this method.

WACHTEL The different voices featured in *A Strangeness in My Mind* include those of the women, the wives of those who come from the village to make a life in the city with their families, some happily, some less so. Can you comment on the power relations between men and women within the society depicted in the book? How they changed, not just through time, but because of that move from the village to the city.

PAMUK I also wanted to represent the anger of the women who were pushed back into their houses, the way men suppressed them, the way men use religion, Islam, to suppress and curtail the voices of the women. I grew up with a mother who had an older sister and a younger sister, and I enjoyed their conversations in my childhood: the way they made fun of their husbands, criticized their family life, the way they had a needling language, making fun of everything, always fighting back against the repressions of men. It was a challenge to represent the anger of women in the book.

WACHTEL Mevlut is, as you've said, a simple man at heart: honest, hard-working, devoted to family. But his personal story is complicated right from the start by the fact that he marries the wrong girl. In effect, she becomes the right girl, but not the girl that he thought he was running away with. It's a kind of plot device that usually lends itself to romantic comedy or even black comedy, but you take it in another direction. What attracted you to this idea?

PAMUK Just recently, I read a Turkish statistic claiming that 52 per cent of marriages in Turkey are arranged. What do we mean by "arranged marriage"? It has many, many levels. In an Islamic country, men and women do not get together easily before marriage. Flirting, as we understand it in the West, does not exist in a normal conservative Islamic society. There is also a romanticized idea of modernity being equal. So the point about Mevlut's marriage is that his marriage is not arranged. He elopes with a girl, and that's romantic, implying that they're not slaves to their families. The strange thing both in Mevlut's mind and in the story is perhaps that he sees a girl at a wedding, and weddings are the only places where a girl and boy can meet outside of marriage, even if it's for ten seconds or one minute. It is a custom and ritual to romanticize that one look and write poetry about that. The whole of Ottoman poetry is based on romanticizing how her eyes look. Why? Because that's the only part of her that you can see. If you want to marry, you have to develop this romantic rhetoric about love, and Mevlut is actually doing that. After he writes love letters to a girl for three years, his family helps him to elope with her, but he realizes in the middle of the night that they actually cheated him and sent him the elder sister, who is not that good looking. In the whole history of modernization in late Ottoman times and early Turkish, secular, republican times, the subject of arranged marriages was crucial, and pro-modern writers criticized arranged marriages. Perhaps my book is also a take on that old-fashioned subject in an ironical way. Mevlut elopes with a girl, but it turns out to be someone different. The strangeness, or the twist, in my story is that he is not worried about that. He is in fact happy with the older girl, and that constitutes the whole mode and the storyline of the novel.

WACHTEL Your last novel, *The Museum of Innocence*, also takes place in Istanbul over more or less the same period. It begins a little later and ends a little earlier, but it's set in a very different world, a world closer to your own. It's about a young man from an established, westernized Istanbul family who has an affair with a younger cousin, a beautiful shop girl, and he becomes so obsessed with his love for her that he collects endless objects associated with their time together and builds a museum dedicated to her. The novel is part of an extraordinary long-term project. There is the book, and there's an actual museum associated with it, and then there's a catalogue to the museum. Can you describe some of the background, the inspiration for this unusual enterprise?

PAMUK Doing strange things in literature, in art—I like that. One day you have an idea. I don't try to see the origin of the idea. I like the idea. I give my whole time, my energy, to expand, to dramatize, to make this idea real, such as writing a novel and opening a museum that has the same name, Museum of Innocence. The novel is a love story really, an obsessive story of an upper-middle-class Istanbul boy who is infatuated, who is deeply in love with his twice-removed cousin, who comes from the poor side of the family. In the novel, we also see that, because of his infatuation, Kemal, the protagonist of *The Museum of Innocence*, collects everything that his beloved, Füsun, sees or touches, everything that reminds him of her. And in the end, as the love story in *The Museum of Innocence* goes bad, ends tragically, he decides to exhibit in a museum all the things that remind him of her, the things that he has already collected as the story unfolds, and builds a museum in the last hundred pages of the novel. Kemal also explains the poetics of it, the architecture, and, all through the novel, the story of each object.

At the beginning, when I was writing *The Museum of Innocence*, I thought that I would open the museum and publish the novel on the same day, the novel posing as a sort of annotated museum catalogue. In the end, I finished the novel and decided that the museum would take more time. *The Museum of Innocence* was published in Turkey in 2008, and the museum took another four years. In those four years, I was also busy with Mevlut's story, *A Strangeness in My Mind*. I had to build the museum, put all the objects inside in a beautiful way, caring about composition and the beauty of the vitrines, or boxes. I'm happy I did what I did. But if you're asking me why I did it, I don't know. A jinn entered my head and I did what it told me to do. And really, in literature and in art, you just follow what the jinn says. I regularly joke that I don't know why I did it—I will need another five or six years to understand why.

WACHTEL As you were saying earlier, you were originally a painter. How has it been fulfilling for you as an artist as well as a writer to create your own museum?

PAMUK But it's not a museum, Eleanor, about me. It's a museum about my fictional characters and also all the real objects that my fictional characters touch. So the experience of coming to the museum is also interesting and dizzying, between fact and fiction. We read novels, and some part of our minds are always dizzy. As we read novels, is this a detail that the writer imagined, or is this a detail that the writer experienced? If it's a very convincing detail, even if it's imagined, we say, "Wow! It's so convincing. Probably he lived something like that." In fact, after the publication of *The Museum of Innocence*, the most frequent question I've been asked is "Mr. Pamuk, did you live all these details of the love story, with so much infatuation with the girls? Did you collect all the objects that she touched?"

WACHTEL Thousands of cigarette butts, for a start.

PAMUK Yes. My character Kemal is so infatuated by Füsun, his beloved, that he collects all the cigarette butts that she leaves in an ashtray because these objects offer him a sort of a consolation. Also, objects have the power to bring us back to the times that have passed, the memories we may have lost. I argue that we are, in our cities, attached to our architecture, old buildings, squares, trees, fountains, bridges. We are attached to them because they remind us of our memories. If you live in a city, like me, for sixty-three years, all the visions—buildings, trees, squares of that city—turn out to be indexes that will return the memories that I tend to forget.

WACHTEL I visited the museum in Istanbul. It's extraordinary, so engaging. And the care that's been put into creating each vitrine is like a work of art. You said somewhere that it's a lifetime project, that it's never-ending. How? What more can you do?

PAMUK Don't forget that the logic of the museum is that each chapter of the book is given a sort of a vitrine, or box, but in the end, what you saw there is only sixty-five boxes. I have to do another fifteen boxes.

Three chapters are the penthouse. Then I have some fifteen chapters to do, and I will gradually add them, make them big projects. I'm also collaborating with international, contemporary artists, going to them and making suggestions for the remaining chapters… I'm thinking of a box like this and an artwork like that. So until I die, I will do more vitrines and artworks, contemporary artworks of mine or in collaboration with internationally known artists. I'm very happy that I'm doing this. The dead artist in me is still trying to resurrect, so I'm placating him.

WACHTEL When you say that every square or fountain, every street, has a whole cluster of memories associated with it, is it painful for you to see modern Istanbul just steamroll over this?

PAMUK Yes, it is painful. But then I also want to be a balanced man. I don't want to be a reactionary, nostalgic person who says, "Well, the old Istanbul was better." Definitely, the conditions of the poor in old Istanbul were not better. Shanty houses or even old, wooden buildings sometimes didn't have electricity, didn't have sewage systems, water and all the comforts that we expect from life today. Yes, I am upset by these high-rises. I am upset that Erdoğan's government, although they're conservative, do not care much about preservation—they're demolishing historical buildings. But on the other hand, I want to balance my sentiment of nostalgia with my desire to understand other people who may not be like me, who came to Istanbul between, say, 1970 and 2000, as my character Mevlut did. My attempt to understand Mevlut, to see the world through his eyes, is related to identifying with other people, seeing the world through other people's pain, happiness, different culture, or different religion. Novels are not only self-expression; they are also attempts to see, to jump into the shoes of other people.

WACHTEL In Kemal's westernized social set, everything European is desirable, including the latest gadgets, even if they don't know how to use them, and headscarves are associated with provincial types. But at the same time it's confusing, because no matter how modern it seems, young women are still subjected to a double standard when it comes to sexuality…

PAMUK *The Museum of Innocence* is related to the cult of virginity, which is, of course, related to patriarchal, traditional society, partly related to Islam. The "innocence" in the title is also related to the purity of the main female character that Kemal is so much in love with. Without underlining it too much, the book was also suggesting that, even if you aspire to be ultra-modern or come from the upper classes, with pretensions to embrace Western values, when it comes to the deep, moral ideas, or strange ideas, or traditional ideas—such as the cult of virginity or authoritarianism—these ideas do not change easily.

You may see that the upper-class, westernized, highly sophisticated man's mind can still be obsessed with the cult of virginity, or he may be extremely authoritarian, looking down at the lower classes, although he may believe that he is a secular, liberal person. All my life in my fiction, I have paid a lot of attention to this kind of contradiction rather than merely observing the obvious facts.

WACHTEL You often make surprise appearances in your books, and *The Museum of Innocence* is no exception. In fact, the whole fidgety Pamuk family is seated at the back of the room at Kemal's lavish engagement party at the Hilton, including—and I'm quoting here—"the chain-smoking, twenty-three-year-old Orhan—nothing special about him beyond his propensity to act nervous and impatient, affecting a mocking smile." And he even dances…

PAMUK I was like that, really. Thank you for quoting that. I was a nervous, cynical boy who was interested in everything, who wanted to be invisible so that his eyes could enjoy the world. And, of course, I was a boy that Füsun would never be interested in, though, yes, I…

WACHTEL You danced with her!

But by the last chapter of *The Museum of Innocence*, you become the "esteemed Orhan Pamuk," chosen by Kemal to tell his story. What are you doing here? It's obviously fun.

PAMUK Okay. I appear in my novels but that's not a big deal. I appear sometimes, as in *Snow* or *The Museum of Innocence*, because sometimes the characters, through whom I have seen the whole story, die, and someone needs to pull things together, to take the narrative to its conclusion. That's, for example, why I have Orhan, who also explains the connection between the museum and the novel. It adds one final twist to the fictionality of my fiction. Sometimes I appear like Hitchcock to give it a sort of signature. Sometimes I appear like a Borgesian character just to make the reader aware of the fact that this is fiction and that there is a metaphysical side to it or, like a Brecht character, underlining the fact that, "Reader, don't be too sentimental, and don't run after the joys of catharsis, but be more cerebral, and judge the story rather than enjoy the sentiment." So there are many, many reasons why I appear in my novels, but they are not that significant. Even if the reader doesn't notice them, the value of the book doesn't change. It's like many, many thousands of things in my novels. It's something by the side and something I don't want to dramatize, but then all of the details in my books are perhaps like that. They are there for themselves, but I don't want to make anything a big deal.

WACHTEL You've been critical of westernized, secular Turkish intellectuals for what they reject or fail to value in the world around them: the complexity, the richness…

PAMUK Yes. I have to underline that while I'm critical of them, I am myself a secular liberal. I argue that modernity doesn't mean forgetting, shouldn't mean forgetting. You can be modern, even postmodern, but you can also be attached to some details of the past. Turkish modernization projects, especially in the first years of the Republic, as it was understood by the ruling elite and intellectuals, were deleting the past, forgetting the past. In fact, my strongest statement to the previous generation was about this forgetting and deleting. I sometimes argue that I am the forgotten and repressed past that is coming back in disguise, not in conservative dress, but in postmodern clothing.

October 2015
Original interviews produced by Sandra Rabinovitch

ALEKSANDAR HEMON

When you read about Aleksandar Hemon's own story, you real- ize it's almost as striking as his fiction. And it's a story shared by several of his fictional alter egos: Josef Pronek, in his book of sto- ries, *The Question of Bruno* (2000) and in his first novel, *Nowhere Man* (2002); Vladimir Brik, a central character in his 2008 novel, *The Lazarus Project*; and the unnamed narrators in his collections, *Love and Obstacles* (2009) and *The Book of My Lives* (2013).

Aleksandar Hemon was born in Sarajevo in 1964, the son of a Bosnian-Serb mother and a father whose background is Ukrainian. Hemon has referred to himself as an atheist of Christian heritage. Like his character Josef Pronek, who when asked, "Are you a Serb or a Muslim?" answers, "I am complicated."

Aleksandar grew up in an upper-middle-class household. His father was an electrical engineer who taught at the University of Sarajevo and also worked for an international company. Sasha (as he prefers to be called) studied comparative literature at university and then worked for a radio station that morphed into a liberal newsmagazine. In 1992, with war brewing at home, he accepted an invitation by the United States to be part of a cultural exchange program for journalists. He spent a month in Chicago, and just as his visit was winding up, the siege of Sarajevo began. He applied for political asylum, stayed in Chicago, and took a variety of odd jobs. He didn't yet realize how long he would remain in the US, but he resolved not only to learn English but to write in English. He gave himself five years, but was ready after three. His success was extraordinary: rave reviews for his debut book of stories and novel; work published in *The New Yorker* magazine; and he won a Guggenheim Award and a half-million-dollar MacArthur "genius" grant.

His experience of exile and then publishing fiction in English prompted comparisons with Vladimir Nabokov, among others. My favourite response is when Hemon said: "If Nabokov managed to make love with the English language, I'm happy with heavy petting." It's typical of the sardonic humour that colours his work, alongside the darkness of war. When we first spoke in 2008, the focus was his ambitious second novel, *The Lazarus Project*, set partly in the Chicago of a hundred years ago and drawing on the true story of a young Jewish immigrant, Lazarus Averbuch. Alternating with that tragic tale is an account of a Bosnian writer who is tracing the life and history of Lazarus. The result is a complex interweaving of politics and the immigrant experience.

We met next on stage at the International Festival of Authors in 2013, with the publication of his work *The Book of My Lives* (2013). Although there's always been a blur between fiction and non-fiction in his writing, he called this one "a collection of true stories." His publisher described it as his first book of non-fiction.

WACHTEL In your first book, *The Question of Bruno*, you, or someone who sounds a lot like you, write about imagining as a child that your father was a spy and about wanting to become a spy yourself. Was this a serious fantasy for you?

HEMON It wasn't as intense as in the story "The Sorge Spy Ring," but I did have a phase, as it were, when I read a lot of historical books, mainly about spying affairs in World War II, and so at that time, I was really into spying. I was always fascinated with the fact that spies, to deliver secret messages or packages for example, would find a hole in a tree in a park, and then they would mark a nearby bench with chalk to say that there is a message in the hole in the tree. To make sure that the chalk mark is not erased, they might turn over a Pepsi can to the left of the bench and so on. In other words, the world could become an entirely coded place if there was a message to be delivered. And this is, in some ways, the first step towards poetry, where you have to pay attention to the smallest, most insignificant things, and you have to read them and try to find the meaning in them. All the big events, as they were, are either misleading or really irrelevant. I tuned my sensibility that way. This is why I'm still fascinated by spies and their complicated identities and the necessity to pay attention to everything. But it's also that through pursuing these interests, I tuned my sensibilities in my work and perhaps as a person.

WACHTEL You or your character describe writing a poem at age sixteen about Sorge the spy with the title "The Loneliest Man in the World." You quote the first stanza: "Tokyo is breathing and I am not / The curtain of rain glued to my face / I don't live a life, I live a plot / Having two selves in one place." Now, this idea of having two selves, the double life, the secret life, seems to be an ongoing theme in your work. Why do you think it grips you in that way?

HEMON When I was a child, spies fascinated me for a different reason. But then when I started writing and when I started living in the United States, and particularly in the circumstances in which I was living in the nineties and even now perhaps, what became interesting to me in relation to spies is the fact that they have two simultaneous selves, so to speak. One of them would be public. That is what they put out as the front. Part of this public self would be what in spy lingo is called "the legend"; that is, an invented, previous life. And then they will have their real self, which is invisible to almost everyone, perhaps even the people that they work with. This very situation questions the notion that we are so beholden to: that we have solid, monolithic selves as individual human beings. If you don't, then it's some sort of distortion that needs to be redressed in various ways.

That was fascinating to me for metaphysical reasons, but also because immigration, at least the way I experienced it, is very similar. You have a sense that there is a previous life and then this life. There is also a sense that what you represent to other people here—"here" being Canada, the United States or wherever—and who you really are are two different things. Unlike spies, immigrants—or so I thought—have no control over that distribution of selves; that is, I did not organize myself to present my various selves to people here. It was beyond my control in some ways. And at the same time, this inner self is also under duress. It feels shaky. You don't know who you really are. To work out this problem requires a lot of things, and I'm not sure what the best way to go is. One way is to find a means of uniting those two selves into one solid, simple self so you're the same person publicly and privately. Or you can just let your selves multiply.

WACHTEL Which is more your inclination.

HEMON Yes, it is, yes, temperamentally. But also as a writer: that's the perfect setup. People ask me whether I'm Pronek, one of the characters in my books, or Brik from *The Lazarus Project*. But the fact of the matter is that I'm all of the people in my books. Every single person.

WACHTEL I'd like to find out a bit more about your childhood in Sarajevo, when Bosnia was part of the Socialist Federal Republic of Yugoslavia. You've described Sarajevo in the 1980s as a beautiful place to be young. What was it like to grow up there? What was the city like?

HEMON It was great! I didn't know it would turn out this way. It was a good time in the former Yugoslavia, and in Sarajevo in particular because it was the time between communism and nationalism, when a lot of energies that had been pent up until that point were being released, and the disaster was still far on the horizon. I was lucky enough to be a teenager at that time; that is, I had my own pent-up energies and had all kinds of ideas about what the world should be and how we should go about making it that way. And so I belonged... I belong still to an incredibly creative and talented political generation of Sarajevans. So I did not feel repressed. I was repressed, but repression is a good thing for a teenager because then you have to fight it. It provokes you; it was inspiring in some ways. For instance, when I was in my early twenties, I worked at a radio station in Sarajevo which was geared towards young people, but it was also created by young people. It was a revolutionary idea, and we did things that previous generations had not dared do at all. Most of those people are still my friends, and I'm in close contact with them. We have collaborated on various things, and we just stay in touch.

WACHTEL Tito, of course, was the leader of Yugoslavia for thirty-five years, from 1945 until his death in 1980. But in 1980 you were still young, you were just sixteen. In one story, you write that, "My childhood was saturated with histories of his just enterprises." What was the atmosphere like under Tito? What role did he play or occupy in your consciousness even as a child?

HEMON I think it's in "The Sorge Spy Ring" story; I remember as a kid that one of the older kids claimed that if you swear by Tito's name, you must not lie because Tito, he said, has monitors in his palace in Belgrade on which he watched every single citizen of Yugoslavia, including the kids. And so if he sees that you use his name to swear that something is true, and then it turns out not to be true, he dies to punish you. So first of all, this notion that the Great Leader was watching us all, this sort of omnipresent surveillance was one thing. But also that somehow he cared about what we kids had to say.

WACHTEL You mean it's surprisingly reassuring rather than making you feel paranoid. The children never feel alone, even if their parents have gone out.

HEMON I'm taken care of as long as I don't lie. The moment I lie, he dies, and I'm alone in the world, and that's another set of problems.

So when I was a kid, Tito was like a comic book character or a movie character. In fact, there were movies in which Tito was a character. There was a movie where Richard Burton played Tito. He was always handsome and wise and good and had a dog and... whatnot. It was appealing to us. And I never really hated Tito. I was too young when he died. And I still don't hate him. He just wanted to keep power, like a lot of those people.

What was interesting to me—it's still interesting to me—is this notion that, if we have a leader who cares about us, it was reassuring, and it was easy to think that once you remove this leader, people would automatically be free. But the fact of the matter is, once you pull that rug out from under people's feet, a whole structure, a whole infrastructure falls apart. Aside from the symbolic value of Tito's presence in your life, it was a state that was run reasonably well, compared to the former Yugoslavian states of today or Iraq or other such places. A lot of people from former Yugoslavia long for Tito. They're nostalgic about those times, when at least you knew what the structure was, and you could live assuming that it would last for a long while, that changes were not going to be sudden.

WACHTEL Your own identity is complicated, as your fictional alter-ego, Josef Pronek, puts it. He says "It's complicated." Your father's background is Ukrainian. Your mother is a Bosnian Serb. Can you tell me a bit more about your family, their roots and social position and so on?

HEMON My father was born in Bosnia, but his parents were born in what is today Western Ukraine and used to be part of the Eastern Austro-Hungarian Empire. Bosnia was occupied and annexed by the Austro-Hungarian Empire at the end of the nineteenth century, and so, at the turn of the century, the empire tried to colonize the new land. They imported a large number of people from other parts of the empire, including Galicia, what is now western Ukraine. There were all kinds of people in the part of Bosnia my father was born and grew up in, including Czechs and Italians and Germans and Russians who left after World War II. But even western Ukraine, or Galicia, was complicated when my grandparents left, so my great-grandmother was Ukrainian, but my great-grandfather, my grandmother's father, was Polish. In those days, that was not a problem. They did not have to choose an identity as a family. So the boys, my grandmother's brothers, were Polish, and the girls were Ukrainian. I remember seeing a picture in which the boys were dressed as Polish boys, with those square hats, and the girls had Ukrainian dresses. My family in Canada is exclusively from my father's side and still speak Ukrainian in the family. My dad sings in a Ukrainian choir, and they go to a Ukrainian church, my father and uncles and some others.

On my mother's side, they are ethnically Serb, but they were in Bosnia for generations. They never lived in Serbia, and by and large, they are Bosnian loyalists, not pro-Serbian. My mother, as a matter of fact, both before and after the war, considered herself to be a Yugoslav, which is not an ethnicity, but a citizenship. It's like calling yourself American or Canadian, for that matter.

And then within these two families, there are all kinds of inter-connections.

WACHTEL So it's "complicated," partly because if you say Bosnian, then people assume Muslim rather than Christian, or…

HEMON Right. Bosnian is much like American or Canadian. It's not an ethnicity. It's a citizenship, or at least it's about a relation to a state or an idea of a state or a country. So ethnically, Bosnian really means nothing. The Bosnian Muslims are known as Bosniacs, and then there are Serbs and Croats.

WACHTEL Your father was an electrical engineer who travelled a lot.

HEMON With a Yugoslav passport, you could go anywhere. No visa required. My father travelled all over the world. He would always bring back stories and chocolate. So we felt connected to the world. We were not behind the Iron Curtain in Yugoslavia. The Iron Curtain was to the east of us.

WACHTEL I like chocolate and stories. In your fiction, it's the fathers who love to tell stories. Was it like that in your own household?

HEMON Yes. My dad told stories. When I was a kid, my bedtime stories were about his childhood, featuring all kinds of domestic animals. He also was in charge of the visuals in the family, and from his trips, particularly from the Soviet Union, he would bring these rolls of slides which told fairy tales in Russian. He could read Russian, so then he would show us these slides. They were not films, not moving images. He would just roll it and keep one slide on the wall and then read what was happening in the fairy tale. So he told stories, not just out of his head, but he brought these things from abroad.

WACHTEL There are observations in your fiction about a distinctive Bosnian style of storytelling. For instance, the way that nobody asked you anything. You had to make your story be heard. Can you tell me more about that, what you call the simple pleasure of being in the story?

HEMON I sense a difference when I go to Sarajevo and people start telling me just the most banal stories about going to the supermarket. A lot of people, at least people I meet, turn it into an interesting story, and this is not an artistic endeavour. They just tell you what happened. And somehow that is not so frequent here. There is something about this desire or willingness not only to entertain the listener but to live through an experience while collecting fragments that would constitute the story later. In other words, you're processing. I do it all the time; I do it because I'm a writer, but I have always done it. A lot of my friends who are not writers, who do not write fiction or have an interest in literature in any profound sort of way, do the same thing. They collect their experiences, and then they process them into a story. And a lot of those stories are so funny and so much fun that I still can't figure out where exactly that is coming from. I would like to think it's a cultural thing, but of course I have to be aware that my sample is limited. These are my friends.

In North America and maybe in all of the Western world, there is this omnipresence of media and narratives being imposed upon an individual to define himself or herself as such. These stories are external, that is, they come from the outside. In former Yugoslavia when I was growing up, we had one-and-a-half channels of television and most of it was unwatchable, so we just had to sit around and tell stories or read books. In other words, you made up stories in which you cast yourself. This is changing rapidly, I think. I have no idea what younger generations in Bosnia think of themselves, how they talk about themselves.

WACHTEL Then there are the Bosnian jokes that come up in your novel *The Lazarus Project*, featuring these stock characters Mujo and Suljo. How would you describe these jokes?

HEMON Throughout the war, people would send me jokes about Mujo and Suljo. One of the jokes, as an example—it's not as funny as it used to be, if it was ever funny—is: what do Suljo and Mujo do on a seesaw? The answer is, they're teasing the snipers. This was very funny to people during the siege perhaps, but it was—

WACHTEL A kind of black humour.

HEMON Yeah. But it's not just black humour, it's also a way to process the bare-bone experience. There is something about being able to laugh. When I went back to Sarajevo for the first time in '97 and met a large number of friends and family and people I had worried about during the siege, they would tell me these stories, and by and large, they would tell them as funny stories. They would tell a story about how they had nothing to eat, how there was no food, and they all lived together in one apartment, ten of them, and then somebody brought in a potato, but only one potato. They hadn't seen a potato for God knows how long. It was a shrivelled, small potato. They couldn't cook it. But they hadn't seen a potato for so long that they in fact put the potato in the middle of the table, and then all ten of them sat around the table and watched it. There was no television to watch. They watched the potato. When this was told to me, there was roaring laughter, as if it was the funniest thing you ever heard, but of course it bespeaks hunger and despair. But the fact that they could tell me this and laugh—that's triumphant.

And in this joke about Suljo and Mujo teasing the snipers, the agency is given to Suljo and Mujo. It's not that the snipers are shooting them. It's that they're teasing the snipers. And so in this way of story-telling or joke-telling, the agency is reclaimed rhetorically. This is what storytelling does, and this is what joke-telling does, if I tell you a funny story about how we survived.

WACHTEL There's also the music, which seems to have a unique sensibility. You've written about *sevdah*, the Bosnian version of the blues. "It's so sad, it makes you free"—a line in *Nowhere Man*. Tell me more about that. What's that music like?

HEMON There is a word in Bosnian that describes a feeling and then the things that you do to produce or enjoy that feeling. The feeling that you might have at dusk: the word is *akshamruk*. It's derived from the word *aksham*, which is the word in Turkish for dusk or evening, and in Bosnian its use is poetic and archaic. But *akshamruk* is not a Turkish word. It's entirely Bosnian, and it denotes this feeling and the activities related to this feeling that you might have at dusk, at the end of the day and when you hear the evening calls to prayer. One song that talks about this is called, "There Is No Sorrow as When the Dusk Falls." It describes a moment where you can hear the courtyard fountains shudder, so subtle and so small, these shudders of courtyard fountains. Why they would shudder, I'll never know. And when the birds stop singing for a moment. But these are fine, gentle moments that you can experience only if you pay attention. In other words, only if you pay attention to your melancholy at that moment.

There's a whole industry in this country, the United States, and in all Western countries, that is trying to prevent you from absorbing or dealing with your own sorrow. Sorrow or being sad in the world is just abnormal. You have to redress it instantly. If you look at the world and think this is a sad place, you need a pill or you need Oprah or you need... whatever you need.

But there is a tradition in Bosnia. Not every Bosnian does this, and this music is not widely sung, and it's archaic; that is, there are no new songs that express *sevdah* the way the old songs did, so there's always a nostalgic element to that. But there's a cultural tradition in Bosnia that embraces these moments of sorrow. Here they are, let's see what they are and enjoy them for a moment, strangely, as you might enjoy dusk, which is the end of something before the night falls.

WACHTEL When you were nineteen, you did one year of mandatory national service, conscripted into the Yugoslav People's Army. You went to the former Yugoslavia Republic of Macedonia, and this experience, as described in your fiction, seems to have served up endless helpings of humiliation along with the usual miserable food. Was there any upside to your time in the army?

HEMON No.

WACHTEL What kind of impact did it have on you?

HEMON The general mythology of army service is that it turns you into a man, and it teaches you this and that and makes you tough. All I remember, all I experienced, was constant, incessant humiliation. This was in '83–'84, and it was clear to me then that the Yugoslav People's

Army, at least the officers who were my commanding officers, would commit war crimes as soon as there was a war. I did not know what war they would fight. While I was in Štip, in Macedonia, my unit was supposed to stop the Bulgarian advance, and we would all have been sacrificed in that, but fortunately the Bulgarians did not advance. But it was clear to me that, if we fought the Bulgarian army, we would commit war crimes.

WACHTEL How was that clear?

HEMON The inherent violence and sexism of the army as I experienced it. The principle of army training is that they beat you into obedience, essentially. They humiliate you until they break you. Or if you resist and they can't break you, they give you a commanding position so you can break others. The system never allows you to occupy a position from which you can say no—you simply can't do that—nor does the system allow you to retain your moral consciousness through all the humiliation, not to mention throughout a war. I learned nothing in the army other than I should stay away from the army. And it wasn't even the general idea that human beings are awful. It was more that: in a particular context, human beings are awful. At some point, you just worry about your own survival.

WACHTEL In July 1991, you made a visit to Ukraine where you have family. While you were there you witnessed the collapse of the Soviet Union. What was that like for you? Did you see it coming?

HEMON The collapse of the Soviet Union? No. I could see the descent from where I was. Yugoslavia was not part of the Soviet Union or the Warsaw Pact, but we could see that things were getting weaker. We could also see the general decline of socialism as an idea. The Tiananmen massacre was in June '89. Then there was the Romanian revolution, which we watched live on TV because the signal was broadcast from Romania, from the studio that the rebels occupied. But I was there for a summer school in Ukrainian language and culture. And then one morning we woke up, and I saw the staff crying, and there was this morose, glum man reading a pronouncement on TV, and then we figured out… we were told that there was in fact a coup. But then in Kiev, we went to the main square, Nezalezhnosti, where there were demonstrations already, and we participated in those demonstrations or at least went there for a few days. For two or three days, Kravchuk, the president of the Ukrainian Socialist Republic, didn't really declare himself either way. He was going to see who was winning before he did that. And so the demonstrators were surrounded by the KGB and the army, who were also waiting to see who was going to win. We went back to the place we were staying, but a lot of people actually slept for days at Nezalezhnosti because they were afraid that, if they left the main square, if they went home, they could be arrested individually. So it was very dramatic, and we did not know what was happening and what would happen. There were rumours. We could not get information. But my father called me from Sarajevo somehow and told me that there were a million people demonstrating in Leningrad and Moscow, that the whole thing was falling apart.

And then Ukraine declared independence while I was there. There had been demonstrators putting pressure on the parliament, the Rada, to declare independence, which they did. I was in front of the Ukrainian parliament when it happened. Wherever I go, I cause trouble.

WACHTEL It was later that year, 1991, that you got an invitation to visit the United States. Was that a welcome opportunity to you? Did you feel a need to get away from Sarajevo?

HEMON Yes, I did, but I did not think I would go for the rest of my life. My hope was that I would leave for a few months just to free my brain a little because it was coming down hard. The war in Croatia was on. It was brutal. Preparations were being made in Bosnia, and there were all these incidents and so on. But what was worse was this constant propaganda and pressure, in the sense that what we hold dear is under attack in various ways, whether it's the city of Sarajevo or rock 'n' roll or whatnot. I just needed to be elsewhere, I thought, so I could think clearly. War muddles your brain, and the preparation for war muddles your brain.

At one point, I got an application form from the Canadian Embassy, but the form was so brutally discouraging that I just never filled it out. But then miraculously I received an invitation from the American Cultural Centre. I was a young journalist, and there was a program that invited young journalists from Eastern Europe to visit and stay for about a month. So I accepted the invitation and came in January of '92.

WACHTEL And then?

HEMON Then the war started in April. I was supposed to fly out of Chicago on the first of May. The siege of Sarajevo started on the second of May, in the sense that the city was closed and nobody could get in and out, and the train station was destroyed in a rocket attack and so on. If I had flown back on the first of May, I would have arrived just in time for the siege, but I didn't go, and here I am in Chicago.

WACHTEL When you were watching news reports, how were you able to keep contact with friends or family?

HEMON Early on, phones would work occasionally, and so I was calling randomly. I had no job outside of the fact that I taught my room-mates—one of them I met in Ukraine in '81—to play this card game. I would win the card game, and their money, and then I would give their money back to them for the phone and so on. Then I got jobs and all that. Later on I was able to call my parents and friends when the phone lines went down because a lot of my friends were working as journalists and had access to satellite phones. And sometimes during a truce, the phone lines would just work. I also wrote letters. Because my friends were foreign journalists or were with the Red Cross and such, they could bring things in and out of the city. So I stayed in touch.

WACHTEL At some point, you realized you were going to be staying in the United States for some time, and you made a commitment not only to learn English but to write in English. How did you—?

HEMON It was clear to me, at some point, that I was going to live here for a very long time, possibly for the rest of my life, and that I would have to write in English because of that. Somehow—it was completely arbi-trary—I gave myself a five-year period in which to write a publishable story in English. And then I set out to read a lot in English, and I made lists of words from the books that I was reading, lists of words that I did not know, and then I would look them up. I also found my first legal job in the United States, as a canvasser for Greenpeace. I cannot believe that I ever actually applied for the job, never mind getting it and then having it for two-and-a-half years, because it's a very hard job. It's the worst job ever for someone who doesn't speak English.

WACHTEL I know. You go door to door and pitch something.

HEMON Yes, I got this job, which is to say that I spoke to people every day for two-and-a-half years, and I had to drop being self-conscious, and I had to pay attention to what people were saying, and I was learn-ing all these intricacies of everyday life. If you read books, you can read philosophy in English and then get philosophical concepts from the dictionary. But all these words that you get from people who live in the experience that produces these words: I was in touch with that daily, and I read at the same time and enrolled in a graduate program that allowed me to read even more.

WACHTEL Your novel, *The Lazarus Project*, features a factual story within a fictional one. Vladimir Brik, a Bosnian immigrant who shares a certain amount of your own experience, stumbles upon a news story from 1908 about Lazarus Averbuch, a young Jew who was shot when he went to the home of the Chicago chief of police, and was then cast as an anarchist, a would-be assassin. Brik becomes fascinated with this story, and presumably so did you. What caught your imagination here?

HEMON It's a sad story, and I'm attracted to sad stories generally. But it was also the photo. Somebody passed on a book to me about the Averbuch affair, the factual story of the killing of Lazarus Averbuch, and in it there were a couple of photos featuring the dead Averbuch and a police captain holding him up in a chair. These photos are stunning. I'm seen them obviously millions of times since, but I still am shocked by the brutality of that photo, and the sadness. This captain is showing off the body of a dead foreigner, telling the viewer we killed him, don't worry. He's so gloatingly alive, the police captain, with Averbuch in a torn jacket and socks, sitting there, his eyes closed. In one of the photos, because they were shot indoors and required long exposure, the police captain moved, and his face is blurred. So he strangely looks like a ghost. Whereas Averbuch, who has not moved, looks more present because his facial features are sharp and clear. These photos are haunting, and when I saw them, I realized not only that I would have to write about Averbuch, but that I would have to put those photos in the book somehow, and so I did.

WACHTEL No one knows exactly why Lazarus Averbuch went to see the Chicago chief of police or what happened, but you're not ambiguous about that. You make it clear that the police chief murdered him.

HEMON That seems to me to be the most plausible explanation. The Chicago police often have this attitude that you shoot first and ask questions later. People with guns do that. But there is no evidence whatsoever of any anarchist plot in which Averbuch was part. In the book *An Accidental Anarchist* by Walter Roth and Joe Kraus, they note that the anarchist angle is entirely dropped by the police; that is, they stopped insisting that this was an assassination plot. They just went on to exonerate the chief of police and to declare the killing accidental.

They stopped arresting people in the real story because the story did not hold up. There was a coroner's hearing that exonerated Chief Shippy, and the whole thing ended. They were arresting people for various reasons, and there were immigration laws and changes in immigration laws that were a consequence of this. But at some point, with all the bias, with all the newspaper control, they just stopped insisting that he was a violent anarchist. I left it out of the book for a number of reasons. But there is no evidence whatsoever, not even fabricated evidence, that he was an anarchist. They pushed the story early on in the affair, but then they could not sustain it.

WACHTEL One of the facts about Averbuch was that he had escaped a pogrom in 1903 in Kishinev, in what's now Moldova, and then he was in a refugee camp in Czernowitz before he came to America. He was only nineteen when he died. Is that part of the poignancy of the story?

HEMON Yes, that's the saddest aspect of the story: that he survived the pogrom, and he came to America, which is supposed to be the land of freedom, and then he was shot by the chief of police seven months after his arrival. The American Dream did not work out for him at all. His sister, Olga—it's suggested in *An Accidental Anarchist*, and in my book also—went back to Europe. She could not handle the grief. She went back to Europe and then vanished, probably in the Holocaust. It's a very sad story. Those stories are left out of the narrative of the American Dream.

WACHTEL Your writer character in the novel goes on a journey to Eastern Europe with his old friend, a photographer, and you made your own journey in 1999, with your old friend who is also a photographer, although a different kind of person from the fictional version. What did you find most moving about that trip? What affected you?

HEMON The Jewish cemetery in Chişinău, in Kishinev, which is by and large torn up, three-quarters of it dug up by the Soviets, who built a park and playground on some parts of it. Other parts they just levelled. And so when you enter it, you enter another world. Parts of it are neglected and old, overgrown. The families have been gone for God knows how long. And then there are some tombstones, although many of them are desecrated. Some of the tombstones—this is in the book, too—have writing in Russian that says, Do not take down. There is family. The implication is that those untended stones can be taken down, that nobody cares. It's a very sad place.

WACHTEL *The Lazarus Project* is about this person whose real name is Lazarus Averbuch, and then of course there is in a sense the biblical resonance of his name, which you allude to in the epigraph. Do you see him, in a sense, as resurrected through your own storytelling?

HEMON He is temporarily resurrected in the book, but not completely and fully. The body is absent. That is the saddest thing. We can't live retroactively in narratives. In some ways, the only way you can really mourn a death is by telling stories about them. It's the only way you can have access to their lives as they used to be. I'm not religious. I don't believe in alternative destinies and other worlds and so on. Where we live, we live here and now, and then we're dead and that's it. But then what do you do with all those lost lives? So many people have lived. More people have died than there are people living now. So what do you do with that? The only way is to keep them alive, to tell stories about them, not to forget about them.

WACHTEL Chicago is famously an immigrant city, and it's the city where you've now made your home. Do you see yourself staying in America?

HEMON My primary loyalty is to the city, so I'm loyal to Sarajevo and then by extension to Bosnia, and I love Chicago and by extension I'm an American. It would be very hard for me to leave Chicago. We lived in Paris for about ten months, and Paris is beautiful and wonderful, but in Paris, which I adore and adored back then, I would follow snowstorms in Chicago on the Internet—the most insane thing to be nostalgic about. I'd say to my now wife, "Look! Six feet of snow in Chicago. It's minus 40. How lovely! I wish I were there." That's a little demented but I love the city.

WACHTEL And do you also check the weather in Sarajevo?

HEMON No. I know what it is. There are no dramatic, climatic upheavals in Sarajevo. Now it's changing because of global warming and all that, but there are no dramatic storms. It's one of the things I love about Chicago: the drama of weather. Last night, there was an incredible storm here. You think you're never going to live through this, and then you live through it. And similarly in the winter, it's minus 30. Disaster euphoria reigns in the winter. This is appealing to me. It is entirely wrong, I acknowledge.

WACHTEL But your fictional characters: Josef Pronek wants to return to Sarajevo, where you can be anybody. Brik wants to stay in Sarajevo, leaving his Chicago wife behind.

HEMON Ideally, I would divide time between Chicago and Sarajevo and Paris because I miss Sarajevo and I miss my friends and the simple, little things and the fact that I don't have to explain myself to anybody. But I would not be able to choose Sarajevo as the only place I live. Unfortunately, the way it is now, it is far from the world, but also I have a substantial chunk of my life that has taken place in Chicago, and I have a little daughter who was born here and has spent her whole life of ten months in Chicago so far. And so I have again multiple selves. I have a Chicago self and a Sarajevo self.

July 2008

§

WACHTEL You've described yourself as a man whose imagination is always on the go: constantly, compulsively thinking up stories. What's that like? What goes on in your head on any given day?

HEMON Well, there has to be a syndrome that describes that state, that compulsive narrativization of experience. I operate like a typical human being most of the time, but there's a part of my brain that is constantly converting experience into narrative, and I do not have to think about it. I would imagine that dancers, whenever they walk, can feel the rhythm of their steps. When they move, they can imagine a progression of moves that would follow the initial move, but then they just do whatever they have to do. So there is a part of my brain always narrativizing the experience that I'm involved in and extending that experience into the realm of the imagined, so that I can imagine a story that will come out of this moment. I almost never get around to actually telling the story, never mind writing it. As an example, I was once in a coffee shop idling and saw a bee buzzing around a woman's head. Her partner, or the man who was with her, chased the bee away, and that was the end of the real experience. But I sat there and imagined the beginning of a story in which the bee stung the woman, and the man failed to protect the woman from the bee, and some conflict came out of it. And within five minutes I was churning up some kind of story...

WACHTEL Their whole relationship was unravelling before your eyes.

HEMON Right, because of the bee. And I only remember this because I caught myself doing it. This happens to me all day long, all the time. But there's also the part of imagining the possibilities inherent in the moment that's scary—I imagine catastrophes all the time, something that I have to learn to keep in check.

WACHTEL How do you manage to do that?

HEMON It's very difficult because every day I imagine what the world will be like thirty, forty, fifty years from now. I have children now, and to me it's horrifying to think about what they will have to face fifty years from now while we're all going about our business of ignoring climate change.

WACHTEL But how do you curb that catastrophe syndrome?

HEMON I don't know. I just start thinking about soccer or something. I focus myself on the real at the moment. But it is something that just goes through me; it never disables me. It is part of the way, or it is the way, my mind works. I've learned to live with that. Sometimes when it gets worse, when there's a real possibility, when I'm in the doldrums, I imagine outcomes of this moment that are terrifying. But one of the ways to manage this is to convert it into fiction, or into actual narratives that can be written down and passed around to other people so they can share my concerns.

WACHTEL And the process of narrativizing, is it a distancing process? Does it remove you?

HEMON No, I don't think it's a distancing process. In fact, in some ways it brings me closer to the experience. It's a way to process the experience. If I don't, it's chaotic and confusing and more scary. I've learned in my life and in what I do that the most terrifying thing is what you cannot imagine. However active or inventive your imagination is, the scariest parts are beyond that. People ask me, "Did you know that the war was coming in Bosnia?" I did and I didn't. I worked as a journalist, all of my friends were journalists, we had all the facts that you needed to have to know that war was practically, at a certain point, inevitable. But what I couldn't do—it was a failure on my part—was imagine what it would be like. I began to imagine it, but it was too late. The only people who could imagine it were the people who were organizing it. They were deploying their imagination, as it were, to organize the war. And even now, or even then, in fact, it required a work of imagination to know what was happening because I would get only fragments of it and then had to reconstruct it with my imagination into some sort of a narrative. So to be able to imagine, to engage—I think it's part of our survival evolutionary machinery.

WACHTEL I always thought if you imagined the worst, then it wouldn't happen. It was a kind of way to…

HEMON No, if you imagine the worst, the worst will happen, but then there is worse beyond that. That's the positive approach.

WACHTEL *Sasha Hemon Tells You True and Untrue Stories* is the playful title of a radio show you hosted as a young man in Sarajevo, and somehow this question of true or untrue stories inevitably comes up in conversations about your work. Why is that? Did you imagine when you dreamt up that series title that it would come back to haunt you?

HEMON No, I suppose it determined or described my interest, which has lasted since then. The trick of media, particularly radio perhaps, is that however outrageous the story you might be telling, the authority of the medium is backing it up and people will believe you. To me that was very, very interesting. One of the things that I did was come up with this outrageous story about a character named Alphonse Kauders, and then people believed that such a person existed. But it was also the time in former Yugoslavia when the most outrageous lies were the propaganda that people believed, and that resulted in catastrophe. The notion of relating a truth in narratives is something I have to deal with constantly. That is, is there truth in fiction, or is it only the problem of non-fiction? Is that the dividing line between fiction and non-fiction? And how do you construct the truth in fiction or non-fiction? How do you arrive at that? It's a technical issue for what I do because I cannot lie. That is, I do not wish to lie when I'm writing fiction. But I make it up, so how do you use lies, made-up stories, to arrive at something that could be experienced by the reader as truthful? And similarly with non-fiction. A reasonable person knows that whatever experience you might be describing, it is never just *your* experience. And certainly with my family, my circle of friends in Sarajevo, nothing ever happened just to me so that I was the only one who owned the story. There were a number of pieces in my book that I had to run by my friends and family—Is this what happened? Is this how it was?—because we have different memories. So even in what could presumably be self-evidently true, what we refer to as non-fiction needed the validation of truth.

WACHTEL But given that truth is so subjective and everyone's memories are different, how could you—I mean, I understand your feeling of almost moral responsibility because of the collective experience—but how do you then determine what is true?

HEMON Well, I'm not a postmodernist in the sense that the truth is always slippery, that you never know what it is. There's history in the sense of a documented consensus of what really happened. So, the Holocaust is not up for discussion, nor is what happened in Bosnia. But the truth in the sense of organic connection with common reality—that is, if we share this moment, we can go back to it and find the consensual truth of it, what really happened in this moment—to my mind, narrating this is one way to arrive at it, and narrating it as a communal, or at least not an individual, effort. It would require editing, but we would be able to cover all the moments and all the experiences, and we would have to put it into a sequence of events. We would convert it into story, and in the process of narration, truth emerges, I think—the truth of common experience—but it has to be negotiated in the same process, it's not necessarily self-evident.

WACHTEL You've said that Bosnians have no words to distinguish fiction from non-fiction. How do you explain or understand the difference?

HEMON There's no word for fiction and there's no word for non-fiction, but there's also no pair of words that would match the distinction between fiction and non-fiction. It was a problem because my translator asked me how to translate the acknowledgments at the beginning of the book where I talk about my relation to fiction and non-fiction. And we decided to cut the acknowledgments because it was too difficult. The closest that I could come up with, and the truest—although *personal essay* is in the running—to me, is true stories. So these are true stories, with some essayistic parts perhaps, but even that's picky. They're the stories that I had been telling to people and wanted to tell in various ways, but they had this particular quality so that I didn't have to make up additional stuff. I could just lay down what happened and ensure through the consensus of people involved that this is actually what happened, or it was close enough.

WACHTEL Bosnians also, apparently, have no word for privacy. What are the implications?

HEMON Well, there's no privacy. Privacy, in this Anglo-Saxon, Western sense, where you have this sovereign territory around yourself, spatially speaking, that belongs to you and no one else and that you determine who's coming in and out of, that's limited in Bosnia. At the least your family has access to that territory. Once when I was back in Belgrade waiting in a line to get a bus ticket to Sarajevo, I left about a yard between me and the person ahead of me, and about four people moved into that space. You have to rub your pelvises to ensure that no one will cut in, because if there's a yard, they think you're not interested in standing in line. Prior to communication, people touch one another, not necessarily aggressively. I still do it, in many ways. Individuals, human beings, they do not invent themselves. Self-invention is a standard notion in the United States, it's part of the notion of individual sovereignty, which I admire and try to live by. But you have to be part of a network of people to exist at all. No one exists outside of a family, no one exists outside of a neighbourhood, no one exists outside of a larger group of people, of friends and acquaintances. So if you isolate yourself from that, then you're not really fully existing, you're only partially existing. That's the upside of the absence of privacy. The downside is, well, the absence of privacy.

WACHTEL The issue of truth versus fiction is central to one of your stories in your collection *Love and Obstacles*. The narrator's father, who sounds a lot like your own father, is deeply and personally offended by anything he considers unreal. He regards the whole concept of literature as a scam. Do you get his strong reaction to fiction? Why he would take that position?

HEMON That character is not my father. My father doesn't spend that much time on real and unreal because he's very immersed in the real all the time. When you're living with a group of people who are close to you, physically and otherwise, then you cannot simply step out of the reality that you share and move into the realm of the imagined without losing some legitimacy as a serious person. So in some ways you have to constantly negotiate what is your right to tell made-up stories. For me, it goes back to what I mentioned earlier, it's a fundamental human question: How do you tell a story that is true? Under what circumstances? And this works in any situation with any life experience, but if you are connected as I was with something like war, that requires a respect for truth—you cannot just make up stories and numbers of people killed, or claim that the Holocaust didn't happen, or the siege of Sarajevo didn't happen, or that people ran up the hills to attack people who were besieging the city—you know, you have to respect that truth, but at the same time that truth is not necessarily self-evident.

And then part of the story of displacement, whether you're a refugee or just an immigrant, is that your connection with your previous life becomes tenuous or even lost, so that it's hard to know what stories about your previous life you invented and what really happened. There's a continuity between stories, memory, and history in that cluster of issues. So I had to deal with that on a personal level because there was a time when I was in Chicago that this network of people that constituted me—my friends, my family, anyone who knew me in fact—was beyond my reach, and I realized I could make up my entire life; there were no witnesses in the 1990s in Chicago of who I used to be.

WACHTEL During that time, did you feel unmoored when you were in Chicago without, in a sense, an identity?

HEMON I did because only upon displacement did I realize how much I was constituted by other people. But this individualist notion, the individual sovereignty, is also something that literature deals with and establishes really well because there has to be a central consciousness, or at least a limited number of them, in each work of fiction. It is what we really engage with.

WACHTEL The literary enterprise itself is a theme of your most recent story collection, *Love and Obstacles*, and once again like some of your fictional alter egos, the unnamed narrator of these interlinked stories follows something like your own journey: the coming of age in Sarajevo, travelling to Chicago, finding his life ruptured by the outbreak of war, struggling to make a new life, new language, new culture. You're quite ironic about this fellow's literary aspirations. On the very first page there's a reference to Joseph Conrad. Why is that?

HEMON Why am I ironic?

WACHTEL Yes.

HEMON I don't know if I would use the word *ironic*. The thing is, the simple rule of writing, and perhaps of writing life, is that it's all shit until it isn't. The culture of writing programs results in a notion that somehow if you work steadily and chip at it slowly, then it becomes incrementally better and little by little you'll get to be good. But my experience is that I struggle along and then hope it turns good enough for me, good enough to be published and have a conversation like this one, but before that it's all embarrassing all the time. That's true when

I write a book or a piece, and it's also true over my writing life. I wrote very, very bad stuff for many, many years, twenty years at least. I had an entire life of writing poetry that was in the running for the worst poetry ever written. When I read that poetry after years of not looking at it, it was so funny to me that there were tears running down my cheeks. At the same time I'm proud of those failed attempts. It requires a particular kind of commitment, I think, to constantly fail for many, many years, or at least even for a period of time, for six months or nine months or two years, while writing a book, and then it turns good because in some ways you've made all the mistakes that you could possibly make, and then all that is left are the right things to do. So in that sense, this boy in the book is not like me in a number of ways, but he's close enough for me to understand him. I enjoy making fun of him, but it is not disrespectful.

WACHTEL In your story "Everything," there are various misadventures your character follows, but he's particularly interested in writing a poem called "Love and Obstacles," and in another story he tries to impress girls by offering to recite his poem "Love and Obstacles." Later it became the title of a short story in *The New Yorker*, and then you chose it as the title of your collection of stories. What is it about the title that appeals to you?

HEMON When I was writing all the bad poetry, I had a rock band, and the only way to deploy that poetry—because no one would read it, let alone publish it—was to use it as lyrics for the songs. But even then I had to at some point sit down with the drummer and explain what it all meant, except I didn't know, so it was dazzling bullshit that I provided for him. But I liked the title "Love and Obstacles." I don't remember what the lyrics were or what this poem was about. I just liked the title. It lays out an entire universe of plots: Love and Obstacles. And so in the book it functions as a hint, as it were, or a symbolic hint. It is what the boy deals with, this constant situation in which he seeks love, but there are some obstacles. And that's in relation to girls or women, and then with some men whom he admires for the wrong reasons, and also in his relationship to the United States, which he wants to love, but it's not easy.

WACHTEL In another story in *Love and Obstacles*, the narrator finds himself in the complicated position of being a published author who feels like a fraud with no right to talk about the suffering of others. He says, "I was Bosnian, I looked and conducted myself like a Bosnian, everyone was content to think that I was in constant, uninterrupted communication with the tormented soul of my homeland." Did you experience that?

HEMON That I did experience, yes. I would be at a dinner party, and they'd ask me, "Where are you from?" And I'd say, "Bosnia." And they'd say, "What is going on there?" And then I'd have to, I guess, in ten words or less lay out for them the entire history and the complications there, and the individual stories of all the people I know and love—the whole universe going on there. So there was a time when if someone asked me where I was from and I didn't care to talk about it, I would say I was from Luxembourg. They would have heard about Luxembourg, but no one really knows where it is, no one ever goes there unless they're money laundering. Now I do a little better at that. I don't know how to explain the situation, and I still do avoid identifying myself, not because I'm ashamed, far from it, but rather I don't want to be a cut-rate explainer for a very complicated thing.

WACHTEL Your story "The Conductor" introduces a character, an associate of the narrator, who becomes the greatest living Bosnian poet, Muhamed D.—he's nicknamed Dedo, old man. This poet survived the siege and wrote about it. The narrator uses Dedo's poetry to get women into bed. You quote from it. Did these poems exist? Was there a model for Dedo?

HEMON No, no. To this day, many Bosnians don't believe that I did not refer obliquely to some other poet. I wrote all the poetry for Dedo. I have a friend who's a very good Bosnian poet, and he liked the poems, and he wanted to see the rest of them, but there was no rest. He urged me to complete them, but once I stopped writing Dedo, I had no position from which to write poems. The thing is, it does not hurt me in any way when people say that my fiction is autobiographical, but I never see it that way myself. I imagine the situations I was in with entirely different outcomes, so it does not conform to my life. But also, I'm everyone in my books. That is, I had to put myself in the head of Dedo and deploy parts of my brain that would not have been deployed otherwise to write that poetry.

WACHTEL You made Dedo a Bosnian Muslim. Does that make a difference to his stature as a poet? Does it add greater authority to his voice?

HEMON Not necessarily, not directly, no. I can't remember why I did that. I mean, it was a poke in the eye of all the bigots who dismiss

Muslims automatically as a lesser culture. There's plenty of secular culture or religious culture that is not fundamentalist that came out of Islam, and it was evident to me throughout my life in Bosnia, and even after the war. So I think that was part of it, because I wrote that book at the same time as I was writing *The Lazarus Project*, and I was very invested, or rather enraged, with what was going on in the United States at that time.

WACHTEL You mean the war in Iraq.

HEMON Right, the lies and—talk about truth in fiction. And so I think that was the reason, but I would not think of it in terms of authority.

WACHTEL Your non-fiction collection, *The Book of My Lives*, explores the before and after of your journey from Sarajevo to Chicago, your different identities as a son, a brother, a displaced person, a husband, a soccer player. One of the most striking stories is called "The Book of My Life," and it describes your obsession and later disillusion with someone who'd been a role model for you at university. It's a story that shows the clash of literature and ideology. Tell me about your literature professor.

HEMON Nikola Koljevic was my favourite literature professor when I was in college. I enjoyed his courses very much. I think the only writing course I ever took was the one that he taught, an essay-writing course. He was also my thesis supervisor. And then after I graduated, I called him up, and we went for a walk by the river and discussed literature, and I actually showed my first literary attempts to him. So he was the one, in some ways, before the war, before it all happened, who led me into the realm of literature, and I enjoyed being led by him. But then at some point he joined and became a leading person in the Serbian Nationalist Party. He was very close to Karadžic at the beginning of the war, and he would have been more than likely indicted as a war criminal had he not shot himself in 1997. Once I saw him becoming a fascist, I had to question all the things that I had learned from him, or in this realm that he delimited by his presence, and I had to test the whole notion of literature and the many, many books against the fact of his fascism, against the fact that being exposed to the noble project of literature in no way stopped him from going in that direction. Before the war, I believed, and many people still believe now, that literature and art are ennobling. That is, if you expose yourself to it, it'll make you a better person. And so the more you read, the more music you listen to, the further away you are from being a war criminal or orchestrating a genocide, or just being a mean person. But the sad and simple fact of life is that this is not the case; and that the kindest people in war may not be interested in reading books or caring about art or literature in any way, and wars and genocide can be orchestrated by well-read, educated people who can quote Kant or Shakespeare, no problem at all.

WACHTEL How do you unlearn what he taught you in terms of—?

HEMON Well, I read and reread books. This coincided with my project of acquiring English so that I could write in English. So I read books with this in mind. Many books would just not hold up to the reality that I discovered once I abandoned this dreamy realm of ennobling literature. But I also had to answer: Why do this? I had been a writer before, I wanted to be a literary writer, and I also worked as a journalist. Why do this? What is the point? If it's not ennobling, why do it?

WACHTEL And?

HEMON The alternative of not doing it is not available, or not acceptable, for one thing. I think what literature does is construct a field of human experience in a language that people have access to, and in that field you can have access to knowledge that is not available otherwise, and the important factor in having access to that knowledge, is imagination. You can imagine your alternative lives, you can imagine the lives of other people who have nothing in common with you, and then you can stay engaged with the world by means of literature in a way that is not available otherwise. That allows fascists to enter this field too. It does not keep them out, and they might find things that they're already looking for, so it does not end up ennobling. But it is where we come together to try to do some good things, and if we fail at it, we fail at it. It's a continuous project rather than a production of masterworks that makes us better all the time, and this continuous engagement, to me, is what matters. It never ends. In some ways it's a utopian project. I know rationally that it's never going to come off in a way that we're all going to become good people, but where else would you go? Where else would I go? What else would I do? The other possibility is just to sit at home and do nothing and give up on humanity.

WACHTEL Do you blame yourself in some way for not noticing your professor's genocidal proclivities?

HEMON I did blame myself, and I thought about this a lot. Everyone I know had an example of a friend, or even family member, people who were nice and pleasant and intelligent and honest, and suddenly they turned murderous. And it's a great problem to deal with this if you assume psychological and moral continuity in people. What a comfortable life and stable society produces is a notion that we have always been who we are now, that when I was four or five, the person that I am now was beginning to develop, and there's this continuous trajectory of self-development. It's a comfortable, perhaps necessary, delusion. But what happens at times of historical, societal rupture is that this continuity is blown up, and people who were good until the war started turned into killers, and once the war ends they turned back into being nice people. This, to me, has become the explanation for the situation: he was a nice person until he wasn't. This does not, of course, relieve anyone of responsibility for the acts they may have committed in these extraordinary circumstances, but it puts pressure on all of us to block the possibility of people converting to murderous individuals. In other words, this is the work of democracy; this is the work of engaging with other people in the realm of equality and respect.

WACHTEL That sounds like a utopian project too.

HEMON Ah yes, all I ever do, all day long, is utopian projects.

WACHTEL You've said that everyone in Sarajevo has a story about betrayal. How have these wounds been absorbed in the culture? Is it something that you feel now?

HEMON I don't because it's been sorted out. People who betrayed me, I got over that. But then there's this reinforced loyalty and closeness with people, whether it's my family or my friends. Everywhere I go, including Toronto, I have friends who are so close to me they're practically family. They are family. We behave the same way, we stay in touch, we do things, and we have such strong connections that this is beyond any kind of damage. You lose some, you win some, as it were. But the stories of betrayal... If you assume moral and psychological continuity, then the alternative explanation for the switch from being nice to being a killer is that they were always that way, but we never knew. And "they" being, in Bosnia's case, ethnically defined, so you can never again trust them, even when they seem nice. And so the outcome of that, unfortunately in many ways, is the segregation, often the institutional segregation, between people of different ethnicities. In Bosnia, this is what many of us are struggling against, directly or intellectually.

WACHTEL In an essay called "The Lives of a Flâneur," you describe the Sarajevo you knew before the war and your love of the city. You intended to tell stories about it to your children and grandchildren, to grow old and die there. Is it still a shock to you that your life took this dramatic turn?

HEMON It's no longer a shock. I got over that. I'm inside my life, I don't think of it phenomenologically, as it were. But it is eventful in a way that I would not have chosen. I just try to make the best of it as much as I can. But it's also… In my family, on my father's side at least, no one has said, "I want to die in the country where I was born" for a number of years, a number of generations, maybe centuries; maybe my children will just live one life in one place in a sense of continuity, but that's not something we carry around. It's not just my family; it's a common story.

WACHTEL When you first arrived in Chicago in 1992, you were trying to learn English of course, but you couldn't write in your own language. Why?

HEMON I couldn't because a language encompasses the experience of the people who use it, and it reflects it. It reflects not just the experience of the past but the experience of the present. Words emerge from the experience, and I was cut off from that experience. I wasn't speaking the same language—or at least not enough for me to write—as people who were under siege or involved in the war. I had been writing for a magazine in Sarajevo; the people I was working with continued publishing this magazine, and early in the summer of 1992, when the war started, there were two or three pieces that I wrote and then dictated to them over satellite phone. They wanted me to write, even to review movies. They wanted me to go to a theatre in Chicago and see a movie. It was important to them to know that there were movies being made, and that they would get to see them sooner or later. But I simply was not comfortable using that language. They were inside, and I was outside. And so the notion that I would be telling them what is right, what is wrong, what is good, what is not, just about movies—I could not. To write and tell a story, you have to assume a position of some sort of authority, not necessarily superiority but just, "I know a little more about what I've written in these pieces than you." This is the direction of the exchange, and then ideally the reader responds, and then we get into a conversation. But I could not start a conversation from that position of authority, because I was in a much better position, on the one hand, in terms of safety and life—no one was shooting at me— but also I had no access to the language they were speaking. And so I stopped writing in my own language for a few years and started writing in English. But I've been writing a column for a Bosnian publication again on and off since 1996.

WACHTEL You came to America initially on a one-month journalistic project, and the day you were supposed to return was when the siege of Sarajevo began. When you left Sarajevo, did you have an inkling that you might end up staying longer than you—?

HEMON No. I had written a book of bad stories, and I'd submitted it to a publisher in Sarajevo, and there was a book of stories that was supposed to come out in the summer of 1992. Fortunately the publisher vanished and so did the book, so you're all safe from that. But my plan was to somehow establish some connections, people in universities or whatever, and then I would come back to Sarajevo, publish a book, and then with that book and those connections I could perhaps try to find a way to the United States. So I did not have money or clothes.

WACHTEL So this was an instance where you knew and you didn't know, as you mentioned earlier. You knew war was coming, but there was a level—

HEMON Right, you do not know when it's coming because you can't imagine what it really is to know when it's there. I imagine wars, or most of us imagine wars, as battles. We're on this side and on that side, and then we shoot at each other. But that's not how it works. War starts well before that, both in military terms and also intellectual, emotional, and many other terms.

WACHTEL You describe your return to Sarajevo in the spring of 1997, a year and a half after the end of the war, as an irreversibly displaced visitor. In what way did you feel that most strongly?

HEMON The first few days that I was in Sarajevo, I walked around the city intensely before I talked to any friends; I didn't go out to places where I thought I could find them; I didn't contact them. I was alone with the city first. Then I started re-engaging with people I hadn't seen for five years. The five years felt like a very, very long time. And so, everything was the same and not the same. Buildings were damaged, but they were in the same place. I knew the geography of it all, I knew how to get from this point to that point, but it was different in many ways. I ran into an old friend of mine from elementary school. I'd known her since the age of seven, and so I was happy to see her, and in this excitement I asked, "How are you? How's your mother?" and she said, "My mother was shot by a sniper the first month of the war." As I was asking her, the tone, the approach that I had, was as though nothing had happened. This was a default way of speaking without the fact of war there. She was not insulted, she was not upset about it, because we were friends. We're still friends. But I had to adjust to that reality. She was the same friend as before the war, she was the same person, but that fact, that her personhood existed in a particular context, I had to adjust to. So she was the same but not the same at all.

WACHTEL At one time you described yourself as a militant Sarajevan. You can now say the same, maybe, almost, of your adopted hometown of Chicago?

HEMON You could say that, yes. Militant is an awkward—

WACHTEL Maybe a bad choice of words.

HEMON I was more militant about Sarajevo back then, and exclusive. I made a distinction that was a form of bigotry frankly, in which people who were born in Sarajevo, the urban people, they could understand the city in a way that non-urban people couldn't begin to comprehend, and so there was an inherent superiority in my urbanness; it was indeed militant. I do love Chicago very dearly, and I do still love Sarajevo, but I would never again posit that I'm better at being in a city than someone else and that I'm more important in the city than someone else.

WACHTEL But, as you say, you wanted from Chicago what you'd gotten from Sarajevo, which is a geography of the soul. How does that work?

HEMON In some ways I understood this in retrospect. Although I was well on the way to understanding it, I needed to relate to the city in nearly metaphysical ways. That is, on the one hand, if who I was was constructed by this collective entity of the city—growing up in a particular geographic, architectural, cultural, and human context—once I was taken out of it, I realized how much I depended on all those exchanges and interactions that were necessitated by the space of a city. I needed to be in a city I understood, not only to know who I was but also to be someone at all. And this, most importantly, included being able to tell stories about the city I was living in. The way I formulated my love for Sarajevo before the war is that I wanted to tell stories to my grandchildren and children about things that happened to me in the city—this is where I met your mother, this is where we were making out the first time, or whatever, this is where I was beaten up once—to organize a physical space into a narrative space, as it were. And to do that in Chicago I had to spend a lot of time there, and then also I had to organize it narratively, to move to this space and then find ways to tell stories in that space and out of it. To me that is the geography of the soul. Metaphysical geography is laid down in language.

WACHTEL In your own language.

HEMON Well, in this case the English language, in Chicago. But in Sarajevo I did the same thing in these columns I wrote. And then after the war, when I was writing in English, I wrote a number of columns that dealt with Sarajevo and Chicago.

WACHTEL And was that easy, to transpose yourself?

HEMON It's not easy, but it's not supposed to be easy. I don't think literature or writing should be easy. In fact, I don't think that life should be easy. Of course, we want it that way, but it never is somehow. So I think a part of being a mature and adult person is not to be pissed at life or whatever you do because it's not easy.

WACHTEL I meant more from the perspective of Chicago, to be writing in your native language about Sarajevo.

HEMON It was difficult in that standard way of things being difficult, but resolving those difficulties is the creative part of any writing. Writing, to a large extent, is solving problems that you created yourself. And so to find ways to engage with Sarajevo from Chicago was the point of writing those columns. To me, one should go in only the difficult directions, in terms of writing at least. Otherwise, why do it? You know, watch movies or television, or do nothing at all.

WACHTEL What do you appreciate most today about life in Chicago?

HEMON I appreciate the network of people that I organized for myself and put together without people actually knowing they're part of a network. It's like a perfect spy organization. Everyone is a mole, and I can activate them at any point, but they don't know when. I have a barber, a butcher, soccer players, bars. We live in a neighbourhood where you can actually stop by a store and say, "Hi, how are you today?" without buying anything, and they know our names, our children's names, our dog's name. I know a lot of people in Chicago, and this is exactly the transposed structure of urban living I practised in Sarajevo. I can play soccer with busboys and illegal immigrants, and then at some dinner meet a billionaire who would never remember my name, but for a writer that's a perfect situation. How would I know what a billionaire looks like? I sneak up on them at various dinners and watch what they do, what their shirts look like, and what they do with their hands. So there is this vast space that I have access to. Chicago is as big as the whole country of Bosnia, pretty much—I mean, the number of people. So I have this network, and to me that's an asset that's not transferable to any other place. If I had to leave Chicago right now for some reason, that would be traumatic for me. Not as traumatic as leaving Sarajevo because there was a war involved, but I would have a feeling that I had lost something of great value.

WACHTEL The most powerful, painful story in your latest book is "The Aquarium," which deals with the illness and death of your baby daughter, Isabel. You said you wrote this story because you couldn't not write it. Why?

HEMON I had to formulate why I would write that story, because in terms of responsibility to other people it's my wife's experience too, and I knew that people would ask me, "Why would you write this?" And it was not an easy thing to write, as you might imagine. So why do it? If I failed to write it, then I would have failed in two respects at least. One of them, I fail as a father because thinking about my daughter's life and death would have been too difficult for me, and that means there is a ceiling to my love for her. There would have been, that is, and there's no ceiling. So unfortunately, part of her life and her being was her death, and for me to step away from that would violate something in our love for her, in my wife's and my love. I would also have failed as a writer because that means that I would have chosen a path in which I avoided dealing with difficult things. I had thought this before I found myself in the situation of writing about Isabel's life and death—that literature allows access to things that are not available otherwise, or knowledge that is not available otherwise, and this is the reason to go in difficult directions. So to avoid that direction means turning in a different direction, the opposite direction, of dealing with easy things. That means I would've been a hack. I might as well write TV commercials. And so I saw no choice but to write about it.

WACHTEL You describe Mingus—and you'll explain about Mingus—as imaginary and real at the same time. Can you tell me a bit about him and the role he came to play, not just in the life of your older daughter, Ella, but within the family?

HEMON Mingus is my older daughter's imaginary brother, who emerged at the time of the diagnosis of Isabel's illness. Isabel had a brain tumour. Mingus's appearance coincided with it, and maybe it was accelerated by the diagnosis and the crisis our family was going through. It's honestly common with children of that age to have imaginary siblings, but in my daughter's case, Mingus was growing as the crisis was growing, as Isabel's tumour was growing. And so we paid attention to her as much as we could in the situation, and we were worried about the way she was handling the whole situation because we were absent a lot. It was traumatic, and so I paid particular attention to Mingus.

WACHTEL You even gave him the name Mingus—

HEMON When we asked her, "What is his name?" she didn't know or she would say "Goo-goo, ga-ga," which is something that her cousin used as words for things he didn't know the name of. So we suggested Mingus, after Charlie Mingus. Her name is Ella, so it's a whole jazz constellation. And so Ella accepted Mingus as the name, and from there on in she talked about Mingus. The first emanation of Mingus is this blue alien on the cover of my book. At some point, Mingus was not material. But she would talk to Mingus, she would play with him, and he would have tumours, but he would get better in two weeks. And she would hear these things that we talked about in relation to Isabel's illness, and she would deploy them in the stories about Mingus. At some point, I realized that she was using Mingus and the stories about him as a way to process her experience. She was making up these stories that would never end—there was never closure to any of them, just rambling-on stories as children that age are prone to—but she was dealing with the whole situation, and I realized this is what I do. I come up with stories and avatars. And it was to the point that Mingus was so close to her, as my characters are close to me, that she would sit down and play with him. Once I asked her, "Where's Mingus now?" when we were sitting at the table having dinner. And she said, "He's in the other room throwing a tantrum." Simultaneously. And then it got complicated. She said Mingus had three siblings and a mother who makes movies and projects them on an imaginary television in Ella's room. It's a whole universe. But the process of narrativizing experience as a means of processing it, particularly if it's difficult, it's evolutional, I realized. This is what my daughter did at the age of three and a half, four years old; this is what I do in books and complicated narratives that have closure and arrive at something. And to me it was a perfect and complete revelation. I understood how it all worked, and I learned it from my four-year-old daughter.

WACHTEL You've written elsewhere about the distinctive Bosnian form of music called *sevdah,* a kind of Bosnian version of the blues, so sad that it makes you free, and you've talked about its coming from a cultural tradition that embraces moments of sorrow. Is there any connection for you in your decision to write about this event?

HEMON No, because there's a pleasure in *sevdah.* It is something that you do at certain times with your friends and some alcohol perhaps, and you relish the controlled sadness of the experience. It's a way to process certain tragic aspects of life, like the passing of time and the passing of youth, and the passing of love and all that. *Sevdah* is primarily practised in songs called *sevdahlinka,* so that when you sing, that sorrow of existence is converted into a song. But I did not feel pleasure writing this. I have a responsibility to the piece, as I have a responsibility to my writing and my daughter, but I do not enjoy reading it in a way that I enjoy reading some other of my things. It does not perform the function of *sevdah,* no.

WACHTEL We talked earlier about your compulsive imaginings, along with the what-ifs that spark your stories. There is the larger what-if in your own life—what if you hadn't been in the States when the war broke out in Sarajevo, what if you hadn't mastered English and learned to write in it and found an angle on your own experience, your complicated identities, and so on—that continues to fuel your fiction. Do you ever imagine "what if "?

HEMON That's what I do all day long. That's the narrativization of experience, it includes imagining the what-if moments.

WACHTEL But "what if " in terms of the whole shape of your experience?

HEMON Yes, I mean, it can be applied at any moment in your life, including now. It is a practice, I think, that conditions or is conditioned by the fact that I am a writer, but at the same time it is very likely that I became a writer because I could never not do it. It comes to me spontaneously. I don't have to will it. I once asked Ella, "How come I never see Mingus? You talk about Mingus all the time. I would like to meet Mingus." And she laughed at me and said, "Tata, Mingus is imaginary." And of course, I realized there was no contradiction, at least at that moment, between the real and the imaginary. The fact that he was imaginary did not mean that he was not real. It just meant that I couldn't meet him at that particular moment. And so the reality of our life requires imagining other lives, and within this life imagining what would've happened if, for instance, I had not said this to my wife at this particular moment; it would have been so much better, this dinner or this day. The imaginary delimits the real, but the imagination also allows us to construct, assemble, and turn the real into a narrative that we can process. And so there's this dialectic between the real and the imaginary that I cannot escape. This is why I do what I do. My entire life is the what-ifs of my life.

October 2013
Original interviews produced by Sandra Rabinovitch

ANNE CARSON

I've admired Canadian poet, essayist, Greek and Latin scholar, and librettist Anne Carson for a long time now. I first heard about her as a professor of classics at McGill University who was writing amazing stuff, starting with her quirky academic treatise, *Eros the Bittersweet* (1986), where she mixed classical philosophy with witty, ironic brilliance.

Next she produced two remarkable books of poetry combined with essays. She was hailed as an original by Harold Bloom, Susan Sontag, and Annie Dillard. She won both a Guggenheim and a Lannan Foundation Fellowship, and the MacArthur "genius" award. With her 2001 book, *The Beauty of the Husband: A Fictional Essay in 29 Tangos*, she became the first woman to win England's T. S. Eliot Prize for Poetry. Carson also took Canada's inaugural Griffin Prize. Along the way, she had a crossover success with another unusual book, *Autobiography of Red: A Novel in Verse* (1998). It blends a modern homosexual romance with Greek myth, set in small-town Ontario and Peru.

Anne Carson's 2010 book *Nox*, the Latin for "night," is yet another surprising and haunting work. An elegy to her brother—"an epitaph" as she called it, a notebook of memories and fragments of photographs, letters, and paintings—it's a moving reflection on absence. As she writes in her first entry: "I wanted to fill my elegy with light of all kinds. But death makes us stingy. There is nothing more to be expended on that, we think. He's dead. Love cannot alter it. Words cannot add to it. No matter how I try to evoke the starry lad he was, it remains a plain, odd history."

Anne Carson's recent books are *Antigonick* (2012); *Red Doc>* (2013), a sequel to her novel, *Autobiography of Red*, which won her second Griffin Poetry Prize; and a translation of *Iphigenia among the Taurians* (2014).

We met in June 2011 at the Banff Centre, where she was part of their International Literary Translators residency.

WACHTEL Much of your work invokes the ancient Classical period, references to Greek myths, translations from Greek or Latin, essays on ancient thought. What first drew you to that world?

CARSON I think it was in a shopping mall in Hamilton, Ontario, in about 1965; I was travelling around the bookstore and for some reason they had a bilingual edition of *Sappho* by Willis Barnstone, the translator and editor, with the Greek on the left, the English on the right, and it just looked so fascinating I thought I should learn this. The next year we moved to Port Hope and I went to a high school where the Latin teacher knew Greek. When she found out I was interested she offered to teach me on my lunch hour. So I owe my career and happiness to Alice Cowan in Port Hope High School.

WACHTEL And what fascinated you? Was it that the language looked so alien, or enticing?

CARSON It was partly the look and just the aesthetic, but also at that time I was fancying myself a reborn Oscar Wilde, and the whole world of intellectual life in Oscar Wilde's time, which included a lot of Latin and Greek, was sort of a myth to me and I thought, If I learn Greek I could be all the more like Oscar Wilde. It seemed the natural next step.

WACHTEL A reborn Oscar Wilde.

CARSON I had an Oscar Wilde costume that I wore now and again for special occasions. I thought he was the most interesting fellow.

WACHTEL Did you drop bons mots and witticisms?

CARSON As we will discover in the course of this interview, no, I'm not quick-witted but I appreciate wit.

WACHTEL Once you started to study Latin and Greek, especially Greek, do you remember what the first myths you heard were?

CARSON I think probably the ones that Sappho refers to, which are not in general the standard ones. Niobe, for example, who was turned into a rock because she wept so much; and most pointedly I remember from that book the myth of Tithonus. Tithonus was the young man who fell in love with the goddess of the dawn and they were having a pleasant affair; then one day he asked her to make him immortal. He wanted to be a god and live with her forever. So she went to Zeus and said, "Can you make Tithonus immortal?" And Zeus said, "Sure," and made him immortal but he didn't make him ageless. So poor Tithonus withered away into a little cricket of himself and that wasn't much fun for the goddess of the dawn anymore.

WACHTEL Pay attention to the fine print.

CARSON The wording, yes. The wording is key.

WACHTEL Tell me a bit more about studying Greek. I mean, obviously you stuck with it and it became your subject, but can you say more about what attracted you to it: the culture, the language, the complexity?

CARSON I think it's partly the content of the works. They're some of the most thoughtful pieces of literature anyone's ever come up with. But also the mental activity of being inside a translation is something I simply love. It's like doing an endless crossword puzzle but with a valuable product. And that puzzle mode of mind is simply the best thing.

WACHTEL You've said that the ancients don't necessarily have much relevance to our world today, and I have to say that surprised me, because we always seem to be able to extract relevance from everything in the past.

CARSON I didn't mean it that way, I meant it upside down—that it's more our task to be relevant to them, to go back and see what they were really doing, from their side. John Cage says, "No one can have an idea once he really starts listening," and I think that's what's important about studying the past, to listen to the ancients rather than replacing them with your own ideas of how they are relevant to you.

WACHTEL And is it partly that they saw the world so differently, or they're just so far away from us in time and in the language that we use to apprehend?

CARSON They're at the root of things that then grew up and formed the trees where we now live—they're fresh, the ideas still have dew on them. And thousands of years later our ideas have some of that left in them but they're all crusted over and with centuries in between. The newness of the world keeps dawning on the Greeks.

WACHTEL Do you know at what point you determined that this would be your life subject?

CARSON Immediately when I studied it with Mrs. Cowan. It was unquestionable.

WACHTEL A *coup de foudre*.

CARSON Yes. And she was a very unusual person. She smelled of celery all the time. And after that year she disappeared. Quit, I guess, and somebody told me she ended up in Africa. Some decades later when I did a reading somewhere—I think Montreal—and mentioned her because I read some Greek stuff, a woman came up to me afterwards and said, "Alice Cowan's my mother and she now lives on a farm in northern Ontario. She's kind of a hermit. She'd probably like to hear from you but she won't answer." So I wrote her a letter and indeed she didn't answer. So that's all I know about Alice Cowan.

WACHTEL Your latest book, *Nox*, is a kind of grief project, an epitaph for your brother who died in 2000. You structure the work by translating word by word a poem by Catullus, a Roman poet who lived in the first century B.C. Each Latin word of the poem gets its own page, and then you set your own poetry, thoughts, images, all kinds of things, on the opposite page. Where did that idea come from?

CARSON Probably from the structure of the bilingual translation, because I spend a lot of my life looking at books with left-hand-page Greek or Latin, and right-hand-page English, and you get used to it, you get used to thinking in the little channel in between the two languages where the perfect language exists.

WACHTEL I can see that it would also appeal because it forces one to slow down when you have each word with its expanded lexicographical definition—

CARSON Oh, well I'm glad to hear that. I wondered when I did it if people would bother to read the left-hand page or just look at it and think, I don't want to plow through that, and go on to the next. So I hope it slows them down. The lexical entries are drawn from the lexicon but a bit fiddled with, and I did want people to gradually notice that and follow the clues of it; it's a bit of a puzzle.

WACHTEL Because you manipulate the Oxford Latin lexicon entries a bit.

CARSON Yes, I manipulate them to put in more *nox*.

WACHTEL I read somewhere you quote Jacques Lacan, the French psychoanalyst and philosopher, who said we don't go to poetry for wisdom but for the dismantling of wisdom. How does poetry do that?

CARSON I feel it's a kind of fervour of mine to get away from whatever body of information I rest on when I give opinions. And I think poetic activity is a method for doing that—you leap off the building when you think poetically; you don't amass your data and then move from point to point, you have to just know what you know in that moment. Something freeing about that.

WACHTEL Maybe I'm being too literal-minded when I think of dismantling because when I think of taking the poem apart word by word—

CARSON Yes, it is a mantle, the confidence that you can ever know what words mean because really we don't. They're just these signs that we pretend to nail down in dictionaries, tokens of usage, but frankly they're all wild integers. Disassembling it is a way of exposing that myth at the bottom of language.

WACHTEL Is that the myth you're referring to?

CARSON The myth that you can ever know it definitively. Use it, yes. Make sense, yes. But know it, I'm not sure.

WACHTEL Now this isn't your first attempt to translate Catullus's poem 101. When did you first try?

CARSON I think probably in that same year with Mrs. Cowan. It's probably Catullus's most well-known poem, so everybody tries it. It's deceptively simple on the surface, impossible to capture underneath. The ideal poem.

WACHTEL And why is it so difficult to translate?

CARSON Well, that's complicated. Partly because of the nature of Catullus's diction, which is a reinvention, in a way, of Latin poetic language through an infusion of common talk. He wrote a lot of poetry in street language, much of it scatological or obscene, and he keeps the energy of street language even in his more formal works. But also he just has a way of, it feels to me, economizing a situation and telling you exactly the bones of it and no more, which is hard to capture in another language.

WACHTEL Although I think both aspects would appeal to you: the conjunction of idiomatic language and the more dignified or elegiac verse.

CARSON It's true I do mix registers of discourse, maybe inadvertently. I believe Catullus did it as a program, sort of a renovation of his language because he was tired of the way people were doing poetry. I'm not sure I'm that committed. But there is this same energy.

WACHTEL And is that difficulty of translation the very thing, or among the things, you admire about Catullus?

CARSON I don't admire it as give-me-a-problem-I-can't-solve, but as having something to flail away at daily.

WACHTEL And this time, you felt you could finally translate it? I know you've said you tried hundreds of times to translate this poem, but this time, in the case of *Nox*, you could, or did you just resign yourself to a certain way of translating?

CARSON It was more a resignation. I think a translation always has a context and this one needed to fit into that book and it needed, therefore, to be somewhat plain. I didn't want to decorate anything.

WACHTEL Tell me a bit about the poem, the context for it, like how Catullus came to—

CARSON He wrote it in honour of his brother, whom we don't know much about except he died in the Troad, a Roman settlement on the site of what they thought was the ancient city of Troy, in Asia Minor. Catullus travelled from Italy to Asia Minor to bury his brother and stand at the grave. He wrote the elegy sometime around then.

WACHTEL A sense of mystery infuses *Nox*. I mean, there is the difficulty of elegizing a brother who had disappeared from your life long before his death. What did you know about his life around the time he left?

CARSON I didn't know very much. We both went to university—different ones—more or less at the same time. I was immersed in my Greek and Latin, a world he had no interest in or patience with. And he diverged from me in taste and moral standards and everything else that makes you a person, so I didn't really know him anymore. Then he began to deal drugs and that seemed stupid to me so we argued about it. And then he got arrested and decided to jump bail and leave the country.

WACHTEL That was 1978, which was the last time that you saw him.

CARSON Right.

WACHTEL In your book, there's a photo of your brother when he was around ten years old, and he's standing on the ground with some other boys above him in a tree house. What do you see when you look at that?

CARSON It just breaks my heart, frankly, because he always wanted to hang out with boys too old for him; I guess because it, I don't know, enhanced his view of himself. They always picked on him and exploited him. So there he is at the bottom of the tree. They've taken up the ladder so he can't come up. And he looks just so stalwart about it. He looks like it's just another one of those setbacks; he's going to get through it and come out to a brighter day. He always was like that. He had a certain absolutely unfounded optimism that things would get better. They didn't.

WACHTEL In the text you say that, years later when your brother began to deal drugs, you'd get a sinking feeling because of a sideways invisible look that he wore in that photo. Why is that look so troubling to you?

CARSON I'm not sure. Photographs are stunning that way. They give you so much information that you can't paraphrase. But when I looked at that photograph after he died, it seemed to me his whole life is in that look. He'll never win and he'll never believe that the next throw of the dice isn't going to be a win.

WACHTEL It's interesting you say optimism because in so many of the photos he's bashed up. He's wearing a sling or a bandage or something.

CARSON Isn't that odd? I didn't notice that until I got the photographs out to make the book; I was struck by the fact that he always has a broken arm or a bandage on his leg. I don't remember all those injuries but there it is. Yet he was not deterred. He'd break his arm and go right on, join the hockey team.

WACHTEL Partly, I think, hanging around with the older boys would do it. Did he have trouble making friends?

CARSON No, he was very charming. He could make friends with anyone, so I don't know why they beat him up so much. There are these mysteries with one's siblings.

WACHTEL Your brother was four years older than you, and when you were in your teens and both in high school, he liked you to do his homework, but also he called you "professor" or "pinhead." How would you describe your relationship?

CARSON Rueful. I think he put up with me once I started doing his homework for him—he kept failing French and got put back in school a few times. I had an ambivalent attitude towards him, I guess. When we were younger he was my total hero and I followed him around everywhere, got told to go home. But later I didn't understand his decisions and couldn't reason with him, and it all got to be fractious. I think I still saw him as a kind of mythic person because of that strange optimism. And he had a sort of glow. He would come into a room and everybody would look at him. He was very handsome—tall and blond—and as I say he had this charm. I was never charming. Certainly not glowing.

WACHTEL Twice in the book you mention this "pinhead" thing. You write, "His voice was like his voice with something else crusted on it, black, dense—it lighted up for a moment when he said pinhead (so, pinhead, d'you attain wisdom yet?), then went dark again. All the years and time that had passed over him came streaming into me, all that history. What is a voice?" And on the following page you write, "I love all the old questions." Does that refer back to this?

CARSON What is a voice? Yes. I've been so long fascinated by all the information conveyed in a voice.

WACHTEL And do you think that "pinhead–professor" was an affectionate play?

CARSON I think it was, yes. When I turned sixteen he also gave me *Roget's Thesaurus* because he wanted me to be a writer and I wanted to be a writer. I still have this book. But it was in two volumes and he only gave me volume one. Never got around to volume two. It's a clue to certain things about my writing.

WACHTEL You favour the first half of the alphabet?

CARSON Yes, I'm much more versatile with that half, for some reason.

WACHTEL *Nox* itself is presented as an artifact. It's a fold-out, accordion-style book with pieces of paper stapled or glued on, sometimes with text, or photos, or painted images, or fragments of a handwritten letter. It's very tactile. In fact, I kept touching it, thinking there would be a staple there. But of course each page is a reproduction of all those things. Why this presentation, why did you physically want to build a book?

CARSON Because I made the book myself at first. I bought an empty book and filled it with stuff, painted it, glued it, stapled it, and so on. It was a grand day when I discovered you could staple instead of gluing, that was really an advance in method. Anyway, [Robert] Currie, my husband, said that the thing about this book is, because it's handmade, when you read it, you're pulled into these people and these thoughts and the thing that it is. If you want to reproduce it, it has to have that quality still. So he fooled around with ways of Xeroxing to make the pages look, as you say, three-dimensional. If you photocopy or scan something perfectly, it looks glossy like a cookbook but if you let a little light into the machine and make it a bad Xerox, you get all those edges and life, you get what Currie calls the "decay" put back in. So it was really important to me to have that in the experience of the reader.

WACHTEL You even soaked some of the typescript in tea to make it look like parchment. Why? You made the book in the year 2000. Why did you want it to look ancient?

CARSON It was a fancy of mine to make the left-hand pages, the Catullus pages, look like an old dictionary because when I was learning these languages I always had very old, faded dictionaries with yellowed pages. The experience of reading Latin, to me, is an old dusty page you can hardly make out. So I thought, Well, I'll just stain them with tea and it'll look magical. And they did look magical for about twenty-four hours, and then the tea dried and they all turned white again.

WACHTEL And the original process for you of making the book, what was that like? Was it a way of working through grief? How did it engage you?

CARSON It was not so much grief as it was the puzzle of understanding him. Because actually, just before he died, he had telephoned me for the first time since 1978. This was in the year 2000. We had a very strange, awkward conversation and I arranged to go to Copenhagen, where he turned out to be living, to meet with him. But a week before I was to go I got a phone call from a woman who said, "You don't know me, but your brother has just died in my bathroom." That was his wife in Copenhagen, whom he'd been married to for seventeen years.

WACHTEL He didn't mention that on the phone.

CARSON He did mention it, but on the phone his wife didn't identify herself, she just said, "You don't know me." So I went to Copenhagen and met her and the dog and found out some things about his life, but the more I found out the more I didn't understand who he had been those twenty-two years he was gone. So I started the book as an effort of understanding, just trying to put strands of things I could say about him into one place and see what it added up to. As it went on, it became what I called an epitaph, a way of praising him.

WACHTEL When he called, did you know what prompted that call? Was it a premonition of his own death?

CARSON No idea, he never said. He was laconic. Just felt like getting in touch, after all those years. You see it's puzzling.

WACHTEL How did he die?

CARSON Aneurysm. I think he'd lived a hard life, drugs and so on, his system gave out. He was only in his fifties.

WACHTEL Some of the photos that you use are fragments, and many don't have people in them. One features a shadow of a person more than the humans in the distance. A chair, a shed, an empty swing, some stairs, a wall. There is a sense of absence. What do you see when you look at them?

CARSON The puzzle of him. Breaking it down, two things. When I was young and idolized him he was always gone—he didn't want to spend time with me, he managed to vanish. Later on when I was puzzling over who he had been in his later years, I just couldn't get it. It was like Aeneas in the Underworld, you know, when he meets his dead mother and tries to embrace her. Three times he holds out his arms and tries to hold her, three times she vanishes from his grip. So I wanted to put the vanishing into the pictures, and if you cut out the people, there's a lot of vanishing there. And some of them were empty anyway, oddly—another thing you discover when you look at your old family photographs, a lot of them are pictures of nothing. Very evocative pictures of nothing.

WACHTEL And did you tear some of them for the book?

CARSON I did. I tore them, cut them.

WACHTEL Was that hard, to tear?

CARSON Surprisingly no. I'd go into work mode and rip on through it.

WACHTEL The information about your brother the last time you saw him—when he ran away in 1978 travelling on a false passport, only one letter home in all those years—is repeated several times in a row, sometimes with slightly different punctuation or minute differences in the marks on the paper. On the fourth repetition, it becomes almost a fragment itself. Why that repetition?

CARSON The repetition is only in the printed book. In the original, the letter is glued in as a folded thing, so to make the fold visible in the printed book we had to repeat the information. It's a mechanical solution to the problem of not having the original book.

WACHTEL I thought the repetition might have something to do with trying to understand the revealed in repetition. Sometimes we say what we know over and over in a way to make sense of it.

CARSON Sometimes it helps to hear what you think by saying it more than once. That came to me as we were doing it. Incidental benefit of my imperfect method. But I can't say I thought of it before.

WACHTEL And you say that you didn't understand your brother's decisions in those days of self-exile. Did you try to imagine what his life was like?

CARSON I got anecdotes from his widow and other people in Copenhagen who were his friends. But it was like reading bits of a synopsis of a movie that you never see; it just didn't add up. Somebody would say,

"Oh yeah, I knew your brother in his gold-smuggling days." Well that was news to me! Things like that. Little chips of data. They didn't make any pattern.

WACHTEL About halfway through the book there's a line that says, "Always comforting to assume there is a secret behind what torments you."

CARSON A secret—meaning something that would make sense—the answer rather than just all these bits. I mean, most of us, to be honest, are just a collection of bits that don't make sense. It's a nice idea that there's a coherent self in each of us with a story that another person could tell, but it's a fiction. And with somebody like my brother, you really come up against that fiction. Because he did not want to be known.

WACHTEL I think that must be the difference because even though all of us might be these fragments that are a fiction, we try to present narratives that make it seem to have coherence.

CARSON We do. At some point he gave up on that, I think.

WACHTEL Your mother described your brother as the light of her life, and he wrote occasional postcards and one letter to her. She didn't see him for the last twenty years of her life. Can you talk about their relationship, how his absence affected her?

CARSON It ruined her life. She died not knowing if he was still alive. And she was simply sad for all those years. On the other hand she never gave up hoping he'd reappear. I did. But she never quite abandoned that notion, and it made her life be sort of the wrong life. The right life would have been the one where he came in the door. He was her golden child. She had a little lock of his hair from when he was a baby. I don't know how to measure that sort of sorrow. And when he called me that time I mentioned this. He just said, "Yes, I guess that's true."

WACHTEL She had already died by then.

CARSON She had died three years before. And I said, "She had a lot of pain because of you." And he said, "Yes, I guess that's true." So, cut off from himself at some level.

WACHTEL And you describe how eventually you and your mother stopped talking about your brother, which you say was a relief. Why, what had it been like when you did talk about him?

CARSON I said in the book it was like the smell of burning hair dropping through every conversation. There was nowhere for it to go. It blackened the day, and I didn't think it was a problem with any solution.

WACHTEL Although you describe, every time a car would pull up, she'd look up out the window—

CARSON Gravel on the road. She thought it might be him. Sad.

WACHTEL At one point you ask, "Why do we blush before death?" I found that a surprising word. Have you found an answer to that?

CARSON No. It surprised me too. I found that in another poem of Catullus. I don't remember the exact passage, but he's talking about death, it's an elegy for a friend, and he uses the blush. It's a puzzling passage. It often happens to me trying to translate something in Latin or Greek that I come to a piece that doesn't make sense, but it still seems true, it seems like a nub of something I should get to, so I just secrete it into writing and hope it'll work its truth by itself without me knowing how to control it. I'm still thinking about the blush.

WACHTEL And there's an interesting image nearby, it's not on the same page, I don't think, but there's some quite lurid red that's…

CARSON Well I thought *blush*, good! I'll use my red paint. Nothing subtle about me. You know I loved making that book, despite the context. I gave myself the task of trying to do something different on each page than I had done on any page previous, mechanically, physically. It was just a joy.

WACHTEL Without being too literal, did that enable you to turn the page in a way?

CARSON In a way, yes.

WACHTEL You quote the seventh-century BC historian Herodotus, who said that history is by far the strangest thing humans do, all this asking and searching, because it doesn't give a clear or helpful account. Do you agree with that?

CARSON They call Herodotus the first historian, when what he invented was a picture of history as all these chips of data that don't make sense. He collects them and hands them over.

WACHTEL And this reflected on what you felt you were doing.

CARSON Yes, that sort of assembling without any final control of its sense.

WACHTEL But Herodotus also suggests that, as a historian, he didn't have to believe everything everyone reported. He says, "So much for what is said by the Egyptians. Let anyone who finds such things credible make use of them." Or, "I have to say what is said, I don't have to believe it myself."

CARSON He has a good sense of humour, Herodotus. But I think he's not kidding. He does hand over opinions, as well as facts, and he doesn't try to distinguish too much among opinions as to the good ones and the bad ones. He trusts the reader to do that. An admirable tolerance.

WACHTEL Did this reflect on your own search in some way?

CARSON I think in that book, or in everything I write, there is an attempt at tolerance, to put down as much as I can figure out and let the reader make what sense they make.

WACHTEL Sometimes the sense is, as you alluded to earlier, in the crack between the pages, because on the very next page of "I have to say what is said, I don't have to believe it myself," is, in your brother's handwriting, "love you, love you, Michael," a fragment from a letter.

CARSON Isn't that haunting, when people write things twice. Why would he write it twice? I don't know.

WACHTEL You also say history and elegy are kin. How are they connected?

CARSON They're both a way of telling a story, giving the shape of a person or an event by—as Herodotus says—this searching, asking, without arriving. It's the non-arrival that makes them akin, the struggle and then the non-arriving.

WACHTEL Did anything change for you after finishing *Nox*, either in how you saw your brother or the whole idea of elegy and investigation?

CARSON I don't think anything changed in my view of him. It was more storied but not more complete. Elegy, I don't know. It's a difficult form, I would say. It's hard to keep the dignity of the subject without getting your own fingerprints all over it.

WACHTEL That's an interesting way to put it because it seems to me a very apt description of elegy, that whoever—and maybe I'm conflating it with eulogizing—but whoever is doing the eulogy has their fingerprints all over it. It seems like it's about them, it's not even about the deceased.

CARSON It's very hard to get the right place to stand, to elegize or eulogize somebody. But I thought by making these pages instead of just writing them, it helped me do that, because making, somehow, seems less egotistical, I don't know why.

WACHTEL At one point you say, "A brother never ends. I prowl him."

CARSON I had this sense of him as a room where I was groping around, finding in the dark, here a chair, there a book, there a switch, and not getting a sense of the floor plan ever, but just being in that room every day, working with it. And the poem was like that too, disassembling the poem, also a dark process.

WACHTEL Do you see Catullus's poem differently now? I mean, of course, as an elegy for a brother; your own brother's death would lend a certain resonance.

CARSON Yes, it has a resonance. But I always thought it one of the best things in the world and I still do. There it lies, untranslatable.

WACHTEL Well, there's not that much that's explicit in *Nox*. It's still a very personal, intimate work. What made you decide to make it public?

CARSON The fact that it got lost. For a number of years, seven or eight years, I used to show the book to people one by one and then I met by chance a German publisher who does art books and fashion books who said, "I think I can do that in a respectful way, why don't we try?" So I said okay and he took it to Germany, then lost it for three years. He didn't answer emails and he had no phone so there was a certain interval of anguish about this object I thought I'd never see again. Then one day it showed up in a FedEx package. So I thought, Time to make this permanent. Then Currie figured out how to make it work as a replicated book.

WACHTEL We alluded to it earlier, but it's interesting, on the left-hand pages with the definitions of the Latin word, you almost always add idiomatic expressions with the word *nox*, meaning night. But when it comes to defining *frater*, brother, the subject of the book, there's no idiomatic expression with *nox*. That was deliberate, obviously.

CARSON I couldn't add to that one. It didn't seem respectable, or fair. And a way of putting the boundaries around him that he wanted put there. He wasn't noble, didn't want to be noble, and *frater* is an impersonal word for that.

WACHTEL Your 1998 book, *Autobiography of Red*, is your first novel in verse. It also takes a story from the ancients as its starting point, the myth of Herakles and the monster Geryon. Can you tell me a bit about that story?

CARSON Herakles is that person you probably know from Saturday-morning cartoons who did the famous labours. Hercules they call him in American. One of his labours was to travel to the island of a supposed monster named Geryon and capture his magic red cattle. So he did that, killed Geryon, took the cattle. I just changed that story a bit.

WACHTEL A bit?

CARSON A moderate bit.

WACHTEL Well, the mythical Geryon has wings, and so does your incarnation. They're another marker of his difference. What attracted you to this story?

CARSON I Iis monstrosity. We all feel we're monsters most of the time. But also there is a very tantalizing set of fragments about this myth from the Greek poet Stesichorus, who isn't very much read or known. He doesn't write attractive love poetry like Sappho, but these fragments are quite beautiful. I got involved in translating them for my own pleasure, then got frustrated because I couldn't work into the translations most of what I thought was interesting in the original language. For some reason.

WACHTEL What do you mean?

CARSON The differences between Greek and English set up some barriers to what you can say and how you can say it. Plus the myth being somewhat unknown to most readers meant that the context was missing. I couldn't talk about Geryon and have the audience say, "Oh yes, the red guy with wings." So a lot of explanatory blah-blah-blah would have been necessary to make the fragments intelligible as such and I didn't want to do that, so I thought maybe I could do it in another form. What's another form? I've never written a novel, let's try that.

WACHTEL Did you actually first try it as a straight prose novel?

CARSON Yes, I tried it a lot of ways. Prose, various kinds of prose, and then one day, messing around with the lines, I worked out those couplets that are long and short alternations, which seemed to work so I went ahead with it. And then it proved to be quite nice to do. Before, it was a bit hellish, whole paragraphs of prose. I really wanted to write a novel, you know, an Arthur Hailey novel that people would read in airports.

WACHTEL An Arthur Hailey novel?

CARSON I mean something huge and substantial with lots of manly activity, and of course I couldn't do it. But anyhow, the verse form eventually extracted itself from my efforts and that was obviously right.

WACHTEL In *Autobiography of Red*, Geryon and Herakles are modern-day lovers. What did you see in the ancient myth that inspired this interpretation?

CARSON Absolutely nothing. In the ancient myth Herakles goes there, confronts Geryon and kills him and the story is over. But in other ancient sources, for example *The Iliad*, there's a certain amount of reference to homoerotic tenderness and it's interesting to me how that works in a story and I wanted to give Geryon a fun part to his life.

WACHTEL There's a great line: "They were two superior eels at the bottom of the tank and they recognized each other like italics." What is the nature of the attraction that you imagined between them?

CARSON Probably mutual strangeness. I think that's why I used italics. Everyone else is Roman font, then these two people show up slanted and they see that. Automatic lightning.

WACHTEL You give another view of love in your book *The Beauty of the Husband*. It's described as a fictional essay in twenty-nine tangos. At one point the wife in the story describes their interaction as characteristic or ideal. In what way ideal?

CARSON Based on beauty. Beauty being a romantic ideal that works itself out in various ways. You desire the one you've invented rather than the one who exists.

WACHTEL Because the one who exists knows "more about the Battle of Borodino than he [does] about his own wife's body." It's such a cutting line!

CARSON Yet his beauty partly consists in that.

WACHTEL This is a complex relationship that's described here. The husband lies and cheats, but he's not ashamed of this. He says he loves her, he even says he wants to be worthy of her. What kind of love is this for him?

CARSON It may be ideal from his point of view in the sense that he idealizes himself as the agent of perfect or beautiful actions, but I'm not sure that either the wife or the novel knows what his view of it is. Or what he's looking for. There are a few places in there where the narrative structure tries to put things from a husband's point of view, but it becomes external; it's mostly what he says and what he does, not what he thinks.

WACHTEL And for some years the wife continues to sustain the relationship. What kind of love is it for her?

CARSON I think desperate. I think the kind of love—as with Herakles and Geryon—based on that original moment of recognizing the other person in italics, without whom you can't be your own italic self, so you have to keep that going as long as possible.

WACHTEL Although it's giving power to the Other over oneself.

CARSON That's the paradox of it, isn't it? But I think, again, because there's a desperation in it, there's nothing else to do.

WACHTEL It's refreshing to hear the wife admit that she wasn't ashamed to say she loved her husband for his beauty. For some reason we very often are reluctant to admit beauty's power over us.

CARSON Isn't that odd? And it's so much a part of Western culture, that beauty's what makes love happen. Even if the person isn't beautiful you convince yourself they are.

WACHTEL You quote a passage from Keats before each tango or section, and it was Keats of course who wrote famously, "Beauty is truth, truth beauty." How does beauty speak of truth?

CARSON I don't think it does. I think that's all a big mistake, but there's so much power in believing it, and so many of the decisions of life, especially early life—with the adolescent emotions—identify those two, and think that the person who's beautiful is also true, and the feelings that come from beauty lead you to truth. I don't believe it works out usually.

WACHTEL Certainly not in the beauty of this husband.

CARSON No.

WACHTEL I don't want to presume autobiography here, but did you bring some of your experience to *The Beauty of the Husband*?

CARSON Some of it. But it's very manipulated and beautified, not to put too fine a point on it.

WACHTEL Did your first husband take your notebooks? Did he return your notebooks? That's what I want to know.

CARSON He did. And eventually he did.

WACHTEL The poet, or the wife, sometimes tells her story to a listener whom she addresses as *You*. Is that a particular You? Who was the You?

CARSON Not a particular You. It's the generalized You of lyric poetry. Catullus invented this, I think, for the Romans, and the You is sometimes unnamed, a persona who forms as the poem forms, a sort of ideal listener.

WACHTEL And that started with Catullus? Because you're right, it's certainly a convention in lyric poetry.

CARSON He used it extensively. Probably took it from Sappho.

WACHTEL Near the end of *The Beauty of the Husband*, the wife contrasts her earlier view of beauty, her pure early thought, with a later experience of it. Before she wanted to recognize it without desiring it. Now her advice is "Hold, hold beauty." What has changed for her?

CARSON I guess her sense of where she stands in the whole question. She can hold it if she doesn't need it.

WACHTEL Which has to do with not wanting to desire.

CARSON Yes, it has to do with getting the desperation out of it.

WACHTEL Although at one point the wife wonders what not wanting to desire means, and one could associate that with a kind of freedom, but on the other hand it feels like giving up.

CARSON A kind of deadness.

WACHTEL Utter resignation or something.

CARSON Or turning entirely inward. I think that's not where she wants to end up. But I believe it's left open whether she does end up there or not.

WACHTEL In your 2006 book, *Decreation*, you said your earliest memory is of a dream. Can you describe that for me?

CARSON Oh yes. I was there and it was a dream of being asleep. I went downstairs in our house and it was our living room as it had been in the daytime but it was also all changed, somehow intangibly weird. I don't know how to describe that change. How can a room change and still be the same room? But later, looking back on that dream, it seemed like I was imagining a room gone mad, the same room but gone mad inside itself. And I guess I came to that because it happened to my father; he got dementia and he was his same self and yet utterly changed inside. The room seemed to have undergone that same weirdening.

WACHTEL Although you also say that despite the spooky element of the dream there was something consoling about it.

CARSON Still it was the room. I mean, even if your father's mad, he's still your father and you want to, you know, try to keep talking. There's something about the familiar that's absolutely necessary no matter how weird it gets.

WACHTEL In "Father's Old Blue Cardigan," you say, "His laws were a secret." What was your father like?

CARSON He was very quiet. He didn't explain himself much. We had not a lot of conversation in our life. But I very much liked him as a person. We had not at all the same taste or intellectual ambitions but we shared the same sense of humour, we liked the same stupid jokes and that's a nice bond with someone.

WACHTEL Do you or did you get comfort from that cardigan?

CARSON Yes, I still have it. I wear it in the winter. I always liked to imitate him. But I especially love that sweater.

WACHTEL Imitating him in what way?

CARSON Oh, wearing the same kind of boots, trying to walk like him, or, yes, just being… I don't know… manly and reticent.

WACHTEL And he was a banker?

CARSON Yes, he was a bank manager in various towns of Ontario.

WACHTEL Which meant the family moved around a lot.

CARSON Yes, we moved quite often. I don't know, six or seven times within my childhood.

WACHTEL Was that hard on you?

CARSON I guess it was hard. I didn't like leaving my friends but I think you gradually withdraw a bit from attachment, which perhaps is a good thing.

WACHTEL That sounds like a person who learned the hard way that it really was a good thing.

CARSON Well that could be. Anyway, I did learn it. And it brought me to Mrs. Cowan. So that was good.

WACHTEL You say that you didn't have much in the way of conversation with your father, but he liked numbers.

CARSON He was always figuring on napkins because he was a bank manager, and I think also because he was shot down in the war and in a prison camp for some time, about a year. He didn't have horrific experiences there but he, I'm sure, was just bored to death and one of the things he had with him for some reason was an accounting textbook. So he passed the time doing all the problems in it. Which set up a habit in him of whenever he had empty time, he'd just fiddle with algebra problems on a napkin. So all the napkins in our house or when we went to restaurants were covered with little numbers in his script. I was never any good at math.

WACHTEL And do you think it interested him because he originally wanted to be an engineer?

CARSON It did, I think. Engineers use a lot of math. And it was a form of mastery for him, numbers.

WACHTEL When you say you wanted to be like him in that silent, manly way, that's the opposite of Oscar Wilde.

CARSON I think Oscar and my dad would have admired each other as different monsters. But yes, it's true, it's a different type. My dad was a deeper model. I think Oscar Wilde was perhaps the phase of rebellion against being my father. So I came and went from rebellion but always wanted to be like my father underneath.

WACHTEL You and your mother seem to have been very close.

CARSON Maybe. Not the same kind of people, but we got close. As the others were gradually pared away, we came to be close.

WACHTEL You mean your brother disappearing.

CARSON And my father dying, yes. My father disappearing before dying. We did have a lot of "quality time," as they say, together, perforce.

WACHTEL When you say you aren't the same type and your mother is not the mother in *Autobiography of Red*, what kind of person was your mother?

CARSON Frustrated. Very clever—in high school she won the Latin medal in her graduating class and could have gone on to university but had to work. Her father had died and the family needed income so she got a job in an insurance agency as a secretary. I think that loss of the intellectual channel was always a frustration to her. So we lived very different lives because I took that channel, and she admired me for doing that, but I think there was a loneliness in it. She was a little lonely for the person she would have been if she'd had a different fate. So we didn't have a lot to talk about, but we made our peace with that gradually.

WACHTEL Did she read your books?

CARSON She read usually the first chapter and then turned that page down and put them all on a shelf by the door. She was proud to show them to people but I'm not sure she read any of them all the way through.

WACHTEL There's a line in *Decreation* describing a mother as "love of my life."

CARSON I think she became that in the years when my father was nuts and my brother wasn't there. We had so many struggles in common that she became the most important person to me.

WACHTEL Your mother was a Roman Catholic, and you say your attendance at church is or was in part a habit. Do you still attend?

CARSON I don't, no. I can't tolerate papal things in general.

WACHTEL But you used to go.

CARSON I did. I found great comfort in going with her. It was a habit we had. She was a believer. Sometimes that's enough, you know, for comfort, to be with a believer and share the actions.

WACHTEL And smell her coat.

CARSON And smell her coat!

WACHTEL There's something about that I can relate to. I don't know if it's the Canadian winter or what, but...

CARSON Yes, I remember that coat still. It was a fake fur coat and I'd lean into it all the time the priest was droning on.

WACHTEL One of the books you received as a very young girl was a version of *The Lives of the Saints*. And you had an interesting response to it.

CARSON I wanted to eat it. I still remember how luscious those pages were. I don't know if it was some kind of specially printed book or I just hadn't seen many books with a lot of colour in them but each saint had a crown or garland on the head and some kind of complicated cloak thing, all different colours, and they looked like jujubes. I just wanted to stuff them in my mouth.

WACHTEL Do you think it's significant that these were saints that you wanted to eat?

CARSON Not particularly. I think that just happened to be the book that I had.

WACHTEL In your poem "My Religion," you say, "My religion makes no sense and does not help me, therefore I pursue it." That was written about twenty years ago, but the idea of God is one that percolates its way through some of your other work. Are you still in pursuit?

CARSON Not so directly as then. At that time I was teaching a course about that sort of searching and was interested in the writings of various mystics. I searched around in that for years, but in the end I didn't find it was the place where I could do my best thinking.

WACHTEL What is your idea of God?

CARSON I don't have an idea of it anymore at all. Maybe I once did, at least an idea of unknowability as a divine atmosphere, but I don't even know that that's solid in me anymore.

WACHTEL Because in *Autobiography of Red*, one character says he's a sceptic and Geryon asks him, "You doubt God?" And he replies, "More to the point, I credit God with the good sense to doubt me."

CARSON That's an Oscar Wilde moment. I do credit God with that. I don't think I'll get much further with it than a shallow witticism. It's just not my gift.

WACHTEL You've noted that attention is a form of prayer, and from paying attention to who one is, one can step beyond the border of oneself and then move from there to the creation of a work of art. Can you link that chain for me, tell me more about how that works?

CARSON Yes, well, maybe I can. I don't remember when I wrote that or what it meant at the time, but lately I've been studying John Cage and I think that's something I very much appreciate in him, that he moves or tries to move to a place of complete stillness and attention within himself. He says, "I want to get every Me out of the way in order to start doing whatever the work will be." And that is an ongoing struggle, to get every Me out of the way.

WACHTEL For you? You would like to eliminate the Me?

CARSON Yes, I would.

WACHTEL The Me is a kind of interesting flicker through the work.

CARSON It's hard to keep it at the flicker level though. It tends to take over, it becomes the only principle of reasoning. I want to reason about something else. Life is short.

WACHTEL Isn't that what the Classics, particularly Greek and Latin translation, gives you, because it's so far out of yourself?

CARSON Yes, but anything can… I mean, looking at a pencil can give it to you. It's just a matter of causing your mind to focus on that thing, that question, whatever you choose to consider a question. Translation, yes, is an ideal process because it's so big it envelops your whole day but you can do it with very small things too.

WACHTEL How?

CARSON Well, looking at a stone. Attention is a choice of where you put your mind.

WACHTEL And looking at a stone to the extent that you forget you're doing the looking.

CARSON Yes exactly. Well put.

WACHTEL In *Plainwater* (1995), you write, "I will do anything to avoid boredom. It's the task of a lifetime." Are you winning?

CARSON So far.

WACHTEL Do you get bored easily?

CARSON I don't think I get bored easily, but I fear boredom.

WACHTEL Why?

CARSON Largely because it's the condition next to death.

WACHTEL Some people view it as a kind of fallow, proto-creative state.

CARSON John Cage would. John Cage pursued boredom but I'm just not that highly evolved. I fear it.

June 2011
Original interview produced by Mary Stinson

DORIS LESSING

When Doris Lessing won the Nobel Prize in Literature in 2007, she was eighty-eight years old, making her the oldest winner and also only the eleventh woman to win in its 106-year history. Lessing was described as the surprise winner—surprise only because she'd been touted to win for so long that it was starting to look like she'd been passed over permanently. She famously greeted reporters with something like exasperation. "Oh Christ," she said when they met her at her doorstep and told her the news. Yet as a writer, she continued to produce provocative new fiction and autobiography. In her Nobel speech (delivered by her publisher), she said, "The storyteller is deep inside every one of us. The story-maker is always with us. It is our stories that will recreate us, when we are torn, hurt, even destroyed. It is the storyteller, the dream-maker, the myth-maker, that is our phoenix, that represents us at our best, and at our most creative."

Doris Lessing was one of the great visionary writers of the twentieth century—and with an astounding range. Her groundbreaking 1962 novel, *The Golden Notebook*, was an unusual exploration of women's relationships, politics, and choices, but it was as much about the writing of fiction, the determination to capture the multifaceted aspects of a life, as it was any particular story. Published well before the feminist movement of the late '60s and '70s, *The Golden Notebook* was enormously powerful. Lessing said that at the time, just to write down what women were thinking, feeling, and experiencing was revolutionary.

But she consistently resisted the role of feminist heroine. With models such as Tolstoy and Stendhal, she wanted to write a social history—to record the intellectual and moral climate of the times.

In the early 1970s, in novels such as *The Summer Before the Dark* (1973), Lessing portrayed a society that was both recognizable and apocalyptic. Madness or catastrophe lay just around the corner, but meanwhile her characters could lead quite ordinary lives—and Lessing was attuned to every detail. Whether she was writing speculative fiction, novels about aging, or revolutionary fervour, Lessing's work was vivid and persuasive.

When I first met her in Toronto in the early 1990s, she'd recently written *The Fifth Child* (1988), an odd story of a monster child. She went on to publish sixteen books in as many years—while she was in her seventies and eighties, among them a sequel to *The Fifth Child* called *Ben, in the World* (2000). She wrote a collection of sketches and stories set in London, *The Real Thing* (1992), and *African Laughter* (1994), a travel memoir set in Zimbabwe. There was another futuristic adventure, *Mara and Dann* (1999), and an unusual look at romantic passion at sixty-five, *Love, Again* (1996). At the same time she wrote two compelling volumes of autobiography, followed by a novel, *The Sweetest Dream* (2001), that picked up—in the early 1960s—where the autobiographies left off. It revolved around "a kind of house mother for deeply troubled teenagers," which is how Lessing described herself in the early 1960s.

Doris Lessing was born in Persia, now Iran, in 1919. Her parents were English, her mother a nurse who married her patient, a man who'd lost his leg during the First World War. Lessing grew up on a remote, unprosperous homestead in the British colony of Southern Rhodesia, now Zimbabwe. She published her first novel, *The Grass Is Singing* (1950), a book set in Africa, just after she'd moved to England—travelling, famously, with her young son from her second marriage in one arm and the manuscript in the other.

Doris Lessing won many prizes over the years. She turned down the honour Dame of the British Empire—she couldn't quite stomach the title—but she did accept the higher Companion of Honour. And then, in 2007, the Nobel. She died in 2013, aged ninety-four.

Ten years earlier, just before she published a collection of four novellas, *The Grandmothers* (2003), I went to see Doris Lessing at her home in West Hampstead, at the very top of the hill, above a reservoir. It was a tall, three-storey house, very cluttered, very full: rugs, sculptures, books everywhere—she was an omnivorous reader. There was a biography of Nelson beside the couch; in the upstairs bathroom, a Russian grammar and dictionary on the floor. Lessing was able to continue to live in that house until her death.

When we spoke, she was full of energy, even cheerful. When her cat nestled up against me, she remarked that it rarely liked strangers, so I was in.

WACHTEL The early impressions which you describe in *Under My Skin*, the first volume of your autobiography, are very powerful, with an intense physicality, which you say is the truth of childhood. As you describe yourself growing up, first in Persia and then in Africa, it seems that you were aware from an early age of the uniqueness of your own perspective and how it differed from that of the adults around you. Do you think that all children feel that gap between their own perceptions and what they're told they should think or feel, or was it especially strong for you?

LESSING I don't know. I'm always surprised, when you ask people how early they can remember, how often they say, "Oh, well, I don't remember anything before I was seven or eight." Somewhere very, very, early, I made a private resolution, which I remember renewing throughout my childhood, that I was not to succumb to what they said was true—that obviously had to be my mother—and to preserve what I remembered. I used to have a whole gallery of little pictures, events that I, as it were, polished to make sure they were still there.

WACHTEL Your mental pictures—

LESSING Yes, mental. The physicality, for example, of objects, which I preserved. And this went on until I was in late adolescence, with adults insisting this is what happened, not what you said had happened. Children very easily succumb to what their parents say happened, and that, I think, is what most memories are for children.

But the real ones, you see, can be sorted out from the false ones simply by the quality of physicality, the touch of things, the smell of things, the sound, the taste. Children are so sensitive to taste; no wonder they complain about food. We've forgotten how strong their food tastes. A child's life is intensely sensual, and we've forgotten it.

WACHTEL When did you realize that the adult version was at odds with your own? I mean, do you know what made you so confident of the truth of your own perceptions of that reality?

LESSING I knew what was true and what wasn't very early. I think there must have been a very strong assault on my ego, to use this fashionable word, and I had to fight for my own version; otherwise, how do you account for it? I don't know. It's stubborn self-preservation. But then you have to ask, what was this assault?

I had a nurse who was Assyrian, and she turned up again last week, actually in a book annotated by my mother, described as a "dear, sweet, little thing." This is not how I remember her.

WACHTEL Is this the Marta you didn't like?

LESSING Marta, an Assyrian, who came to Kermanshah as a refugee from the innumerable wars that were going on in the Middle East. And so she became a nurse. Now I ask myself, what was this poor refugee doing, a nursemaid to two English children? What was her life? I have no idea and we'll never know now.

WACHTEL You have an exceptional memory, I think. Does it ever play tricks on you?

LESSING Oh, of course, it does. If you keep a journal and you look back at things you've written, sometimes you don't remember them at all, or you remember them differently. So your memory plays tricks all right, very creatively.

This is how I started thinking. When I wrote volume 1 of the autobiography, it occurred to me that I had never, ever thought about the reality of memory before—what was true and what wasn't. I spent an immense amount of time thinking about it, and I concluded that most childhood memories come from your parents' version of events.

But I had this other journal running in my memory, which I think was true. If you're very small and the table is right above your head, that is likely to be a true memory. But the memories your parents impart are not clear at all. What you are remembering is what they have said, like, "Oh, we used to go to the beach, and you loved it." It's always, "You loved it." Or, "We always had a picnic, and you did this and you did this." What you're remembering are your parents' words.

WACHTEL Are you ever surprised by what you remember, by what floats up, and by how memories come to you?

LESSING When I was writing this, a lot of things surfaced. But then they surface when you write any book. When I wrote *Mara and Dann*, an adventure story about a little girl and her younger brother, I had the most powerful memories from my early childhood because I adored my little brother, which surprised me later because by then I didn't enjoy him at all. But I adored him quite passionately, this little boy, and I'd forgotten all that, how powerful it was.

WACHTEL In your book on Africa, a collection of essays titled *African Laughter*, you describe family trips in the bush and sleeping out under the stars and a sense even then about the need to hold onto moments. You said, "I knew already how Time gave you everything with one hand while taking it back with the other." Why do you think, at such an early age, there was a need to hold onto the moment like that?

LESSING I don't know. But I was always thinking, hold us, hold us, hold us, it's going to disappear. I have no idea why. I think it must have had something to do with that very early childhood in Iran, in a very ancient trading town, full of refugees of all nationalities. The Spanish flu had just raced through it. This was the town I was born in. I believe that children are affected by an atmosphere of impermanence and threat. I must have been.

WACHTEL You also talk about being obsessed with time.

LESSING It's true. I have been all of my life. Always.

WACHTEL You talk about keeping a list of moments in your head, "to be checked, often, so they did not fade and go." It's like you're referring to an inventory, a file. Do you think you're still obsessed by time? It's a different world now.

LESSING Now what's happening is that you hardly start a week before it's ended. This is common to old people. What the reason for it is, I don't know. But I remember very clearly the way time stretched out when I was a child. Each day was endless, especially the six-week summer holidays. I've never had an explanation for the way the organism measures time differently. When I came to England—I was then just thirty—time went much faster, of course, than when I was a child. But compared to now, it was very slow. So it's an exponential speeding-up, which is very odd, isn't it?

WACHTEL Your brother shared those experiences, sleeping out under the stars and so on. You described how you had a pact to help each other stay awake so as not to miss any moments. But then you also describe, when you went back to visit him years later in Africa, that he didn't even remember.

LESSING He remembered nothing. All this time, we were basically at odds because he was a strong supporter of the white cause, and I was a strong supporter of the black cause, so we just didn't communicate. When we met, thirty years had passed, and I said, "At any rate, we remember that incredible childhood," but he remembered nothing at all. Nothing. He said his first memories were really when he was about ten or eleven, and his first memory, which is typical for this culture, was of going off into the bush with a cook's son— that's a black cook's son—with a rifle and sleeping out under the stars. They would take some mealie meal cakes or cook what they shot. He said he used to go out into the bush for days at a time, and that was the most wonderful experience of his entire life. I would recite some of the things that we had done. Nothing. An absolute blank. It was very painful.

WACHTEL Was this a kind of subtraction from your own experience?

LESSING It was nice to have shared something. We certainly didn't share anything later. These incredible experiences—there were so many— going out together into the very early morning, when our parents were still asleep. We'd leave the second the sun was coming up. Off we'd rush into the bush. We might spend hours there, seeing all the animals and having quite incredible adventures. "Do you remember," I said, "being chased up a tree by the wild pig?" We laughed so hard, we nearly fell out of the tree into the jaws of the wild pig, but he remembered not a thing. Jaws is wrong. They would have trampled us, not bitten us.

WACHTEL I'd like to stay with the subject of time and memory a bit more, because there's something you wonder about, relating to why we remember certain things. You ask, "How do you know that what you remember is more interesting than what you don't?" I think it's such an intriguing question. How *do* you know?

LESSING I've got a good memory, but there are great blanks, weeks when I remember nothing at all, but I can remember a weekend in which nothing particular happened. Why do I remember that weekend? I think—this is my tentative conclusion—that if you happen to be particularly awake for some reason during that weekend, whatever it was, you remember it. It doesn't mean to say it's important. And you might be forgetting some very important thing. The convention is that you remember what's important. I don't think that's necessarily true at all. I think you could be remembering things that were dramatic.

WACHTEL Of course, then you have to figure out why it is you were awake at that particular time or why you were especially aware.

LESSING Oh, now we come into cosmic thoughts. I'm wondering if you're not sometimes more alert because of—I don't know—flares from the sun or something. This is not a dogma, you understand. I'm just questioning: why should you be particularly awake during a certain period? The obvious things that you remember, like the day war is declared or great public events, that's easy. But why, in this terribly unimportant stretch of time, do you remember a great deal and another time nothing? There must be an answer to it.

WACHTEL On some of your return visits to Africa, you puzzle over the tricks that your memory plays and why places that you knew even as an adult should be so diminished.

LESSING That's very true. I think that, as a young adult, you're living in a kind of story of great dramatic importance. It doesn't stay though, does it? Things get much more humdrum. I can remember all kinds of enormously vivid scenes from the war, for example, but that, I think, probably comes under the heading of "public events." Why should I not remember anything at all about the periods of time I know I spent with people? I remember nothing at all. Were they really so boring? Was I so boring? It's an interesting question.

WACHTEL In going back to Harare, Zimbabwe, which was then Salisbury, Southern Rhodesia, you visit what had been a club or a bar, a restaurant where terrifically exciting things had happened, or where you'd danced, and then ten, fifteen years ago, you find it so shabby or diminished—

LESSING I think I was talking about the Salisbury Club, which is now the Harare Club. It's a nice little building with a pleasant veranda. But it had always been lit by great, dramatic, emotional events when I was young. That was the year before I married. I remember it extremely clearly, but I wonder how accurately I remember it.

WACHTEL "We make up our pasts," you say. Do you actually see yourself consciously making up the past?

LESSING No, no, not consciously. We always reinterpret the past in our favour, don't we? We always make ourselves out better than we were. Like any of you who have read a diary written in your youth, I think, oh, my God, was I really like that? Yes, we were like that, but we try to pretend we weren't.

It's particularly political, I think, that we soften things up. All my generation, too. I know people now by the dozen, raving Reds and Stalinists, who say things like, "Oh, yes, I was a bit of a Red once." My God, I think. You nearly drove us all mad for years. So this is what we do.

WACHTEL When you describe your early experience, what you saw and heard and understood, what comes through is that you had, even then, a very strong, private self, an observer's self at the core. You write, "They call it loneliness, that here is this place unsharable with anyone at all, but it's all we have to fall back on. Me, I, this feeling of me. The observer, never to be touched." This intense self-awareness—is it something that you enjoyed? Did it make you feel strong? Or did you feel isolated by it?

LESSING Oh, not isolated, no. It's what I was as a child and what I am now. This is a constant, this sense of self. People seem to think that memories are identity, but I think the sense of self is identity. For all I know, we've got other identities. That's what religious people say. But this is the only thing that you can rely on, this feeling, which makes old people look in mirrors and say, "That's not me," and why they put pictures of their younger selves around their rooms, which I think is a bit pathetic. "But what you're looking at is not me at all. There I am over there, age twenty"—that's what they do. Well, they couldn't do that if they didn't have a sense of self which is quite apart from that image of what they are now. It's the great joke of old age which everybody old shares. That we have been so many things in our lives that this one is just temporary. What's it going to be next year—it would be interest-ing—or in five years' time, if we live?

WACHTEL Do you have a sense that the true you is you at a particular age?

LESSING No. I have a sense of self which is quite apart from time, quite apart from anything. You know when you're deeply, deeply asleep and you wake up in the dark and you don't quite know where you are, but you are there—it's that feeling. Yes, it's identity. It must be.

WACHTEL In volume 2 of your autobiography, *Walking in the Shade*, you write that "There was a point when it occurred to me that my early life had been extraordinary and would make a novel. I had not under-stood how extraordinary until I had left Southern Africa and come to

England." What aspects of your early upbringing seem most extraordinary to you now?

LESSING Now? I was brought up in the bush on the veldt in an Africa that has vanished, not only because it was white-dominated, but because the bush has taken such punishment. So nothing I remember as a child is still there. The birds and the animals—everything has diminished or gone. I remember a lost paradise. Then there was a war, which was extraordinary. I'm always surprised that nobody remembers it. Britain sent in vast numbers of air force personnel to train because flying conditions were better in these parts of the world. So there were air force camps all over Southern Africa and Kenya and Australia, hundreds and thousands of men, the flyers who were only there for a short time and the ground staff who were there for a long time.

I've just written a story about these events, "The Love Child." The RAF men used to tell me about these trips. It's amazing that it's been forgotten. We're so focussed on Germany and what happened in Germany that we don't remember what a spread the war had, what an astonishing thing it was everywhere.

WACHTEL Yes, in your story, the Allied troops have to stay in India and put down the Indian rebellion.

LESSING Yes, there was a great political furor going on towards the end of the war. The troops said, "We're not here to put down Indian freedom. We joined up to beat the Germans." And naturally the authorities didn't go for this much and said, "You joined up and you will do as you're told." Then it was taken up in the House of Commons and they were sent home. But it was quite a nasty little time for a while with mutinous activity among the soldiers in the camps.

WACHTEL You have a particular perspective, a kind of double-vision as the daughter of British settlers in Southern Rhodesia. You have a sense of "absolutely belonging and absolutely not belonging, which," as you put it, "is extremely valuable for a writer."

LESSING It is very good for a writer. I can absolutely understand the end of the Raj. People like my parents believed totally and sincerely in the virtues of the British Empire and its function, uplifting and civilizing, inspired by God. So I can understand it very well. People from the Indian army, for example: my character in the Indian army says he has spent a lifetime doing work which now nobody values—I used to meet these people, bitter people. A lot of them came to Southern Rhodesia.

They had been doing their duty and now nobody valued them. I can see their point of view. But I don't share it, of course.

In Salisbury, now Harare, there were only half-a-dozen people who celebrated Indian independence. We were the only people drinking Cape wine to toast Indian independence. And we would have been regarded as absolute traitors to want such a thing. It's hard to believe now, isn't it?

WACHTEL In 1947.

LESSING Yes. It was before I left. There was a handful of people who thought, my God, this is an incredible thing, the end of the Indian empire. We drank to it, but quietly, because we didn't want to lose all our friends.

WACHTEL You had a difficult relationship with your mother, whom you describe as a "good, conventional, British Empire-loving woman." And in fact, you say you were the wrong kind of daughter for her. Why is that?

LESSING Of course I was. I'm really very sorry for her. Genuinely. It was tragic for her to have a daughter like me because she had very little in life. She had a terrible life. Her life was absolutely wrong for her from the moment she left Persia and went to Africa. Not only did she have an invalid husband, she had a daughter who fought her every inch of the way and a son who simply switched off. He was bland and polite and took no notice of her at all. I fought her. We must have been hell for her all the time. What she wanted was nice English children. She knew exactly what she wanted: the kinds of schools we should have gone to and how we would have ended up. Just look at it from her point of view: I left school at fourteen and I was bright—it wasn't that I was stupid. I just refused to be what she wanted. There was a terrible pressure on me all the time to conform. And then I got married in a foolish manner, and left home.

WACHTEL Why was it foolish?

LESSING She never wanted me to marry a Rhodesian civil servant. She probably wanted me to marry a—I don't know. I'm not really cari-caturing it—a naval officer or an army officer, British, and return to living my proper life in England as a good British girl. This is what she wanted. And then I left that marriage and married a German refugee. The fact that he was anti-Nazi meant nothing to them. They were very polite, but they never liked him. I really put her through it. Then I left everything and came to England with a child. For her, I was a tragedy. There's no softening it.

WACHTEL But to you, her life was tragic.

LESSING It was tragic. She made a very good job of something that for her must have been really terrible. I admire her. I'm just sorry for her. But I know, if she came here, we'd be quarrelling within five minutes.

WACHTEL Would you?

LESSING Yes.

WACHTEL Because at one point in your autobiography, you wonder, if she showed up now, what you would have to say to each other as two older women.

LESSING Nothing, but it's hard to say. The world has changed so much for both of us. What would she make of it?

WACHTEL You say that it took you until you were in your seventies to come to terms with her, not feeling that you had to fight her all the time. How did you come to understand her?

LESSING Simply by getting older and understanding what kind of life she'd had. When she arrived at that farm in Southern Rhodesia, she'd come with beautiful clothes and found herself in the middle of the bush in what was virtually a mud hut. She had a breakdown. But it was called "trouble with her heart." There was nothing wrong with her heart. She was suffering from terrible anxiety. It's easy now to see it. And then she got out of bed and went on living, and I admire her for that because she hated her life. There was nothing in it that gave her pleasure. She did not enjoy the bush. She did not enjoy the things that my father and my brother and I enjoyed. She didn't like Africans. She never could get on with them. It was a feature of the white Mrs. of that time, the continual nagging and fighting that went on with our servants, which now is almost funny, so ludicrous. But it was not funny living with it. It was unfair, without saying. Black people just out of some village landing a job as a servant in a white house with a white woman who complained that the forks were not on the right side or that the tumblers were not placed properly or that the roast beef hadn't been served with the right kind of… I don't know. It was a continual battle to preserve middle-class standards in a setting where they had no relevance at all. This was going on all over the country. One could recognize this voice from a hundred yards, this high, desperate, nagging voice: "If I've told you once, I've told you a hundred times." Yap, yap, yap, yap, yap. It drove you mad, this kind of thing.

WACHTEL It took your getting older to really appreciate what she'd been through?

LESSING Yes. Because she was trapped, wasn't she? You have to be trapped yourself to understand what being trapped is. And don't ask me—I'm not going to tell you. We all get trapped in our lives, one way or another, in situations you can't get out of. So I understood that. I can't think of a more trapped woman than my mother. She had all this energy. She was such a competent woman. She was such a clever woman. She had nothing to use it on, except two children who just wished she were somewhere else. Tragic.

WACHTEL And your mother didn't like what you wrote. Can you still hear her voice in your head as you imagine her responses?

LESSING More in sorrow than in anger. "Oh, my dear, this is so unfair," she would say about something, like *The Grass Is Singing*. Of course she couldn't like it. The whites loathed it. And I was regarded as a traitor to the white cause and a nigger lover, a kaffir lover. How could she possibly like it?

WACHTEL What about your autobiography? Would she have liked that?

LESSING No.

WACHTEL What would she have made of your being offered the title of Dame of the British Empire?

LESSING Oh, she'd have been so happy.

WACHTEL And then you turned it down.

LESSING I couldn't be a Dame of the British Empire. Anyway, I'm a Companion of Honour, which is better, but I still don't know what I'm a Companion of.

WACHTEL As you say, you have to be really grown up, not merely in years, to understand your parents. And you say that it took you until you were middle aged to also get a sense that you never understood your father and who he really was, or what he might have been without the terrible war. What happened to him? Of course, he was injured in the First World War, and that's how he met your mother. But in what deeper ways do you feel he was changed by the war?

LESSING The thing that emerges from all his reminiscences as a young man. He played cricket for his county. He played billiards. He played football. God knows what he did. He was a man. And he used to walk. In those days, they thought nothing of walking five or six miles to a dance and then walking home afterwards. Who would do that now? But then it was normal.

It wasn't just that he was wounded in the trenches. Clearly he had a breakdown but they didn't use that word. He was deeply and clinically depressed. The doctor who treated him was obviously a very kind man. He didn't belittle his condition, which was a common response in those days. He supported my father. It was called shell shock. In fact, my father was depressed. He'd had his leg cut off, this very physical man. He was depressed.

Then he went out to Persia, where he worked in a bank. Now, my mother adored every second of Persia because social life was just her kind of thing, but he was a rather solitary man, and he loathed parties and jolly musical evenings and things like that. He hated it.

So he escaped to the bush, where he slowly failed because he was ill most of the time. He got diabetes and he had to inject himself with insulin several times a day. Can you imagine? The insulin had to come out from Salisbury by slow train, then to the farm by oxcart. No refrigerators. It was a continual balancing act. Was the insulin going to arrive in time? Now you just pop it into the refrigerator.

Although he had a very bad time, I don't think he had it nearly as bad as my mother, because he loved Africa whereas she didn't. While he was quietly failing as a farmer, she suffered terribly.

WACHTEL You've talked about the literature you were exposed to when you were growing up.

LESSING Oh, I have to thank my mother for that. She ordered books from England for us, absolutely everything, including things like *Anne of Green Gables*. There were always books in the bookcases, all the classics, and then later on I ordered books for myself. It was a wonderful thing she did. There were even children's newspapers then. My brother wasn't interested, so it was really for me.

WACHTEL What worlds did it open up to you?

LESSING Everything. And then I started ordering books for myself on an amazing pattern: if a book was mentioned in one novel, I ordered it, because I didn't know what to order. So I was continually ordering books that were a great surprise to me. They'd come out by sea, of course, and the greatest days of my life were when the books arrived. I have read a great deal. That was my education.

WACHTEL I want to go back to one aspect of your journey away from Africa, which is the shaping influence of Communism and being exposed to Reds, as you put it, and an involvement that continued for many years. It was the spirit of the times, you say, that made Communism a natural choice for you, but can you recall that zeitgeist for me? What was it that attracted you?

LESSING If I'd been in England, it would have been different for me because then the strongest influence was the Spanish Civil War, as I discovered when I arrived. Communists were the only people I'd ever met in my life who had read everything, because in those days it was a reading culture. They were politically oriented. They read everything and they'd read everything I had read. It was greatly exciting for me, but it is a culture that has gone completely, as I described in "The Love Child."

In the late thirties, the whole of England was abuzz with young people reading, listening to music and attending summer schools. This was not a class thing. It included a lot of the working class, because I met them. When you read memoirs, this always emerges, this cohort of young workers who had had a political education and who ran debating societies and political clubs in the army. It was these people who voted the Labour Party into office after the war.

WACHTEL But how did you find them in Salisbury?

LESSING They were in the RAF camps around there, bored young men with not enough women. We ran all kinds of clubs: debating clubs and left-wing clubs, and we held lectures.

WACHTEL Is that also where you got your political education, learning from them, while they learned from what you had been reading?

LESSING They read. I didn't have to teach them anything. I was a raw girl, a very raw colonial girl, so they were a great revelation to me.

WACHTEL You describe your decision to join the Communist Party as the "most neurotic act of my life."

LESSING I was totally disillusioned with the comrades by then, so why I did it, I can't think. I didn't actually ever go to any political meetings. I only went to the Communist Party Writers Group, which had some very interesting characters in it, and that was about to fold as well. That only went on for a couple of years, and then it folded. Everything was ending.

When I came to England, there was a completely different culture. First of all, everybody was either a Communist or had been a Communist or was violently anti-Communist. This was the atmosphere. Everyone had just come back from the war. People taught me about the war because they had experienced the war here and couldn't talk about anything but the bombing, or they had come back from war somewhere. That went on until about 1956, and it ended just like that because there was a new generation who didn't want to hear about the war. That was such a surprise to me that I was rather shocked in those days, but now I think it's probably a good thing.

WACHTEL A good thing to move on?

LESSING When I went to Zimbabwe in 1982, everyone talked about the war of liberation day and night. Whites and blacks, they could talk of nothing else. Obsessively. I went again three or four years later, and nobody talked about it at all. This was a new generation. Exactly the same thing. It's inevitable. And it's painful when it happens because you think of all the unrewarded heroes being forgotten.

WACHTEL Do you think that Communists were wrong to identify socialist ideals with the Soviet Union? Would it have been possible to hold on to such ideals if they hadn't been so enmeshed in the Soviet Union, which you, then, had to defend, despite its crimes and failures?

LESSING Yes, this is what I wonder. It's interesting that, when I brought this up many, many years later, I couldn't find anybody who was prepared even to think such a thought, excepting one or two oddballs. My thesis was that, if the left hadn't been identified with the Soviet Union, it would have been much better, but instead we were identified with everything crooked and rotten, the lies and the trials and everything perverted. It's very easy now to say, isn't it? Hindsight is always easy. But it would have been impossible, I suppose, because the Soviet Union was such a great emotional event. There was a whole element within the Labour Party that hated the Soviet Union; they were always fighting against it. But supposing the whole Soviet thing hadn't happened. The left would not now be in the terrible state it's in—it is in a terrible state—having identified so closely with the Soviet Union.

WACHTEL Then you end up with Mao's China, which was the next generation's—

LESSING People didn't seem to be so involved with China. There were some, yes.

WACHTEL Like Sartre.

LESSING Not to the same extent as the Soviet Union. There were people who were in love with Mao. Quite extraordinary. But it wasn't the same thing.

WACHTEL You'd still end up in an indefensible position.

LESSING With China? I know. Anyone who identified with any Communist regime ends up in an indefensible position. But looking back on it all, it's as if you're looking at people who are completely crazy. That is because of the atmosphere of the time: what is forgotten is the terrible disillusionment that was prevalent. First, our government virtually supported the wrong side of the Spanish Civil War by non-intervention, which meant that nobody supported the rightful government, but instead supported Franco as did the fascists and Hitler. France and England kept aloof instead of intervening. This caused such anger. We used to feel shame about our governments in those days. Now they're so awful we don't bother to feel shame.

So there was the Spanish Civil War, which had an effect that no one now seems to appreciate, and then the terrible poverty in Britain, which everyone has forgotten. All this made it very easy to become Communist. The war was coming, and our governments were not exactly eager then to stand up against Hitler. So all this created an atmosphere of dislike for your own side, which now is a different kind of dislike.

WACHTEL It's almost the reverse.

LESSING Now the fact that we have sleazy government seems to be taken for granted. Quite interesting. Where can you find a government that isn't sleazy? There isn't one. But we seem to be living with it as if this is normal, which was certainly not the case back then because there was patriotism, a pride in your country, which got this powerful knock, and this is why people became Communist so easily.

WACHTEL You talk about how losing faith in Communism is parallel to people who can't let go of their dream of being in love. What has replaced it, do you think? What's happened to the idea of revolution that was so central to that time?

LESSING For years, people talked about the revolution. Now it seems so silly and childish. This went right on into the sixties. What revolution? No one bothered to even spell it out. It was a kind of mantra: come the revolution. But all that's gone, and a good thing, too, since I don't hold much brief for revolution. The hardest thing in the world is to try and convey a political atmosphere in retrospect. It's gone so completely. The whole Cold War is gone, and yet at the time it was terrible, poisoning everything. But it's gone. Now you can hardly imagine it.

WACHTEL In your novel of the sixties, *The Sweetest Dream* (2001), your character Comrade Johnny becomes a holy man.

LESSING A lot of the comrades became holy men. I don't know if you've noticed. A lot of the old Reds have become gurus. Very funny. The irony is, of course, that they're still telling other people what to do, and they are in the right, and they are sufferers. That's what the great bond is, I think. I now know quite a few saintly ex-comrades. It's funny, isn't it?

WACHTEL So are there any philosophies today that one can pay allegiance to?

LESSING You mean political philosophy? No. If you look at the dilemmas of people like Tony Blair, they have to come up with something like The Middle Way. It doesn't mean anything. It makes him sound like a philosopher. I don't know about the States. Bush, he's extremely right wing, but I don't know what his philosophy is. I don't think there are any political philosophies that are any good anyway. I've never seen anything wrong with pragmatism. It seems to me that a very sensible way of running a country is to look at a situation as it is and act accordingly. That's pragmatism, and it's generally regarded as cowardice, but I think it's very sensible. Why do we have to have political philosophies, that always end in sorrow and tears?

WACHTEL Another movement claimed you, though not necessarily by your choice, when your novel *The Golden Notebook* became the Bible of the women's movement. But I'm more interested in the book's genesis, because when you write about it in your autobiography, you say there were emotional pressures that fuelled the writing of it. "I was at a crossroads. I was in the melting pot and ready to be remade." You were determined that your emotional life would be different from that point. Can you tell me about that?

LESSING Yes. I started writing it at the end of the 1950s, when Communism was collapsing everywhere. I was surrounded by people in various states of collapse, for one reason or other. All the old Communists were having breakdowns or taking to religion or drink or something. It was very evident that this was the end of an era. Embedded in this, it was obvious it was the end of something, and that was ideology. At the very beginning of *The Golden Notebook*, I propose these opposites—black/white, old/young, men/women. This is a book about compartmentalization and the dangers of it, because it was not only politics—don't forget where I was brought up—but religion, a lot of religions in Africa, some of them very lively. I had noticed that extremely religious people tend to have bad breakdowns, like extremely political people do. Ideology. That was what *The Golden Notebook* was about. At that time, I was a youngish woman and emotionally embroiled in everything, in sexual and emotional problems. So it was that which fuelled the book—the word "fuel" is an accurate word, I'm not being emotional—and it's that which got it all the attention. No one will ever believe me, but when I was writing that book, it never crossed my mind that I was writing a book about women's liberation or anything like that. I was simply writing about what I had experienced. All the comrades were talking about women's problems all the time. It wasn't invented in the sixties.

WACHTEL What did you want to change? You say you wanted your own emotional life to be different or take a different direction at the time that you were writing the book, and that it changed you more than just the writing of any book changes you.

LESSING What did I want to change? I didn't like my emotional life. I was then getting on for forty. I was not going to go on in this ridiculous manner. There was a great deal of emotional pressure behind that book.

WACHTEL What did you want to change in particular? When you say you were coming up to forty, it doesn't seem that old to either of us right now.

LESSING I did get married at nineteen. I'd had three children, two marriages, lots of lovers and things like that. I decided that I would do things differently from now on, and I did on the whole. But what I was really doing was writing myself out of the entire Communist package. It's a package, a mindset, which is still around now, but much less so, which is materialism—more chickens in the pot—and the various varieties of Marxism, because there are quite a few. The package espoused atheism and a belief in inevitable progress, because that was very strong at that time. It was never questioned that everything in the world was going to get better and better. I just couldn't believe in any of it anymore, which wasn't my intention, of course, because, when you write books, things often happen quite differently from what you expect.

WACHTEL But you ended up in a place where you wanted to be, in a sense. You wrote yourself to that place.

LESSING You make it sound like an island, like I had a plan. No, not at all. I wrote myself out of where I had been and I was ready for new thoughts. But then as usual, one thinks that one is unique, but one isn't at all because everyone is doing the same thing. The freefall of the sixties was just ahead, characterized by the notion of "anything goes," a wonderful, zany generosity, an openness when young people could travel anywhere and just knock on some door in America and say, "Hi. I'm a friend of Hank's. Can I come in?" "Yes, do come in." This kind of thing was going on all over the West, and I thought it was absolutely marvellous, and I still think so. It was a great culture while it lasted. Admittedly, the price paid was heavy because you had to belong. You had to wear a uniform: the jeans and jersey, preferably with a hole in the elbow, and Mao jackets, and you had to have a certain vocabulary and certain opinions. It was a very, very uniform culture. That wasn't good at all, but the rest of it was.

WACHTEL You write about it in your novel *The Sweetest Dream*, where the central character, Frances, is a kind of housemother to these young people, which is something that you did. How did you fall into that?

LESSING It was very easy. I had just bought a house, because, unlike other parts of the world, here the pressure on you to own a house is extraordinary. Anywhere else in the world, you can rent something; here you must have a house and I had a house with a lot of room in it. My son Peter was more often not there because, you know, I was the enemy. The joke was, he would be off at other people's parents, and other people's children would be living with me. So it went on for quite a time, a very interesting time. The thing that strikes me now as most extraordinary was how little questioning went on. I don't remember any parent ringing me up and saying, "How is my little Freddy who's been with you for six months?" And I would never ring the parents where Peter was staying, which seems to me now amazing. Everyone was so trusting. But it all worked, didn't it, so it was all right.

WACHTEL What did you like best about the sixties?

LESSING I enjoyed the kids very much. There they were, mostly in bad trouble. I think people glamourize the sixties. These kids, they were all war children, after all. Everybody in their sweetest dream is badly affected by war, which is the theme of the book, actually. All of these kids were using marijuana, which I don't count, and alcohol. They were having trouble with the police. They were having breakdowns. God knows what wasn't going on. Now all of these people are highly respected citizens and perfectly okay.

WACHTEL Frances, the central character of *The Sweetest Dream*, is surrounded by people who are in many ways quite disturbed. And that interest in madness and breakdown shows up in other aspects of your fiction, with Kate, for instance, in *The Summer Before the Dark*. You've written that you've never personally been mad or had a breakdown, although you do describe one instance when you tried to make yourself crazy by not sleeping or eating. Do you feel that any inclination towards madness has been staved off by writing?

LESSING That's what I think, yes, but it's because I've always had things I had to do, like bringing up a child and so on. My entire life has been shadowed by people being crazy, like my father. He was very ill. The word "depression" wasn't around in those days. A great pity, because you didn't know how to describe what you saw. Now I would say that my father was very depressed, and he was never treated for it, which was terrible. So for one reason or another, I've had a lot to do with mental illness in my life.

WACHTEL One of the ironic things is that some of the most troubled characters in *The Sweetest Dream* become therapists themselves.

LESSING It's the current thing, it's what women do. It's very interesting. I know at least—my God—it must be getting on to twenty people who are now therapists, and these are people who have had disastrous lives. It's very easy to become a therapist obviously, since these people have done it. But this is what women do now when they're not qualified. And good luck to them.

WACHTEL On a more serious note, you describe yourself as benefiting from psychotherapy at particular times in your life. Is it possible to say how it affected your writing, for instance?

LESSING It didn't affect my writing at all. Not at all. It just got me through a very sticky patch, as my mother was arriving in England and I wasn't getting out bed. I suddenly realized that something had to be done. I had a boyfriend who was a psychiatrist and a very, very critical man, and I was being assaulted. I also had a girlfriend who was very critical. I was under great stress. And I had this wonderful therapist woman who supported me all the time. She was obviously a genius. She knew what I needed was to be supported. I needed to be told I was okay, because I was under such stress from everyone, and that's what she did for me. It wasn't an orthodox psychotherapy. What I was doing, I now see, was buying a friend, someone who said I was all right. Is it possible this is what a lot of therapy is? Because, as you probably know, if you know someone who is ill, in a breakdown or anything like that, they are always intolerable. What you're listening to is a complaint against life that is virtually unbearable, and this is why you have to have therapists. They're paid to listen to other people's misery.

§

WACHTEL I'd like to go back to Africa for a moment. You've described how every writer has a myth country, with "myth" being defined as a concentration of truth. You first returned to Southern Rhodesia in 1956, only to discover that you'd been branded a prohibited immigrant. Then you went back in 1982 to what was now Zimbabwe. How did that myth country, imbued with all the memories that you'd been carrying with you, measure up against what you saw?

LESSING Like everything else in my life, that place wasn't there. I went back to the farm with a friend who'd said to me, "Look, you've got to stop this nonsense. You've got to go back." So we went back and found that the old house, of course, had gone long ago in a fire, and a totally hideous little bungalow had been built, full of black people, black children. They didn't have so much as a pencil or a piece of paper between them, which I still think of with anguish—a good description of Zimbabwe, let me tell you. And somebody had cut off the top of the hill. It was a good twenty feet lower. It was all a bit absurd.

WACHTEL In *Under My Skin*, your first volume of autobiography, you say, "I'm trying to write this book honestly. But were I to write it aged eighty-five, how different would it be?" You're closer to that age now. Would you approach it any differently?

LESSING It would inevitably suffer from a feeling of loss. I suppose it's what we experience throughout our lives, anyway—a feeling of all that has gone for nothing, because nothing good that I can see has been left behind. I feel rather in fact like the people running the Indian Empire. Was all this a waste of time? Well, it probably was. Yes, I think a feeling of loss and waste.

WACHTEL One of the characters in *The Sweetest Dream* is a disturbed anorexic, Sylvia, who turns herself around through the support of the household and in particular her grandmother. She becomes a doctor, and she's the focus of the second part of the novel, which is set in Africa in a country you call Zimlia. The problems Sylvia encounters in Africa are overwhelming, as you say: "Mistakes written into a landscape, a country, a history." But she finds purpose in hands-on action, in doing, in giving to the people there. Even then she's undermined. And there's so much government corruption; even the international aid organizations are ineffectual and decadent.

LESSING They're not all ineffectual. The interesting thing is that all the big attempts, the big things, are just a waste of money. But little things, little attempts, they seem to work and are very valuable.

I was taken to meet some young women not far from Harare. There were a few sheds in the bush, and there was this young woman doctor, who was semi-religious, living at a mission, but not actually part of it. She was using her own money to do what could be done. She had the only clinic for many a mile, but later I discovered that the government had closed it down because it wasn't good enough, leaving them nothing. That was all true.

I have been involved for some years now with an organization trying to provide books to Zimbabwe, not in the towns but in the bush. If you take books out to some village stuck in the middle of nowhere, they will be greeted with tears; entire villages can be transformed. They've got civics classes and literacy classes, and they're reading each other's books. They're even writing them. It's amazing what a box of books can do. This has had to come to an end because it's now dangerous to go out into the bush as you can be killed by Mugabe's Zanu Patriotic Front bullyboys. Maybe it'll be revived again.

WACHTEL Engagement with others and responsibility to others—connectedness—are themes in your books, and it would seem also in your life. The characters who isolate themselves in *The Sweetest Dream* have healing to do. To be alone is problematic. Frances's home is remembered as a place of kindness, a blessed place. Do you still need that kind of connection?

LESSING I'm getting old, and I don't have the energy that I used to have. I have a fairly complicated personal life, but I'm not going to go into it. It's harder and harder for me to find time to write, which is really interesting because I used to think, when you got old, you would have all the time in the world. But it didn't happen like that. So make the most of time now, when you're young.

WACHTEL But you're so remarkably productive.

LESSING Nothing compared with what I used to be. I'm always having to fight for a morning here, an afternoon there... anyway, that's another story.

WACHTEL I won't ask you about your complicated life, but I do have to ask you about love and romantic love because you have written about that in all its variety and complications in your 1996 novel *Love Again* and in *The Grandmothers*, which is another unconventional look at love between older women and younger men.

LESSING It's such a taboo subject. But after I wrote *Love Again*, I got so many letters, some of them very funny, about relationships between older women and younger men, which definitely is a love that dare not speak its name. These things go on secretly.

WACHTEL You've said that you were writing out of personal experience when you wrote *Love Again*.

LESSING Not exactly, directly, but I used personal experience. In *Love Again*, all the loves are out of reach—did you notice?—every one, without exception, which is the essence of romantic love, isn't it? It has to be out of reach.

WACHTEL Whereas in *The Grandmothers*, it's very much within reach.

LESSING That was a real life, a story that was told to me that I've been saving up all these years to write.

WACHTEL Is there something about illicit love or passion, these taboo subjects, that appeals to you or to the storyteller in you?

LESSING Yes. It's more interesting to write about something forbidden unless you want to write the equivalent of George Gissing about modern marriage, which I'm sometimes tempted to do because they're interesting, marriages now.

WACHTEL In the story "Victoria and the Staveneys" in your new novella collection, there's a young black girl whose encounter with a middle-class liberal family opens up prospects and places that she didn't even know were there. I'm interested in how fantasy and obsession come to shape your characters' lives in ways both good and bad. Does that theme have a particular resonance for you?

LESSING I hadn't thought of it like that. This is also a true story, set in America, but I didn't want to set it there so I set it in Britain. And instantly, class comes into it in a way it never does in America.

WACHTEL Is it about race then?

LESSING Even that is not so. The American story is that of a poor black girl who has an affair with a white American boy and, six years later, rings up and says, "There's this child." The entire family embraces the situation in a way which she must find pretty overwhelming. So I thought I would transfer it to England. Now, you have to have a family like the Staveneys, of whom there are many examples in Britain. the liberal, middle-class family who embrace good causes by the dozen. But at the end of that story there has to be a choice. What did happen to that little girl? She would either stay indefinitely a disadvantaged little black girl, or she would become part of the middle-class family, which I think is probably more likely to happen. But that choice is not in the American story, as told to me. England goes on being England in an amazing way.

WACHTEL Other than the truth of these stories, what is it about them that interested you in particular?

LESSING Three of the stories, which I've been saving up for years, appealed to me, because they were true. When you're writing such stories, you always have to remember who told it to you because the story gets filtered through that person, and then you imagine the same story being told to you by a different kind of person. That's a different story, particularly in the case of "The Grandmothers" because you can imagine being told it by someone totally disapproving. It becomes a very different story from the original as told to me.

WACHTEL In the final, longest story in that collection, "A Love Child," you give us another aspect of the legacy of the First World War. But it's also about romantic obsession.

LESSING Yes, it is. As I said, it's a true story that couldn't have happened without the war, the troop ships docking for four or five days in Durban and Capetown. There were many love affairs, as there were bound to be. And this young man was convinced that a child was his child, and after the war, he went back to Durban, but he could never find the woman again, which meant she didn't want to be found— understandably, after all. But he kept looking for the child. Now, this is a romantic obsession, if you like, and it went on for years, so one can say this man is totally bonkers, which he probably was. But then most people are bonkers about something, don't you think? This is just more visible.

WACHTEL It ends on a sad note.

LESSING I thought that it was very terrible. He says, "If you think that's love…" Of course, it was love. But he's still in his dream of four days of bliss somewhere.

WACHTEL We began with memory. Some people say that memories of childhood are closer and sharper as we get older. Do you find that?

LESSING No, not necessarily. They are sharp because I'm determined to keep them sharp. That's a different thing. As for the short-term memory that they say you lose—I don't think I've lost mine yet, but I dare say it's a pleasure to come.

WACHTEL You said a few years ago that you felt you were at the end of a certain phase of your life and what you're on the lookout for now is the unexpected, and for things that come from outside that you never thought might happen. As a storyteller, what sparks your curiosity?

LESSING It's amazing. I'm writing a story now where something happened that hasn't happened to me for many, many years. A character just strolled in from nowhere and took over, which is fascinating because I didn't expect it. Where do these characters come from? Where did Julia in *The Sweetest Dream* come from? I did have a German mother-in-law, but I never met her, and she certainly wasn't like Julia. So you have to ask where Julia comes from. Is it me in disguise? That's an interesting question. Just imagine, could I really be that tidy and well-organized? Don't bother to look around the room.

WACHTEL This is the sort of matriarch who lives at the top of the house in *The Sweetest Dream*.

LESSING Yes. So it's very interesting, all these characters inside you of whom you know nothing.

WACHTEL And do you like this one who's just wandered in?

LESSING Yes, I do. I'm fascinated by him. I really like him. He's a great surprise to me.

July 2003
Original interview produced by Sandra Rabinovitch

HILARY MANTEL

I have to say that it was gratifying when, in 2009, Hilary Mantel won the Man Booker Prize for her ambitious historical novel, *Wolf Hall*. I can't exactly claim to have discovered her, but here was a writer whose work I'd been following—and admiring—for more than twenty years, finally getting some major recognition. But what I hadn't reckoned was that *Wolf Hall* would break records and become the biggest selling Man Booker Prize winner ever—220,000 hardback copies in the UK alone, 1.5 million worldwide—sweeping onto more literary prize shortlists than any British novel had ever done. It also picked up an American National Book Critics Circle Award and was a favourite of book clubs. I know that Tudor England is a popular subject—from *Henry VIII and His Six Wives*, and *The Other Boleyn Girl*, to Thomas More and *A Man for All Seasons*. But the figure at the centre of Mantel's novel, Thomas Cromwell, was so relatively unknown that people often confused him with his more famous great-great-great nephew, Oliver—the seventeenth-century man who ruled England as Lord Protector after the overthrow and execution of Charles I.

Thomas Cromwell lived from 1485 to 1540. He was Henry VIII's fixer, a blacksmith's son who rose to become Secretary to the King, as well as Master of the Rolls, Chancellor of Cambridge University, and deputy to the king as head of the Church of England. One of the marvels of *Wolf Hall* and its sequel, *Bring Up the Bodies* (2012), is the intimacy in the way the story unfolds through the consciousness of

Thomas Cromwell. This not only creates sympathy for an otherwise cold, ruthless man, but it also puts us right into the middle of the action, in the present, without our quite knowing what will happen next. Even if we do. *Bring Up the Bodies* also won the Man Booker Prize, making Hilary Mantel the first woman to win the prize twice (after J.M. Coetzee and Peter Carey), and she captured the Costa Book Award. And what started out as a single, big novel turned into a major three-volume project, plus two extraordinarily successful plays—at Stratford in the UK, in London's West End, and on Broadway—and a BBC television mini-series.

I first encountered Hilary Mantel with her novel *Fludd* (1989), a charming, witty, and moving story about Roman Catholicism in a windswept town in Northern England. *Fludd* is young Father Fludd, a mysterious but attractive curate, a transforming power, both angel and devil. So I associated Mantel with writers like Muriel Spark or Beryl Bainbridge or Barbara Pym. But then I read *Eight Months on Ghazzah Street* (1988), an ominous, claustrophobic nightmare, set in Saudi Arabia. It follows the experiences of an expatriate woman, and the tension is relentless. Then there was Mantel's epic novel, *A Place of Greater Safety* (1992), an ambitious, idiosyncratic book set in revolutionary France, which won the *Sunday Express* Book Award.

The more I read, the more I realized that with an adventurous novelist like Hilary Mantel, each book is something completely different: *A Change of Climate* (1994), set in 1950s South Africa and 1970s Norfolk; *An Experiment in Love* (1995), about convent-school girls in the 1960s; *The Giant, O'Brien* (1998), based on the life of a real giant, an Irishman who went to London in 1782 to exhibit himself, and who died there the following year; and her vivid and unsettling novel, *Beyond Black* (2005), about evil spirits and the occult, a bighearted psychic and her coldhearted sidekick, abuse and grotesquerie, and maybe most disturbing of all, her depiction of modern England. Mantel is a satirist with a keen sense of humour.

One of the things I always like about her work is her nuance and complexity, as well as the political dimension. She's interested in the nature of good and evil, personal and public. In 2003, in keeping with her wide-ranging output, she wrote an unconventional memoir, *Giving Up the Ghost*, along with a book of autobiographical short stories, *Learning to Talk*. Her autobiography is unlike any other, but it does provide the context for a lot of that fiction: the childhood in Derbyshire, the convent education, living in Africa and the Middle East, Irish ancestors, and so on. Less expected are her accounts of devastating illness, misdiagnosis, shattering consequences, and ghosts—of the dead and of the imagined—and even a surprising discovery on the very day of our conversation in 2003—which you'll see below.

Hilary Mantel was born in Northern England in 1952. She studied law at the London School of Economics and Sheffield University, but then had to give it up for health reasons, so she turned to fiction. Since the success of the Man Booker, she has moved to a seaside town in Devon. In 2014, she was appointed Dame Commander of the Order of the British Empire, the female equivalent of a knighthood.

Here are two of our conversations, the first from 2003, focussing on her autobiography, *Giving Up the Ghost*, and then from 2012, when we discussed *Wolf Hall* and *Bring Up the Bodies*.

WACHTEL You say that you used to think autobiography was a form of weakness. How is that?

MANTEL The confessional urge that overtakes people, a splurge onto the page, the "poor me" aspect of it, washing your dirty linen in public—all those other metaphors. I badly didn't want to get into that. I had to think long and hard, to ask myself, Is this book really necessary? Has it got any utility outside mere self-indulgence? And in the end, I decided it might have. It was probably worth the attempt, though I feared it might be excruciatingly self-conscious.

WACHTEL You say it's difficult to know where to begin with the story of one's own life, that it's not a matter of simple chronology, and memory doesn't work that way anyway. How did you figure out how to tell the story?

MANTEL I suppose I had a set of memories constellated around the house I grew up in, which was my grandmother's house, on Terrace Street, Milltown, in the north of England. The back yard, the neighbours—these were the backdrops to my earliest memories. I seem to have lived very intensely before I was four years old. And I suppose it was because there were a lot of adults around me, more adults than children, that my memories have content from the adults' world that was going on above my head.

WACHTEL Tell me about that household you grew up in and the extended family.

MANTEL My grandfather was a railway worker. My grandmother, who came from a large Irish family, had been a millworker. My mother was their only child. We lived together, the five of us, my grandparents, my mother, my father, Henry. I was the only child for a long while because my brother was five years younger. It was perfectly happy. I can't tell you how brilliant a start in life it was in many ways, with the caring attention of the older people: my grandmother's sister and her family lived next door to her. It was secure, it was fascinating, and it was the best start in life that you could have had, I think. It only got rather blighted when I went to school.

WACHTEL Is that the terrible thing that happened when you were four? Because you say you lived very intensely until you were four.

MANTEL Yes. Things shut down after that. As a child, I was so busy. I had so many occupations on the go. One of them really was imitating my grandfather or helping him out, as I thought, because I'd made up my mind to be a railwayman. I was convinced that, when I was four, I was going to turn into a boy, and that would solve all my problems. And I had certain military pursuits. I was an Indian brave, and used to spend a great deal of time in a small wigwam erected in my grandmother's sitting room, with the adults stepping around me. I had a sort of sideline in training camels because my grandfather had been a soldier in Palestine, so machine-gunning and training camels figured highly in my life. And then being a Knight of the Round Table also. So you can imagine, with all this going on, it was a bit of a disappointment to be suddenly put into this institution, where it was religion, reading, sums, dinner—what came next?—writing, and then they told you a story. It was so small, it was so dull. And I didn't see why you had to do all this stuff. I thought I was much more use at home, and I just couldn't grasp the compulsory idea of it.

WACHTEL You said you thought you would just check school out, and if you didn't care for it—

MANTEL Yes. If it didn't suit you, you just gave it up, and you went back to your old life. I really didn't see any necessity for education. I seemed to know everything I needed to know, and if you didn't know, you just asked somebody.

WACHTEL Being a knight-errant seemed to be a particular enthusiasm of yours, I think.

MANTEL I didn't learn to read very early, but I had this book of King Arthur and his Knights of the Round Table. And with all these willing adults around, I could get people to read it to me. Once they'd read me a story a number of times, I knew it off by heart, including the dialogue. So when I went to school, I'd address people as "Thou, base Varlet!" if they got on the wrong side of me, and call them a low cur and challenge them—"Throw down the gauntlet!"—that sort of thing. So I was highly unpopular, as you can imagine. But to me, it was just the way you talked. And I continued to live my knightly life inside my head while my outer shell conformed with the sums and the wax crayons and all the rest of it.

WACHTEL You've said that you didn't think you were particularly suited for childhood. Why?

MANTEL No. I seem to have been born old, really.

WACHTEL But all those enthusiasms you've just described are characteristic of young children.

MANTEL They are, yes. There was a fantasy aspect, but I took these enthusiasms quite seriously in that they set out a code of conduct for adult life. They set out a code of honour and a standard of personal conduct, and they say that you have a certain place in the world and particularly one's knightly occupations. It's slaying monsters, rescuing maidens. It may be childish to a degree, but basically it has to do with fairness in the world, equity, getting justice for people.

Of course, the world of childhood is a deeply unfair one, so I lived in a ferment of frustration, knowing what should be done, but being too small and powerless to act. My preoccupations, therefore, were rather precocious. One of the first things I realized when I went to school was that there was a class system of sorts in operation. This was a grim little Catholic village primary school. None of the children were particularly well-off, but there was a kind of hierarchy. Certain children were just looked down on. Funnily enough, given the Church's policy on contraception, they were usually the children from large families.

By the time we were six, we were doing work on two different blackboards, one for the smart ones and one for the dumb ones, so you were chosen at that age, and it seemed to me that there was some kind of prejudice involved. It made me very unhappy, very uncomfortable.

WACHTEL Even though you were one of the smart ones.

MANTEL Well, I was sitting on that side of the room, which seemed accidental to me because I often felt that I was treated as if I were stupid. I think that was partly my own fault because if people asked me what

I considered a stupid question, I simply wouldn't answer it. I was very uncompromising, so I'd just sit there and stare, I suppose, with a contemptuous expression on my face. I was completely oblivious to public opinion.

WACHTEL Is that because of the enormous confidence that was instilled in you in those early years by your extended family?

MANTEL I don't think I was really a confident child. I was rather timid in many ways. But not at the core. I was outwardly timid. My pre-school years mattered a lot because they gave me a place to stand, a place to move away from. But I think I also became hardened against public opinion by the things that went on in my household, the irregular life that my mother and father fell into, which was the cause of a lot of comment and gossip in our village. I had no choice but to go inside my hard shell.

WACHTEL Can you tell me what happened when a boarder moved into your home and never left?

MANTEL When I was six, we moved out of my grandmother's house. My next brother was on the way and we needed more room, so my mother and father moved. When I was seven, a visitor named Jack came, for tea. This visitation went on for a little while, and then one day he came for tea, and he simply stayed. He moved into the main bedroom with my mother, and my father moved into a back bedroom. They lived in that way for three or four years, seemingly unable to cut through the knotty problem of what to do next. And so, as you can imagine in a small village, where everybody minded everybody else's business, this was an occasion for a great deal of finger-pointing and name-calling.

WACHTEL Do you understand why your father stayed?

MANTEL No, I don't really have insight into that. It was as if they didn't know what else to do, economically perhaps. My father was a warehouse clerk. There wasn't much money coming into the household. And divorce was very difficult in those days, quite apart from the fact that we were Catholic. People didn't have money for solicitors either. And yet when all that is said, it was a most peculiar setup because you would think something's going to explode. How can people live in that situation? Surely jealousy and anger must come to the fore and necessitate a parting.

But what actually happened was more of a simmer than a boil, a low simmer of resentment and disinformation and—how can I put it?—an atmosphere of concealment. But as a little child, I was only able to take in what my mother said. No one else gave me any information about the situation. Of course, she tried to pretend that what she was doing was perfectly normal.

WACHTEL Tell me a bit about your mother. She had to leave school at fourteen to work in a textile mill.

MANTEL That's right. The village industry was a textile mill. Most of the women and many of the men were employed there. She was very bright, very pretty, talented, artistic, musical. She would have made a very good actress, I think. But all these opportunities were stifled, and she went right into the mill. You had to earn. So her formal education was cut off, and she was very frustrated, I think, by the fact that life seemed to have closed down on her. She always said that her marriage with my father, Henry, had been over almost as soon as it started, and that she had made a terrible, terrible mistake. While she lived with the consequences, she wasn't going to let it blight her whole life. She was going to have this second chance with Jack.

WACHTEL And what was your father, Henry, like?

MANTEL Quiet, studious, introverted. I say "studious," although he'd had no education either, but he was a reader, he played chess, he was a crossword puzzle fanatic. Just very quiet and reserved and passive, I suppose. He must have been, otherwise I can't make any sense of him living in this situation.

WACHTEL Looking back, have you been able to figure out why your parents' marriage didn't work?

MANTEL My mother's story was that, soon after they were married, she found a cache of letters to my father from another woman, one that he had been seeing during the period of their engagement. Being proud, she wasn't disposed to forgive this, so it seemed that it was all over, she had been deceived, and there could be no going back. Of course, I never heard it from my father's point of view.

WACHTEL As a small child, you felt responsible for your parents' unhappiness. Why do you think that was?

MANTEL I did. Maybe it's the sense I had for a long time of being the "only child," feeling myself to be more adult and to have equal responsibility. I think it was also because I perceived quite early that, if my parents didn't have me, they would be more free, that their lives would be less cluttered and not bound by responsibility. So I thought that my mere existence was a very big factor in their unhappiness because I think, by the time I was four, I powerfully sensed that all was not well with them.

WACHTEL After your mother left your father, taking you and your brothers with her, you never saw him again, and he was never mentioned. You say he might as well have been dead, except that the dead are talked about more.

MANTEL That's right. In 1963, Jack and my mother, my two little brothers and myself moved to another town. I was just coming up to my eleventh birthday. There was a parting of the ways and I never saw or heard from Henry again. And then this morning, just as I was about to leave for our interview, the mail arrived. There was a letter from a woman living in the Manchester area who told me that Henry is dead. It appears that in 1971 he married again, to a widow with daughters from her first marriage. It is one of these daughters who has now written to me. She had read the memoir, and realized that this is the same Henry. She's offering to give me any information I would like about his second marriage and his later life.

I had almost anticipated that something would come of the memoir when it went out into the world, that I would hear something, and now it arrived this morning. I'm still rather shocked. But, of course, I won't know very much more until I get in touch.

It's a very friendly letter, very tactful, very sensitive. And I can't wait to know the story.

Of course, all these years, I've been wondering if I had half-brothers and half-sisters. It appears not. It appears that Henry took on a ready-made family, and there's no mention of other children.

I'm rather shocked to find that he's dead. I somehow imagined he wasn't. Although he would be seventy-seven, he seemed like one of those very lean and fit men who would make old bones, but there you are. So I'm still coming to grips with that, really.

WACHTEL And in all those years, you never tried to find him?

MANTEL No, I didn't. I had been very much turned against him, I suppose, by my mother. During my teenage years, there was a constant litany of his derelictions and stories of how unhappy she'd been, and naturally I took her side because I wasn't being given anything else. But I did remain fond of him because, as much as was in him, he was a good father. It seemed like he was a child himself in some ways. He didn't take responsibility for what was happening in our household; he was more like a kind uncle, I suppose, and in a way he civilized me. If he hadn't taken me to the library and taught me to play chess, no one would have, I suspect. So I feel I owe a lot to him.

When I reached my twenties and was a free agent, I worried that I might be the unwelcome intruder. I assumed that he would marry again. And I wondered, because a lot of people from my past have traced me in recent years, whether he might find me, and it appears from this letter I just received that Henry saw me on television once, and recognized me as his daughter and the very image of his first wife, but it didn't go any further. I wonder if the fact that I'd taken my step-father's name and used it in my professional life seemed to him not so much an act of hostility but an indication that I had chosen. And so I suspect mutual embarrassment kept us apart.

WACHTEL You and your husband were married when you were both still undergraduates, and although marriage gave you a certain stability, it caused a rift between you and the rest of your family. Why?

MANTEL It's inexplicable in any logical terms. My mother was ambitious for me—she didn't mind my having boyfriends, but for some reason, they took against Gerald. He was a perfectly respectable young lad from one of the Manchester Catholic schools, from a stable, professional family whose station in life was well above ours.

When we became serious, both my stepfather, Jack, and my mother turned against him and banned him from the house—well, it's a recipe for failure, isn't it? We'd made our minds up. Theirs was not an advisable course of action, but there it was.

So we got married. People said two could live as cheaply as one, and that was what we tried to do.

WACHTEL How did things get patched up with your family over the years?

MANTEL I think after a time they just accepted that Gerald was there. It was difficult because I've always felt very close to my mother; I was and I am very, very fond of her. To be estranged in this way seemed unnatural. I didn't get on with Jack, so it was just another layer of not getting on. Over the years, they tolerated Gerald but it's only in very recent years that my mother's come to appreciate him as a person.

WACHTEL In your short story "The Clean Slate," the narrator visits her mother, who's in hospital with what seems to be a serious illness. The narrator is trying to come to terms with their relationship. How do you see your relationship with your mother now? Has she read your memoir?

MANTEL She has, but she's not admitting it. She's complaining madly about it to anyone in the family who will listen, but she won't talk to me about it. So silence has fallen, and I find that uncomfortable.

I wrote to her some months before it was published and asked her if she would read it because I hoped that it might open up a discussion, and I hoped, dare I say, since Jack has now been dead for some seven years, that we could do some talking and maybe reconcile our memories by filling in the bits that we don't know about each other's lives. I also hoped she would enlighten me on the family back story. I had wanted to dedicate the book to her and in memory of my stepfather, but she said she didn't want to read the manuscript, so I wasn't able to do that. It was published, I sent her a copy, and since then we haven't spoken about it. After the silence had gone on for some time, I did ask her if she'd read it, but she said no. And you mustn't drive people into lying, I feel, so the best thing is just to drop the topic. My hopes that the memoir might have opened doors for my family have been dashed.

WACHTEL You have an illness you've written about called endometriosis, which you've said stole your life. What happened?

MANTEL When I was eleven my first period happened along, and it was a pretty horrible experience. But in those days, one simply didn't talk about these things, and I thought, well, maybe this is the way it's meant to be, and everyone else is going through this, and I'm a wimp. But actually it was abnormal, and it wasn't until I was twenty-seven that I was diagnosed as having endometriosis, which accounted for the pain. But by the time the diagnosis came along, a great deal had gone wrong in my body, and I had to have surgery, which meant I could never have a child, so a whole part of my life was over.

WACHTEL You were also misdiagnosed as suffering from depression.

MANTEL That's right. I was told that I was mentally ill. I couldn't have these pains. They were not known to medical science. They were caused by stress. Why was I under stress? I was too clever for my own good. I was pursuing an unwomanly course, studying law. I really ought to know my place. I really ought to go and work in a dress shop. And this was the era—we're talking about the early seventies—when young women were routinely treated in that way. The medical establishment was fearfully male, fearfully patronizing.

My GP sent me to a psychiatrist, who put me in a student clinic, where they gave me some seriously heavy-duty tranquilizers that had devastating side effects. For me, the side effects looked uncommonly like madness. So you're in a terrible bind, and you really lose your grip on what is happening to you. You are just trying to avoid being medicated further.

WACHTEL After that surgery when you were twenty-seven, you were supposed to be cured.

MANTEL Yes, but I wasn't. I thought that the surgery would eradicate the endometriosis, but it was impossible to get rid of it at a microscopic level. I'm sure they did their best, but they should actually have warned me that it might come back. Within eighteen months I was in a great deal of pain again, and very frightened until I found out what was happening.

WACHTEL And you've been on drugs that caused you to put on weight, and you write about how physical change affects personality. What's your experience with that?

MANTEL After the endometriosis recurred, I was given drugs to try to damp it down, if possible to eradicate it. The first nine months of treatment transformed me from Cinderella into a pumpkin. I started off treatment at something under 7½ stone and ended up at about 12½, like an amazing, expanding woman. Clothes I got into one week didn't fit me the next week. So I was pretty soon living in a body that I didn't recognize. And when I came off all that treatment, my weight didn't go down again. Of course, it does affect the way people look at you, because in our culture a fat woman is a kind of un-person, and people make all sorts of assumptions about you: that you're a slob, that you're completely undisciplined, that you overeat, that you're not too bright, and that you're lower class. I can probably hold my hand up to that one. But you have to go through it to know. I've seen it from both sides. When I was young and slim, the little girls were all so jealous of me. People would insinuate that I had an eating disorder or a thyroid problem. And they were catty. And I was always accused of living on the end of my nerves. It was as if I was keeping slim by some kind of unfair practice.

Maybe that's another reason why I wanted to write my memoir. I feel this is not me, you know. I needed to tell people that I didn't get like this by sitting on the sofa eating crisps and swigging lager. It just happened. I'm obviously not so oblivious to public opinion as I was when I was a girl.

I also thought that it would be good to talk about the illness that has really shaped my life. Endometriosis is an illness that needs publicity; if it's diagnosed early, it can be cured, but it's a condition that people don't know about. I was beating the drum on behalf of fellow sufferers, I suppose, but to make it meaningful, it had to be put in context.

WACHTEL You've also said that one of the reasons you wanted to write this memoir was to address the issue of childlessness.

MANTEL I have certain thoughts about childlessness, that I haven't seen in print. People talk an awful lot about childlessness, but I don't really find myself responding to what they've said. So I thought, let's have a go at this hot topic. Let's see what I can make of it. It seemed to me that to talk about childlessness meant I had to talk about myself as a child, about the things that happened to me. The reader has to know your hopes and fears and your way of looking at life, and I suppose that's what I was hoping to capture.

WACHTEL You speculate as to what a child might have been like. You even give her a name, Catriona, after a Robert Louis Stevenson novel. What presence does this daughter have in your life now?

MANTEL When Gerald and I first got together, we were only seventeen, and it seems unusual for a young man at that age to be thinking about his possible future children. But we very quickly decided to get married, and he said, "If we had a daughter, could we name her Catriona?" I was very happy about that—we were big Robert Louis Stevenson fans. She acquired a sort of presence, a body, not something I've obsessed about or fantasized about, but as someone who half came into being, a chance missed, or a road you didn't go down. I've sometimes seen this child in dreams. So, yes, she has a sort of presence for me, but not in a morbid way.

WACHTEL You were saying that there were things about childlessness that you felt weren't addressed anywhere that you wanted to talk about.

MANTEL The problem of what happens to women who lose a child in pregnancy is not really addressed because it cuts against the ethics of success. And sometimes women who wish to be reconciled to their childless state find it difficult. The social mood is almost that you can't throw up your hands and say, "Okay. I'm childless. It's not precisely by choice, but I'm going to make the best of it." It's quite hard to do that.

It's not, in a way, socially sanctioned. But I wasn't going to spend the rest of my life mourning the unborn. I realize I have done it at some level, and I think it comes out in the memoir, but you have to get on with your life and know that you exist to be you, not just to reproduce.

WACHTEL Your title for this memoir is *Giving Up the Ghost*, and at one point there's an implication that writing gives life to one's ghosts. Where are yours now?

MANTEL There are various ghosts in the book: the unborn children; chances missed; books I didn't write; words I didn't choose; my father, Henry, of whom, until today, I knew nothing; my stepfather, Jack, who died some years ago; all of my family, all of my Irish family, the ones I remember, the ones who are just names. I often feel conscious of the powerful pulse and flow of their lives through me, but it won't go on, of course. I'm the last. So where they are is between the covers of this book. It's my monument to them.

October 2003

§

WACHTEL Tudor England is such a rich period: Henry VIII and his six wives, the Reformation, the beheadings, the burnings. There have been countless books, movies, television series, even opera. Why did you want to enter the fray?

MANTEL I'm always conscious of untold stories. Historical fiction is in many ways a project of recovery, rediscovery, and sometimes rehabilitation. I felt that Thomas Cromwell's story hadn't been told. He's very central to Henry's reign. He was his chief minister for almost ten years, during the tumultuous decade of the 1530s which saw Katherine of Aragon out, Anne Boleyn in, Jane Seymour in, then Anne of Cleves. So just on wives alone, you have enough for a novel. But, of course, there's a lot more to it, as Cromwell was minister for everything, and he's a fascinating man in his own right. His viewpoint has not been explored.

WACHTEL On first impression, there isn't a lot of romance around Thomas Cromwell. Why him in such depth?

MANTEL He's not a glamour boy, is he? And his private life is very guarded, very hidden. We know he married and had three children. He lost his wife and his two daughters in one of the epidemics of the late 1520s, but never remarried. And yet he's the man who tells Henry VIII who he can go to bed with. A very interesting, precarious position to be in.

WACHTEL Yes, but this is after Henry VIII says, "This is who I want to go to bed with." He facilitates that…

MANTEL Yes, that's quite true. He makes it possible for Henry to fulfil his desires. But at the same time when you look specifically at the Anne Boleyn story, you see there comes a point where Henry no longer desires Anne, but there's much more to it than that because Anne has become a political liability and a threat to Cromwell. So the whole story has political as well as personal ramifications.

What strikes me about Cromwell is the wonderful arc of his story: blacksmith's boy to Earl of Essex—how did he do that?

WACHTEL When did you first encounter Thomas Cromwell?

MANTEL I think it would have been while studying history at school. I went to a Catholic convent school, so although our history teacher was a woman of great integrity, and she didn't feed us a biased version, there were certain assumptions that underlay the history we were taught, which was very conventional. We were to regard Henry's break with Rome as a disaster and a tragedy and heresy. Thomas More was a saint, of course, and Thomas Cromwell was the villain, but there was something about Cromwell that piqued my interest. I do remember writing an enormous essay as a sixth former about the dissolution of the monasteries, which went on for pages and pages. My history teacher was very patient with me.

WACHTEL Were you a good Catholic?

MANTEL This is the thing. I'd long ago become a free thinker of sorts, but I had to hide much of my free thinking under my straw hat and my little navy-blue uniform. But somehow when it came to history, I felt I could break out a little and say what I was beginning to think. I was beginning to read around the syllabus a bit, and I'd become very interested in the way nascent capitalism and nascent Protestantism seemed to work together. If anyone had fed me more facts about Thomas Cromwell at that stage, I think I would have been delighted.

I continued to think about him. And when I was writing my big historical novel, *A Place of Greater Safety*—

WACHTEL About the French Revolution.

MANTEL That's right, yes. That was my first novel, really. I saw myself as a historical novelist, and I thought, oh, maybe Thomas Cromwell next, but life then developed a logic of its own, and I became a contemporary novelist as well. Then I wrote another historical novel, *The Giant, O'Brien*, set in the eighteenth century, and I began to write bits of non-fiction and criticism, all connected with revolution. And I thought, I do not have the energy to start cold with a new period of history where I just don't know where to put my feet, and I don't know what it looks like, and I don't know how it sounds. And then there came the time when I thought, right, it's now or never.

WACHTEL Do you know what the trigger was at that moment?

MANTEL I had made my publisher a proposal for two novels, a more or less contemporary one and the Thomas Cromwell novel, which was supposed to come second. I thought, I'd do the modern one first: no research, easier, and to a great extent based on my own experience. But when I began writing it, it scared the life out of me—it was too close to my own experience. I began to have nightmares about it, and I'd only been writing for weeks. Then one day I decided to give myself a day off, just to see what Thomas Cromwell sounded like. When I'd written the first two paragraphs, almost without premeditation, I felt the most enormous joy. And that might sound strange given the book's violent beginning.

WACHTEL I was just going to say—it's young Thomas Cromwell being beaten up by his father.

MANTEL Yes. Suddenly I realized that I knew everything about the book because we'd be looking through Cromwell's eyes. When I wrote that paragraph, he was lying on the ground, and we were looking, through his eyes, up at his father's boot in very close focus, looking at the twine that held the sole to the boot and the knot in the twine and young Thomas's own blood. And then I thought, this is singular, isn't it? I'll go on for another couple of paragraphs and see how they speak, and I've never had a writing experience quite like it. I suddenly felt, this is what I was meant to do all these years. This is the book I was meant to be writing. I suppose in some way I was subconsciously very well prepared for it, but it just seemed to happen visually, unrolling before me. Nothing after that was easy, but that bit was.

WACHTEL The first line is, "So now get up," which is what the rest of the trilogy is about. He's getting up, not just off the floor, but through social class and through life and so on.

MANTEL Yes. And that's absolutely the key because, when we come to the end of the trilogy, and Cromwell is on the scaffold, we know that he was a man who had had time to reckon with his imminent death and that the same thought would be running through his head: "Now get up, now get up." Once I realized that, ha! Simple. All I've got to do is write the middle.

WACHTEL There's an almost palpable sense of smell and sound and feel to your Cromwell novels. Why is the physical environment especially important to you?

MANTEL Cromwell is a man who experiences the world through sensation. He's a clever man, and he's learned, but he's not an intellectual. His viewpoints aren't rarefied and he's not someone who thinks in abstractions. He's a man with a solid, earthy body and a big fist that grasps materially what he wants. He's a man who's travelled, and he knows the sound of many languages. He knows the smell and sight of the sea. He knows the quality of fabric. He's been a wool trader, and he's lived in Venice, where luxury fabrics are traded. When he sees someone, he immediately assesses what they're wearing. He knows the quality and drape of the fabric. He's not actually touching it, but he's handling it with his eyes, as it were, and it seems to me that the book should be like this: let's know what people eat and drink, how the world presents itself through the senses to them. He'd spent time in Italy, and he could never quite get over that. The sounds and sights of Italy, the sundrenched landscape that still saturates the senses. And he's amazed to find himself living in cold, grey, rainy England. He really feels the cold for all his big body, which he is always feeding on the most delicious things. His uncle was a cook, and it's my supposition, based on a little soupçon of evidence, that he could cook himself and that the pleasures of the table were among the things he valued.

WACHTEL I understand the appeal of Cromwell in terms of moving up from his class and that this would be part of the attraction for you. But your Cromwell doesn't quite fit the cold or ruthless image that's been presented over the centuries. How did you come to see him in such an appealing light?

MANTEL To begin with, I took at face value what is normally presented to you in populist drama and fiction. I thought he was a villain, but an interesting villain. But then I jettisoned all this and thought, Let's write on a blank page, let's try and set aside the prejudices. It was when I went back to first principles and started to read the calendar of state papers, as well as his letters, that I encountered him through his actual words. I got a slightly different perspective on him: here's a man who's got a highly sophisticated intellect. He's obviously eloquent in speech and writing, and he's got an edge of sardonic, black humour, which really appealed to me. I began to study his work and try to see his preoccupations through his work. And what I felt then is, yes, he was a ruthless man, but he was no more ruthless than most of the great men in the reign. And he is, I think, a man driven by a large vision, not just by personal ambition—though I admire him for that—but also by a larger vision of England's future, most of which he couldn't make manifest because he was working against terrific opposition from all sides. But it seems to me that he was a radical in his thinking, and that appeals to me too.

WACHTEL I did read somewhere that he'd pushed more legislation through Parliament than anyone would for the next three hundred years.

MANTEL Yes, that's probably true. He was a beautiful manager of Parliament, which was not always subservient to the king in his desires. There were bits of legislation that he didn't pull off, like his Poor Law of 1534–1535, which, if he had been able to implement it, had the very faint glimmerings of a welfare state that had to care for the economic casualties of the system. To bring in his reforms, his Poor Law, which would have created work, would have meant imposing income tax, and he can imagine how the House of Commons would have liked that. Even though the king went to the Commons to speak for the measure, they simply wouldn't have it, but Cromwell didn't give up. He kept trying to sneak this into legislation, but his political path was destined to get harder and harder as Henry's own political troubles multiplied. It's difficult to imagine the world bogged down in tradition, the static, hierarchical world that he lived in, how hard it was to be a modernizer because people did not regard modern as a term of approbation. They wanted things to be the way they always had been. So someone like Thomas Cromwell came along and mightily and profoundly upset everyone, but in a good cause, I would argue.

WACHTEL *Bring Up the Bodies*, the second in your trilogy, takes place in 1535. Thomas Cromwell is fifty. He's in control of his emotions and has an outward calm and rationality that's in contrast with the passionately driven people who surround him. Did you ever see evidence or suspect any passions in Cromwell?

MANTEL Oh, yes. Although perhaps my reader will see this more in the third part of the trilogy. Just occasionally between the lines of his letters or—no—actually *within* the lines of his letters, you see an explosion of passion. When Jane Seymour dies, it's the only time you find him irrational. He is not only in mourning, he's also angry, and he's irrationally blaming Jane's attendants. This made me think, well, strong feelings are involved here. Maybe he did care about Jane as more than just Henry's third spouse.

WACHTEL But you could see why he might be upset. Jane Seymour wasn't gotten rid of by Henry VIII; she died of postnatal complications after giving birth to a son. So for all kinds of rational reasons, he wouldn't want her to die.

MANTEL Yes, indeed. But it's unlike Cromwell to attribute blame in an irrational fashion, and that's the point I'm making. He had every political reason to be sorry for Jane's demise, but he really seems to be engaged here. So, yes, a man of generally controlled feeling, a man who keeps his feelings tightly bridled, but not a man without feelings, not a machine.

WACHTEL In *Bring Up the Bodies*, you slip in one paragraph that suggests Cromwell has taken up with a woman, an innkeeper, and has had her husband killed. It's almost a throwaway, a rumour, but it's rather shocking. What are we to make of this?

MANTEL The encounter is fictitious. He's on his way up-country at Henry's bidding to find out whether Katherine of Aragon is dying or not. They stay overnight at an inn, and he sleeps with the innkeeper's wife. The next morning they're gone, it's over. The point I'm making is that ridiculous rumours will proliferate, that Cromwell had her husband tried for a crime that no one's ever heard of because Cromwell has just invented it. The story goes that he brought the woman to London, that he set her up in a house and that the husband has been found dead in his cell, hanged, strangled, poisoned, bludgeoned to death. This was the climate of rumour at the time. There is a serious point to it because this is the kind of rumour that surrounds the Boleyns and runs throughout London. What I'm really saying is that when the man on the street gets hold of the story, the merest fact is distorted, it's magnified, it runs away with itself, and you can't recognize the original event in there at all.

WACHTEL The nobility in Henry VIII's court liked to denigrate Cromwell for his low beginnings. Can you talk a bit about how he was viewed by those above him, below him, and his peers?

MANTEL Yes. The thing is, he had no natural constituency because he was just Cromwell, a singular man. He is resented by those above him and resented by those below him. The great lords think it should be their privilege to advise Henry. The common people, instead of applauding the ambition of someone like Cromwell, think that something unnatural has happened. You did what your father did. You didn't rise through the levels of society. You kept on doing what your family had always done. So if a man like Cromwell, from nowhere, could get the ear of the king, how had that happened? Was he a sorcerer? So with the rivalry of those courtiers on a level with him, and enmity from above and below, you can see why, at one stage in the book, he reflects that the king is his only friend. What a friend to have! And that's fine, except what if something were to happen to Henry? What then?

WACHTEL As you were saying earlier, this period, the mid-sixteenth century, was a time of ideological conflict and great political change in England. The country had just recently separated its Church from Rome. This set Henry up as the head of the Church of England, not the Pope in the Vatican, and although this passed in English law, it wasn't without a lot of conflict. How divided did the country remain over this?

MANTEL It's a very good question because there was a strong evangelical movement in England, which had been very well suppressed, certainly as long as Thomas More was Chancellor and was persecuting the people that he called "heretics." There was a sizeable evangelical community in London ready to receive the break with Rome. There were evangelical communities in other towns, particularly weaving towns, but as you go to East Anglia, Essex, and some of the southern counties, it's very uneven. There are other parts of the kingdom, particularly the north, where evangelical ideas don't really seem to have penetrated. So when the divide comes, these people are uncomprehending. Of course, Henry's split is a political one. It's not about doctrine. He's declared himself head of the Church of England, but he's not bringing in Protestant beliefs, and he even resisted for some years the English Bible. However, simply the break with Rome is regarded as schismatic. For most of the old nobility, this is something that they do not understand and will not tolerate. They do not know what Henry's new Church is or what it might become, but they suspect that, because Thomas Cromwell has a strong hand in it, it will become something that's not greatly to their advantage. And, of course, they're right.

So there were many currents. As to Thomas Cromwell himself, it's very hard to say what his affiliation was. He was no more revealing about his spiritual life than any other aspect of his life. But his great cause was the English Bible, and he did finally manage to persuade Henry to agree to the placing of an English Bible in all parish churches. This was one of the great legacies that he left for England, a matter in which he did succeed.

WACHTEL I was going to ask you what sense you have of Cromwell as a believer or not.

MANTEL I think myself he was an evangelical in the broadest sense. I don't think he was a Lutheran. But people would give me an argument about that. He was once asked by ambassadors from Lutheran Germany what he believed, and he nodded across the room to Henry and said, "I believe what he believes." That wasn't necessarily quite the case, but he had to walk a line between his evangelical convictions and Henry's conservatism.

WACHTEL The sixteenth century does seem to be something of a turning point in terms of how people fundamentally saw the world. What distinguishes the sixteenth-century mind from how we see the world today?

MANTEL In some ways—and an author has to be careful about this— their system of metaphor is still medieval. It may be an age of discovery of new views of the solar system, new views of what the universe is all about, a great age of navigation and exploration. But these things take time to come down to the man in the street, who's going to retain his worldview for a couple of generations. So you have to be careful with the metaphors they can make, the way that their senses can register the universe and the ways they experience themselves, as well. You can't have them talking about their subconscious minds, at least not in so many words. It's a truism to say that the individual does seem to come to the fore. Thanks to the printing press and the proliferation of writing, we get to know people in a way that we didn't in earlier eras, when they remained frozen in their posture as Lord Chancellor or bishop or cardinal.

And then comes a flood of personal writing. It's not by individuals yet, but rather by people who observe those individuals; the first real biography in English was written about Cardinal Wolsey from the intimate point of view of one of his household servants. It's as if statues begin to move and speak. At the same time, you've got Holbein fitting individual faces to people who would only otherwise be names.

WACHTEL This is the painter Hans Holbein.

MANTEL Yes. Holbein is Henry's court painter, going with him on all his summer holidays, enjoying all the young gentlemen and all the young ladies and unfortunately not putting their names on the pictures because everybody would know who they were. This is an insiders' world. They weren't doing this for posterity, just for themselves. But the delineation of individual personality becomes worthwhile. It becomes a fit subject for an artist. He's moving away from the prescribed subjects for religious art into observing the quirks of personality.

WACHTEL There are two other key characters in *Bring Up the Bodies*: Henry VIII and Anne Boleyn. Your Henry is a multifaceted personality. Tell me a bit about how you see him.

MANTEL He's a hard character to bring onto the page. When Cromwell first sees him, he sees him flat against the light, like a playing card king, huge and brightly dressed and filling all the space around him. There's just that little pause before Henry begins to move and to speak. He's like all the characters, like Cromwell himself. He's a work in progress to me, an almost impossible character to make decisions about, to give a judgment on, because he's so volatile, he's so capricious. And he has this hearty exterior; no one is more sporting and athletic and "Hail, fellow, well met" and hard and masculine than Henry. Inside him you feel there's a seething mass of insecurity but also a fine mind, which is something we tend to forget about Henry. He was beautifully educated. He had intellectual interests, and he prided himself on his facility with languages, his knowledge of theology.

WACHTEL He wrote poetry.

MANTEL He wrote poetry and he was a musician. He was a man of culture, in other words. At Henry's court, such qualities were not incompatible with being brilliant at jousting and tennis and hunting. These courtiers were Renaissance men. But you do feel that a lot of the time Henry is forced into the company of people who are not his intellectual equals, and therefore he grasps at someone like Wolsey and exalts him in the hierarchy, just as he grasps at someone like Thomas Cromwell. These are the people who can tell him something, whose quality he recognizes. He was, of course, the focus of all ambition, particularly for Cromwell, who didn't come up through the Church.

But what strikes me—and it's one of the things I wanted to write about—is this: what can it have been like to deal with Henry day by day? You never knew what you were going to find, what stratagems he would have come up with, whether he'd be the same man as yesterday, what strange demands he would make on you. You had to be very adroit and very resilient.

WACHTEL How would you describe their relationship? For a time, Henry does seem to trust Cromwell.

MANTEL When Cromwell fell from power in the summer of 1540 it was quite abrupt, and Thomas Cranmer, the Archbishop of Canterbury, wrote the king a very courageous letter. Cranmer asked, "Who will Your Grace trust hereafter if you cannot trust him?" I think it was a fairly good question because Henry never found another servant like Cromwell. He recognized this only a short time after Cromwell's death, and he accused other people of having manipulated the situation and poisoned his mind against "the most faithful servant I ever had." The point was that Cromwell could not have an agenda of his own. Everything came to him through Henry, and only Henry could keep him in his position and add to his honours, unlike Cardinal Wolsey who could look to be pope. Cromwell couldn't look to be king, although strangely that was what he was ultimately accused of.

WACHTEL Obviously you're involved in writing the third instalment now because you're pointing more towards Cromwell's end than in *Wolf Hall* and *Bring Up the Bodies*. But when you were writing the first two volumes, you knew that in the not-too-distant future, that this man on the rise, the man near the top, was going to precipitously fall. How does that affect your perception as you're writing these other books?

MANTEL Just as Cromwell doesn't know his end, it's my job for the moment not to know his end because there's a great deal more writing to be done before the fall. In the earlier part of the next volume, he goes from strength to strength. Even when we reach 1540, the year of his ultimate fall, at that point in the spring when it seemed as if circumstances had turned decisively against Cromwell, Henry turned around and made him Earl of Essex, and he was in greater standing than ever before. The fall then followed within weeks. He didn't have very long to enjoy that dignity.

But it's not the story of a fall; it's the story of the rise and rise and rise and then the sudden fall, which will be contained, I should think, in the final chapter of the book. I still remain interested in his climb. But I know, as Cromwell knew, how precarious all this is. Even within the ambit of the time covered by *Bring Up the Bodies*, Chapuys, the imperial ambassador, reported a conversation he'd had with Cromwell, in which he asked, "What will you do if Henry turns on you one day?" Cromwell replied, "I will possess myself in patience, and I will leave it to God," which ultimately was all you could do. One slip at Henry's court could be fatal. The stakes were so high. Nowadays if a government minister makes an error, he gets to apologize, he may have to resign. In those days, you could find yourself in the Tower. And it wasn't just a question of making an error. It was a question of, Could you continue to please Henry? Which meant that you had always to be guessing how you could please him. In some ways, you had to be one step ahead of him.

WACHTEL Henry VIII famously or infamously had his first marriage to Spain's Katherine of Aragon annulled because he wanted to marry Anne Boleyn, whom he hoped would produce a male heir. This happens at the end of *Wolf Hall*. What do we know about Anne Boleyn?

MANTEL We know quite a lot about her for a sixteenth-century woman. We don't know her actual date of birth. We're guessing around 1501, making her in her mid-thirties at the time of her death. We know a fair bit about her family because her father, Thomas Boleyn, was a leading courtier and a diplomat. We know a little about her girlhood, when she spent time at the French court as a lady-in-waiting and became thoroughly Frenchified. We know about her debut at the English court, dancing in a yellow dress and wearing a mask. We know about her sister, Mary Boleyn, who was Henry's mistress before his fancy lighted on Anne. And then she really comes into the record as the king makes a move on her. We have some of her books, some of her letters. She has a voice in a way that many women of the time didn't. And then we see her through the eyes of other people: a glamorous woman, chic, as we would say nowadays, not conventionally good-looking, but with wonderful eyes, a magnetic glance, really sexy, charismatic, daring, ambitious for herself, bold in her manoeuvres, a woman of quite subtle judgment. And one thing Anne did know or appeared to know at that stage was how to manipulate Henry, keeping him from losing interest in her personally and sexually during the years when their cause was just stuck and, Henry couldn't get his divorce. This dragged on year after year, but still Anne kept him fascinated.

In *Bring Up the Bodies*, I have one of her attendants say, "You know, she thought every day will be like her coronation," and of course it isn't. Even a queen must face the realities of married life. And Anne isn't lucky. She's promised Henry an heir. She gives him an heir but it's a daughter. And then she miscarries two children. She becomes afraid. She lashes out and becomes shrewish. She's on the run. She makes enemies. She was never liked by the grandees of Henry's court who saw her as an upstart responsible for pushing the sainted Katherine out of the way. They didn't like what she represented, and they were ready to unite and force her out when the moment came.

WACHTEL You suggest we might recognize ourselves in the historical figures in *Wolf Hall* and *Bring Up the Bodies*. What about you? Do you see yourself in any of them?

MANTEL Oh, no. I think it's the author's job to efface herself of the text and the story.

WACHTEL Yes, but really. A little bit of Cromwell?

MANTEL I wouldn't be giving away any secrets if I say I'm more interested in people who have a long way to climb in the world than in people who are born to the purple. So I'm less interested in Henry himself or his wives than I am in someone like Cardinal Wolsey, the butcher's son, or Thomas Cromwell, the blacksmith's son, because ambition has always interested me. I've always possessed it. And I have to realize that I've had it easy because in my lifetime ambition has been thought of as a virtue whereas the sixteenth century saw it as a vice. So it's a completely different world. But, yes, my sympathies are with those who have a long way to climb. I think also I look at Cromwell wistfully because he's so bouncy, he's so resilient, he's so thick-skinned, whereas all authors—it's commonly known—have one skin too few. And there's a kind of merriment in writing about someone who's so different from your shrinking little self, and I look at him with envy and, as I said, a kind of wistfulness. Oh, why can't I be more like Thomas Cromwell?

June 2012
Original interviews produced by Mary Stinson

W.G. SEBALD

After scarcely a five-year career in the English-speaking world—from the translation of *The Emigrants* in 1996 to the publication (in German and English) of *Austerlitz* in 2001—W.G. Sebald died in a car accident near his home in Norwich, England, on December 14, 2001. He was driving his daughter, a schoolteacher, when his car jumped lanes at a curve and crashed into an oncoming truck. (His daughter was seriously injured, but has since recovered.) It's believed that he suffered an aneurysm. Before his death, *Austerlitz* had been named one of the best nine books of the year by *The New York Times*; after he died, it won the American National Book Critics Award and the *Independent* newspaper's Foreign Fiction Prize. Sebald had been widely praised, his work declared a masterpiece, and even touted as possible Nobel Prize material. And it all happened so fast.

I felt a personal sadness at his death. Sebald was the master of desolation, absence, of quietly beautiful, haunting prose—not only in those two titles that evoke the Holocaust but also in more allusive work like *The Rings of Saturn* (1995, trans. 1998) and *Vertigo* (1990, trans. 1999). Then, only fifty-seven, he himself was absent, lost. But as his books continued to appear, translated into English out of chronological order, I was reminded of what he'd said during our conversation. Describing his village high in the Alps, he talked about how, because the ground was frozen, you couldn't bury the dead in winter. First they remained in the house, in the living room for a while, and then in the woodshed for a month or two. That is how, he said, he grew up with a certain familiarity with the dead and dying, and more than that, a sense that "these people aren't really gone, they just hover somewhere at the perimeter of our lives and keep coming in on brief visits." So, his works such as *After Nature* (1988, trans. 2002) and *On the Natural History of Destruction* (1999, trans. 2003) brought his voice back with particular astuteness.

Winfried Georg Maximilian Sebald, who liked to be called Max, was born in May 1944 in Wertach im Allgäu in the Bavarian Alps, into a working-class Catholic family. Because the time and place were so freighted with history, he wanted to trace his life back to the point of its conception. His father had joined the army in 1929 and prospered as a career soldier during the 1930s, marrying in 1936. Sebald describes a photograph taken during a furlough in August 1943—picturing his parents carefree in a botanical garden, with a swan reflected in the pond, "a perfect emblem of peace," his father in lederhosen and loden jacket, his mother in an open coat—which he determines is when he was conceived. The next day, his father was posted to Dresden. Two days later, during the night, 582 aircraft firebombed Nuremberg (a subject Sebald returned to).

His father ended the war a prisoner in France, not getting back to Germany until 1947, so Sebald didn't see him until he was three. "At the end of the war," he wrote, "I was just one year old, so I can hardly have any impressions of that period of destruction based on personal experience. Yet to this day, when I see photographs or documentary films dating from the war I feel as if I were its child, so to speak, as if those horrors I did not experience cast a shadow over me, and one from which I shall never entirely emerge." When he was eight, his family moved from Wertach to Sonthofen, a small town nineteen kilometres away, where he encountered the teacher Paul Bereyter, whose life became one of his subjects in *The Emigrants*.

Ten years later, he left to study German literature at the University of Freiburg. Two things troubled him there: physically, it was terribly overcrowded with lecture halls filled with 1200 students and seminars of 150; intellectually, he felt the faculty was tainted by association with the Nazi past. "Those who had chairs at the time and even aspiring younger teachers had done their doctorates in the '30s or '40s and in one way or another, the study of German literature was very much an implicated discipline; that is, they actively condoned and supported the regime," he told me. "The structures were authoritarian and we were given only a quarter of the truth."

He always assumed he'd go to America, as many members of his family had, but during the anti-Vietnam '60s, the United States had lost its lustre, and hearing about a language assistantship in Manchester, he went there for graduate work. He taught briefly in Switzerland and then worked for the Goethe Institute in Munich. He even briefly considered the latter as a career. It's curious to try to imagine him, with his oblique, private, critical, elegiac sensibility, as a professional, an official representative and promoter of German culture. But he returned to England and an academic career. For the next twenty years, Sebald was a professor of European literature at the University of East Anglia, publishing scholarly works in German, although hints of his famous melancholy—he was born, as he pointed out, under the sign of Saturn—surfaced in such titles as *Describing Unhappiness*, a collection of essays on Austrian writers from Adelbert Stifter to Peter Handke.

In 1988, while continuing to teach, he published his first work of creative writing—as he himself put it—a three-part prose poem, *After Nature*—narratives about three very different men: the sixteenth-century painter Mathias Grunewald; the eighteenth-century botanist-explorer Georg Steller, and Sebald himself. When questioned later about this shift from academic writing, he attributed it to a need to escape the unpleasant teaching conditions and work pressures of Thatcherite England. But his non-academic output over the next dozen years—four "novels," two books of poetry, essays—bespeaks a quiet passion, even obsession, whose sources go deeper. He chose a form that was much more common in Europe than in the Anglo-Saxon world, creating a genre of documentary fiction that involved the crossing of boundaries between fiction and non-fiction. Mediated through a sensibility, a dislocated voice that seems to be Sebald's own, an elusive persona that is often unwell or recovering from some nameless illness or uneasiness, the books have no ordinary plot. They also feature uncaptioned, often blurry, black and white photographs, as if from another time, of houses, landscapes, documents and diaries, family groups, school children, and hotel postcards.

I spoke to Max Sebald in 1998 when only one of his books, *The Emigrants*, was available in English.

WACHTEL *The Emigrants* is variously called a novel, a narrative quartet, or simply unclassifiable. How would you describe it?

SEBALD It's a form of prose fiction. I imagine it exists more frequently on the European continent than in the Anglo-Saxon world, i.e. dialogue plays hardly any part in it at all. Everything is related round various corners in a periscopic sort of way. In that sense it doesn't conform to the patterns that standard fiction has established. There isn't an authorial narrator. And there are various limitations of this kind that seem to push the book into a special category. But what exactly to call it, I don't know.

WACHTEL You've put together four stories of four different lives that have connections and resonate but seem to be discrete in the telling. Why did you want to write about them together in *The Emigrants?*

SEBALD Because the patterns are remarkably similar. They are all stories about suicide or, to be more precise, suicides at an advanced age, which is relatively rare but quite frequent as a symptom of what we know as the survivor syndrome.

I was familiar with that particular symptom in the abstract, through such cases as Jean Améry, Primo Levi, Paul Celan, Tadeusz Borowski, and various others who failed to escape the shadows which were cast over their lives by the Shoah and ultimately succumbed to the weight of memory. That tends to happen quite late in these people's lives, when they're in retirement age, as it were, when all of a sudden some kind of void opens up. The duties of professional life recede into the background and then, you know, time for thought is there all of a sudden. As I was working at one point round about 1989, 1990, on Jean Améry, in particular because he originated from an area not far from the area in which I grew up, it occurred to me that in fact I did know four people who fitted that particular category almost exactly. And it was at that point that I became preoccupied with these lives, started looking into them, travelled, tried to find all the traces I could possibly find, and in the end, had to write this down.

The stories as they appear in the book follow pretty much the lines or the trajectories of these four lives as they were in reality. The changes that I made, i.e. extending certain vectors, foreshortening certain things, adding here and there, taking something away, are marginal changes, changes of style rather than changes of substance. In the first three stories there is almost a one-to-one relationship between these lives and the lives of the people I knew. In the case of the fourth story I used two different foils, one of a painter who currently still works in England and the other a landlord I had in Manchester when I first moved there. And because the landlord I had in Manchester is still alive today, I didn't want him to appear, as it were, in an undisguised form in what is essentially a work of documentary fiction, so I introduced this second foil in order to make it less obvious. But they're pretty much the same life stations that these people went through that I knew very well.

WACHTEL You say at one point that it's "as if the dead were coming back, or as if we were on the point of joining them." This idea seems to preoccupy you.

SEBALD Well, I don't quite know what the reason for that is, except that death entered my own life at a very early point. I grew up in a very small village, very high up in the Alps, about three thousand feet above sea level. And in the immediate postwar years when I grew up there, it was in many ways quite an archaic place. For instance, you couldn't bury the dead in the winter because the ground was frozen and there was no way of digging it up. So you had to leave them in the woodshed for a month or two until the thaw came. You grew up with this knowledge that death is around you, and when and if someone died, it happened in the middle or in the centre of the house, as it were, the dead person went through their agonies in the living room, and then before the burial they would be still part of the family for possibly three, four days. So I was from a very early point on very familiar, much more familiar than people are nowadays, with the dead and the dying. I have always had at the back of my mind this notion that of course these people aren't really gone, they just hover somewhere at the perimeter of our lives and keep coming in on brief visits. And photographs are for me one of the emanations of the dead, especially these older photographs of people no longer with us. Nevertheless, through these pictures, they do have what seems to me some sort of a spectral presence. And I've always been intrigued by that. It's got nothing to do with the mystical or the mysterious. It is just a remnant of a much more archaic way of looking at things.

If you go, for instance, to a place like Corsica... Nowadays of course it's not quite the same, but very recently, twenty years ago, the dead in Corsican culture had an unquestioned presence in the lives of the living. They were always reckoned with, they were always seen to be just round the corner, they were always seen to be coming into the house of an evening to get a crust of bread or to march down the main street as a gang with drums and fifes. And in more atavistic cultures, of which there were pockets in Europe until, I would think, about the 1960s, there is always a presence of these departed. And certainly there were areas in the Alps in the postwar years where that was also the case. Now it's all obliterated, of course. But somehow it got stuck in my mind, and I think it's possibly from that quarter that my preoccupation stems.

WACHTEL You include many photographs with your text—of the people, the places, cityscapes or landscapes, and they're very evocative, they're haunting. In the narrative they seem to trigger a search. You see a photograph or you look at an album or someone shows you something, and then that takes you somewhere.

SEBALD Well, the pictures have a number of different sources of origin and also a number of different purposes. But the majority of the photographs do come from the albums that certainly middle-class people kept in the thirties and forties. And they are from the authentic source. Ninety per cent of the images inserted into the text could be said to be authentic, i.e. they are not from other sources used for the purpose of telling the tale.

I think they have possibly two purposes in the text. The first and obvious notion is that of verification—we all tend to believe in pictures more than we do in letters. Once you bring up a photograph as proof of something, then people generally tend to accept that, well, this must have been so. And certainly even the most implausible pictures in *The Emigrants* would seem to support that, the more implausible they are. For instance, the photograph of the narrator's great-uncle in Arab costume in Jerusalem in 1913 is an authentic photograph. It's not invented, it's not an accident, not one that was found and later inserted. So the photographs allow the narrator, as it were, to legitimize the story that he tells. I think this has always been a concern in realist fiction, and this is a form of realist fiction. In the nineteenth century, certainly in the German tradition, the author is always at pains to say, Well, this is where I got it from, I found this manuscript on top of a cupboard in this or that town in such and such a house and so on and so forth, in order to give his whole approach an air of legitimacy.

The other function that I see is possibly that of arresting time. Fiction is an art form that moves in time, that is inclined towards the end, that works on a negative gradient, and it is very, very difficult in that particular form in the narrative to arrest the passage of time. And as we all know, this is what we like so much about certain forms of visual art—you stand in a museum and you look at one of those wonderful pictures somebody did in the sixteenth or the eighteenth century. You are taken out of time, and that is in a sense a form of redemption, if you can release yourself from the passage of time. And the photographs can also do this—they act like barriers or weirs which stem the flow. I think that is something that is positive, slowing down the speed of reading, as it were.

WACHTEL One critic describes you as a ghost hunter. Do you see yourself that way?

SEBALD Yes, I do. I think that's pretty precise. It's nothing ghoulish at all, just an odd sense that in some way the lives of people who are perhaps no longer here—and these can be relatives or people I vaguely knew, or writer colleagues from the past, or painters who worked in the sixteenth century—have an odd presence for me, simply through the fact that I may get interested in them. And when you get interested in someone, you invest a considerable amount of emotional energy and you begin to occupy this person's territory, after a fashion. You establish a presence in another life through emotional identification. And it doesn't matter how far back that is in time. This seems to be quite immaterial somehow. And if you only have a few scraps of information about a certain sixteenth-century painter, if you are sufficiently interested, it nevertheless allows you to be present in that life or to retrieve it into the present present, as it were.

One of the first things I wrote was a long prose poem [*After Nature*] about the early sixteenth-century painter Matthias Grunewald, about whom we know hardly anything at all apart from his pictures. And it's these lacunae of ignorance and the very few facts that we have that were sufficient somehow for me to move into this territory and to look around there and to feel, after a while, quite at home. It interests me considerably more than the present day... I mean, going to Rio de Janeiro or to Sydney is something that I find entirely alien. You couldn't entice me there. The fact that I'm now in America seems extremely strange to me.

WACHTEL One of your subjects in *The Emigrants* is a former school-teacher of yours named Paul Bereyter. What made you want to get beyond your own, as you put it, very fond memories and discover the story that you didn't know?

SEBALD In the town in which I grew up—we moved when I was seven or eight years old from a village to the nearest small town—I went to the primary school where I was taught by this particular teacher. And in this town throughout the postwar years when I grew up, between the ages of eight and eighteen, no one ever mentioned that this man had gone through years of persecution, had been ousted from his teaching post in 1935, and then had come back after 1945 to pick up the loose threads again. Everybody knew about it. A small town that had, I don't know, eight thousand inhabitants—everybody knew everybody else's business. The teacher himself of course—and that is the most perplexing aspect of that whole tale—never mentioned it either. And so clearly, as I was very attached to him as a boy—I admired this man greatly—I did want to find out the truth about it. And at that level you might describe it almost in the first instance as a piece of investigative journalism. Once you get hold of a thread you want to pull it out and you want to see, you know, what the colours of the pattern are. And the more difficult it gets—as it did in this case, because nobody in the town was prepared to talk to me about that life—the more intrigued you become, the more you know that there is something buried there. And the less you want to give up on it.

WACHTEL Why wouldn't they to talk to you? This is forty, fifty years later.

SEBALD Yes. Well, you know, the conspiracy of silence still lasts. It is something which people in other countries can scarcely imagine. It continues to puzzle me that when I grew up there, even when I was beginning to be capable of rational thought, as it were, at the age of sixteen or seventeen or so, this was scarcely fifteen years after the war. If I think back from the present moment in time, from 1997, sixteen or seventeen years back to 1980, it seems to me like yesterday. And so for my parents, for my teachers in 1960 or thereabouts, these calamitous years from 1941 to 1946, 1947, or so must have seemed like yesterday. And if you imagine that you have gone through such a dreadful phase of history, implicated in it in the most horrendous way, you might think that there would be an urge to talk about it. But I think that conspiracy of silence... it just came about, as it were. And it held, I think, even between married partners. I cannot imagine my parents, for instance, ever talking about these matters between themselves. It was just a taboo zone which you didn't enter. I think these self-generated taboo zones are always the most powerful ones.

WACHTEL Because Bereyter was one-quarter Jewish he was not allowed to teach, he was rejected by the townspeople, he went to live abroad. But then he came back to Germany in 1939. Why?

SEBALD I think there are quite good reasons for that, if you imagine the actual scenario. He must have been about twenty-two, twenty-three, at the time. There is a photograph in the text which shows him with this family near Besançon on a Sunday afternoon, where he had gone to be a private tutor in a middle-class household after he had been ousted from his teaching post. He looks extremely thin and emaciated in that picture. One can conclude even just from that, that he must have been through what for him was quite a harrowing transition. Now, if you imagine France in the late 1930s and the young—what he was to all intents and purposes—a young German, partly Jewish schoolteacher sharing the dinner table of his employers every day, having taught the children in the morning, listening to the conversation around that dinner table, extended conversations as they tended to be in France... Midday meals would last for a couple of hours, and there would be plenty of opportunity for the paterfamilias to hold forth about his political views and opinions. And in French middle-class life I think the general inclination at the time was very much towards the right, i.e. the messages which came out of Germany through the news, through the radio, through the papers were very frequently endorsed: This is how you do it, this is what we should be doing. So by going to France, in a sense he didn't escape it. Ironically, all these things have come very much into the foreground over the last few weeks and months. Today in *The New York Times* you have a report about the Maurice Papon trial in Bordeaux. And this is all, as it were, connected with this particular tale.

So I think he must have felt quite an acute sense of discomfort in France. And of course by the late summer of 1939 one began to have an idea that, well, things were going to be very critical soon. So perhaps he did return to Germany because simply this was the place he knew best. And also I think, as the text makes clear at one or two points, he was very much in the German mold, this young teacher. An idealist coming out of the Wandervogel movement, as it were, a little bit like the young Wittgenstein when *he* went to upper Austria to teach the peasant children there, full of idealism, educational zeal, and so on. And this return to Germany in that sense is not altogether surprising.

The curious thing, of course, is that he was then drafted into the German army—as a three-quarter Aryan you were allowed, it was possible to serve in the army—and that he survived the whole war and did go back to the town where he had begun his career as a schoolteacher. That is to my mind the more puzzling side of this particular person's life: the return to Germany in 1945 or the staying there, and repressing, as it were, or being silent about all those dreadful things.

WACHTEL And then even later, after he retired, Paul Bereyter went to Switzerland. But he kept a flat in that same town where at this point he loathed the people.

SEBALD Yes, quite.

WACHTEL Could you understand why?

SEBALD Well, it's all in the nature of the double bind, isn't it? The psychologists know all about this. You want nothing more than to leave your parents, but you can't bring yourself to do it because you fear that they will despise you for leaving them alone. It's that sort of pattern. I mean, whatever you do is going to be wrong. And I think double binds govern, to a greater or lesser extent, almost all lives. Of course this is a particularly devastating form of double bind, if you are bound, as it were, to the nation that has done harm to you. But there are many Jewish-German stories which are exactly of that ilk.

WACHTEL A friend of Bereyter's talks about "the contrarieties that are in our longings."

SEBALD Yes. The history of Jewish-German assimilation, which goes back to the late eighteenth century, is full of this kind of ambivalence. Jewish names like Schiller and Lessing for instance—Jewish people took those on in admiration of the writers who they saw as the champions of enlightenment and tolerance. There was a very, very close identification between the Jewish population in Germany and the gentile population. And especially between the Jewish population and the country, the topography of the country, through their surnames. They were called Frankfurt or Hamburger or Wiener. They were, as it were, identified with these places. And it must have been extremely hard for them to abandon all this and to forget about it.

I'm essentially interested in cultural and social history, and the relationship between the Jewish minority in Germany and the larger population is one of the most central and most important chapters of German cultural history from the eighteenth century to the present day in one form or another. And if you have a wish to understand, as I did have quite early on, the cultural environment in which you're brought up, with all its flaws and terrible aspects, then there is no way past this issue. I talked before about the conspiracy of silence in, for instance, my hometown. And of course when I went up to university at the age of nineteen, I thought it might be different there. But it wasn't, not at all. The conspiracy of silence certainly dominated German universities throughout the 1960s.

At the same time of course, i.e. precisely at the time when I began to use my own brain, as it were, the great war crime trials, the Auschwitz trial in Frankfurt which lasted for many months, the Treblinka trial in Düsseldorf, and various other trials of this kind took place, and the problem for the first time for my generation became a very public one. It was in the newspapers every day, there were lengthy reports about court proceedings and so on. And so you had to contend with this. There was evidence of what had occurred, evidence in no uncertain terms. And yet at the time you were sitting in your seminars at university, you know, reading a piece of romantic fiction, E.T.A. Hoffmann or something, and never referring in any of those cases to the real historical background, to the social conditions, to the psychological complications caused by social conditions and so on. That is, what we were doing at university was pure and unadulterated philology, and this didn't get us any closer to what we wanted to know. Certainly for me it was always so. I think all children know this—if something is withheld from you, you want it all the more. And certainly from the age of eighteen or nineteen onwards, I was always bent on trying to find out about these matters.

WACHTEL Many of your family chose to emigrate to America, but you chose England eventually. Why?

SEBALD In a historical accident. As a boy, my ambition was to go to America because America was the ideal country, at that time. But later on I had this, as it were, anti-American phase, which was part of growing up in Europe in the 1960s, where everything was very anti-American, and that must have cured me of my desire to go to America. When I was about twenty-one—this is round about the time I left the European continent—I had no clear idea as to where I wanted to go. And Manchester, which is where I ended up, happened quite accidentally. I was looking for a job which would allow me to earn some money and continue my studies. I knew there were these language-assistant posts in British universities, and I wrote off to some of them and Manchester replied positively. So I packed my case and went there, thinking that I might be there for a year or two or three until I got a doctorate and so on. But then eventually I got stuck in that country, because as it turned out, it's even nowadays a very pleasant country to live in.

WACHTEL Although at one point, after studying in Manchester, you said you tried to live in Switzerland and also in Munich, and it didn't work. Why not?

SEBALD The episode in Switzerland was in the German-speaking part, in a small town called Saint Gallen. I taught at a private school there, which was run by some mafioso, you know, who got much more money from the students per month, or from one student per month, than he would pay a teacher. The whole setup was bizarre, and I knew from the first day I was there that I wouldn't do it for more than nine months, and this was what happened. Also the German part of Switzerland, beautiful though it is still—you do come across an enormous number of people who are terribly interfering. If you dig your garden on a Sunday, they'll denounce you to the police. I just cannot live with this kind of thing.

The year I spent in Munich and thereabouts I was working for a German cultural institute, the quite well-known Goethe Institute. This was after I had taken my doctorate in England and I was looking for a career, and I thought I might do that. But as it turned out, I found it too officious, representing Germany, however obliquely, in a public sort of way abroad. I felt, when I saw it from closer up, that it wasn't me and that I'd rather go back and live in hiding, as it were.

WACHTEL In hiding?

SEBALD Well, where I am now is very much out in the sticks. It's in a small village near Norwich in the east of England. And I do feel that I'm better there than I am elsewhere in the centre of things. I do like to be on the margins if possible.

WACHTEL What attachment do you feel to Germany now?

SEBALD Well, I know it's my country. Even after all those years. I've been out of it now for... it must be well over thirty years. Longer out of it than in it. Although of course I come from the edges, as it were, the southern edges of Germany. My granddad's house was on the Austrian border, almost directly. I hardly knew Germany. When I left it I knew the territory where I had grown up and I knew Freiburg and I had been to Munich once or twice. But one didn't really travel terribly much in the mid-'60s or early '60s. And so I hardly knew it. I didn't know Frankfurt, I didn't know Hamburg, I didn't know anything in the north or the middle—Hanover, Berlin, were all totally alien to me. So in a sense it's not my country. But because of its peculiar history and the bad dive that history took in this century or, to be more precise, from about 1870 onwards, I feel you can't simply abdicate and say, well, it's nothing to do with me. I have inherited that backpack and I have to carry it whether I like it or not.

WACHTEL And you still write in German.

SEBALD And I still write in German, yes. There are very few writers who write in two languages, even people as accomplished as Nabokov. Once Nabokov had moved across from Russian to English, he stayed in English. He still used Russian for translation purposes. But he didn't, as far as I know, write in that language after he had made the transition. Making the transition as Nabokov does is a very, very risky and harrowing business. And so far I have tried to avoid making that decision. There aren't many other writers that I can think of who had to contend with that particular problem. There is Elias Canetti, who lived for many decades in London before he returned to Zurich, who spoke English perfectly well but never wrote a line in English, to the best of my knowledge. I think it is quite difficult to reach a level of sophisticated competence in a language. Even if you can babble on, it doesn't mean that you can write it well. That's quite a different proposal.

WACHTEL Since you mention Vladimir Nabokov, there are references in *The Emigrants* to a man with a butterfly net, the boy with the butterfly net, Nabokov himself. Why does he hover over this book?

SEBALD I think the idea came to me when I was thinking of writing the story of that painter. This particular story, as you know, contains among other things, as a secondary narrative, the childhood memoirs of the painter's mother. These are to quite a substantial extent authentic, based on authentic materials. I had the disjointed notes which that lady had written in the time between her son's emigration to England and her own deportation; she had about eighteen months to write these notes. As you know from the text, this family had lived in a small village in northern Bavaria, upper Franconia, called Steinach, then around 1900 moved to the nearest town, the spa town of Bad Kissingen. And if you read Nabokov's *Speak, Memory*, his autobiography, which to my mind is a wonderful book, there is an episode in it where he says that his family went to Bad Kissingen several times in exactly those years. So the temptation was very great to let these two exiles meet unbeknownst to each other in the story. And I also knew— and this is based on fact, it's not something that I artificially adjusted later on—that my great-uncle Ambros Adelwarth had interned himself in an asylum in Ithaca, which is where Nabokov taught for many years. And where, as one knows from his writings, he was always in his spare time going out with his butterfly net. So it seemed a very, very strange coincidence that two locations in the stories that I would have to write about were also Nabokov locations. Of course I also knew extremely well, from my time in the French part of Switzerland, the area around Lac Le Mans and Montreux and Vevey and Basel-Stadt and Lausanne. I knew all these places quite intimately. I didn't know of Nabokov, of course, when I was a student there; I hadn't got quite that far. I didn't know he lived there, and even if I had known, I wouldn't have dared to call on him, as you can imagine. But I knew the whole territory and I knew these lifts going up into the mountains that he talks about. And so it seemed an obvious thing to do and, again, an opportunity to create something which has a kind of haunting, spectral quality to it, something that appears, forms of apparitions of virtual presence that have, vanishing though they are, a certain intensity which can otherwise be not very easily achieved.

WACHTEL I think one critic sees it as a sign of joy and another as foretelling death.

SEBALD It's both, of course. People always want what seems to them to be symbolic elements in a text to have single meanings. But of course that isn't how symbols work. If they are any good at all they are usually multivalent. They are simply there to give you a sense that there must be something of significance here at that point, but what it is and what the significance is, is entirely a different matter.

I think that it was a question of trying to find, in a text of this kind, ways of expressing heightened sensations, as it were, in the form of symbols which are perhaps not obvious. But certainly the railway business, for instance. The railway played a very, very prominent part, as one knows, in the whole process of deportation. If you look at Claude Lanzmann's *Shoah* film, which to my mind is one of the most impressive documents of this whole fraught business, there are trains all the time, between each episode. They run along the tracks, you see the wagons, and you see the signals and you see railway lines in Poland and in the Czech Republic and in Austria and in Italy and in Belgium. The whole logistics of deportation was based on the logistics of the railway system. And I do pick that up at one point when I talk about my primary schoolteacher's obsession with the railways. So it seemed a fairly obvious thing to do. It always depends of course on how you put this into practice. The more obvious you make a symbol in a text, the less genuine it becomes, so you have to try and do it very obliquely, so that the reader might read over it without really noticing it. You just try and set up certain reverberations in a text and the whole acquires significance that it might not otherwise have. And that is the same with other images in the text: the track, certainly, the smoke, and certainly the dust.

WACHTEL Memory seems harder to escape the older your subjects get. And most of them succumb, in a sense, through withdrawal or suicide. Why is memory so ineluctable and so destructive?

SEBALD It's a question of specific weight, I think. The older you get, in a sense, the more you forget. That is certainly true. Vast tracts of your life sort of vanish in oblivion. But that which survives in your mind acquires a very considerable degree of density, a very high degree of specific weight. And of course once you are weighed down with these kinds of weight, it's not unlikely that they will sink you. Memories of that sort do have a tendency to encumber you emotionally.

WACHTEL I'm thinking of your uncle Ambros, who suffered so acutely from his memories that he voluntarily submitted himself to shock treatment. And his psychiatrist describes how he wanted "an extinction as total and irreversible as possible of his capacity to think and remember." Why so extreme?

SEBALD It's in many senses quite an extreme tale. What is hinted at in this story is that there was, between this Ambros Adelwarth and his employer's son, Cosmo Solomon, a relationship which went beyond the strictly professional, that they were to each other, to say the least, like brothers, possibly even like lovers. And that particular story and the way in which it unfolded in the grand years before the First World War went against the grain of history, across the fissures of history, and contained within it at least something like a semblance of salvation. And you are permitted as a reader to imagine—the text never tells you to and never really makes it explicit—but you are permitted as a reader to imagine that these two young men, when they were together in Istanbul and down by the Dead Sea, lived through what for them were very blissful times. And it is the weight of that which brings him down, I think, in the end. You know, it's the old Dante notion that nothing is as horrendous as imagining the times of happiness from an environment which is that of hell.

WACHTEL So many of your characters take such extreme action against memory. Is there any alternative? Is there any way to live with a memory? One of your characters, Max Ferber, says that while physical pain has a limit because eventually you'll lose consciousness, mental pain is without end.

SEBALD Well, it is. There is a great deal of mental anguish in the world, and some of it we see and some of it we try to deal with. And it is increasing. I think the physical and the mental pain in a sense are increasing. If you imagine the amount of painkillers that are consumed, say, in the city of New York every year, you might be able to make a mountain out of them on which you could go skiing—you know, all the aspirin, powders. Of course we do see some of it, but people usually suffer in silence or in privacy. And certainly when it's a question of mental anguish, not all of it, only very little of it, is ever revealed. We live, as it were, unaware; those of us who are spared this live unaware of the fact that there are these huge mental asylums everywhere and that there is a fluctuating part of the population which is forever wandering through them. It is a characteristic of humans, in evolutionary terms, that we are a species in despair, for a number of reasons. Because we have created an environment which isn't what it should be. And we're out of our depth all the time. We're living exactly on the borderline between the natural world from which we are being driven out, or we're driving ourselves out of, and that other world which is generated by our brain cells. And so clearly that fault line runs right through our physical and emotional makeup. And probably where these tectonic plates rub against each other is where the sources of pain are. Memory is one of those phenomena. It's what qualifies us as emotional creatures, psychozootica, or however one might describe them. And I think there is no way in which we can escape it. The only thing that you can do, and that most people seem to be able to do very successfully, is to subdue it. And if you can do that by, I don't know, playing baseball or watching football on television, then that's possibly a good thing, I don't know.

WACHTEL What do you do?

SEBALD I walk with the dog. But that doesn't really get me off the hook. And I have, in fact, not a great desire to be let off the hook. I think we have to try to stay upright through all that, if it's at all possible.

WACHTEL Even as a young man, your uncle Ambros—you quote from his journal—says that memory seems to him like "a kind of dumbness;" that it makes his head "heavy and giddy, as if one were not looking back down the receding perspectives of time but rather down on the earth from a great height." How does that work?

SEBALD It's that sensation, if you turn the opera glass around... I think all children, when they're first given a field glass to look through, will try this experiment. You look through it the right way around, and you see magnified in front of you whatever you were looking at, and then you turn it round, and curiously, although it's further removed, the image seems much more precise. It's like looking down a well shaft. Looking in the past has always given me that vertiginous sense. It's the desire, almost, or the temptation that you might throw yourself over the parapets. There is something terribly alluring to me about the past. I'm hardly interested in the future. I don't think it will hold many good things. But at least about the past you can have certain illusions.

WACHTEL What are your illusions?

SEBALD You do tend to think that the people who lived in New England in the late eighteenth century must have had a more agreeable life than nowadays. But then if you think about women having eight children and having to do all their washing in a bowl in the kitchen with a fire of sticks of wood, it's perhaps not quite as idyllic as one tends to imagine. So there is of course a degree of self-deception at work when you're looking at the past, even if you redesign it in terms of tragedy, because tragedy is still a pattern of order and an attempt to give meaning to something, to a life or to a series of lives. It's still, as it were, a positive way of looking at things. Whereas, in fact, it might just have been one damn thing after another with no sense to it at all.

WACHTEL In *The Emigrants,* the painter in Manchester, whom you call Max Ferber, thinks he's found his destiny when he sees sooty Manchester with all its smokestacks, and he feels he's come there to "serve under the chimney." Why is he so drawn to dust? What does that mean for him?

SEBALD We know the biblical phrase, ashes to ashes and dust to dust, so the allegorical significance of dust is clear. The other thing is that dust is a sign of silence somehow. And there are various references in other stories in the book to dusting and cleanliness. That of course has been in a sense a German and Jewish obsession, you know, keeping things kosher and clean. This is one of the things that those two, in many ways quite closely allied nations, shared. And there is the episode in the story of Adelwarth where the narrator goes through Deauville and a woman's hand appears through one of those scarcely open shutters on the first floor and shakes out a duster.

There are some people who feel a sense of discomfort in tidy, well-kept, constantly looked-after houses. I belong to those people. I've always felt it difficult to be in a house where this sort of cold order is maintained, the cold order which was typical of the middle-class salon which would only be opened once or twice a year for certain days like Christmas, perhaps, or an anniversary of one kind or another, and where the grand piano would stand in dead silence throughout the year and the furniture possibly be covered with dust sheets and so on. By contrast, if I get into a house where the dust has been allowed to settle, I do find that comforting somehow. I remember distinctly that about the time I wrote the particular passage that you are referring to, I visited a publisher in London. He lived in Kensington. He had still some business to attend to when I arrived, and his wife took me up to a sort of library room at the very top of this very tall, very large, terraced house. The room was all full of books, and there was one chair. And there was dust everywhere; it had settled over many years on all those books, on the carpet, on the windowsill, and only from the door to the chair where you would sit down to read, there was a path, like a path through snow, as it were, you know, worn, where you could see that there wasn't any dust because occasionally somebody would walk up to that chair and sit down and read a book. And I have never spent a more peaceful quarter of an hour than sitting in that particular chair. It was that experience that brought home to me that dust has something very, very peaceful about it.

WACHTEL One of the painter Max Ferber's techniques to achieve his goal of creating dust is to put on layers of paint and then scrape it off and then rub it out and put it on and scrape it off. And there's a point when you describe your own writing of this book where you seem to be adopting, almost, or finding yourself in the same position of writing and erasing and even questioning the whole, as you say, questionable business of writing.

SEBALD Yes, it is a questionable business because it's intrusive. You do intrude into other people's lives, as I had to when I was trying to find out about these stories, and you don't know whether you're doing a good or a bad thing. It's a received wisdom that it's good to talk about traumas, but it's not always true. Especially if you are the instigator of making people remember, talk about their pasts and so on, you are not certain whether your intrusion into someone's life may not cause a degree of collateral damage which that person might otherwise have been spared. So there's an ethical problem there. And then the whole business of writing of course—you make things up, you smooth certain contradictory elements that you come across. The whole thing is fraught with vanity, with motives that you really don't understand yourself.

This form of creative writing doesn't date back very far with me, but I have always been scribbling in one way or another. So it's a habitual thing. It's very closely linked, as far as I can tell, to neurotic disorders, that you *have* to do it for certain periods of time and then you *don't* do it for other periods of time, and then you *have* to do it again and you do it in an obsessive manner. It is a behavioural problem in one way. Of course it has other more positive aspects, but those are well known. What is less well known are these darker sides of it.

WACHTEL I think at one point that someone says, referring to another text, that the book was a heartbreaking but necessary work. It felt to me like that's what you were doing here, that this was heartbreaking but necessary work.

SEBALD Well, I'm glad to hear that some people think that. I find that reassuring up to a point, but it's not going to allay all the misgivings that I have about it. And one of the most acute problems after a while is, of course, contending with the culture business that invariably then surrounds you, and you have to deal with it. Because when you do begin to write seriously, then it is very much like an escape route—you find yourself in some kind of compound, your professional life, and you start doing something about which nobody knows. You go into your potting shed... For me, when I wrote my first texts, it was a very, very private affair. I didn't read them to anybody; I have no writer friends. So the privacy which that ensured for me was something that I treasured a great deal, and it isn't so now. So my instinct is now to abandon it all again until people have forgotten about it, and then perhaps I can regain that position where I can work again in my potting shed, undisturbed.

April 1998
Original interview produced by Mary Stinson

ALICE MUNRO

Described as "Canada's Chekhov" or "Canada's Flaubert," Alice Munro has been called a writer's writer—and many writers, both in Canada and internationally, love and admire her work. But she is also a reader's writer; she writes with intelligence, depth, and compassion, guiding her reader in her exploration of character, in search of some kind of understanding—just trying to figure things out, no neat resolutions—in an elegant, moving way.

Whenever I would see that *The New Yorker* had a story by Alice Munro, I'd save it up as a treat, a reliable pleasure to talk about afterwards with friends: What is she doing now? I remember years ago, the summer fiction issue was extra special: it had three connected stories by Munro. Cumulatively tough and very affecting, they became part of her eleventh collection of stories, *Runaway* (2004).

Munro has won virtually every prize available to a Canadian short story writer. From three Governor General's Awards, starting with her very first book, *Dance of the Happy Shades* (1968), to the American National Book Critics Circle Award, the Trillium, and two Giller Prizes. She was the first Canadian to win both the PEN/Malamud Award for Excellence in short fiction and the Rea Award for the Short Story. In 2009, she won the $100,000 Man Booker International Prize and then, in 2013, she became the first Canadian to win the $1.3 million Nobel Prize in Literature.

Alice Munro was born in Wingham, in southwestern Ontario, in 1931. She studied at the University of Western Ontario for two years, then married at twenty and moved to Vancouver. In 1976, she returned to Ontario, settling in the town of Clinton. Back in October 2004, I went to Goderich, a slightly bigger town just up the road from Clinton, and still in "Alice Munro Country," to meet with her at Bailey's restaurant. I would call it "Alice's Restaurant" if that didn't sound too much like an old song, but it's the place where she likes to have lunch and meet friends, as well as visiting journalists, even biographers. She has a regular table at the back and a particular seat at that table. The occasion that day was that *Runaway* was on the shortlist for another Giller—which she won. Given that she's reluctant to do interviews, she was remarkably candid, relaxed, and forthcoming. Although she'd said back then that she was going to stop writing, she produced three more books: *The View from Castle Rock* (2006), *Too Much Happiness* (2009), and *Dear Life* (2012).

WACHTEL The title of your book *Runaway* actually fits many of these stories. They're about women in flight, running to or from relationships and ways of living. Did you feel that current underneath the stories as you were writing them?

MUNRO No, I didn't feel that. I never start out with any kind of connecting theme or any plan, and every story just falls the way it falls, usually. But I like the title, I like it very much now. And you noticed, I suppose, that all the titles are one word. Now, that's a reaction against the last book which, if you remember, was *Hateship, Friendship, Courtship, Loveship, Marriage*. Nobody could ever remember that title. Now I knew one wouldn't be able to remember it, but I liked it so much I insisted on it. So this time, I went back to one-word titles for each of the stories, including the title. I thought of the power of one word, and I liked that a lot.

WACHTEL Keeping with the idea of *Runaway*, in your 1998 collection *The Love of a Good Woman* you have a line about a woman who flees her marriage for another man, and you write, "So her life was falling forwards.... She was becoming one of these people who ran away. A woman who shockingly and incomprehensibly gave everything up. For love, observers would say wryly. Meaning sex." What is it these women run away from? Is it convention and expectation?

MUNRO I think they run away from a life... they look ahead and they can see what their whole life is going to be. You wouldn't call that a prison exactly; they run away from some kind of predictability, not just about things that will happen in their lives but things that happen in themselves. Though, I don't think most of my characters plan to do this; they don't say, "There's a certain stage of my life when I'll get out of this." And in fact I think the people who run away are often the people who've got into things the most enthusiastically. They think, This is it!—and then, they want more. They just demand more of life than what is happening at the moment. Sometimes this is a great mistake, of course, it's *always* a little bit, a good deal, different than you'd expect. Women in my generation particularly tended to do this because we'd married young, we'd married with a settled idea of what life is supposed to be like, and we were in a hurry to get to that safe married spot. Then something happened to us when we were around forty, and all sorts of women decided that their lives had to have a new pattern. I don't know if that will happen to women of the next generation, or the generation after that—I think of my granddaughters' generation—because so much has happened to them by the time they're forty, maybe it's enough. And they pick a life and go on with it, without these rather girlish hopes of finding love, finding excitement.

WACHTEL Why girlish hopes? What do you mean?

MUNRO Well, women often harbour rather youthful ideas—ideas that somewhere there is a passion that will last, or there is a passion that surpasses everything else in life, that you can just tear everything apart, and pick up, and go on somehow. I think that's rather a youthful idea. But I think that women of my age didn't hit this youthful phase until we'd first had our middle age. We had our kids and our homes and our husbands and our... our quite programmed lives. But there remained this voice that said there's got to be more in my life than that!

WACHTEL And they were attracted to a certain recklessness.

MUNRO In men or in themselves? In both, yes, I think in both. The very idea that one is doing a reckless thing! The character you're talking about, the one from "The Children Stay," finds that running away has considerable penalties she didn't count on. The way she finds this out is one of the things you discover.

WACHTEL All women do.

MUNRO Well, runaways find this, that's one of the things you discover. I don't think they find out anything that they altogether regret, but they regret a lot, and I think that's maybe the thing you find out about life, that whichever road you take—I'm saying things that are so banal I can hardly believe it—there are difficulties, there are problems, there are things you'll have to give up and things you'll miss, and that's what I've written about a good deal.

WACHTEL Are men the main route of escape or transformation for these women?

MUNRO In my generation they certainly were. We didn't see any other way. Men were the traditional route. Men for women and women for men, and falling in love is still one of the big, big ways to change your life, and to give yourself a tremendous charge of excitement, and hope. It's still one of the most important things we have.

WACHTEL In several stories, a romantic connection is thwarted by circumstances and what seems to be leading to a sexual union turns into something else entirely. But something emotionally important, or even life-changing, still happens.

MUNRO Yes, I like that to work in stories. I like the change not to be the change that you thought you were getting into, and for something to come that is completely unexpected, as if life had a mind of its own and would take hold of you and present you with something you hadn't anticipated. I always hope that will happen.

WACHTEL You were telling me about the importance of falling in love. I haven't done a count here, but a reviewer of your last book noted that infidelity, romantic encounters outside marriage, occurred in seven of the nine stories.

MUNRO What happened in the other two?

WACHTEL What does that subject give you as a writer?

MUNRO Writers are always writing about infidelity—it's so dramatic. At least, maybe writers, again, of my generation because we just didn't have as much adventure before we were married. And there's the wickedness of it, the secrecy, the complications, finding that you thought you were one person and you are also this other person. The innocent life and the guilty life—my God, it's just full of stuff for a writer. I doubt if it will ever go out of fashion.

WACHTEL Canadian writer Audrey Thomas says you're the only writer who "really, truly examines women's sexuality." American novelist Mona Simpson says you've "done for female sexuality what Philip Roth did for male sexuality, covering much the same period (though it would seem they knew vastly different women)." Does it surprise you?

MUNRO It surprises me mightily. I wouldn't have thought that at all. I think I write about sex just the way almost everybody I read writes about sex. I write about it with a great deal of interest, trying to be as truthful as I can. I try to think about what people really go through, and what they think and how they feel about it. I think that every writer does that. John Updike writes a lot about sex—who else? All of us do. It's just a main subject, and has been for a long time. Charlotte Brontë was writing about sex. I suppose Jane Austen was too—where do you get a hero like Darcy, unless you're writing about sex? No, I don't think about this at all. In fact, I don't ever think about what kind of fiction I write, or what I'm trying to write about. When I talk to you now, I try to think about this, to come up with some explanation. But when I'm writing, what I do is think about a story that I want to tell. For instance, in the story "Passion," I wanted to tell first about the girl's relation with the family and then about this wonderful moment when she runs away with a man who, after all, is married, has great problems of his own, and how during the course of that day, she understands what his problems are—and they're not particularly connected with sex. They're really connected with not being able to bear a life. And so I wanted to take her much further, into what she understands about other people. And then, of course, there's a turn-around at the end— because in my life as a young girl, and in the life of this young girl, money was so terribly important. Just to have a little money. I wanted to bring that into what seemed to be a story about feelings, but I didn't say these things to myself. I just thought, What happens next? And, of course, that was what happened next. But in the end, she is given a start in life, which, I think, are the last words of the story, by another person's tragedy and by her own flightiness and inconsistency. I like it when stories turn out in an unexpected way that does not seem too forced, and that story pleased me because I thought it did.

WACHTEL You take her further than she expected is what you're saying, because the initial attraction is sexual and the brother is more attractive to her than her own fiancé.

MUNRO This is often true with women, I think, that the man who has troubles, the man who is brooding and dark, unhappy, and whom you could perhaps make happy, is very attractive. And so he is very attractive to her. He is full of mystery, and he is older. So she thinks that something is going to happen, probably some sexual awakening will be the answer to her life, and it's going to happen on this day. She doesn't really think that too clearly, but her feelings are urging her that way. He teaches her to drive, which is an unexpected bonus, and so, things are not as we expect.

WACHTEL Just as an aside on writing about sex. You are credited with being the first person to get the "F" word into a short story in *The New Yorker*.

MUNRO Yes, but I can't remember in what context it was used.

WACHTEL But obviously necessary, because you persuaded *The New Yorker* editor, Mr. Shawn, to admit it.

MUNRO Yes, I was so innocent and ignorant. I didn't know about Mr. Shawn. Everybody who knew about *The New Yorker* knew about Mr. Shawn, and the way he had made these rules about the things you couldn't write about and the words you couldn't use. I didn't know this. I thought that they were making Mr. Shawn up, that he was this mythic figure who wouldn't allow these things into *The New Yorker*. But of course he was very real. I think that it was in dialogue that it came up. I just had to use it, and I wouldn't give in, so they agreed. And then, for a while, in every story there was something like this. There was a story called "Lichen" which had an image of pubic hair, and that was a very dicey thing with Mr. Shawn. By this time I knew he was real. But he finally gave in on that, too. So it was much more difficult in those days. But I never started out thinking that this will be unacceptable, I was always rather surprised, because I just hadn't figured things out.

WACHTEL You did say that you were terribly disturbed when you first read D.H. Lawrence.

MUNRO Oh yes, I was awfully disturbed, I thought he was such a wonderful writer. He's a very purple sort of writer, writing very heavy prose. But it seemed that he was trying to find out things that no one else had discovered, and I thought he was great. And then, one of the things he found out, as far as I can figure it, is that women shouldn't have any consciousness. There's this story—is it called "The Fox"?—about how a woman should always be like reeds washing under water, so she never breaks the water of her mind. She's just in a stage, in Lawrence's mind, and it sounds quite like a vegetable stage. That way, she is somehow living through the man, anchoring the man in her nature, her unconsciousness, her life-in-the-body, which the man needs. But the life-in-the-world is his. She strengthens him so that he can have it. I don't find this at all an agreeable idea. In fact, I find it horrifying, because it came from a writer whom I so admired. And Lawrence's ideas tied in with so much that I had already learned about what women should be, only he seemed to take it even further with these ideas. It frightened me. I suppose I thought, What if it's true? What if it's true? This is the gospel of sex that one should follow, and yet it seemed to be downright impossible. The woman, you remember, was not to have a sexual climax, this was wrong somehow; she was just to be in this state of readiness, a floating state, all the time. But she did nothing for her self, the idea of her self had to be submerged, and I found that disturbing.

I found a lot of what I read disturbing—Tolstoy's idea of women, too. Do you remember the end of *War and Peace*, how Natasha is so happy because she's always wanted to be only a mother and to only think about her children, their little childhood illnesses and so on. Even worse, in *Anna Karenina*, Levin has a big religious struggle towards the end: what does he believe? And how is he to exist? What is his relationship to God and man? He goes for a walk and meets Kitty, the nursemaid, and the baby coming out of the woods. Kitty doesn't have to think about any of that: she accepts everything, she doesn't have a mind that functions like his. And that means, of course, that she is nearer to nature and to God, and how nice for her, and he admires her for it. But this attitude also depressed me a lot, along with other things he says about how Anna can't go into society because she is living with Vronsky, that she is an adulteress, that she can't go out to tea parties with other ladies. Because of this, she teaches a little peasant girl to read, but she does so just to fill her time because, really, she is cast off from society. She, too, one of Tolstoy's most intelligent women, doesn't have, cannot have, real interests—I'm just rattling on about this because it bothered me so much! I think this doesn't affect women now at all, because they read this like it's something from the Middle Ages. But to me it was very real, something that was there like claws trying to fasten me down.

WACHTEL In *Runaway*, many of the stories are quite harrowing—the threat of violence, death, suicide, and loss is frequently present. There's always been this quality under the surface of your fiction, but do you have a sense that your stories are becoming darker?

MUNRO I think that they are. This, again, is not at all on purpose. I would like to be writing very cheerful stories so that people felt better when they read them. But I hope that people *do* feel better when they read my stories. I don't think having this content means that stories need to be, or fiction generally needs to be, depressing. I really don't believe that, because that sort of fiction doesn't depress me. As you become older, maybe there are more things like this coming close to your life, things you know about. It could be that. But again, it's nothing I intended. I am trying to think of how it would happen in some of those stories. Well, in a story that ends up with the mother losing her daughter, I was really trying to talk about how that could happen and how it could be almost a natural thing. I think that some things that are seen as tragic can also simply be the things people do. In that story, the daughter has a choice—I don't know if people picked up on this—she has a choice to live quite honestly, which means just ditching her mother, or to live with a number of conventions, and very mixed emotions, which is the way most of us live with our parents, maybe all of us. Instead, she gets out. Not because her mother is a terrible person, not because she has any great grievance—she has a whole lot of grievances—but everybody does. She just goes, and this is terrible for her mother in a way; she probably doesn't even understand, because it is only when you get quite old that the bonds with your children become emotionally so central to your life. And when you're in middle age, or a little younger than middle age, the bonds to your parents are there, but they are mostly nuisances. They're partly nuisances, they're extreme difficulties. They're not your major emotional gratification. So that's what the story was really about. I guess that it seems such a sad story, but not to me. There's sadness in it, but that isn't the same thing as being a sad story.

WACHTEL It's part of a trilogy of stories—"Chance," "Soon," and "Silence"—and one of the subjects that runs throughout seems to be faith. The main character, Juliet, has an explosive argument with her parents about the existence of God. Later her daughter, apparently, goes on a spiritual search, having been raised in a house that wasn't a faith-based home.

MUNRO Yes, but I didn't intend this to be central. Well, of course it's important, but in the story Juliet, as a young woman, has an argument about the existence of God and cannot affirm her mother's faith, because it would be denying her self, her whole being, which is still young and fragile. I feel that she has to do that, but her mother, no doubt, suffers because of it. Then it happens that her own daughter leaves her. I think the daughter's looking for faith is just a sign of wanting to get away, wanting to make her own life. It's not that it's faith in particular she is searching for; she's searching for whatever is there and has been explicitly denied her. Say, if her home had been very repressed and sex had been the thing that was never mentioned, she'd be going after that, I think. She's getting away. And then she gets so far away, she can't come back. Maybe because her mother, the central character, is harder to get away from because she's not very repressive. But, she's still too much.

WACHTEL You write about a lot of places, but you continue to set stories around southwestern Ontario, where you were born and have lived for a large part of your life. How do you stand back and see the fictional possibilities of a place when it is so familiar to you?

MUNRO I just always feel there's more to be discovered about this place, the changes that have occurred and the things I know about it. I never think that I've finished with it. I don't like to be described as a regional writer and I'm annoyed sometimes when people think I write about an idyllic world, a sort of pastoral. It almost seems to me by accident that I write about those people, it's because I know their houses and I know certain things about their lives, but I don't think of them as particularly different from people you might find anywhere in the world. It's just something I do without thinking about it. I don't know if I could write as easily about more exotic characters—nearly everybody I write about has lived, or lives, in a place that I have lived in. Maybe I'm not very imaginative. Except that I once did a story about Albania, and I liked writing about Albania a lot. But usually I don't use unfamiliar characters or settings. I might like to, but there's always something that I have to do first, something that isn't exotic at all.

WACHTEL How has small-town life changed?

MUNRO Oh, it's changed enormously. There's so much tolerance now. When I went to school, people laughed at anyone who was disadvantaged. Now, everybody knows that you don't make fun of people for their problems. At least, you don't do it publicly, and you don't do it in a very obvious way. But when I went to school, we did. Also religion was very central—nobody would ever claim to be an agnostic in a small town. But now it's acceptable. And the rules about sex have changed completely. Women my age now live with their lovers. That's quite amazing, the freedom to live a pleasanter life, one that's much more compassionate, much more understanding. You could probably even announce that you liked poetry.

WACHTEL You lived in British Columbia for more than twenty years, and you still winter on Vancouver Island. Do different landscapes suggest different stories or characters for you?

MUNRO No, no. You see I don't think about the whole story as coming all in one piece, and when I wrote, say, "The Children Stay," I just saw it happening on Vancouver Island, and particularly at Miracle Beach, because I had to have them go somewhere, and there it was. So I saw them there. But I don't know if a particular kind of story comes out of those places or not, because I'm simply not very analytical about what I do.

WACHTEL What was it like for you to move back to small-town, southwestern Ontario after having been away—that was in the mid-seventies—for twenty-odd years?

MUNRO That did influence my writing because I had written about growing up here, and I thought I was finished with this area. When I moved back, however, I started seeing things entirely differently. I didn't see them right away in present-day time, but I saw a lot of things that had to do with social class, and the way people behave towards each other, that a child doesn't see. So I wanted to go over all of it again, and that's what I did. For me, personally, it was surprising, it was unexpected. But I liked a lot of things about it, I love the countryside, that I can't get over. And I like cross-country skiing in the winter, all that kind of thing. I liked living with my husband and making our life, I liked our house, I liked our backyard, all kinds of things were good. And also, I was now an independent woman. I was not someone who had grown up there and had never left. And if people were talking about me, or judging me, I didn't know. So that was okay.

WACHTEL What was it about social class that you became aware of?

MUNRO Oh, I wanted to write more about the class I lived amongst when I went to school. In Wingham, I lived on the outskirts of town, which was full of people who were suffering from the Depression, only I did not know that at the time. The school that I went to was very rough. I hadn't really thought about these discrepancies for a long time, about the way these people lived and the differences between them and the people who lived in the town over the bridge and had marginally better lives, some of them even a good deal better. But, as a child, it doesn't matter whether you're growing up poor or rich, I think. You don't take much notice of the way you're growing up, and what the rules are around you, in terms of money and the kind of job you have, and so on. So I did go into that again, and I described the school a lot, because it was both pretty horrific and so richly interesting. There were boys going there until they were sixteen or seventeen because they couldn't get jobs. And I'm not talking about high school, I'm talking about elementary school, so these boys were pretty well running things. There was a great deal of physical violence, and it was amazing to me because I was being raised at the edge of this community as a kind of little middle-class girl, an only child. And it was probably so painful that for a long time I didn't think about it. But then I wanted to write about the way it was, because there were wonderful things about it, too. Our favourite game was funerals. Somebody got to be the corpse, that was the choice part, and the person would be lying out and we'd pick flowers—weeds really—and put great armfuls on the corpse. This doesn't sound dreadful at all, it sounds rather touching. And we'd line up and we'd all get a chance to march past the dead person, to cry and carry on. But the trouble was that the most important people got to be the corpse first, and then everybody else got a turn, but by the time it was my turn, everyone had lost interest in the game. The mourners were few, the flowers were few, and the other kids were playing something else. We made up a lot of things like that. Oh yes, it was really pretty wild. The teachers just didn't come out at all. I think they locked the doors during recess.

WACHTEL When you say violence, was it violence against you?

MUNRO Oh yes. I was beaten with shingles, I remember. I was a terrible coward and not very good about this at all, but I did learn things. I learned things that I wouldn't have learned so quickly any other way, about how people are when they lived really, really deprived lives. Maybe they were like this because it was fun, but these people didn't have enough fuel for the winter. People would stay in bed all day, things like that. It was rather like a Chekhov village.

215

WACHTEL You're saying you were an only child because you were the eldest, so at that point—

MUNRO Yes, that's dreadful, saying an "only child." That's how an elder child talks. I wasn't an only child. I had a baby brother and a baby sister at home, but I wasn't counting them at the time.

WACHTEL You have great empathy for the characters in your stories who are limited by their circumstances, whether it's a matter of economics or society's expectations, or obligations of family.

MUNRO Well, I mostly grew up with people like that. For instance, when I finished high school, I got a scholarship and I could go to university, but had I not got a scholarship... You see, to get a job in the city, you had to get away to the city, you had to be able to support yourself for maybe two weeks before you found a job. Impossible. So these are things that people don't understand so well now. I didn't think of that as particularly unfair, and I still think of my life as really interesting, a great life for a writer. It gave me a lot of confidence because I was the only person I knew who tried to write as a teenager, and I didn't know anybody else who read as much, so I thought I was a uniquely gifted person; it was only going to be a matter of a few years—I would be twenty-one or twenty-two years old before my first novel would burst on the world. You know, if I'd been going to Jarvis Collegiate in Toronto, I might have had a very different idea of the competition!

WACHTEL What gave you the ability to pursue your aspirations back then?

MUNRO It never occurred to me not to. A big ego, I would think. At first, when I was about eight, I planned to be a movie star, and this continued for two or three years. Then I slipped into writing—a slight downgrade because I still think being a movie star would have been more wonderful. No, I wanted to make up stories and I was making up stories in my head. By the time I was eleven, I really thought that I had to write them down. That's what you did with stories, you didn't just let them fade, you wrote them. And it was not even the idea that people would end up reading them but the book—with your story in it—was the thing itself. It really never occurred to me until much later, when I was around thirty, that I might not be able to do this. So the confidence lasted for a long time, and then it just went with a big whoosh. That was hard. I think children who grow up in an environment where they feel strange and a bit outlawed can develop, if they're lucky, and if there aren't too many bad things happening to them. I think they can develop an alternate world which is going to remain for them. And I was lucky. I've mentioned being beaten up at school but I always had enough to eat. I was taken to the doctor when I was sick, and my mother got me into the town school, so I didn't have to go to that school for more than two years. I was allowed to go to high school—many people had to quit and get jobs. It never occurred to me. I think gifted people are sometimes quite selfish, because it didn't occur to me that I should go and work in the glove factory, or work in Stedman's store, something like that, in order to help my family. No. I was going to have this magical life; I was going to do this thing that was so important.

WACHTEL It also meant—going back to your theme right from the beginning of our conversation—running away, in some sense, from family responsibility, as the oldest daughter.

MUNRO Yes. This is the thing that I'll feel guilty about for the rest of my life, that I did not stay home. I did not look after my mother, I did not keep house though my brother and sister were still quite young. I just left them. Well, I came home from university every couple of months and did major housecleaning and household jobs, but I still left, and without—at that time—any qualms. My parents were really quite good. They never asked me to stay.

WACHTEL When did the guilt come?

MUNRO Oh, by the time I was safe. You never feel guilty while there's still a possibility or an opportunity to make up for what you've done. When I could have gone back home, I didn't feel guilty. But as soon as I was free, and nobody could make me go back, I felt guilty. I could afford to feel guilty then, and I've felt guilty ever since. I say I feel guilty, but I'm glad I did what I did, because I think if I'd stayed and became a housekeeper (and certainly no one would have married me, I was too weird), I would have become too frightened to leave. By the time my mother died, I would have been too afraid to go out into the world.

WACHTEL This has become your subject.

MUNRO This has become my subject. Yes. Writers are very economical, nothing is wasted.

WACHTEL And your mother has become your subject.

MUNRO Very much so, yes.

WACHTEL What about your father?

MUNRO Well, fathers and mothers had separate spheres. My father was outside, and I was inside with my mother, doing housework. All my conflicts were with my mother, and I allowed my father to be a figure outside this. When I was older I had a great relationship with my father because he also read, and he wrote a book when he was dying. We were terribly good friends, and he was very understanding. He never criticized anything I did. My first books were not easy for him to take, still living in a town where people didn't read fiction and didn't know where fiction came from. And there was all this language, and all this sex, and he had to put up with it. But he never blamed me for it, he liked my books, yes.

WACHTEL Did you have any idea he had a book in him?

MUNRO I began to when I was older. I didn't know him that well when I was a child. He wrote columns for a local magazine and things like that. And then he started to write this book and he became really involved in it. The last time I visited him in the hospital, he was sitting up in bed in his pyjamas, saying, "What do you think about that character so and so?" So I told him that, if he didn't pull out of the operation, I would make sure that the book got published and I did. I was really happy about that. It gave him such delight! But I think he wouldn't have thought that there was a connection between himself and that world where books were written and publishers existed if he hadn't seen that I had done it. And then he thought that it was possible for anybody to do it. I remember when I told him that Margaret Laurence was a friend of mine. He'd been reading a book of hers that he got out of the library, and he said, "But Alice, she's a really good writer!" That meant that he felt the connection, that it wasn't something unreal. And so he could try it himself.

WACHTEL A while back you said that you didn't know how you'd feel if your daughters wrote about you.

MUNRO Did I say that? Well, one of my daughters *has* written about me!

WACHTEL Exactly, a memoir. How did you feel?

MUNRO In a way I felt very lucky because I thought that it was honest and fairly gentle. When she was doing it, I felt good, too, because I knew that it was courageous. We try to say it isn't, but growing up the child of someone who has been successful, and is sort of famous, is difficult, especially if the thing the parent does is the thing you want to do yourself, or that you have a talent for. And so I thought that it was very good that she just decided to come right out with this. I also know that if you dish it out, you have to take it. So there we were! And we're very good friends.

WACHTEL Memory shapes many of the stories: that relationship between the older and younger selves in a life. Grace, in "Passion" for instance, is literally revisiting the places where she spent time with the Travers family, and ran off with their son, Neil, some forty years earlier. What do you find interesting about having a character look back and reconsider her past?

MUNRO I suppose in that particular story I wanted to show where Grace had ended up, but also I like to have people trying to find something of their past, and then looking at what they actually find, like changes in landscape and a house that no longer holds the same meaning. I just thought that was a good way to get into the story. Also, I suppose I'm a little self-conscious about writing of the past, so I anchor it in the present, because there is a feeling sometimes that people who write about the past are writing about a time that is much easier to understand, and is safe. A reviewer did say that I chose the past to write about because I would be safe there. Now I don't feel that I am safe there, but I know that people have this quite false nostalgic idea about the past being a pleasanter, gentler time—my God, gentler!

WACHTEL There's a line in another story ["Powers"] where there's an older woman whose children say, "be careful you don't live in the past," and she says, no, no, what she wants to do "is not so much to live in the past as to open it up and get one good look at it."

MUNRO This is what I want to do too, obviously, and I try to do it over and over again. But there is a sort of feeling, like the feeling her children have, that you have to keep going all the time. And I am so involved in everything that I've lived that I never want to let go of it until I've done something with it. And that is not just to write and sell a story, but to see—to find out what I can see in it. And so I don't suppose I'll ever catch up with myself.

WACHTEL What tense do you live in now?

MUNRO Oh, I inhabit the present now, and I inhabit it with a great sense of grabbing it. I don't inhabit the future much for obvious reasons. I don't know how much there is of it. For the same reason, and this will sound very clichéd, I want to appreciate every bit of life I can. It's not as if I do that all the time, but I am conscious of wanting to do that.

It's almost like another "I should," I should be perfectly happy because, after all, I'm not dying and my heart is fixed up, and I live in this nice place, things like that! But I can be just as irritable, burdened with things to do, as I ever was. So, life doesn't really change that much.

WACHTEL Last fall you said that that you'd decided there was not going to be another book, and yet here is *Runaway*.

MUNRO Did I say that last fall?

WACHTEL It was quoted in *The Guardian* in October 2003.

MUNRO All right, I must have done that interview sooner than that. I must have been insane, I really must have been! But I guess I try to live in two realities, because I'm always afraid of bringing out a book. I'm afraid of being responsible for all this stuff, and having to stand behind it; I want to go on and write more stuff. And yet the obvious thing is to bring out a book. When I get enough stories, that's what I do. But I honestly believe that, except for the book that I've almost finished and which will probably come out in two or three years, I won't do any more after that. I feel that there is some kind of wonderful plateau you get to where you don't have to write anymore, and you don't have to go around being interviewed anymore. You're just happy all the time. This is my idea of retirement. I don't know if it works or not.

WACHTEL Why do I not believe you?

MUNRO Because you've known me for a long time, and you know I lie. But I'm not lying about this. There is a thought in me, it has been for a long time, that there's a kind of happiness that consists in not having to work hard at something, in not striving at something. There is just a place you get to where everything is comfortable, and you are satisfied. And you're not trying anymore to do something. Because when you try to write you always think, this is impossible, I'm not bringing it off, it's not working, and when I get through this, I'll be so happy. Well then, you get through. Why don't you stop? I don't know...

WACHTEL It's been fifty years since you first published a story. Thirty-five years of publishing books and being celebrated internationally by critics and readers as someone who never disappoints. Does that help or hinder the writing?

MUNRO Oh, it hinders it. I think, *OK*, wait 'til next time. Sometime this is going to come crashing down, and I hope I'll be so old I won't care. Or I will have got to that plateau we were talking about. Oh, what will

I do there? Play golf? No, I can't play golf, so I don't know. Maybe go for long walks and really appreciate things.

WACHTEL You already do that.

MUNRO Yes, I do. But often I'm distracted, thinking about something else. That's it. To be not thinking. Isn't this an ideal state, only thinking and feeling about the present, not thinking about what you have to do, or what may happen. Isn't that a kind of Nirvana or something?... I'm asking you! I'm interviewing you!

WACHTEL I can't imagine it—that's why I'm having trouble answering you.

November 2004
Original interview produced by Lisa Godfrey and Mary Stinson

J.M. COETZEE

John Maxwell Coetzee is an elegant, disturbing, and provocative writer. When he won the 2003 Nobel Prize in Literature, the Swedish Academy praised his ability to write fiction that "in innumerable guises portrays the surprising involvement of the outsider." His 1999 novel, *Disgrace*—which won both his *second* Booker Prize and the Commonwealth Writers Prize—is a compulsively readable, but troubling, unforgiving work. As in his memoirs, *Boyhood* (1997) and *Youth* (2002), this was Coetzee at the top of his form.

J.M. Coetzee was born in Cape Town in 1940 and educated in South Africa and the United States. His novels, such as *Waiting for the Barbarians* (1980), *Life & Times of Michael K* (1983), and *The Master of Petersburg* (1994) have won virtually every major literary prize in England and internationally. Coetzee is also a fine critic. When he was invited to give the Tanner Lectures on human values at Princeton University, he melded ethics with aesthetics, and created a kind of novella, *The Lives of Animals* (1999). His fictional novelist examines animal rights, argues for vegetarianism, and concludes that "there is no limit to the extent to which we can think ourselves into the being of another. There are no bounds to the sympathetic imagination." Coetzee later incorporated some of this material into his novel *Elizabeth Costello* (2003), a character he returned to again in his book, *Slow Man* (2005).

J.M. Coetzee has frequently expressed his uneasiness with the media and he's famous for his reticence [see my introduction to this book].

When he won the Booker prizes, he didn't go to London to collect them, and he refused virtually all interviews.

I first met him in Toronto during the very first season of *Writers & Company*. His 1990 novel, *Age of Iron*, had just been published and was one of the best books I'd read that fall. Spare, compelling, it's set in South Africa in 1986, during a time of countrywide black insurrection and harsh counter-violence by security forces. The story centres on Elizabeth Curren, an old woman who's dying of cancer but not quite ready to let go of life. Politically aware and politically outraged by everything she sees, at one point she says, "I'm trying to keep a soul alive in times not hospitable to the soul."

In February 2000, I went to South Africa to talk to writers for a special series on the dramatic changes that were transforming the country. Coetzee was, as usual, reluctant, but he didn't turn me down entirely because, he said, he had positive memories of our earlier conversation. But he did stipulate that he wouldn't discuss his own work, his life, or the political situation in South Africa. We could talk about writing, and he would read from *Disgrace*.

So I went to see J.M. Coetzee at his office at the University of Cape Town on a hot summer February afternoon, just as classes were resuming for the semester.

Two years later, in 2002, Coetzee emigrated to Adelaide, Australia, where he holds an honorary position at the University.

WACHTEL In a review of your novel *Waiting for the Barbarians*, the American critic Irving Howe wrote, "Imagine what it must be like to live as a serious writer in South Africa, an endless clamour of news about racial injustice, the feeling that one's life is mortgaged to a society gone rotten with hatred, an indignation that exhausts itself into depression and the fear that one's anger may overwhelm and destroy one's fiction." Is Irving Howe imagining correctly? Is he describing you?

COETZEE No, he isn't describing me, but I recognize very well the syndrome he's talking about. I don't think South Africa is a society gone rotten with hatred. There's a lot of hatred around and a lot of people have become rotten with it, but not enough to infect the whole.

WACHTEL Is it something that you've had to struggle with personally?

COETZEE I think "struggle" is slightly too strong a word. I think it's certainly a menace lurking at one's shoulder. But I think a strong awareness of it is enough to keep it at bay.

WACHTEL What is it like to be a serious writer in South Africa today, a white writer? Are you concerned about who is listening or who you're addressing, or if your audience is at home or abroad?

COETZEE I have no real standard of comparison for what it's like to be a writer in South Africa. That's the only place I've ever been a writer. There's been a relaxation of censorship, particularly for so-called "literature," in the last ten years or so. That isn't to say that there's been a relaxation of the regulations governing journalists and people in the media in general. But censorship, I think, was one of the great obstacles for South African writers, particularly in the 1960s and '70s, not so much in the '80s.

As for the question of audience, frankly I try not to think too much about my audience when I'm writing, simply because in the past my experience of trying to write for someone in particular, some group in particular, has been that it's not good for one's writing.

WACHTEL An early novel of yours, *In the Heart of the Country*, is a mix of Afrikaans and English. The narration is in English, and the dialogue is in Afrikaans, at least in the original South African edition. I wonder, does this split reflect some tension, some sense of division in your own background?

COETZEE I think "division" may not be exactly the right word. In general I tend to think of mixtures and cosmopolitanism as thoroughly good things. My own personal background was indeed linguistically mixed, if I can use that word; I spoke English in some circumstances and Afrikaans in others. I thought that was a very, very good thing. It's reflected certainly in the novel you're referring to, but I don't think it reflects any division or split within myself.

WACHTEL You say there were some occasions when you would speak Afrikaans, and in others you would speak English. You were educated as a linguist. Is English different from Afrikaans in its world view?

COETZEE I don't think English has a particular world view because it now inhabits so many environments across the globe. In fact, some sociolinguists no longer talk about English. They talk about Englishes.

I think Afrikaans certainly does. It has a highly determined world view, and particularly in the last fifty years or so; it's had a very intense ideological imprint forced upon it. I really lived in an Afrikaans environment in the 1940s and early '50s, just before that heavy ideological boot came down. So I still retain a certain affection for the language and hope that the day will come when Afrikaans will be able to return to where it really belongs: namely, as not a national language at all and really not a language with any particular pretensions to wide currency, but rather a patois, a second language for lots and lots of people and a language that closely fits the South African landscape, geography, climate. I look forward to that day.

WACHTEL Your new novel, *Age of Iron*, is very spare and very powerful. It's about an old woman who is dying of cancer, but she develops a peculiar relationship with a black, homeless alcoholic who appears in the alley behind her house. This is a woman who hates the government and lives in a perpetual state of shame. But she says she has to find her own words and that she can't borrow anyone else's rage, or it wouldn't be true. Why is that important?

COETZEE It's a question of authenticity. One must come to one's own realizations. And if one is a writer, as she is in the book—the book is cast in the form of a long letter from her to her daughter—if one is a writer, one must express one's awareness not in someone else's words but in one's own. These are the only authentic words there are, one's own words. They can't be borrowed.

WACHTEL One of the things that she realizes, this old, dying woman, is that to be good isn't enough, that there are plenty of good people, but that the times require heroism.

COETZEE Yes, that's the form in which she puts her dilemma to herself. And it's a particularly difficult dilemma for her because, of course, she sees plenty of examples of heroism around her, but they are forms of heroism that involve the violence that she can't find in herself to imitate. She's thinking here, of course, particularly of the heroism of young black revolutionaries, teenage black revolutionaries. She sees them as children who have not yet lived, and really don't know the meaning of life, in the sense that they, as she understands it, are incapable of imagining death. So she's torn between outrage at their foolhardy or reckless actions in their own lives and this overpowering realization that, as you say in the words you quoted, being a good person, living in terms of love and charity, let us say, is actually not enough in the particular historical situation of South Africa.

WACHTEL The image of the title *The Age of Iron* in a way refers to South Africa's future as embodied by its black youth, and it's a tough and relentless picture. The woman has a vision of "millions of figures of pig iron floating under the skin of the earth, the Age of Iron waiting to return."

COETZEE Of course, she's reflecting on one of the archaic legends of the ages of mankind: the Golden Age, Silver Age, Bronze Age, and Age of Iron and so forth. And at that moment in the story, she is, I think, heartily sick of all the metal frankly.

WACHTEL She yearns for a softer age, an age of clay or an age of earth.

COETZEE And if there's anything a bit despairing about the book, I think it is held in that feeling of hers that it's going to be a long time before there are soft ages again, that for the foreseeable future, it's going to be one version or another of metallic.

WACHTEL Do you feel like Elizabeth Curren?

COETZEE No, I don't. Elizabeth Curren is a representative, I think, of a generation that was particularly betrayed by its leaders and really didn't live long enough to do anything about it, but instead lived long enough to understand that (a) their generation had been betrayed, and (b) it had no excuse for having been betrayed. They should have known better.

I see Elizabeth Curren as representative of the generation that was born, I suppose, around 1910, 1920, a generation in whose name, largely, the whole massive system of apartheid was erected and who didn't do enough to prevent it.

WACHTEL A number of your earlier books, such as *Waiting for the Barbarians* and *Life & Times of Michael K*, are set in unnamed places. They're somewhat allegorical. But *Age of Iron* is more particular, more explicitly South Africa. Why is that?

COETZEE I've never used that word "allegory" about my own work, so I won't comment on allegory, except to say, to emphasize, that it's not my word.

Michael K is, of course, a novel very much about South Africa, but not about South Africa at the present. It's about a South Africa in the future or in a potential future. So I don't see *Age of Iron* as really a departure from *Michael K*. I tend to put those two books together and contrast them, indeed, with *Waiting for the Barbarians*, as you say.

WACHTEL At the end of *Waiting for the Barbarians*, the central character, a white magistrate, concludes that his liberalism was no more helpful than the soldiers who made war and tortured people. I wondered if in any way it's a reflection of some disillusion with liberalism generally.

COETZEE *Waiting for the Barbarians*, of course, is set in a very undefined landscape and milieu in which words like "white" and "black" actually no longer mean anything. And insofar as "Liberal," let's say, has a capital "L" and has a particular historical basis and provenance, he lives in a time when no one has heard the word "Liberal," much less knows exactly what Liberalism, with a capital "L," means.

I tend to think of the magistrate rather as a man of humane values. Is he disillusioned with humane values? I don't believe that he is, but I think what he does see is that power is capable of using humane values and people who espouse humane values for its own end. Sometimes the people who believe in and act in terms of humane values get used, and perhaps they ought to be a little more aware.

WACHTEL When you put it in terms of humane values, it makes the magistrate in *Waiting for the Barbarians* similar to Elizabeth Curren in *Age of Iron*, someone who believes in humane values and comes to recognize their futility.

COETZEE If I believed that humane values were futile in every sense of the word, I wouldn't be writing these books. On the other hand, if I believed that humane values were the answer to every problem, I wouldn't be writing these books either. I'm writing these books to pose the question of what good humane values are. And to pose that question without having the answer signalled from the beginning—namely, that humane values are everything or humane values are nothing. We cannot only believe in humane values quite sincerely; we must also act in terms of humane values. The question is, is that going to be enough?

If you were an American and a strong believer in the Constitution of the United States, I would expect you to say, yes, ultimately humane values, if believed in and acted upon by enough people, will be enough. I'd be sceptical about that. But fortunately, you're not an American.

WACHTEL One of the things that I am struck by in your fiction is that so many of the characters have some sort of disability. The Barbarian girl in *Waiting for the Barbarians* is blind. Michael K has a harelip and is slow-witted. Friday in *Foe* is unable to speak; he doesn't have a tongue. Why do these kinds of characters interest you?

COETZEE Let me name an aspect of all these characters that you haven't mentioned, which is that they're not particularly verbal people. Friday is the extreme case. He doesn't speak at all. But none of them is a great believer in speech, in the word. All of these people express, in various ways, a scepticism about values, particularly about words and specifically about the power of words in the real world. Parenthetically, of course, we're talking about the power of novels in the real world, the power of art in general in the real world.

What these people do, in lieu of the words that should have been or could have been, is obtrude these bodies of theirs, these damaged bodies. It seems to me that their damaged bodies are a continual reminder to the highly verbal people who confront them, of their brute physical existence and of their own—I mean the speakers' own—brute physical existence. The magistrate, for instance, is not just the voice of humane values speaking. He is also a brute physical body and has to confront the continual deflationary effect upon himself of the brute, damaged, physical body of the girl he's involved with.

WACHTEL *Age of Iron* is a novel that's on the cusp. It's looking back, and it's looking ahead, because of its prophetic quality. But its vision of the future is certainly uneasy and, to some degree, unclear. Are you hopeful about change in South Africa?

COETZEE I think this is a time in history when it is extremely important for people who carry any kind of influence in South Africa to be hopeful because hope and confidence in the future are the most urgently needed commodities in the social and political life of the country. Therefore, if I were not hopeful, I certainly wouldn't say so.

WACHTEL Is this like one of those Camus-like existential things, that just to keep writing is to be hopeful?

COETZEE No, it's nothing like that, it's nothing as grand as that. It's more like a kind of stock exchange phenomenon, where the more people who believe in the economic future, the more likely that future is to materialize.

WACHTEL So you're obliged to be hopeful.

COETZEE Not "obliged" to be hopeful. It's just a good idea.

January 1991

§

WACHTEL Language, its character, its subtleties, its complexities, is of course the stuff of writing. I'd like to talk a little about language. When you were growing up, on some occasions you'd speak Afrikaans, on others English. What would decide it?

COETZEE I come from a mixed background, mixed in various ways. My mother's family, although not of British descent, had spoken English at home, and my mother's children, my brother and myself, were brought up speaking English. But our father was Afrikaans-speaking, and for much of our childhood we lived in an Afrikaans-speaking environment, and spoke English at home, Afrikaans in our public life.

WACHTEL You have an Afrikaner name, but you thought of yourself as English; at least, the way you describe it in referring to yourself in your memoir, *Boyhood*, you spoke mostly English, lived in fear, at times, of being sent to an Afrikaner school, consigned, as you put it, to an Afrikaans' life. Why, what would that mean?

COETZEE One must remember the period in history in which the book that you refer to, *Boyhood*, is set, around the year 1950, just after the coming to power of the Nationalist government in South Africa. It was a period of deep and officially encouraged polarization of all kinds, including polarization between English speakers and the new ruling Afrikaner elite. The second thing to remember is that there is a distinction, or at least I like to maintain a distinction, between the terms Afrikaner and Afrikaans. Afrikaans, to me, is a purely linguistic term with linguistic and cultural overtones, whereas Afrikaner, at least in my parlance, has a quite heavy political and ideological content. It's a bit like the difference between, let's say, a Briton, which seems to me to have a certain ideological content—someone calling himself a Briton, if people do call themselves such any longer, is quite distinct from someone calling himself merely from Britain. What it meant at the time to be consigned to what I would call an Afrikaner life would have meant, first of all, being consigned to the Afrikaans half of the school I was attending but, more frighteningly, it would have meant being drawn into the bosom of the Dutch Reformed Church and the National Party, into the whole cultural crusade of the times to erect a distinct and unique white Afrikaner national being. For a rather timid child, this was an alarming prospect.

WACHTEL You describe yourself, in *Boyhood*, as naturally drawn to all things English, not just the language but the literature, the values, even the heroes. Growing up in rural South Africa, and later in Cape Town, what was it about English culture that seemed so attractive to you?

COETZEE If I did indeed say I was *naturally* drawn, then let me withdraw the word. I don't think this is a matter of nature at all. It is a matter of acculturation. I was brought up in a family in which books were, to an extent, read. I was certainly an avid reader as a child, and the reading culture into which I was drawn was that of England, but more specifically of the remnants of late Victorian and imperial England in the colonies. I was surrounded by that ethos and certainly didn't know enough about it to be able to distance myself from it in any way. So, indeed, the heroes of Victorian England, the boy who stood on the burning deck and all the rest, seemed like the heroes most worth imitating.

WACHTEL Did embracing all things English bring with it a sense of cultural superiority or did your natural affinity for English culture make you feel marginalized? Or both, I guess, are possible...

COETZEE It was difficult not to feel marginalized in a country town in South Africa in the early '50s, for the simple reason that the people running the show were making every effort to make you feel marginalized and were quite triumphant if they succeeded. The story they told themselves was that they had spent the years between the Boer War, at the turn of the century, and the accession of the Nationalist government in 1948 feeling marginalized in their own country, and now it was their turn to make everyone else feel marginalized. So, yes indeed, I felt marginalized.

WACHTEL But did you have a secret sense of cultural superiority, that you had allied yourself with the richer culture?

COETZEE I wouldn't want to put it too strongly since we're talking about quite a small boy. Certainly, I had no sense that the cultural offerings of, if I may call it, Afrikanerdom, were particularly rich, whereas I certainly did feel that the whole late imperial ethos that England offered was rich. Rich is a word one can continue to use about that period in English history even though one might feel a little sceptical about the variety of richness it offered.

WACHTEL In addition to being a celebrated novelist, you've had a successful career as an academic and a teacher. What do you look for when you're choosing a book to study?

COETZEE I'm not so sure that I've had a distinguished career as a teacher. I've had a middling career, let us say. What do I look for in a book? I would say that I look for something that still interests and intrigues me, even if I'm not sure it will interest and intrigue my students. My hope is always, of course, that it will. There should be something about the book, about the writer, that I haven't quite got the hang of, some secret or mystery, something that it has to teach me and, very often, to teach me as a writer rather than simply as a human being.

WACHTEL Which writers do you consider essential?

COETZEE Essential. That's a difficult enough question, I think, in North America, I would say, as an outsider, particularly in Canada, and even more problematic a question, loaded with hidden meaning, here in Africa, where we're speaking today. We are talking about the canon, and perhaps asking a question about whether there are writers or works of literature that are so important that they are above canonical questions. Then, as someone of, finally, I think, Western culture, even though we're speaking in Africa, I would have to say that the Bible, or some of it, is essential in the sense of being more than just canonical, in the sense of being absolutely foundational. I would throw in *The Iliad,* at this point, and I would say that if one is absolutely unaware of Plato and Aristotle, or what Plato and Aristotle were about—if one were absolutely innocent of Greek philosophy to that extent—one would not be entirely of Western Judeo-Greco-Christian culture.

WACHTEL Do you want to move to anything more recent?

COETZEE No, I don't want to move anywhere more recent because, at that point, I think one would start having to speak about the canonical or the merely canonical, and the import of the question is, Is there an area which is super-canonical?

WACHTEL It doesn't necessarily have to be in more recent terms, it could be at any time. Who's underrated? Are there writers that you feel have been neglected, overlooked, deserved more recognition, more reading?

COETZEE Again that's a rich question because, speaking now, at the turn of the century, there is a sense in which all writers, finally, are underrated or not read enough or are about not to be read enough. We are, dare I say it, moving into, or have already moved into, a phase of history or post-history where the idea that writers are important has begun to seem odd or slightly old-fashioned. So rather than say Writer X or Writer Y is, in my opinion, underrated, I think that, more seriously, writing in general is becoming underrated. And let me add that I speak from the bosom of an educational institution which is in the process of turning itself from one that studies writing to one that studies all kinds of other cultural artifacts, some of them exceedingly transitory in nature.

WACHTEL It's interesting when you say that the idea of writers being important is, perhaps, a thing that's fading. At the same time, and maybe the two are related, writers are becoming celebrities. I mean there's more of a sense of the writer as celebrity.

COETZEE Yes, that's interesting. Writers of course have been celebrities before now, and usually for reasons that don't have all that much to do with their writing. Byron, for example, was a great celebrity in his time and was a celebrity as a writer in the sense that if he had not been a writer he probably would not have been a celebrity, but he wasn't a celebrity because of his writing.

WACHTEL Are there writers who are overrated?

COETZEE Of course there are writers who are overrated, but the list is too long for us to go into it right now.

WACHTEL Can you say what makes a classic?

COETZEE When it comes to the question of What is a classic? I have nothing better to offer than what Horace said, which is that it's a book that has somehow managed to stay around for a long time. The implication is that if people have been reading it for a long time and have not consigned it to the dust heap, then there must be something to be said for it.

WACHTEL You've written extensively about Beckett, Kafka, Dostoevsky, Ford Madox Ford—quite different on the face of it, but they could all be considered outsiders. What are the common elements to their writing?

COETZEE You have named four writers on whom I happen, at various times in my life, to have written, among—may I say it?—many other writers. You could say that those four were outsiders, but they were outsiders for very different reasons. Ford Madox Ford, for example, became an outsider because of various scandals attached to his name that made it difficult for him to continue in the social circles that he was born in. Kafka was a constitutional outsider; he would have been an outsider wherever he was, and his outsiderdom or outsiderhood was only compounded by having been born a Jew in troubled times, even in Austria-Hungary at the end of the nineteenth century. Beckett was an outsider by temperament and election, I suppose, although, what must be said about Beckett and Kafka is that, although they have the image of being cold and remote, they certainly didn't impress their friends that way. We have record of both Kafka and Beckett striking people as extraordinarily warm and friendly and amusing. Dostoevsky, the fourth person you mentioned, was an outsider because of historical circumstance. I suppose the decisive, or external, event of his life was being caught up without full premeditation in a secret student movement and being packed off to Siberia for a long period, and returning, when he did return, with a mark against his name which was difficult to obliterate. So I'm not sure that these four writers you named, insofar as they were outsiders, had that much in common.

WACHTEL You've said that Samuel Beckett's writing gives you a sensuous delight. How so?

COETZEE That's true. Beckett and Joyce, though in different ways, knew the English language with a completeness and mastery that I find hard to attribute to anyone else, at least in modern times. In Joyce, particularly in his *Ulysses* phase, and in Beckett, at least while he was still writing in English, there is a connoisseurship, a delight in the perfection of the writing itself, which I respond to and responded to even more intensely when I was younger. That sensuous side of his own writing was perhaps what Beckett reacted to when he, in effect, gave up writing in English and moved to French: a need for a greater rigour and fewer seductive possibilities, because English has seductive possibilities that have to do with its peculiar history, effects that it's possible to obtain because of that history, namely of being a Germanic language with a very heavy Romance overlay that came in wave after wave. Which means that there are, in one's lexical choices, all kinds of possibilities of playing off the Romance against the Germanic in ways that are not possible in any other language.

WACHTEL So by writing in French, Beckett was choosing greater rigour, greater precision, a discipline that he didn't have in English?

COETZEE Yes. Beckett really never explained fully—and why should he have, there was no need to explain, it was a matter for himself alone—why he made the switch, so it's for us to guess. My guess is that what he felt to be the irrelevant seductions of English at that point—we're talking now about the post-war, post-1945 years—just felt to him to be something he'd done with. He'd played with language enough and it was time to move on.

WACHTEL Your own critical writing doesn't touch much on American literature. Why is that?

COETZEE I think that's purely accidental. There are American writers—let me name Melville, let me name Whitman, Faulkner, Emily Dickinson, too, in a different way—who have meant an enormous amount to me. If I don't happen to have published anything on them, well, maybe I'll fix that one day.

WACHTEL You've said that you read Dostoevsky and Tolstoy on their own terms. What are those terms?

COETZEE I'd find it hard to be exhaustive, but let me at least produce the beginning of an answer. Both Dostoevsky and Tolstoy, in very different ways, are Christian writers. If it's at all relevant, I'm certainly not a believing Christian. So the first step in reading these two writers on their own terms would be to take their very different readings of the Christian gospel seriously, if at all possible, as seriously as they took it themselves. That's no mean task for any reader, because it's easy enough to read either or both of them putting aside that Christian element, and still be overwhelmed by their work. So you might, as a reader, feel it's no great loss, since there is such wealth, to not read them as Christian writers. To return to your question, what I mean by saying that I try to read them on their own terms is that, despite my own religious position or lack of religious position, I make every effort to enter into the religious world they inhabit in their different ways.

WACHTEL Was it George Steiner who said "Tolstoy *or* Dostoevsky"? Why is it that people tend to line up with one or the other?

COETZEE It was Steiner who said so, and I don't know the answer to your question. It's true that there are people who line up with one or the other, even among those who fully appreciate the strengths of both. I would hate to have to make the choice; I'll go on evading the choice as long as I can.

WACHTEL You've written about the nature of confessional writing, and specifically about Tolstoy, Rousseau, and Dostoevsky. As you describe it, Dostoevsky was sceptical that the self could ever tell the truth to itself. Why is self-delusion so apparently inescapable?

COETZEE One's dealing here with a major dialogue taking place across time between Jean-Jacques Rousseau and Dostoevsky. In Rousseau's mind, one had only to be very honest with oneself, and brave—considering the possible consequences—and one could tell the truth about oneself, write down the truth about oneself. Rousseau's confessions are exactly that; they're an exercise in being ruthlessly frank and honest about what Rousseau would have considered his most deeply shameful character traits. The dialogue is taken up by Dostoevsky when he says that it simply is not good enough to look in your heart and write, that what comes out when you write is quite as likely to be some self-serving lie as it is to be the ruthless truth about yourself. I must say that, in this confrontation, my sympathy is wholly with Dostoevsky. The basis of his position is simply that the heart of our own desire is unknown to us and, perhaps even further, that it's in the nature of human desire not to know itself fully, to have some kernel of the unknowable in it. That, perhaps, is what animates desire, namely that it is unknowable to itself.

WACHTEL Although, unknowable seems slightly different from self-delusional, because self-delusional implies a consciousness that isn't there in the unknowability of ourselves.

COETZEE What is self-delusional is to imagine that you can tell the truth about yourself, that it merely takes a certain frankness with oneself and a certain boldness in putting things down on paper and revealing them to other people. That is, at least in Dostoevsky's eyes, a delusion.

WACHTEL As a young academic you thought that languages spoke people or, at the very least, spoke through them. How much does language control a writer?

COETZEE It depends on how strictly you want to gloss the word "control." If you want to give it the strictest of all meanings, then I would say language doesn't control any writer who's worth his or her salt in any significant respect. But if we're using the word "control" more loosely, then one can surely repeat what is, I think, simply a truism, that each language has its so-called genius, and that it's not at all easy to escape from the genius of the language without a kind of intellectual analysis for which there's very often no reason and which could have the effect of deadening or sterilizing you as a writer. There are not only turns of phrase, turns of language, but turns of thought in French, for example, that are not possible in English without real contortions of the mind and contortions of language. And vice versa. That is why literary translation is such a field in itself, such an art in itself.

WACHTEL Have you ever thought about writing in another language?

COETZEE The short answer is that I would be very stupid to try. I've written a fair amount in Afrikaans, but what I read afterwards has no life to me. Perhaps that relates to the crisis that Afrikaans is undergoing at this moment, the historical crisis of language which really no longer quite knows what it is, that is to say, whether it any longer aspires to be a minor European language, which was the program it set itself during the years of nationalist domination here, or whether it really is what it now proclaims itself to be, namely one of the languages of Africa, although with a strong European linguistic base. That is the crisis, as I see it, that Afrikaans is facing at the moment.

WACHTEL Is there a direct relationship between repressive societies and great literature?

COETZEE I'd be very, very hesitant to say that repressive societies breed great writers. There are far too many counter-examples. What one could say instead is that there was a period, a historical period, when writers were very important indeed and became targets of repression in a way that I can't imagine book writers becoming targets nowadays, because what they do is really too peripheral to the interests and concerns of politics. We're talking about a period, therefore, from around 1500 to around 1945.

WACHTEL Hmm. I thought you'd say 1989.

COETZEE Well, 1989, perhaps in South Africa as a belated member of the world society.

WACHTEL Or the Soviet Union and the Eastern Bloc.

COETZEE Yes, indeed, in the Soviet Bloc, a society ruled by people who wanted the clock to have stopped, if one is to judge by the literary tastes of their rulers, in the nineteenth century.

WACHTEL You've admitted a fondness for narrative pleasure, but you're also proficient in difficult, demanding literary theory. Which kind of reading do you do the first time you go through a book?

COETZEE We're talking about novels now, aren't we? I read for the story and feel no shame about that. I wouldn't want to make a distinction between pleasure on the one hand and thought or analysis on the other. In fact, the ultimate fruit, I would say, of a literary education is to produce people to whom intellectual pleasure is possible, including people who are not ashamed of reading for the story, because reading for the story is to them not just unthinking fun, but an intellectual pleasure as well. Writing has everything to do with pleasure, and the kind of thinking one does about writing has a great deal to do with pleasure as well.

February 2000
Original interviews produced by Sandra Rabinovitch

YIYUN LI

Yiyun Li is one of those astonishing success stories. She was born in China in 1972. Her father was a physicist, her mother a school-teacher, and she herself something of a math whiz as a child. She studied immunology at university in Beijing and always planned to go the United States to further her education. When she was twenty-three, she fulfilled that dream and went to graduate school in Iowa. Her first year there, she was lonely. Her boyfriend, soon to be her husband, was still in China, so she enrolled in a community writing course, figuring she'd improve her English. Her very first story was highly praised by her teacher. Yiyun Li was amazed; she'd never written fiction before, in English or Chinese. She continued in science and got a graduate degree before enrolling in the Iowa Writers' Workshop where she received two more MAs—in fiction and creative non-fiction. Before she was done, she had stories published in the *Paris Review* and *The New Yorker*, she had an agent and a six-figure, two-book contract. All in English.

Her first book, a masterful collection of stories called *A Thousand Years of Good Prayers* (2005), won four major prizes, including the Hemingway/PEN Award and the inaugural 50,000-Euro Frank O'Connor International Short Story Award. She was also named by *Granta* magazine as one of the best American novelists under thirty-five.

I first interviewed Yiyun Li when her first novel, *The Vagrants* (2009), was published. Ambitious, harrowing, and simply extraordinary, *The Vagrants* takes place in a new, small city in China, during the uncertainty and flux of the late 1970s. She followed it with another, much-admired collection of stories, *Gold Boy, Emerald Girl* (2010), and around that time she won the half-million-dollar MacArthur "genius" award.

We spoke again in 2014, on the twenty-fifth anniversary of the Tiananmen Square massacre of June 4, 1989, and with the publication of her second novel, *Kinder Than Solitude.* This work is also inspired by real-life events but focuses on the psychological violence that marks the central characters. Yiyun Li was only sixteen at the time of Tiananmen, but she already felt it was her generation on the barricades.

Yiyun Li lives in Oakland, California.

WACHTEL Your grandfather was an important figure in your early life. He lived with you and shared a bedroom with you and your sister. When you think of him now, what images come to mind?

LI He always had a wooden cane, very well carved. He carried it without using it until he was in his late eighties—as a sign of status. That's the image I remember.

WACHTEL Your grandfather sounds like he had a remarkable life. He lived through three regimes, two world wars, two civil wars, famine, revolution. Can you tell me a bit about his story?

LI He was born in 1897 in southern China, near Shanghai, and he was sent to a traditional school to learn Asian scrolls and poetry. His parents had the foresight to send him to a Western-style middle school and high school, and after that he took an exam to become an editor. I'm not certain how, but at some point in the civil war he became an officer in the Nationalist Army, where both his sons were fighting against the Communist Army. One of my uncles went to Taiwan and the other stayed in mainland China with my grandfather. And then he went back to his editing career. He was an editor for probably twenty more years and then he retired. Meanwhile, his domestic life was pretty crazy. His first wife—he really, really loved her—committed suicide three days after she gave birth to her first baby. Then, about a year later, he married my grandmother, who in her early thirties became psychotic; she remained that way all her life and died in an asylum. After my grandmother died and my mother married my father, my grandfather pretty much spent the rest of his life with my family.

WACHTEL Did he talk about any of those more personal events with you?
LI No, he never talked about anything personal with me, or with my sister, or even with my parents. These stories all came out after he had passed away and my mother started to talk to us about his early life.

WACHTEL But he was very talkative with you when you were growing up.
LI He talked about the world in such a fascinating way. He would tell me about someone he met on a walk. And because he always asked questions, he could tell me this man's whole history. So he was talkative about politics and history and culture, everything but his own life.

WACHTEL And you described how he would get up every day at five in the morning and jog for an hour and write poetry and paint. Did he read his poetry to you?
LI When I was three or four, he tried to teach Asian poetry—not his own poems, but Asian poetry—to us. He was an actor so he could act out the poems, and it was great fun. I was a very snoopy child, so I looked at everything on his bookcases, and I found poems that he had written and just stuck in a book. I didn't really understand that he was a poet until much later.

WACHTEL Your grandfather was anti-Communist. You say he fought in the war on the Nationalist side, and that was something that had to be kept secret, but he somehow continued to denounce Chairman Mao. How did he get away with that?
LI He was very outspoken—I think it was in the early fifties—and he had no patience with the new government or new regime, so he said something like, you know, Chairman Mao was the king of hell, and all the party officials were guardians of this hell. He was almost arrested. I don't know how he got away with it. I think he was given an early retirement because of that. And early on in the Cultural Revolution—this was before my mother married my father, when she still lived with my grandfather in their house— these Red Guards would come to his house, and because he was an old-style intellectual with all this history, they would try to find faults with him. He was a very fine calligrapher, so he used his best calligraphy to write this banner in his house saying, "Follow the Communist Party. Be the best child of Chairman Mao." The story was that the Red Guards looked at this banner for a long time and couldn't find anything wrong with his writing or with his attitude, so they let him go.

WACHTEL As a keen young pioneer, did it bother you that your grandfather would denounce Mao?

LI From very early on my sister and I were taught by my parents that there were two sides of life. One was lived in school, in public, and we pretty much echoed everything we were taught there, and the second half was at our home, where my parents and my grandfather would talk about things that from early on we knew were not to be shared with the public. I mean, I was probably baffled, but I wasn't hugely bothered.

WACHTEL Your grandfather was a man of strong habits and beliefs and, as you write, through all that he experienced, what didn't change was his faith in eating. He was a man with a good stomach and extraordinary luck. Why was food so important to him?

LI Look at his life. He lived almost a hundred years through the whole century with these wars and famines and disasters, and I think food was the only thing that was consistent for him. He loved his wife and then he loved another wife, and then he wanted to marry a woman he loved, but couldn't, so he had a lot of emotional lives. When I got to know him, he was in his eighties, so he'd let those things go, but what was left for him was this joy in food. It was pretty amazing, I would say. I don't enjoy food as much as he did.

WACHTEL You grew up with rationing—flour, rice, sugar, salt, oil, tofu, eggs. How did that affect your relationship to food?

LI All these rationed foods give me a very strong impression, but eggs in particular. Eggs always represent something very good that I would never get enough of in life. When I first came to America, I loved to scramble eggs, fry eggs, eat eggs all the time. But as I grew older, I removed myself from that eagerness, from that desire for food, so now I eat very simply. I'm always very aware of the possibility of hunger because hunger was one of the experiences that really stayed with me. So I think I look at food in a very practical way: I need to fill my stomach so I don't feel hungry.

WACHTEL When did you experience the most acute hunger?

LI I was in the Chinese Army for a year, and we didn't have enough food—or not enough sustaining food. This was in central China, and there was no heat where we were in the camp. But there was also that emotional hunger. For a few months, I felt like I'd never be filled. We were always hungry and there was not enough hot water, so we would eat dried milk powder. It was extremely sweet, just nauseatingly sweet, but I guess hunger drove people to do things like that.

WACHTEL Your grandfather experienced the famine between 1958 and 1961, long before you were born. What kinds of stories did he tell you about that?

LI He would describe the neighbour, a very respected old man or perhaps a respected intellectual: "Oh, he would walk in the street and see a little kid with half a bun, and he would be so hungry, he would grab the bun and run." It was even worse than hunger when you lost your dignity, when you robbed a little child, and that was the kind of story he would tell. And then he would go back through history and tell the stories about this or that dynasty; there was this famine here and people would have to eat their own children. But it was hard to eat your own children; neighbours would switch so they could eat other's children. That really freaked me out. I was three when he first told me this story, and I think my early memory started around that. Because I was a very plump child—I was plumper than my sister—I always had a strong belief that if there was a famine, they would trade me with the child next door, who was also a little fatty. So that was very scary, I think. But looking back, I find him very funny.

WACHTEL Through your grandfather you grew up with an appreciation of an older traditional Chinese world that had changed so dramatically. Your own world was quite different. You were born in 1972 in the shadow of the Cultural Revolution. Can you tell me about your childhood, where you lived, how you lived?

LI My father used to work for the core research institute for the nuclear industry in Beijing, so I grew up in this compound. It was very much like a small village: grocery stores, barbershops, school, daycare. And every family's father or both parents worked for the research institute. My sister and I, my parents, and my grandfather shared a two-bedroom apartment, which at the time was rather a luxury because in many families, three generations would live in one room. We had central heating, water, and propane tanks, which were rationed too. People had to have a certain status to have a propane tank. Our neighbour, who was a janitor for the institute, had to use a coal stove.

WACHTEL And were you aware of being privileged?

LI Yes, because the institute was on the outskirts of Beijing, and across our backyard fence were the village children, who had to raise their pigs and their donkeys and horses. We knew they were much less privileged. In a way, we were the city kids among the villagers.

WACHTEL You said that you were taught that you lived in a honey jar.

LI Yes, I think those were the songs we were always taught to sing. You know, "We live in a honey jar, we're so happy." When you first encounter this language as a child, it does have that very concrete meaning for you. I remember I was seven and I came back from school one day, I think in early afternoon. It was spring, the sun was shining, and the whole time I was just bouncing, bouncing, bouncing along the path and singing the song and I felt my life was just blissful. Very, very happy.

WACHTEL The Tiananmen Square massacre, twenty years ago now, was a turning point for you. You've said that's really when you became an adult. What do you remember?

LI I remember the two months leading to that period. My sister was in college then, so on and off she would go to the square to protest or to help with other students who were on a hunger strike. For those two months before the massacre, I think there was this gleefulness in the air. Everybody was so hopeful that things would change. I was in high school, and I would go to colleges and universities to listen to people or to look at the flyers, and I remember sometime in May, my best friend and I were riding bicycles to the university, and she said, "You realize, this is the moment of our time, and these are our lives now." And I was very much impressed when she said that because I hadn't thought about it, and I realized, yes, if we were two years older, we would be the ones active in the square. She made a point that we had to consciously live through every moment that spring, so we did.

Neither of my parents had much faith in the government. Early on—when everybody was so hopeful that things would change—my father said this would lead to bloodshed. My mother disagreed and they would argue. My father was very pessimistic about these things. When things escalated, my parents locked my sister and me in the house. They didn't want us to go to the square, and by the night the bloodshed started, when the killing started, I think my parents already knew and they made a point to lock us in. My mother and father took turns going into the street to see what had happened, but they would not let us out. Immediately after, there was a time of uncertainty and fear and confusion, and so I felt that was the period of time when I started to live every day very consciously.

WACHTEL And afterwards you and your fellow students were questioned about what had happened?

LI Pretty much everybody had to go through a period where you had to report what you did and what other people did. I think my parents were more worried about my sister because she was there quite often. My sister was a medical student at the time, and because she had gone to the square to help the people on hunger strikes, my father instructed her about what to write in her self-report, the self-examination thing. He would say, "Well, you know, you can't say you just went there. But you could say, 'Out of humanitarian consideration, I went there to help people who fainted or who were dehydrated.'" So many ways to work around the system. In high school we did too, but on a less dramatic scale. A friend of mine, a sixteen-year-old boy, actually went to the square that night and he saw things. He came back, he told who-ever he could tell, and a few months later, the police came to get him. They knew exactly what he'd told people. That, to me, was also part of the life-changing experience. He told things to twenty classmates. Who reported him, we would never know. I felt at the time that I would never be able to prove my own innocence to him because I could have reported him. Somehow you experience these things and you grow up rather dramatically.

WACHTEL So even though you hadn't reported him, you still started to avoid him?

LI Right, I just thought—maybe it's me. I think it was partly my per-sonality. I just felt this shame, not for my own sake, but for some rea-son I felt ashamed and I could not face him, so I started to remove myself from him and we just drifted apart.

WACHTEL When you were eighteen, in 1991, you were sent to the army for an involuntary gap year, this forced re-education. What was is like for you? How did you get through it?

LI By then I was rather rebellious and unhappy about my life, and I brought a lot of English-language novels with me. Somehow I felt read-ing another language secretly, and also just reading literature in general, was helpful for me. I've always been a big reader. By then I was becom-ing a very bookish person. When you read literature, you live in two places at the same time, and if you suspend a little more imagination, you can stay in that literary world a bit longer than the reality. So I think that was my way of coping with the stress or the unhappiness or all these dramas in the army.

WACHTEL When you left for the army, your mother told you to imagine a zipper on your mouth and zip it tight. It's a very strong image. But then you didn't listen. You told your squadmates some of the details and the truth about the Tiananmen massacre. What was their reaction?

LI Very interesting, because I was the only one from Beijing in our squad. I went into the army thinking all my fellow soldiers would feel the same way about the Tiananmen Square massacre, and it turned out none of them knew what had happened. I was very shocked and angry. This was at eighteen or nineteen, when you could afford to be angry. Or I could afford to be angry. I was furious, so I couldn't stop talking. It was almost my goal to make everyone admit that these things happened. And part of the squad was iffy—everybody was very cautious around that time, so nobody wanted to talk about these things openly. But I took a stand as an activist in that little space, and I forced people either to listen to me or take a stand, and I was very unhappy.

WACHTEL Were you worried about punishment?

LI I was. That was the closest feeling I had to someone in my novel, like someone willing to sacrifice her life for a cause. I was worried at night. I remember I had this fear that they would not let me return to Beijing, they would keep me in the army, and that was a nightmare for me. But somehow, and these things might be a little psychological, the more fearful I became, the louder I became. I just couldn't stop talking.

WACHTEL Your novel *The Vagrants* is set in 1979, two and a half years after the death of Mao and the end of the Cultural Revolution. You were still very young during that time, seven years old or so. What drew you to this particular period in Chinese history?

LI On a historical level, 1979 was the year when China started to develop technologically and economically and opened the gate to the West. So China became the China we know today because of 1979. Personally, I think that when you're six or seven, you start to view the world as a little person. You start to process a lot of things. I wanted to write about the time when I started to recognize things and to be baffled by the world, so that led to this decision to write about 1979.

WACHTEL The story takes place over a couple of months and it's book-ended by two executions, loosely based on actual events. Can you tell me what you wanted to explore in this story?

LI In this provincial city in China, a woman had been imprisoned for ten years as a counter-revolutionary because she was against Chairman Mao and the Cultural Revolution. Ten years later she got a retrial, and because she did not repent in prison and wrote diaries and letters and essays, she was retried as a counter-revolutionary and sentenced to death. Before she died, her kidneys were taken out for transplant and a lot of horrible things happened to her body afterwards. The city organized a protest on her behalf, and a few weeks later the woman who was the leader of the protest was sentenced to death, too. So that was the case I took from history. When I look at that case, the two women were heroines. They gave up their lives; they sacrificed family life, children, everything, for justice, or for dreams of democracy, or for all these grand themes that come into life. My major interest was not with the two women, however, but with the town, the community; what happened during those six or eight weeks from one execution to the next, in this community. My goal was to look at every possible angle, so I had old people, young people, people who were active in the protest, and people who were against the protest. I just wanted to understand that period and I wanted to understand that world, which as a seven-year-old, I did not understand.

WACHTEL Although you had, as a child, seen denunciations.

LI Yes, and that part of the novel was taken from my life. I think I was between five and six. There were quite a lot of executions at the time, and before they executed people they would send them from community to community for ceremonies. I remember being taken out of daycare and going to these places. As a young child, you don't understand the consequences of someone being executed. It was a very festive event, and life was interrupted in an exciting way. For instance, one time there were four prisoners and one of them was a woman, and I remembered her hair very well. As a child, you store these images in your memory, but you can't understand them. My parents wouldn't talk about these things. So as a grownup, as a writer, you come back to study these things again, to see what did happen at that moment.

WACHTEL Did the fact that the executed counter-revolutionaries were women, including a mother, contribute to your fascination with the story?

LI Yes, I think so. When I started the novel, I knew that the first woman would be executed in chapter one and that we would never know her because she'd already been transformed from a real person into a legend. But the second woman was a young mother, and I was more fascinated with her because to me she represented something that I really needed to understand as a young mother. How could you give up your child for something, even for a higher calling? Where was her fear? Was she ever afraid of death? These questions led to the second character, who was one of the central characters in the novel, and through her I wanted to better understand why people do things as they do.

WACHTEL Gu Shan, the young woman executed in the opening chapter is, as you say, a legend. She's a haunting presence, but she's elusive. Can you tell me about her, how you see her, what you make of her?

LI For one thing, early on in her life in the novel, she was a very active Red Guard, and she did horrible things. She committed atrocities to older people and she kicked this pregnant lady's stomach and caused the baby to be born with birth defects. So she was not a saint, she was not a hero in my mind. She was a very real person until the moment that she died, and then she became a heroine. I was adamant not to make her a glorious figure because if you do that, it becomes propaganda for the other side: See, this is a beautiful young woman giving up her life. No, I think people do things with much more complex motivations. We had to get to know her through all these other characters. And the people she had hurt in her youth would carry that resentment or hatred all their lives.

WACHTEL The horrific details of Gu Shan's imprisonment and execution, and her abuse even after death, are filtered through the very different perspectives of your main characters, but overall the effect is to evoke a society that's brutal and dehumanized. Death is very graphic and visceral on the pages of *The Vagrants*. The treatment of the dead reflects the value placed on human life in the world.

LI You know, I was very aware of that, and as a writer you can't avoid it. You can't turn your eyes away from these details. In the real world, you can say, I don't want to think about these things, I don't want to dwell upon these things. But if you want to write about that time, about the people, you have to get into that whole picture. I did not spare the readers, nor did I spare myself in that process.

WACHTEL Because even animals die brutally in the novel.

LI Yes, that was a very conscious decision. There were so many animals. For one thing, in the 1970s in a small town, or in a small provincial city like Muddy River, animals did coexist with human beings and they had their own world. I always feel that how people treat animals is not too far from how people treat each other, especially under stress or under certain circumstances. So there are a lot of animals in the novel, and many of them die, and some of their deaths are even more heartbreaking to me, I guess, than the deaths of characters.

WACHTEL Teacher Gu, the father of Gu Shan, seems to share some of your grandfather's characteristics, but you've said that he's the character most like you, that you lived in him through the novel. What do you relate to most in him?

LI My grandfather was much more outspoken. I wasn't aware of it until I finished the novel, but Teacher Gu was the only character who had access to philosophy and history. He was a knowledgeable person. He was actually in two cultures and two worlds: the small Chinese one and the bigger one. But that didn't help him because he was trapped in the small world. He was always suppressing his anger; he was nostalgic for all the beauties of the old time. He was a dreamer, but there was nothing for him to dream on, and all these qualities made him a rather complex character—people might say a sad character. When I was writing the novel, I felt very close to him, and when he died I just cried because I felt I had really lived through that journey with him or in him, and I saw everything through his eyes. I don't know. I imagine when you work on a novel with twenty characters you have to put yourself in someone's shoes just to stay embedded in that world.

WACHTEL At one point Teacher Gu says, "Conscience is not part of what one needs to live." He's speaking about saving his daughter, but, I wonder, is that an idea that has larger meaning for you?

LI In a way he's very much resigned to history and his fate, and I was aware of that because people would say my other stories always have that fatalism embedded, and I think his philosophy or his fatalism probably came from me as his creator.

WACHTEL You are fatalistic in that way?

LI Yes, I guess so. It's very disagreeable to hear myself say that, but I do feel that way.

WACHTEL How does that affect your life and what you do?

LI Oh, that's a very good question. I think there are positive influences and negative influences from this fatalism. On the positive side, you never let yourself be deceived by your optimism or your hope, so you're always studying the world or people with a bit of suspicion, or you want to scrutinize people, yourself, and people around you, and strangers, everybody. That is good for a writer, I think, and that is what a fiction writer should be doing, not taking anything for granted. You need to get into that depth of human emotions and motivations. That's the good part. The negative influence, of course, is that it's hard to live as a pessimistic person, and it's especially hard if you're a mother of young children. I feel that parenting requires a huge amount of optimism, and I try to be an optimistic mother, but that optimism does not come from me. I have to force that onto myself.

WACHTEL I'd like to talk for a moment about the actual vagrants in your novel *The Vagrants*, the title characters. The Huas are rubbish collectors, and they're a truly compassionate and dignified couple. They have so little; what accounts for their generosity?

LI A few years ago, I read a very small news report about a couple of rubbish collectors, and through years and years of garbage collecting, they raised thirty-seven deserted babies, all of them girls. And at a certain point, the government would come in and say, "You do not have the birth certificates, so you cannot bring up these girls," and the girls would be transported to orphanages. But the couple never gave up their hope; they just kept doing these things. When I started to write *The Vagrants*, I knew right away I wanted to write these people into the novel. I also knew that even though they were minor in a way, they were the central characters for me. Their story threaded through the novel. It was a little baffling to me because I am a fatalistic person, but I do think that it was hope that sustained them through years and years, through losing one daughter and raising another. I do feel that by writing about the couple, I learned a lot about them or about how to be hopeful, so when it was time to name the novel, I wanted to title it after them.

WACHTEL You've said that people ask you why you have to write about the 1970s when China is no longer that country. Why can't you let go of the past and write about the glorious Olympic Games or the strong and wealthy country that China has become? How do you answer that?

LI Well, I have many answers to that. For one thing, I think literature is literature. Literature should not be propaganda. And if I want to write about the glorious China today or the glorious Olympics, chances are I'm going to see something really dark under that glorious surface, and I think it's a writer's job not to believe in any sort of surface and to go under that surface to see what's really there. The years 1979 and 2009, to me, are not so different, because I think human emotions and human motivations evolve rather slowly. That's why when we read Dickens or Jane Austen, we still understand their characters, even though they live in a different society. So 1979 is almost just a set-up. It's something I'm interested in, but you can move these characters to 2009 and they would react very similarly to the characters in 1979. I'm not a journalist, so I feel that's my freedom as a fiction writer.

WACHTEL Just over a year ago you returned to Beijing for the first time in ten years. What was that like for you?

LI It was an interesting experience. Before I went, everybody said, "Oh, you will not recognize Beijing. You will not recognize China. It's a new country now," which was partly true because the surface of the country has changed so much. Beijing has become a different city on the surface, and I did not recognize my road, I could not find my house. All these things happen if you are away for ten years. But again, as a fiction writer, I truly believe that's only on the surface. When I talked to people—when I went to my parents' neighbourhood, when I met my old friends—I realized people did not change that much. Their life situations had changed. And I always say, you know, twenty years ago, thirty years ago, we were waiting in line to get rationed food, and now people are in the stock market trying to make money. But that, to me, is a surface difference. The human emotions of greed and jealousy, all those things, have not changed. They are all still there. I think people are trapped or determined by their history. To me, it's very reassuring to see these things that haven't changed, because in a way, that's why we write literature.

June 2009

§

WACHTEL The longest story, a novella really, in your last collection, *Gold Boy, Emerald Girl*, is called "Kindness," and the narrator, Moyan, like a lot of your women characters, seems to live life at a remove, with a long-ingrained, carefully maintained attitude of indifference or apparent indifference. This detached emotional stance—why do you find it compelling?

LI I think partly in fiction, as in life, I am drawn to the centre of drama because, if you're looking at the centre of a drama, you can experience a lot of dramatic feelings and moments, but they are like fireworks. They explode. But I'm more drawn to the people on the margins or people who don't want to live in the centre of drama. And these characters, I think, share the traits that they are all very stubborn, and they like to live seriously, and that's one thing that connects them all. They may look removed from life from the outside, but their seriousness and their stubbornness are their rebellion against a life they don't want to conform to.

WACHTEL There's great poignancy to this story, as there is in so much of your fiction, the sense of lives unlived. It might be a form of rebellion or resistance, but it's also a form of self-deprivation, it seems.

LI It is a self-deprivation. On the other hand, it's also their self-preservation. I think that life unlived is exactly what is at the centre of most of my characters. The reason they refuse to live certain kinds of lives or they remove themselves entirely—for instance, in "Kindness," where it's almost Moyan's only way to preserve herself and to preserve her integrity.

WACHTEL Because?

LI Because of the way she was brought up and the way she connects with the world, her love is deepest when she doesn't connect to people. I think she's aware of that, and she doesn't want to give up that position.

WACHTEL Her love is deepest when she *doesn't* connect?

LI Well, yes. In the story, she says, "I have never forgotten a single person who has walked into my life." She says this twice in the novella, at the beginning and at the end, and you realize that's exactly what she does. She remembers, and she loves these people walking into her life, but she cannot express this, except in that silence.

WACHTEL A character who becomes an important influence for Moyan tells her that "the moment you admit someone into your heart, you make yourself a fool." And "when you desire nothing, nothing will defeat you." This echoes the Buddhist saying that you later quote in your novel *Kinder Than Solitude*, "to desire nothing is to have no vulnerability." What kind of wisdom is that? Why does that resonate with you?

LI It is originally from Buddhist teaching that you should desire nothing. But these characters, both received this wisdom at a certain age, as teenagers, which is a time when they should desire a lot of things. They should have a lot of hope for life. Well, I think they're prematurely taught this wisdom to make them feel less desire. I think it would not be a big stretch to say that's the wisdom I grew up with. And it resonates with me.

WACHTEL Except that you somehow transcended that advice because, from when you were very young, you said you knew you wanted to leave China, you wanted to be in America, you knew that. How did you manage not to absorb this advice and end up in that state of self-deprivation?

LI To desire nothing is very hard to do, and as we all know, it's so human to want something. And, of course, I feel lucky that I did not follow that teaching in my life, to desire nothing, because otherwise I would have become nothing.

WACHTEL Who taught you that? Who gave you that lesson?

LI Mostly from teaching, I think, rather than from a particular person. Maybe my father. But mostly just from a culture that is so filled with Buddhist teaching. But also from history because, like my parents, my teachers lived through fifty years of Communist history. To desire nothing seemed a very good way to preserve themselves. For me, my instinct to preserve myself has been very strong since I was young. You have to choose what to preserve and what to give up. And possibly the only things that I preserved from early on are the love of words and love of literature.

WACHTEL One of the most touching moments in "Kindness" is the scene where Moyan, the central character, is a young girl, and she's treasuring two young chicks as pets. And then, when inevitably they die, she tries to fit them back into empty eggshells. As an adult, she reflects, "I have learned, since then, that life is like that, each day ending up like a chick refusing to be returned to the eggshell." It's a curious metaphor and a haunting scene. What inspired it?

LI I used to have this little friend when I was young, and her family bought chicks every year, and every year I saw them die. But the hope she had never died, her hope that one day there would be one chick that would grow up. I think that's an interesting situation, because she was the one who experienced this hope and pain while I was the one watching her, and while I was watching her—I think I was a precocious child—I just thought, If only you could just put those chicks back in the eggs. I think that was a very early thought of mine.

WACHTEL There are parallels in "Kindness" to aspects of your own background, for example, Moyan's army service and her love of English literature. And her most memorable time at army camp is the month her platoon spends in the mountains. "Never before," she says, "had I loved the world as I did then." Did you experience something like that?

LI Yes. I've never been an autobiographical author, but for "Kindness" I borrowed heavily from my own experience in the army. When you walked, marched, in the mountains, it was such a harsh journey. On the other hand, you could see the world around you in a way that I had never seen before, nor have I seen it since. So, yes, I think that's my experience, too.

WACHTEL To give you a certain appreciation of nature or a connection to nature?

LI And also to realize that you're alive in nature. When Moyan was on that journey, she was so alive. She saw fireflies and flowers and raindrops. These things had always been around her, but her life was not connected to nature until that moment.

WACHTEL During your own involuntary army service, you got in trouble not just for reading English books, like Moyan in "Kindness," but for sharing stories of what you had witnessed and heard of the Tiananmen Square massacre. Can you describe what happened that day?

LI June 3rd was a Saturday. My friend and I went to this special school for mathematicians. When we came back, we saw buses overturned across the street, and people gathering. I came home and told my parents that things did not look very good in the street, so my parents insisted that my sister and I not go out that night. My mother asked my father to guard us so we could not run away, and then she ran into the street just to see what had happened. By then the shooting had already begun, and she saw a dead child, one of the youngest victims, probably seven or eight, in his mother's arms. People were driving her and the child to different places where the army had gathered. They wanted to show the army that they were not mobsters, not bad people, and their kids were being killed. My mother came home around eleven o'clock, crying, and said things were really bad.

The next day, they locked us in the house again. We lived quite a distance from Tiananmen Square so my father went to the hospital near us because he wanted to count bodies, he wanted to know what had happened. He said the bodies were in bicycle sheds, and so he counted the bodies. He wanted to calculate approximately how many people got killed. Just near us, he counted about fifty, and we were far from the centre of the city.

WACHTEL What was the aftermath? What happened after those few days?

LI We were not allowed to go to school for a week. Looking back, it was a very strange time. People, I think, were a little shellshocked. If you went into street, you would see tanks and armed vehicles and soldiers everywhere. On the other hand, life had to go on, so my parents had to go out to do groceries. A week after we started back to school, there was a period of time when everybody had to report what they did during this long month and a half. Some of us did not really fare well in this interrogation.

WACHTEL What did you say? You just had to account for yourself or confess to something?

LI You had to account for every day. Did you participate in a march or in a protest? Because we were in high school, the teachers advised us to say certain things to pass the check. We had a friend whose daughter did not follow the official line. She was quite active, a leader at her college, she didn't pass the check. It wasn't serious enough for her to go to prison, but she was expelled from the university, and she would not be allowed to have an official job in China for quite a long time.

WACHTEL I think I recognize this friend as a character in your novel, *Kinder Than Solitude*, but we'll come to that.

What disturbed you most about what you had seen or heard?

LI Partly I think just the fact that people who are not armed would be shot at by the army. That seemed like something we would have read in novels or history books, but it would never happen to us. So that's something that was quite shocking.

I think for me it was also how people reacted. There were courageous people. There were also petty-minded people, because right after the massacre, I think the city government opened hotlines, and you could call in and say who was in a protest, or who threw a rock at the army, and without really extensive investigation these people would be arrested. A lot of people were tortured when they were arrested by the army. Everyone in Beijing had such stories to tell, and that, to me, was also a new thing to learn: how some people could be heroic and others could be really base.

WACHTEL In your latest novel, *Kinder Than Solitude*, the high school students are required to participate in a celebration at Tiananmen Square just a few months after the massacre—the fortieth anniversary of "Mother China" on October 1, 1989. Did you have to do that?

LI Yes, my school went. The timing was very sensitive; it was barely four months after the bloodshed. Looking back, you realized there were so many ironies about the whole celebration. For instance, we were not allowed to wear black and white, the girls and boys. We had to wear colourful clothes. We couldn't wear black and white because those are mourning colours. That the government would orchestrate such a celebration while being so afraid of any kind of subversive activities is interesting to me in retrospect.

WACHTEL A few years ago, you published an essay about your first visit back to China in a decade, where you met a taxi driver who refused to give up the memory of 1989 in his newly prosperous country, and you said then that China has grown into the China we know today partly *because* of what happened in 1989. How so?

LI In so many ways, if you look at the 1980s, young people were quite idealistic, and I would say that this young generation's concern was to have a democratic country and to have a more Westernized economic and political system. I think 1989 stopped a whole generation's dream, and people realized that whatever democracy is, it is not possible in China. A lot of people left China. But for those who chose to stay, like Moyan in the novella, their concern is no longer political. Their concerns are more materialistic; they want to make money in this new economy. So in a way, I think both good things and bad things happened. The country has developed so much; you would never see something like 1989 today, but that's because people are less likely to express their political feelings. They're more concerned about materialistic things.

I think it's interesting because in the 1980s, especially in '88 and '89, when people talked about corruption, it really was a very corrupt government. When people talked about corruption, they hoped for a better government, a less corrupt government. Today I think China is probably equally, if not more, corrupt. And people talk about corruption too, not because they want a better government or less corrupt officials but because they want those corrupt people to be gone so they can replace them and take advantage of possible corruption. So that's a huge change.

WACHTEL The refusal to revisit the events of Tiananmen comes not only from the Chinese government but also from the people themselves. Why do you think there has been no real reckoning or accounting for the repression and brutality?

LI Partly, I think within China it's the political pressure. Every year around June 4—for instance, I follow Chinese news—it's a sensitive time, and I think the human rights activists are all censored, or they're all under house arrest, so it's impossible for such things to happen again in a meaningful way.

On the other hand, I have noticed in the past five or even ten years that China has started to adopt the sentiment of moving on. The Cultural Revolution and 1989 are history. We have to move on, and in a way moving on means you just don't think about it anymore.

WACHTEL So this isn't just the younger generation that lacks historical memory. Even people who experienced or lived through those times have a desire to erase history.

LI Yes, I would say so. Probably my parents' generation cling to that history, but even in my generation, people ask, What's the good of talking about these things? Let's move on. And people move on fairly quickly from tragedy to tragedy because there's a race to become richer and more powerful in a way that we would not have imagined twenty or thirty years ago.

WACHTEL Twenty-five years ago.

LI Twenty-five years ago, yes.

WACHTEL Is it a significant number to you? Is it something that you think back about?

LI When I first came to America, every year on June 4, I would look at all the pictures. You get more access to the documents of the Tiananmen massacre from outside the country than from inside China. I think for about ten years I used to look at the pictures and documents every year on that date. I stopped because they have become a part of my life and I don't have to look at them to remember them. In a way, I think, especially with *Kinder Than Solitude*, it's more directly about the events, and when I was writing it, I wanted to remove myself a little from the real events.

WACHTEL *Kinder Than Solitude* shifts between 1989—a few months after Tiananmen Square—and twenty-one years later, in the year 2000. It deals indirectly with the impact of the massacre, focussing more on the psychological violence that shapes the lives of your characters. Can you explain how the personal and the political connect for you in this story?

LI Yes. This is not a political novel, except it's a novel with a political setting. So it happened in 1989 a few months after the Tiananmen massacre, and one of the characters—you mentioned earlier that you recognized her—was Shaoai. She was an active protester in Tiananmen Square during that period. The Tiananmen massacre happened two or three months before the novel started. But other than Shaoai and a few neighbourhood grownups, most people avoided talking about it, especially the three main characters. They did not talk about it back in 1989, and they would not talk about it twenty-one years later. I did not write the book to negate the events of 1989, but I was fascinated by my characters' refusal to acknowledge them. Any time there is a negative space, it tells a lot about the characters. So the political environment is a negative space in all three characters' lives, and instead they focus on their personal lives, their private tragedies, while actually they live in the big shadow of Tiananmen Square, in the big shadow of the public tragedies, except that they would not acknowledge it.

WACHTEL What's the effect of that shadow, do you think?

LI For these three characters, and even for their parents and their neighbours, the big shadow is more of a fatalistic thing. Again. China already has this fatalism from Buddhism or from Taoism, from five thousand years of history. But this big political shadow was also a source of uncertainty and instability. And so it's a shadow that said life could be turned into nothing, and I think in the end all three characters did not escape that shadow.

WACHTEL The central event in *Kinder Than Solitude* was inspired by an actual case, a chemical poisoning in 1995 of a Chinese college student, Zhu Ling. That crime remains unsolved. What happened?

LI This happened in a college next to the university I went to, and she was poisoned by a heavy metal. She recovered the first time and she returned to school, but then she was poisoned again, and she quickly went into a coma. At the time, there was no diagnosis. This was back in 1995, when the Internet was not very available in China, but a high school friend happened to have access to the Internet, so he sent an SOS email to the world and said there is a woman in Beijing who's been poisoned, and her symptoms include this and this. Within a day, hundreds of email responses confirmed that she was poisoned. So she was saved, but she has been disabled since then. And nobody was arrested or charged, even though it's still widely believed that one of her roommates or maybe all three roommates did it together. And so that's the real case.

WACHTEL And why was no one charged? Do you know?

LI The person who was believed to be mainly responsible comes from a prestigious background. I think her grandfather was a high-ranking official in the party, and they hushed up the whole case. The case was sealed, and even now nobody is allowed access to anything from back in 1995.

WACHTEL What was it in the story that made you want to write about it?

LI My interest is always about psychological wildness. Poisoning happens all the time in China, and in general I was interested in people who poison other people and why they would do that. Poisoning is a very passive-aggressive way to kill people. All murders are plotted, but poisoning has a special kind of plot. It has to be a very intimate crime; not only do you have to have access to poison but you also have to have access to people's food or drink, all these things. I realized poisoning was more than physical violence. It's psychological violence. So I wrote to explore that.

WACHTEL Shaoai, the young activist poisoned in your novel, is not the real-life Zhu Ling. Of the four people whose lives we follow in the story, she is the one whose perspective we never inhabit, but she's still a strong presence. Can you tell me a bit about this character, how you see her?

LI It's interesting you say she's a strong presence. In a way, she's the centre again. After she was poisoned, she remained the same for twenty-one years, and in a way, she's the only one who's been protected from this poisoning. She lost all her abilities to understand the world. She lost most of her sight. She lost most of her bodily functions. But psychologically she was protected. Her parents, her neighbours, all three characters around her—they were not protected. They have had to live through, they have had to endure, these twenty-one years.

So interesting to me. In the end I realized, although she was the one poisoned, that she did not experience the bigger poison, which is time, and time poisons everybody else in the book.

WACHTEL Shaoai is far from idealized. She's passionate, she's argumentative, confrontational. In fact, in some ways, she reminds me of a bit of Gu Shan, the young woman executed in the opening chapters of *The Vagrants*. A political radical from an earlier time, another difficult daughter who alienates her devoted parents—does that make sense?

LI Yes. Except Gu Shan is a bit more idealistic than Shaoai. Shaoai is to me more predatory.

And, yes, in a way I'm never interested in a good or heroic character. They both could be political heroines, but I always want to see the other side of them: why Gu Shan was so willing to give up her child, for instance, or why Shaoai was so unforgiving towards an orphan.

WACHTEL It's also not that hard to see what Shaoai is up against. Her father adheres to the lesson he got from his own father: Do not talk about politics. And her mother says, "Every generation has to learn this lesson. Public protest will never do in this country." It sounds similar to the message of caution that you were also hearing at that time.

LI Very much, very much.

WACHTEL But when Shaoai's father says, "We've had enough revolutions in our lifetime," she says, "Our revolution is going to be completely different." Was that the belief that your generation held as well?

LI That's not my belief, but I would say it was the belief that the Tiananmen Square generation held at the time. I didn't write to judge that, but I want Shaoai to say that so I could hear how it sounds, and you realize every generation's revolution is the same, despite her saying it's different, it's the only revolution that counts. No, it is not.

WACHTEL You not only didn't idealize Shaoai, but you made her quite an unappealing character. What moral complications were you after?

LI Again, this is going back in history. I remember a few days before June 4, 1989, a college friend of ours who was active throughout the protest started to withdraw, and he came to us. I think he was disillusioned in a way. He said, "It's pretty ugly." He said all the student leaders were fighting for this and that. They used the money donated to rent a room in a high-end hotel. He said things that made me think all revolutionaries are human, and they probably all have very unappealing sides. But that doesn't mean Shaoai came from that group of people. Shaoai wanted to be active in the protest. Shaoai wanted to be a heroine. These desires are not far from her desire to control a younger girl. It's that power she's attracted to.

WACHTEL You said you were surprised by one of the teenage friends, the character Moran in your novel *Kinder Than Solitude*, that she lied to you. What do you mean?

LI Moran came in an earlier draft, and she was one of the earliest characters in the novel. She was quite particular about her solitude. And she's also, I would say, the quintessential character, solitary and lonely. But she said certain things about solitude that took me in, and I believed her, and I thought, yes, this is the life she wanted to have. She didn't want to have a close connection to other people because of her history, and while she was not happy, she had peace in this state. That was what she told me when I first started writing the novel.

As I was writing the novel, I always had to push the characters a little. I realized she wasn't honest with me or with herself, probably more with herself. So I kept writing her, and as it turned out, she doesn't really have solitude. She feels extremely isolated and lonely in her state. She wants to be loved, she wants to love people, but she's not able to.

In the end, she realizes she doesn't have solitude, but a lifelong quarantine. And that was the point when I realized she was deceiving both me and herself, and then we stripped that mask.

WACHTEL Moran is probably the most touching character in the novel. We see her change from being an enthusiastic, warm, engaging child to someone who has chosen a life cut off from family and love and community.

LI Yes. She's the least immune to all that happened around the poisoning case. As you say, she was a warm person, and she believed in good things. She believed in loving and being loved. And all her beliefs when she was a teenager were judged. She was judged; she was in a moral court. She also realized that she had made a lot of mistakes around the poisoning, and she cannot resolve her personal conflicts in her head. She had to withdraw from life so she would not experience those pains again.

WACHTEL In a sense, Moran orphans herself, as do many of your characters. There are many different kinds of parent-child relationships in your fiction, but it would be hard not to notice the number of broken bonds: children rejected, abandoned, orphaned, adopted, and so on. Family history seems to be a painful subject for your characters. Why is that?

LI I'm very happy you said Moran orphaned herself. In a way, the novel is about orphans, because in a family and in family history, the burden of emotions is not what every character can handle. I'm always interested in that because we all live in families. We all come from somewhere. Nobody is a true orphan. Even Ruyu said she was like a little bit of grass growing from a crack. Even though she said that, there were still a couple of moments when she thought about her parents because she knew she came from them.

WACHTEL She was given up for adoption at birth.

LI Yes. Her parents abandoned her, but she still had them. She would not allow herself to think about them, but that doesn't mean they did not exist for her. We all come from parents, and our parents come from parents, and family histories become memories of every character.

WACHTEL Kindness is a concern for some of your characters and you too, it would seem, because its meaning, its value, is contrasted with the harshness and cruelty that your characters encounter in the world. How has kindness come to be a preoccupation for you?

LI Kindness seems really at the centre of my concern about the world and life. I have never had a pair of rose-coloured glasses; life is life. There are always hardships. There are good moments and bad moments, and I think all these things, good and bad, are unavoidable. After all, you're going to experience certain suffering and grief. These are all part of life. But kindness is something that we can choose to give or withhold. There are people who are kind not only to others but to themselves. I think that kindness to oneself is also very important. In the end, kindness seems to be one thing that we can choose and show other people, and I like to write about that because it's a choice.

WACHTEL Your novel *Kinder Than Solitude* also tracks the changes over twenty-odd years in your home town of Beijing. Can you give me a picture of your Beijing, the atmosphere or places or landmarks that were important to you when you were growing up?

LI The Beijing of 1989 is the Beijing I knew when I grew up, with all its alleyways. It's just not a developed city; it has the beauty of history.

Any time you look at a tree, it's five hundred years old. Or you walk down an alleyway, and the stone had been there for two hundred years. Those are the parts of the city I grew up to know really well. Of course, the lake area in the novel was quite residential when I was growing up. When we were students, we would go there to watch people living their lives. Now it's very sexy.

WACHTEL "Sexy"? I thought it was touristic.

LI They say it's the sexiest spot in Beijing for tourists, which means it has all the ex-pats and all the pubs. The nightclubs are gathered around this area. "Sexy" is, I guess, what the lake area advertises itself as.

WACHTEL You describe Moran and Boyang in middle school as they become very interested in their city. They collect books about architecture and history as well as anecdotes. How unusual would this be?

LI I suppose I borrowed that from my own life. When I was growing up I was fascinated by the history of Beijing, and Beijing has a rich history. In general, I think children of my generation all know something about history, about this temple, about that palace, and it's part of growing up in the city. The place is in your blood.

WACHTEL What's it like for you to visit Beijing today?

LI It's different. I think the city has had a facelift. Earlier you asked me what the difference was. Most of the alleyways are gone, replaced by skyscrapers. It doesn't feel like home anymore, I would say. It feels like any big city. You can look at Beijing or you can look at Shanghai, you can look at New York and London. I love all big cities. But some parts, some very private, personal parts of Beijing were gone.

WACHTEL You've taken your children back to China to see their grandparents. What do you especially want to show them?

LI I wanted them to see where I came from. They grew up in America and have certain notions about China as an Asian country with pagodas and bamboo shoots or as a very modern country with plastic toys. These are the two extreme ends of their perception of China. I want them to see real people in China. The real people don't change that much.

WACHTEL You have said that you continue to write about China because there are questions you haven't been able to answer. What were you thinking of?

LI I think about family history, and also how personal history and political history intersect. I'm still interested in these things. If you look at

China, a hundred years of public history really has made a huge difference to people's lives. And in that big shadow, there are little shadows I'm still exploring.

May 2014
Original interviews produced by Sandra Rabinovitch

SEAMUS HEANEY

In 1995, Seamus Heaney became Ireland's first Nobel Prize-winning poet since W.B. Yeats. I'd spoken to him earlier and then again, some years later, not long after his seventieth birthday when he was celebrated in Ireland with specials on radio and television, a documentary film, musical compositions inspired by his poetry, and a fifteen-CD boxed set of his work. His following was so large that crowds lining up to hear him were once dubbed "Heaneyboppers." But as Colm Toibin wrote, "Seamus Heaney carried his fame lightly, easily. He was not merely a central figure in the literary life of Ireland, but in its emotional life, in its dream life, in its real life."

Seamus Heaney was born in 1939 into a Catholic family in the mainly Protestant unionist Northern Ireland. He grew up on a farm—the oldest of seven boys and two girls. When he was eleven, he won a scholarship to a boarding school, St. Columb's College in Derry. He went to university in Belfast and then teachers college, publishing his first book of poetry when he was twenty-seven. In 1972, Heaney moved with his young family to a cottage in County Wicklow in the south, in the Republic of Ireland, and he lived there and in Dublin—though for twenty years, he also taught a semester at Harvard.

Heaney's poems engage with the immediacy of the natural world, its physicality; he celebrates the domestic sphere but also with an awareness of the outside world beyond. There are some lines in a poem called "Terminus" that capture some of that. When he digs, he finds an acorn and a rusted bolt. If he looks up, he sees a factory chimney and a mountain. He writes: "Is it any wonder when I thought / I would have second thoughts?" Later he says, "Two buckets were easier carried than one. / I grew up in between."

That "in between" wasn't just a political line but reflected his posture in relation to the world. His embrace was large.

Seamus Heaney was one of the most generous of men: patient, forthcoming. During our conversation in 2010, there was a problem with the sound in the Dublin studio; his forbearance was remarkable. He read from what would be his last book, *Human Chain* (2010). It went on to win the UK's £10,000 Forward Prize, among his many, many honours. He died in 2013, aged seventy-four.

WACHTEL You were born at Mossbawn Farm in County Derry, Northern Ireland. What are your earliest memories of that place?

HEANEY Well, my earliest memory is of my foot touching the ground of Mossbawn, the County Derry earth, or rather a floor laid above the earth. I was in a cot made by the local carpenter, and the bottom of the cot consisted of slats of timber, little smooth boards laid on ledges. They weren't nailed down; obviously you wanted to be able to lift them because the children would be peeing on them or doing worse. I remember lifting one or two of those boards and stepping off the bottom of the cot down onto the smooth, cool cement floor of the house. And I can still feel my little foot inside my old foot here. So that's my very first memory, undoubtedly. The house was a typical thatched, whitewashed, long, low country farmhouse of that era, part of the vernacular architecture of rural Ireland. It faced out to the local county road, and behind it, one field away, was the railway called the London, Midland and Scottish Railway, which stopped operating sometime in the late 1950s, early 1960s. But through the 1940s, the trains were running, and the big powerful noise would come over the field of a steam engine shunting up to the station at Castledawson. I mean, I could talk about this 'til the cows came home.

There were cows at home in the byre across the yard. There was a horse in the stable. The stable was under the same roof with the dwelling house, and one of the big, comforting sounds quite often was the horse going *nhrrrr* in the stable at the other end of the house. We didn't have a fire on the hearth, but we did have water from the pump, and there were wells around the place. What with thatch and well water and horse-drawn vehicles and horse ploughs and so on, when I look back on it, there's a strong sense that it belonged in another age, really.

WACHTEL You were the oldest of nine children. In your poem "A Sofa in the Forties," you evoke the domesticity of your early life with the description of the train game you and your siblings play on the sofa, pretending to be passengers and ticket collectors. But the poem darkens as it reaches out into history. Family play gives way to intimations of a terrible fate as the "ghost trains" and "death gondolas" transport the victims of the Holocaust to their deaths. There is this juxtaposition of innocence and knowledge—

HEANEY As the years went on, I realized that the train was such a sinister vehicle in Europe at the time. I think one of the most terrible images of the twentieth century is of that train pulling in to Auschwitz. So you live and learn.

WACHTEL There's so much in that poem—the inadequate Christmas presents, the resonance of history, and also a wonderful sense of play, of make-believe, imagination. How much was that part of your experience as a child?

HEANEY There was cowboys and Indians of course, Robin Hood with bows and arrows, the train. That kind of thing, I think, is universal for youngsters. We lived a kind of Arcadian life in Mossbawn. If you'd been living in Warsaw or London, or Birmingham, or even Belfast where they were bombed during the war, you'd have a very different sense of what the world was, and maybe your make-believe would have been more defensive. But I often quote William Wordsworth thinking of his childhood before he went to boarding school: "Fair seed-time had my soul," he says, "and I grew up / Fostered alike by beauty and by fear." And actually any fear I had was, on the whole, elemental fear. Wordsworth was afraid in the mountains, I was scared by frogs and rats... and frogs spawning, which went into my first poem, "Death of a Naturalist." That kind of thing was all over the place. The usual rural childhood anxieties. But generally it was a very secure time up 'til the age of twelve, when I went to boarding school.

WACHTEL What frightened you about frogs spawning?

HEANEY I went down into this area where there was a flax-dam, and they were there as physical creatures with their necks pulsing, as I say in the poem. They were croaking, and it was a very sinister kind of croak, a kind of chorus of croaking, and it just was scaresome to me.

I dramatized it a little in the poem. I said I ran away, but I certainly turned. I was afraid of them. I don't quite know what age I was, maybe five, six, seven. It was the sense of the gross, physical frogginess of them all and the sound they made. And the stink of the flax-dam at the same time, that was another factor in the repellent aspect of it.

WACHTEL The land around you comes up frequently in your poetry and your prose. How important is that physical environment when you look back on your childhood?

HEANEY For me it was all-important. When I think back, it's sensation, really, rather than intellection that returns to me. A feel for places. I mean, the body stores so much. I can remember holding the handles of a horse plough for example, with my father's hands over my hands to help me guide it. When the ploughshare would hit a small stone in the furrow, that travelled back up the handles through the grip into your own hand like a little bleep. I still remember that, but I think that's not uncommon, is it? What is stored bodily is very important for memory, and I think that other bodily sensations later on can bring it all back.

WACHTEL I remember that image of the horse plough in your poem "Follower." It's not just the land but the tools for engaging with it that are so vivid—from your earliest poems, such as "Digging," right up to recent ones.

HEANEY Yes, that's true. My head is furnished with medieval tools like sledgehammers and iron spikes to drive into walls and horse collars and so on. There's something in me that responds very physically and emotionally to them. It's as if one has a better grip on things when I get my hand or my tongue around those particular objects.

In my last book I did a poem about a sledgehammer hitting a post, but I think it wasn't just a physical sensation I was trying to get at. It was about the full exercise of merciless, violent power. It was a poem written after Iraq. There were no Iraq references in it, but it is about the sense of transgression you have when you utterly, mercilessly use a sledgehammer, even when hitting a dead post. There's a kind of unrestrained fury, an unforgiving brutality to it that I wanted to get. So I think that you can transmit sensation but hopefully suggest and effect a consequence as well.

WACHTEL Your father was a cattle dealer. Can you tell me a bit about him?

HEANEY His work—his calling, really—involved him going out on the road to fairs, buying cattle there, and then bringing them back home and supplying other farmers. Or he would get orders from local farmers and would go to the fairs to buy the beasts at a certain rate and bring them back and sell them at some profit or other. So he was a kind of middleman between small farmers and other cattle dealers. We're talking about a culture now that has gone completely. I mean, there are no fair days in the way there used to be when local people drove the cattle into the main street of the local village, and there was a big assembly on the first Monday of every month or the second Tuesday of every month or whatever. Now, and in the later days of my father's life, all that negotiation is done in auction rings and it's much more corporate. What he did was find individual beasts and make individual deals at the fair and then on the farm. He was a very good judge of cattle and was much sought by people who wanted decent stock, and I suppose he was trusted also.

WACHTEL You've described him as a solid, quiet country man with country confidence. So he didn't say that much?

HEANEY No, he didn't speak that much, no. I've often said my father regarded speech as a kind of affectation. He suspected the statement of too many good intentions and good sentiments. He assumed that intuitive transmission was the real thing. If it was overstated, he tended to shy away from it.

WACHTEL By overstated you mean stated.

HEANEY Yes, indeed. Statement was overstatement to some extent, that's right.

WACHTEL When your father died in 1986, you said the roof came off the world. Can you tell me what in particular that meant for you?

HEANEY I was forty-seven, I think. My mother died in 1984, and my father died a couple of years later. I think maybe that's just a common experience; that you are next in line, there's nothing over your head in terms of age, in terms of a parent. It coincided in my own life with a wonderful bout of writing a couple of years later—1988, 1989—a sequence of poems eventually called *Squarings*. They were terrifically free, and they began with an image of an unroofed wall-stead of an old ruined house and an image of the soul as a beggar standing in the doorway. I suppose that particular image began to take hold of me—the idea of an unroofed space and the creature, soul-body, down here with nothing between it and the infinite. And all the early formation, all the early religious imagery that I got for life and death, for the meaning of your life on earth and then your afterlife, all that somehow was stirred again. For anybody in my generation, certainly in the Irish Catholic generation, the soul was like a little white handkerchief, unstained, and you would stain it with sin and so on. But more important was the sense that the whole universe was governed by the deity, that there was divine attention being paid not just to the universe but to you yourself. You're like a little drop of water in this great ocean, you're a little speck in the whole scheme of things: nevertheless, you are being watched over, and watched over not only in terms of care but in terms of supervision to see you do nothing wrong. And there was this idea, and my generation got it very early, that there would be two judgments at the end of your life. First, at the end of your particular life, you would be whipped away into eternity and you would undergo a particular judgment; your own life would be scanned, and rewards or punishments, or atonement, would be the result of that. Then again at the end of time, there would be a general judgment, and the whole thing would be ratified on a larger scale. Anybody who undergoes that is marked by it forever, I think. And no matter what kind of secularization occurs, there is a huge coordinate established for consciousness from the beginning, that sense of the outer shimmering rim of everything always being there in your imagination. Maybe that explains it—the soul being whipped away and the roof coming off and you being exposed to that infinity that occurs after the death of your parents.

WACHTEL You mention that this foundation was so strong regardless of the secularization that occurred later, but were you a believer at the time?

HEANEY Of course I was a believer. I don't know what I believe anymore, but I was part of the Irish Catholic machinery until my late teens, early twenties, definitely. The matter of the sacraments, transubstantiation for example, gave me trouble at a certain stage. But the idea that you could gain merit through a system of grace and you could gain merit for other people, that self-denial had a spiritual meaning, and that there was a whole supernatural economy, that had strong appeal to me. Of course you dwell in doubts, as John Keats says, and you can dwell with doubts as well as with beliefs, but I think all that was shaken. When you left the church atmosphere and grew into adulthood, at university, you were between worlds again. You knew that you belonged in a Catholic, medieval, Chaucerian, Dantesque world, and at the same time you were dwelling in a post-Freudian, post-D.H. Lawrence world. One part of you had the experience of going to confession and confessing sins of impurity, the other part of you is writing essays about Lawrence and commending the dark gods and the sensual realities of life that he expressed.

WACHTEL Sex.

HEANEY Yes, sex, exactly. Sex, the whole thing was there.

WACHTEL From your descriptions of home, there wasn't a lot of reading material at hand. When did you first become interested in poetry?

HEANEY Well, poetry as "poetry." Early on I was familiar with recitation. We had little concerts at home as children, where we recited poems we'd learned at school. Then at Christmas and at Easter, elder friends of my father and mother would be in, and there would be sing-songs; and as I came into adolescence I would be asked to do a recitation. I knew several, such as "The Shooting of Dan McGrew," "The Spell of the Yukon," and "The Cremation of Sam McGee," by Robert Service, and then an Irish writer called Percy French who wrote that kind of thing also.

But it was when I went to secondary school, I suppose, and began to get into English literature and poetry as a subject, that something in me came alive to the language, something wakened or was stirred, especially by poets like John Keats, Gerard Manley Hopkins, and so on. In university, that conscious relish of language became stronger, but I was always shy of "poetry." I didn't quite know what it was. And I think it was right to be shy of it, because nobody knows quite what it is. I suppose I wrote some poems as every literary undergraduate does, but it wasn't until I was in my twenty-second or twenty-third year, 1962, that "that something" started in me. I've said this often, but it came from reading poetry by Patrick Kavanagh, an Irish poet with the same kind of background as myself, a wonderful sudden burst of energy from him; and likewise from Ted Hughes, who again touched on subjects that I thought were known only to me, such as dead pigs lying in barrows, and bulls in outhouses, and barns and so on. So that was, as they say, permission. As an undergraduate at Queen's University, of course I had been lectured on contemporary poetry, and I had read Eliot, I had read Auden. But I had also swallowed the standard line that contemporary poetry was urban, ironical, detached. I mean, the intonations of Eliot I could hear as a listener, but they didn't enter me or waken anything in me in the way these other voices did. So once I started in 1962, I was bitten and kept going back for more.

WACHTEL When you were writing as an undergraduate, you went under the name of Incertus, or Uncertain, and then when you got this kind of affirmation to trust your own experience of rural life through, as you say, Ted Hughes or Patrick Kavanagh or even Robert Frost, it gave you this permission. But you say that no place in the world prides itself more on its vigilance and realism than Northern Ireland, and I wondered how you felt that influence on your own work.

HEANEY It would be very hard for me to analyze that. I take it that I am vigilant myself and a bit sceptical, and I hope merrily so, so that's part of the makeup. And allowing yourself to get through that is part of the action. I think that self-forgetfulness, self-entrancement, is part of the action of writing, certainly of writing verse. To dwell silently on something within yourself, to forget that you are there watching yourself in action, that's the achievement and that's the desire. And I think nowadays a lot of people really experience that in front of a screen. A computer screen is an entrancement device. It's hypnotic, that grey glow. Not that I would begin poems on the screen. I have a connection to the shaft of the fountain pen still. I like to get started on white paper with ink gleaming, and then I like the reward of putting it out onto the screen and then hard copy and then fiddling away with that.

WACHTEL You were part of a literary world in Northern Ireland for a while; there was a poetry scene in the 1960s and 1970s. Then you went to California for a year. But when you came back to Northern Ireland, you gave up teaching and moved to the south, to the Republic of Ireland. It made front-page news in *The Irish Times*. What prompted this move in 1972?

HEANEY I had a year in California that meant a lot to me, I have to say. That was 1970, 1971, right in the middle of the Vietnam War, the middle of the countercultural moment. Terrific protests. The whole of that Bay area was really a countercultural area. You had the Black Panthers, you had the Hare Krishnas, you had the loose garments, you had the illegal substances. You had all kinds of fragrances on that campus, all kinds of rhetoric, all kinds of protest. And the poets were very much involved. The year I was there, Robert Bly was up in Inverness, just a little north of Berkeley; Gary Snyder was there, Robert Duncan. When I came back to Belfast, I was first of all fortified in the knowledge that

I could go back to the English department, because the last thing the chairman said to me was, "If you ever need to come back, you'd be very welcome." There was that security blanket, and then there was a feeling of vocation that had grown in me during that year. I taught for another year in Queen's University and finished my third book, and I sensed that it was time to declare myself as a writer. So I thought, okay, go for it. But there was no immediate plan at all that we would go to the Republic of Ireland. That early summer of 1972, Marie and I were driving around the north—County Derry, County Tyrone, County Antrim—looking at places. Then from Canada, we got a letter from our dear friend Ann Saddlemyer, who was teaching at the University of Toronto. She had this cottage in County Wicklow in the Republic, south of Dublin. It was on the old Synge estate—Ann was a scholar of Synge's work, an editor. She wrote, "I heard on the grapevine that you're thinking of leaving the academy for a while and looking for a house. I've got this cottage in County Wicklow." So at Easter, Marie and I and the kids went down to that cottage and we decided, yes, let's make a go of it. I gave in my resignation, and in the month of August we saddled up, filled a van, and went down to the Glanmore cottage, stayed there for four years, and didn't go back to Queen's, didn't go back to the north to dwell there at all. So it was a happy mixture of Ann's philanthropy, as it were, and the growth point in our own lives.

WACHTEL Once you did make the move, did it change how you saw the political situation? What effect did it have on your family, to move to the Republic?

HEANEY I don't think it had very much effect in terms of politics or anything like that. I mean, if I had been in the north, my attitude would have been the same. I wanted the kids, really, to have the kind of childhood I'd had, I suppose; to share the feeling of growing up behind hedges and having eye-level contact with bird's nests and leaves and flowers and so on. And there was something in myself that relished the frugality of life in the cottage, something that belonged in my first life, but it wasn't a matter of fleeing the north. We lived as easily in Belfast as ever we had lived in the years leading up to the Troubles. It wasn't a matter of feeling scared or being hunted out of the place or shaking the dust of the place off. It was very much to do with the option and the freedom of making a choice, embracing something different. In a sense, it was the first choice I deliberately made. I've often said that

Marie and I were part of the scholarship generation. We got the scholarship to secondary school, we got the scholarship to the university, we got the scholarship to the teaching training college, we went into teaching, we got engaged, we got the mortgage, we got the house, we got the young family, and there we were. California was the first step off the conveyor belt, and when we came back we stepped farther off it. So that was a freedom.

WACHTEL There are references to the Troubles in some of your work, but it's not often there as a central focus. How do you see the responsibility of poets to the politics of their time?

HEANEY That is a question that I kept answering ad nauseum between about 1969 and 1989. Almost everything that I've written in prose and much that's in verse is about that question. Poets of the 1930s in England especially felt that. Spender, Auden, and Louis MacNeice—who's an Irish poet of course, but part of that British generation—they had to deal with the Spanish Civil War, the rise of fascism, and so on. They were lyric poets, they had private subjects. They had love, Eros, sex, time, childhood, and yet there was the big war and the need for commitment. Communism was flowering as an ideology. The attraction of working for the wretched of the earth was deep, moral, and compelling. So what was the private lyric poet to do? Was he or she to just keep to the lyric matter of the self and beauty, or was there a bigger obligation? I grew up with an orthodoxy inculcated at the university that these poets made a mistake when they embraced anything propagandist or political. I think there was a confusion, perhaps, in my mind and in the minds of some of my teachers between the propagandist and the political. Political was inculcated as a bad word in relation to art and poetry. Our great exemplar W. B. Yeats was ever against "opinion" in verse, but he was never afraid to deliver opinion. I realized later on that his rhetoric and his practice were slightly at odds. So over the years, I think we had to learn how to incorporate the matter of the Troubles—bombs, killings, the actual landscape of contemporary Ulster—into the kinds of things we were writing. It's a far cry from Mossbawn, if you like, from the big noise of the shunting of an engine to the explosions of car bombs rattling the windows in Belfast; Bloody Sunday to Bloody Friday, both occurring in 1972. None of us had quite got the way of handling it. Many years later, I found a way of letting some people speak in a poem called "Station

Island," which was a kind of a dialogue between a poet/protagonist and various ghosts—some who had been killed in the Troubles, some who had been involved in Irish life in the nineteenth century, and indeed the shade of James Joyce, who warns against too much side-taking, not to be the voice of any people, but to be your own voice.

WACHTEL And when you look back now, not that you need to spend much time revisiting it in your own work, do you feel you walked the right line? It was at some times, I think, a fairly difficult path to negotiate.

HEANEY Well, there's nothing that strikes me as dishonest in anything that was written. It may not have pleased everybody, but it pleased me enough to get on with it, and that's the best you can do as a writer, I think—to write honestly, honestly in terms of the subject and in terms of your attitudes, and in terms of who and what you are. And honestly in terms of your makings, in terms of the art, that it is not faked up, that it belongs as a true imaginative response, that it isn't generated out of will, but arises out of something more deeply lodged in yourself. I feel that anything that is in the books, mistaken or not, middling writing or not, good or bad, got there like that and I have no anxiety about changing it or getting rid of it.

WACHTEL So much has happened, since that time and in more recent years, for the good. How do you feel now? How do you see the future for Northern Ireland?

HEANEY I think that the new institutions are important, but I don't see any great love-in occurring between the two communities for a good while. The main thing would be that in the new local parliament the opposing sides would find a way of talking at least, not bogging themselves down in ideological or sectarian fury again. I think the signs are middlingly good for that. We've moved from the atrocious to the vigilant, small-minded messiness of tit-for-tat politics, and that is an advance. So I am hopeful, yes, and certainly it's a far better prospect now than it was thirty, forty, fifty years ago even. Things have moved on. Little changes are very important, little changes in the individual breast. And getting the institutions up, if not running, at least going at pedestrian speed, has been a great achievement, a great change.

WACHTEL There are so many rich images in your work. I'm wondering, how does a poem start for you?

HEANEY Almost always it starts from some memory, something you'd forgotten that comes up like a living gift of presence. Robert Frost said in his introduction to his *Collected Poems*, "like giants we are always hurling experience ahead of us to pave the future with against the day when we may want to strike a line of purpose across from somewhere." That is generally the way things happen with me. The memory comes up and if I'm lucky, it attaches itself, it crosses itself with some other thing. I mean, I had that poem about playing trains on the sofa in Mossbawn. It luckily didn't end up just a little nostalgic recreation of happy families on the sofa in the 1940s. It crossed with that sense that gradually came as one grew, how lucky we were not to be living the terrible, tragic life of others in mainland Europe and in Britain. The shadow that we didn't know was there could be recognized retrospectively. That is the kind of poem I really like: the stimulus in memory, but the import, hopefully, more than just the content of memory. But without memory, I don't think I could move. Mnemosyne, I believe, is supposed to be the mother of the Muses.

WACHTEL In your Nobel lecture in 1995, you credited poetry for its "truth to life, in every sense of that phrase." What were you thinking about in relation to that phrase?

HEANEY First of all, in a poet like Frost, say, it describes the actual, it has a documentary quality. But that's not the only sense in which you can be true to life. You can be true to it in terms of moral insight, in terms of ethical judgment, in realizing the imaginative dimensions of things. You can be true to it the way Wallace Stevens is true to it in a late poem like "The River of Rivers in Connecticut," or the way he's true to it in an early, crazy little lyric like "The bucks went clattering…" I've forgotten which state they go clattering through. Or "The Emperor of Ice Cream," this kind of grand flourish—sportive, elegant, simply play for its own sake in the domain of language. If you take a contemporary American writer like John Ashbery, who a lot of people had, and probably still have, difficulty with—whimsical, non-sequitur writing, channel surfing the language, going zigzag from sentence to sentence—he is true to life insofar as that is the way people's minds are now, hopping from thing to thing. It's the way the world is, attention spans shortened. The world is full of little sound bites, clamours. There's very little silence on earth for anyone anymore. It takes a lot of effort to find a place to walk silently. Ashbery registers the truth-to-lifeness of the new world we live in. So I think it's not just a matter of poetry being true in a novelistic kind of way, reporting what happens, but it's true to the nature of reality, to the balance between the imagined and the endured, between the moral and the imagined and so on. That must be what I meant when I said it.

WACHTEL I was wondering how winning the Nobel changed your life.

HEANEY I don't really know the answer to that. I mean, it changed it in terms of invitations to do things, in terms of pressure of the mail, in terms of saying no to many things. And in Ireland, because we are a small country, the number of invitations to do things isn't just confined to the literary. For example, I'm going to speak at an international conference of gerontologists in September. So that kind of thing changed, but I don't think it radically changed my sense of myself or what I was about as a writer. I mean, I assume that it was given for work that was done rather than work I was going to do. This happened to me in 1995. At that stage, I was already fairly busy and exposed to the world, and fairly well-known and scrutinized. Living through the Troubles as a writer in the north, living as someone who's part of that generation of poets—Michael Longley, Derek Mahon, and so on—we were constantly under scrutiny. We were under political scrutiny, we were under pressure, we were interviewed. I think the kind of attention that came with the Nobel Prize wasn't any more acute or exacting than what we had suffered ourselves already, so I don't think I'm misrepresenting my response to the prize. What is true is this, that other people see you differently once this garland is hung on you. That's another matter, but that's their problem.

WACHTEL You had a stroke in 2006, which you say wasn't exactly a brush with death. What was it?

HEANEY Well, it was wakening up one morning in County Donegal in a guest house where we had been at a party with friends the night before and not being able to get out of the bed, making moves and nothing happening. I was paralyzed on my left side. Luckily, our very good friends were there on the spot, one of them a physiotherapist, so she came in and had a kind of calm talk. The ambulance services came very quickly and I was snatched straight to the hospital, which was an hour away, and en route I was hooked up to a drip that was very good for the circulation and so on. So I went to hospital, was in intensive care for a day and a half, and then something terrific happened. My big toe moved on the left foot. At that point I was brought by ambulance from the north, from Donegal, about 120 miles down to Dublin. I was in a general hospital there for a week. And then I went to a wonderful rehab hospital for about four weeks, and that was it. I learned balance, learned to walk, got refurbished, and got tablets and instructions.

WACHTEL And you didn't lose speech and it didn't affect your mind at all?

HEANEY No, I was extremely lucky in that way. Didn't lose speech, didn't lose memory, and emerged unmarked. But for a while it was scary enough when I just wondered if I'd remain paralyzed. I was blessed, really. But it was a changing experience all right. I cancelled every appointment I had for readings, lectures, and so on for a year, and that had a good effect. It made me much more cautious about accepting invitations and made me realize how much I was on the road and how I should change my ways a bit.

WACHTEL You wrote a poem called "Miracle," after the stroke. Can you explain its resonance in your life?

HEANEY "Miracle" refers to the biblical story where the man sick with the palsy is carried in to be healed by Christ. His friends can't get him in through the crowd that has gathered around the healer, so they take him up to the roof, they take off the tiles, and they lower the man through the roof to the feet of Christ. So this is a little reminder of that morning when something similar happened to me and I learned the importance of those friends.

WACHTEL The title of your collection *Human Chain* has that kind of solidarity and strength to it.

HEANEY Yes, I was thinking of what happened there in that poem, the friends carrying you down when you're paralyzed. But I've also got grandchildren now since the last book, so there are a couple of poems to grandchildren in this one. There are also poems about my inheritance as an Irish writer; poems about early Irish books, manuscript books; little translations of early Irish scribal poems. I've a poem in my first book called "Digging," and in this book, a poem translated from twelfth-century Irish about a scribe writing with a pen. So there's a sense of continuities and support systems and drip-feeds from different areas of experience and imagination and literature and life. That's in the title, *Human Chain*.

WACHTEL How do you think that whole experience of the stroke and the recovery affected how you see your writing?

HEANEY I'm not sure that it has. I mean, that may sound odd, but it affected my work for the better in that I got a few poems out of it, like "Miracle." But I don't want to tour my stroke, as it were. There were a couple or three necessary poems written afterwards, but I think I had a strong enough sense of mortality already. Elegy has been part of the writing I've done all along, and you don't reach the age of seventy without some sense of the end closing in or coming up, at any rate.

WACHTEL I have the sense that you're not just in between north and south, or Northern Ireland and the Republic, but even your posture as a poet is between the very immediate ground under your feet and then something more skyward or visionary. Does that sound right to you?

HEANEY The poetry helps you to discover yourself, and the poetry in the last twenty years or so, I suppose, helped me to revise my notion of myself as earthbound. I had this character Antaeus, whom I maybe over-identified with early on, a giant born of the earth, who gets his strength from the earth, who is renewed when he is thrown to earth. But he is overcome by Hercules, who is a sky-born hero. Hercules realizes that the way to deal with Antaeus is not to throw him onto the earth but to raise him up out of his origin, and that way he will lose his source of strength. So I think in every one of us there is a Hercules and there is an Antaeus. There is a kind of critic as well as a dreamer. There is an analytic intelligence as well as our capacity for entrancement. And that came into the poetry later on, after I read this little story in a Celtic miscellany, a tale of a ship appearing in the air above the monks of Clonmacnoise. It's an early wonder tale, but it's told deadpan. The annalist just says: In this year, the monks of Clonmacnoise saw a ship in the air above them, the anchor of the ship hooked in the doorway or the altar rails of the church, so the ship was caught above them in the air, couldn't move. And then a little crewman came down the rope to where the monks and the abbot were on the earth below him, and he tried to unloose the anchor but couldn't manage, so the abbot said to the monks, "This man will drown down here if we don't help him." So they helped him to unfasten the anchor from the church door or the altar rails or wherever so the boat could sail on, and the little man climbed back up from the church floor, back up to the marvellous—as far as the monks were concerned—up there. And yet the man had seen something marvellous down on the floor of the church. I thought this story discovered something for myself. It seemed the perfect balance. It had everything, as far as I was concerned. You could allegorize the little fellow as a successful Orpheus who goes down, finds what he needs, and comes back with it. The thing is rescued from the Underworld and everybody's happy. Everybody has a good experience. The wonderful has happened down on earth, the necessary has happened up in the sky, and off we go. I think that poetry assists you towards a new awareness, and that is one of the great virtues of achieving, every now and again, a new poem. It is like a landing on a set of stairs. Whether you're going up the stairs or down the stairs, you come to the landing and it's a different level. And if you're lucky, you write poems that situate you on a slightly different level.

May 2010
Original interview produced by Mary Stinson

TONI MORRISON

In 1993, when Toni Morrison was awarded the Nobel Prize in Literature, she was the eighth woman and first African American to win. The Swedish Academy praised her for giving "life to an essential aspect of American reality" in novels "characterized by visionary force and poetic import. She delves into the language itself, a language she wants to liberate from the fetters of race. And she addresses us with the lustre of poetry."

The *New York Times* described her as "the nearest thing America has to a national novelist." A fact that was underlined—in its way—when Morrison had *two* novels featured on the Oprah Book Club: her 1977 novel *Song of Solomon* was the club's second selection back in 1996, and it promptly sold a million copies; her 1997 novel *Paradise* was later added to the list. In 1998, Oprah made a movie of Morrison's Pulitzer Prize-winner, *Beloved* (1987). More recently, *Beloved* was ranked by a *New York Times* survey as the best novel of the past twenty-five years.

Toni Morrison is the granddaughter of an Alabama slave. The second of four children, she was born in 1931 and christened Chloe Ardelia/Anthony Wofford, but took the nickname Toni from her chosen saint's name, Anthony, at college. She grew up in a racially mixed working-class neighbourhood in the American Midwest, studied at the historically black Howard University in Washington, DC, and then at Cornell. From the mid-1960s, she worked as an editor at Random House Books. Then she wrote her own novels and won prizes, including the National Book Critics Circle Award for *Song of Solomon* (1977). Soon after, she left publishing and focussed on writing and teaching—at Harvard, Yale, and for many years, until her seventy-fifth birthday, Princeton.

I first interviewed Toni Morrison in 1992 when she was at the International Festival of Authors in Toronto with *Jazz* (1992). This was before she won the Nobel, but her powerful presence was already legendary. What struck me back then, and what I associate most strongly with her writing, is a sensuous approach to language and its resonance, a love of the rhythms of jazz, and the admission of great passion and great violence in her work.

We spoke when *Love* (2003) was published and met again, in New York, when *Home* (2012) came out. *Home* revolves around a veteran of the Korean War who returns to racist America after fighting for his country and enduring trauma on the front lines. Despite the abuse he encounters, he finds the strength and tenderness to rescue his sister and take her home, to a small town in Georgia, which he's always hated.

When I asked Morrison about how—despite the tragedy in her own life at that time—she was able to deliver a hopeful ending, she said that she hadn't planned it, but "the world is so beautiful. It is really beautiful. Not just the colours and the shapes and the seasons…. It's all just magnificent. And I think that was part of what I was coming to terms with at the end of *Home*."

WACHTEL When you were writing your first novel, *The Bluest Eye*, you were in your thirties, and you said that you wanted to write the kind of book that you wanted to read, that wasn't out there. Can you tell me what was missing?

MORRISON At the time I thought that there was a persona that I'd never read anything about, except in a derogatory, comic fashion. Quite simply, I had never read a book in which a young black girl was centre stage, when she wasn't a backdrop or somebody's notion of comedy. Had I looked, I learned later, I probably would have found one or two.

But at the time I wrote it because I wanted a book like that to read. It would exist because I had delivered it. It took a long, long time to write, because I wasn't thinking about publishing, but after that I never wanted to be without some project that was gestating like that one.

WACHTEL You'd been reading writers like Ralph Ellison and Richard Wright. I read that you admired them, but you felt they weren't really speaking in their own voices.

MORRISON Yes, I felt that their work was extremely important and made a difference to me, but that they addressed their intended readers or white people, I thought, but certainly not me. I didn't know if it was race- or gender-based. I didn't think in those terms then but I knew that both were explaining things that I didn't need explained. I wondered what it would be like if they had been talking to me.

That very much informed the way I wrote *The Bluest Eye*. I always assumed that the person who would read it would be someone like me, so I didn't have to constantly explain the language or explain the mores. I felt not only freed up by that but also that it was the way in which writers write. That is to say, it was only the racial component that even made me consider that, because it doesn't occur to Tolstoy to wonder about whether he's writing for Russians or not. But I had to think about this. He may have had other kinds of questions about class and so on, but these problems surfaced immediately for me.

The other thing, which was somewhat problematic, was that I wasn't trying to elevate the culture by lying about it. Whitewashing it. And that got me in a lot of trouble with black readers, as well as white ones, because they said, Why do you have to write about that? We are looking for much more positive images. I always thought that was just the most outrageous and demeaning question to ask of me because embedded in the question was the problem. Positive images for whom? At the moment they asked the question, they were thinking about the Other, the mainstream, the white world.

I responded by saying that I didn't care about those people; this writing was for my enlightenment and yours. I thought we were the "tell-it-as-it-is-people," but apparently not. You know, it was that kind of thing that was worrisome; I received an enormous amount of rejection from large communities of black people.

WACHTEL Was that hard for you?

MORRISON No, because I was surprised that there was a huge readership, anyway. I always thought my books were not easy. I thought they would be painful, not sugar-coated like people seem to want. So I always thought that there would be a very small group of people who would like my work, and the fact that people misread it or misunderstood it was not terribly surprising to me. There were places—such as Atlanta, Georgia—where my books were taken off the shelves out of bookstores and libraries. By black people.

WACHTEL Did they say why?

MORRISON The same kinds of reasons. This is *Song of Solomon*. There's a very strong conservative mode by and large, among most black people, anyway. Not that I am anarchic or rebellious; it's just that they were looking for a picture of themselves that they could present to the outside world. That is not just censorship, it's the death of art, it's state art, it's propaganda.

WACHTEL In *Song of Solomon,* do you think your readers were shocked by the fact that there's this group of black men in the novel, a secret society called the Seven Days, who revenge the unpunished murders of blacks by killing whites?

MORRISON Well, white people wrote me nasty letters about that. [Black filmmaker] Spike Lee, as a student, wrote me a note and asked if he could take the Seven Days out of *Song of Solomon* and write a script based on it.

WACHTEL He was a bad boy even then, eh?

MORRISON Yes. I said no. He reminds me of that all the time now.

WACHTEL I'd like to go back to your beginnings. You grew up in Ohio, the Midwest, in an atmosphere where there was respect for the irrational—ghosts, signs, visitations, where your mother would tell you her dreams at breakfast.

MORRISON Yes, they were some combination of very shrewd, down-to-earth realistic people, with cunning about how to live in the world under duress and in critical situations. Folded into that was this enchanted world that they accepted. When my mother talked about dreaming, she never claimed to dream. She would say, "Last night I thought I was in"—she was at home there, you know, in her dreams. She relied on them for part of herself, and the word nightmare was almost non-existent in her world.

I knew what dreams were and of course we all had them, and I had the sense that they were frightening, but somehow they were mine. It wasn't something coming in from other places; I owned them. It's ineffable still, my concept of the dream world. But learning it that way as a real possession and activity of my own mind was like having a secret and private world which I could then articulate.

Now, you can imagine, of course, how exciting it was to hear adults talk about their dreams. I had this connection with their interior life that made my own palpable, liveable, and I was eager, in a sense, to have those dreams.

WACHTEL I like the way you say that there is this practical sensibility alongside the dream one, because apparently your grandmother would ask you about your dreams and she would interpret your dreams in numbers.

MORRISON Yes, she played the numbers, you know. You dream a dream, and you look in the dream book where the plot of the dream has a number. Telling her my dreams was thrilling. She was very interested, totally concentrated. Sometimes she would tell me what they meant in terms of real life, but she was playing the numbers based on them and I had a sort of a run because she won—for about two months. I won too, once. Then my dreams went awry and she lost interest and probably went to some other child to ask what they were dreaming.

WACHTEL What effect do you think it had on you to be brought up on ghost stories, told by people who believed in them?

MORRISON Well, it made all sorts of things that were frightening to other people less frightening to me. Being able to think the unthinkable, for one thing. Also, noticing alarm in natural forces as well as unnatural ones. I liked a peopled world. I liked the notion of things being behind things when I was a child. Now, when I went away to college I just ignored all that, I rejected these ideas. I thought that my parents and their parents and friends were these odd people who must know better. But when I began to write, I didn't find anything meaningful to write about that did not include this perception of the world as a living world in the fullest sense. We're not the only living things here. There's other language for that now. Ghost is the most primitive and elementary. Muse is the most elegant one.

But I know that everybody has had similar experiences. I know that there are very few people who, if they have anything to say about it, will sleep with their hands hanging out of the bed. They know something is underneath that bed. You can't change that. And there are people who know that there are certain basements you go into that make your skin prickle. I don't care what it is, but if I can reproduce that feeling, I can rely on it as being the most common thing in the world among human beings, that area of their sensibility.

And that's why it's important to me to use a technique like this, by which there is some participation on the part of the reader. I have access to the reader's imagination because I can say ghost or spirit, or any of these things, but the language itself reproduces something that is not strange; it reproduces something that is completely familiar.

WACHTEL You know, as I listen to you right now, it feels a little creepy.

MORRISON The creepiness is the good part. It's almost as though something throws up an ugly face to make it difficult for you to penetrate it, because behind the ugliness of the monster there's some bliss. So, you can say to it, Well, show me a better face than that. It's like a challenge. The monster's always a challenge. It's like the way to hide beauty is to hide it behind this most repulsive face. And if you can ever get past that, you'll find this other wonderful thing.

WACHTEL That's what you do in your books.

MORRISON Yes. All of my books go past the monster to find the other thing.

WACHTEL You've called your childhood in Lorain, Ohio, the wellspring of your writing, even when you're not writing autobiographically. Why is that the starting place?

MORRISON It's as though I get a certain amount of authentic true feeling when I imagine the people there. It's a little industrial town twenty-five miles west of Cleveland, with practically nothing to recommend it except the lip of Lake Erie. A town full of workers from all over the United States, Mexicans, poor whites, black people, and so on. There were never any ghettoes in these little industrial towns in the Midwest, although there were major class differences. It's the way I dress up my imagination, and I'm there again, even though my novel may well take place in the Caribbean.

WACHTEL And did you always know you had to leave? Is that one of those places where, by the time you hit high school, you knew you had to get out?

MORRISON Right. I didn't want to stay there at all.

WACHTEL Why is that?

MORRISON I was a very good student. I got As because I read a lot, but I didn't feel very clever. Other than my sister, there were very few young people whom I could talk to as I grew older—about poetry, for example. I wanted to go some place where I thought there were all these incredible, brilliant black people, and I thought that would be Howard University [in Washington, DC].

All I wanted to do was read, really, and I thought if I could go to college, I could read more books and I could talk about them.

WACHTEL And were they all brilliant?

MORRISON Enough. They had a fabulous faculty there. That was even better. So that's what I did. Then, of course, when I left there I didn't quite know what to do either—an English major, right? What was I going to do? I couldn't teach in public schools because you had to have a teacher's certificate and that meant attending a school of education. Instead, I went to graduate school at Cornell.

WACHTEL Since you first started publishing there's been a lot more writing by African Americans, some of whom you acquired yourself as an editor at Random House. And you've written more novels since that first one, *The Bluest Eye*. Yet in the last ten years, each time you finish a book you say, That's it, that's the last one I'm going to write. You even said that after *Beloved*, your novel that won the Pulitzer Prize. Why do you feel that way?

MORRISON It's too hard. I just cannot live like this, I say to myself. This has taken me years. There are so many things to do, places to go.

Writing just consumes me all the time and when I can't make it work, it's miserable. When I can make it work, it's very exciting and the standards I set for myself are very high. I don't want to do the same book again.

There's some other question I have in mind, some critique I want to launch about something that's taken for granted. I want the language to do something else. And that just takes forever. It's hard, wonderful work, but when I am finished, I think that I'll never spend another five years like this. I want to garden, I want to go see some friends. You know, you lose a lot. You lose your contacts and they become secondary to you. And that's why I always say I am not doing this again.

WACHTEL And then what happens?

MORRISON Then I think, Wait a minute. First I don't like myself very much when I'm not thinking about a book. I don't mean myself, I mean my mind is more interesting to me when something's going on. Something *was* going on shortly after *Beloved* and I thought, oh well, I have time. I can do that later. But it kept getting bigger and bigger or deeper and deeper, or stranger and stranger, and I began to play with it.

WACHTEL *Beloved* starts with a true incident, a story that you'd read about a woman who tried to kill her children rather than see them enslaved again. From what I understand, *Jazz* starts with an actual photograph that you saw in *The Harlem Book of the Dead*, of an eighteen-year-old girl who was shot at a party by her ex-boyfriend and then chose to protect him and wouldn't say who he was. What was it about that photograph and its story that seized your imagination?

MORRISON Her Juliet-like notion of love that was so young, so profound, so romantic that she would be willing to let someone who had threatened her life get away. It seemed to be another example of something that Sethe had done, the mother in *Beloved*, women sabotaging themselves in a sense, or locating the true beloved outside themselves: something bigger than the woman, more important than her life. With Sethe it was her children; they were much more important than anything else, so important that she could slaughter them all. I mean that's real ownership, if you think you have that right.

WACHTEL Slaughter them sooner than see them enslaved?

MORRISON Oh, yes. They cannot live like that. I will decide how they live. And she, of course, has a little tentative question. At the end of *Beloved*, she's just beginning to think of the possibility of being the central character in her own life. And it's the same thing with the young girl in *Jazz*, who was based on this girl from a real incident in the '20s in Harlem. A girl who, for some reason—we'll assume, for love—did not get any medical help to make sure that this guy who tried to kill her was not caught. That was another displacement of the self or the beloved into a male/female relationship, a love relationship. I'm very interested in that.

How does one walk that line between a horrid narcissism where you love only yourself, and martyrdom, where you love anyone but yourself? There's got to be some place in between where we—and I say *we* as women, because I'm particularly interested in that, but I'm sure it's not limited to women—can occupy our bodies, inhabit ourselves and freely love ourselves in such a way that it is redistributed to other people.

And how does that happen with black people, black *women*, under the incredible duress that is historical, be it slavery or the exigencies of the city? There was a kind of promise and license and seduction that existed in big cities when people were rushing to live there, when there was something wonderful going on. That's what *Jazz* is about.

WACHTEL When you read about those incidents, did you know that they were going to become novels?

MORRISON No. No, the Margaret Garner story [*Beloved*] I had read much, much earlier, but some of the images kept coming back like refrains—that one did, and so did this girl's story in *Jazz*. But I didn't know at the time that they would eventually become something where I could work out some principles that I wanted to think about. I didn't know. I never know.

WACHTEL And it's women who are giving themselves up for this greater love?

MORRISON Yes, it's a good thing, you know. It's one of the nicer things we do as women—to nurture other people and really worry about other people's welfare. What I'm concerned about is displacing yourself completely so that you have no value if you're not worried about somebody else. When are you going to worry about yourself? But not so much that you become these truly self-absorbed people who have no other thing on their minds except their own comfort, their own welfare. It's the difficulty of bridging those two things.

The book that I was going to write in the beginning was to be called *Beloved*, and this book—*Jazz*—would have been part of it, because it was really about who is the beloved. Is it you? And where is that part of you that you know loves you and will never let you down? And why are we ignoring that part of ourselves? We keep strangling it every minute and it's the one, we know it. It sits there right behind our eyes and in the pit of our stomach and it's us, it's the real us. The one that will always be there, will always love you and makes no judgment. But that's the one we put to sleep all the time and transfer its energy onto some thing outside. I think it's possible, I hope it's possible to love both things.

The next book I do will be an extension of that idea but more recent, say in the '70s. It's a very interesting time for me—the same kind of search but in different terms, in a different language, because there were many more choices open to women in the '70s and later.

But even though there are more choices, women still seem to be shooting themselves in the foot. They are willing to hurt each other in extraordinary ways in corporate America. It's unbelievable. They are willing to engage in a form of self-abuse in forcing themselves to look some odd way, to cut themselves, re-shape themselves, re-figure themselves for a gaze that's someplace else. Some gaze exists somewhere that is saying to them, Well, if you look like this and you weigh this and you're shaped like this, you'll be fine. It's insane. And we're perfectly content—it's like the binding of feet again, so that we cannot walk, but at the same time we want to be fit—fit for what?

WACHTEL Why do you think women are complicit in this? Why do women do this?

MORRISON I don't know. I've read a couple of books and articles about it; as a novelist my question is, What is this impulse to displace the true beloved, never to look for it inside? Maybe it's socialization, maybe it's education, but there's nobody to stop it but us. I don't care if the media reinforces it. I don't care if the physicians in the cosmetic industry reinforce it. I don't care if men like it. They like Crayola women that they can break. Or women who look like children. We have got to change it; we have to think about it differently. It's self-loathing and shame and guilt about the things that one ought to love. And it's a fearful thing.

Those are areas, subterranean areas, in the work that I'm doing, although there are lots of other things going on, but that is a really serious question for me. The sermon in *Beloved*, when Baby Suggs goes out into the forest to preach, and she says you have to love yourself and by that she means your hands, your liver, your heart, your kidneys, your blood. You have to love them. These are people whose bodies were owned by other people and then in the jazz age they began to luxuriate in the license, the freedom, literally the physical freedom from that restraint, that oppression, self-oppression, self-censorship. These are very complicated things, and they are particularly theatrical when you think of how women, as well as black people, solve or negotiate that inner space and that outer space, and that incredible eye, the bluest eye—the one that judges us, who's worthy or not—is almost never us.

WACHTEL I'd like to talk about *Jazz*. I can almost hear the smoky underground '20s jazz that percolates through the novel. How do you come by that, that particular, sensual response to music?

MORRISON My mother sang and her sisters and brothers were singing people.

WACHTEL But your mother sang in a choir, she didn't sing all this smoky jazz stuff.

MORRISON Oh, but she did. My mother sang *Carmen*, she sang blues, she sang jazz, she sang spirituals, gospel. She was really quite a flawless and powerful singer. She sang all day—lots of people did. Those were the days when people sang in the street. There are still cultures where you can go around and hear people singing. And you hear music all the time. My other books have a kind of sound, but it was particularly important in the construction of *Jazz*. The word choices, choosing one word rather than another, over and over again, for the one that was appropriate to the age, but which also has a kick and a sound.

WACHTEL The music is almost a character, the way it weaves through the book. And then the City, the capital "C" City which you evoke as a beautiful and dreamlike creature, it's quite a romantic picture of the city.

MORRISON It was like that. We look at the city as though it were the home of the destitute and the detritus of society. But when you think of the idea of a city, you think of a place where there are lots of different kinds of people, many classes, many groups, variety, excitement, possibilities, promise, even a little naughtiness and danger. That's why people went there and that's what was lovely. Cities evolved that way. I was trying to recreate the way people, whether they were rich or poor, immigrants or native people or indigenous people, used to talk about the city—as though it was truly metropolitan, truly urbane, which suggested a level of sensibility and sophistication and shrewdness that was desirable, as opposed to the way it is now. And that was romantic.

WACHTEL Was it a kind of haven because at that time in the '20s that you're describing, people were coming north to New York City, in particular to Harlem, away from—

MORRISON Horror, devastation, post-reconstruction. Where whole towns were burnt down, lynching was commonplace, and people were in a form of indentured slavery. It wasn't slavery in the sense of what it was before the Civil War, but it was the sharecropping system, which kept people totally indebted. And working-class white people had bought into whiteness instead of identifying with other labourers; they decided they wanted that little extra perk. It was just impossible if you didn't own land to make a living. During various waves of economic depression, people began to go to the cities where there was work.

WACHTEL And where there are other people—there's a real joy in finding other people.

MORRISON Other people like yourself. You could find five hundred more of you within the city, so you had a sense of security in numbers and you felt a possibility for work.

WACHTEL Although, at one point, Violet, one of the central characters in *Jazz*, says that she messed up her life by coming north.

MORRISON Yes. The city is seductive, the city is reinforcing, the city is a haven; but it's still a city and the seduction may be false, you know, the streets are all laid out very neatly but the pressure is great. There are limitations to what a city can provide. But that conflict between the life of nature and the life of the city is part of what they're feeling. There were some possibilities for Violet, some growth perhaps that she could not maintain, but for me, both Violet and Joe were running from something, trying to escape. They managed to escape for a long time and then they couldn't; the past caught up with them.

WACHTEL They lose parents. There's a tremendous sense of loss that comes through here. *Jazz* is loosely based on a sort of love triangle, and all three points of the triangle have lost a mother one way or another.

MORRISON Yes. All of the parents are lost to racial violence or ostracization. Every single one of them.

WACHTEL What's the effect on them of that powerful loss?

MORRISON A feeling of being bereft, of trying to fill up. They decide not to have children, for example. Violet doesn't want to repeat the horror of being evicted when she was a little girl. And they try to fill it up with "the good life" that the city can offer, but the emptiness is not mitigated by this. They achieve a fairly decent, interesting life, but she is hit on the head with mother love. Violet's husband, Joe, suddenly becomes prey to violent sexual passions with a young girl. So the sense of feeling bereft strikes them when they're most vulnerable, when they're getting towards fifty, and what they have to do is come to terms with that. Whether they come to terms with it or not, it's there looming and they're in a place, the city, where the pace is such that these things are worked out very quickly. So there are some wonderful, exciting possibilities in the city, but there's also a down side.

WACHTEL Something terrible happens right at the outset of the book. Joe shoots the young woman that he's involved with, and then two strange things happen. The first is that there's a kind of obsession that develops. Not only Joe, but his wife, Violet, become strangely united in an obsession over the dead girl. There's a photograph of her on the mantle and she haunts them. It reminded me a little of the ghost, the child in *Beloved*, who comes to haunt them. This is another instance of the power of the dead on the living. Is this something you know? Have you been haunted?

MORRISON No. I have enough in these books; I hope I don't have any more. But look at us, we save photographs, we put them on the walls and we look at these faces and we hand these faces down and we cherish these faces and if we didn't have cameras we'd have paintings. We pass things on from one generation to the next. What is that about? It has value that is ghost-like. Ultimately we are very careful about the dead. People treasure and give feeling though the thing itself may be nothing; it's just a picture, but it becomes something that is alive because we have given it life.

Joe and Violet, whatever's going on in their lives, are smart enough to know that it's focussing on this young girl, because he loved her, shot her, a hole in the heart that he couldn't live without. And Violet knows that whatever the problem is, it's in this girl. Who is she? What did she have?

WACHTEL You give us a hopeful view at the end of *Jazz*. There's a sense that love can be redemptive. People who are filled with hate and anger and even madness—Violet seems really quite on the edge—find they have a capacity to heal the wounds through forgiveness and love. Don't get me wrong, I like that. I think that there's a beautiful reconciliation and you describe it in the most moving way. But there is something that troubles me here and I feel I have to ask you about it. The rekindling of love and closeness between Joe and Violet, our fifty-ish couple, has as its source the killing of a girl, even if she's not a very nice girl. And even Violet herself forgives Joe; she has that love outside herself that she bestows on him. How do you cut through that?

MORRISON You have to cut through it. These are hard, hard things to do. It's not loving somebody who is saying yes. It's not loving in circumstances that are conducive; it's loving when it's hard, when it really is hard. I don't care if it's national war, border crossings, or Violet and Joe. It's always "impossible" to love your enemy or to love out of some terrible biblical dictum like that. It's always "impossible." That's why it's important. I'm not talking about love under easy circumstances, but the important kind, that difficult, difficult love.

WACHTEL There's a beautiful poignancy at the end of *Jazz* when the narrator—who has a very slippery voice; we're not quite sure who this nameless "I" person is—seems to know quite a lot about the nature of love. Earlier in the book, you've got this line where a character thinks she can solve the mystery of love, and your narrator says, "Good luck and let me know." At the end, though, this narrator envies the public love of the married couple; it's something the narrator can't have. I like the mystery of it, the ambiguity, but there's also, I don't know, a sense of waiting and passivity.

MORRISON Yes, the know-it-all narrator has a limitation. Starts out full of assumptions of power and knowledge, then makes a mistake in the narrative; the narrator's predictions are wrong, and the characters escape the clutches of that voice. They all go to the seashore and have an interesting life. What the narrative voice learns is the power of its own imagination as well as its limits, and it knows that it longs for the bodily expression of that kind of love because all the love scenes at the end are gentle. The removal of lint from a coat or touching hands when you pass a cup of coffee. Nothing sensual in that except the easy comfort, the marvellous comfort of bodies touching gently.

WACHTEL Are you doing something really, really clever there?

MORRISON Yes, I'm doing something really, really clever.

WACHTEL The narrator is you and it's not you and it's the words on the page in relation to the reader—it's all those things?

MORRISON Yes, it's all those things.

WACHTEL It's very moving. Violet—this middle-aged woman—talks about the dead girl inside herself whom she destroyed, the person she was really was. And you've talked about a dead girl inside you who you've tried to bring back to life. Is that what writing is about for you?

MORRISON It's the way *I* do it. If I was a theologian I might call it soul, call it spirit. I don't care what it is. I have just used that wholly recognizable but repressed person we mean when we say *me*. It's sometimes so silent, so ignored, so unappreciated by the forces that are the world: the family forces, the social forces, the cultural forces. She's dead in the sense of being asleep and nobody can bring that person back to life except the individual in whom she lives.

It seems to be critical and very important for human beings to be able to do that. People confuse it with the absence of strength. It's not that. Or they confuse it with the fulfillment of all their appetites. It's not that. It's something else, which is serene and content and maybe even very frail. But whatever it is, it's within me, and it's the search for that person or thing or concept or idea that is informing a great deal of my work, because I know or sense or feel or want to believe that it's also there where self-esteem is born or destroyed.

December 1992

§

WACHTEL In your novel *Home*, we meet the character Frank Money when he's returned from army service in the Korean War. What made you choose that time and backdrop?

MORRISON In the United States, we think of the '50s as the kind of Golden Age. Right after the war, everybody was making money, the G.I. Bill was sending soldiers onto college campuses, and the television was full of—I don't know—happy stories. Doris Day, all of that. But I didn't think so. I thought that there was a veil being pulled over the '50s and that it really wasn't like that. I was a young woman in the '50s, and I thought I knew all about it. But then I began to think, Wait a minute, there was this huge, foreign war. Something like 58,000 American soldiers killed. They didn't even call it a war. They called it a "police action."

There was also the McCarthy period. Everybody was terrified of Communism, of Russia. And then there was enormous racial violence. Emmett Till was killed in '55. And also, although we didn't learn a great deal about it until the Vietnam War, there were medical experiments on helpless people, like the soldiers who got LSD first, and also prisoners and a lot of black people who were told, if they took this test, they would get free medical care. You remember the syphilis examinations? For years and years, these black men came in; some got medicine, others got placebos so the doctors could find out what would happen if syphilis was untreated. So that kind of thing—it still goes on in other parts of the world.

These were major things that seem to have been erased from our history, but my Korean vet travels back to his home hamlet—it wasn't really a town—and that journey is like a battlefield, but it reveals all of these other things that were going on in the '50s.

WACHTEL The character Frank Money is having a hard time back in the US, and part of it has to do with the trauma of war. Also, as you say, as a black man, he's given no recognition for his patriotic service. He's back to being a second-class citizen. But he also seems to be struggling with the idea of what it means to be a man. What's he wrestling with there?

MORRISON I wanted to examine a young man who had survived a war. You would think, under those circumstances, he would be secure, but he's not. It's interesting that veterans, by and large, almost never talk about their experiences in a war. They talk to each other, but very seldom to people on the outside. He would have all of that in him. He's traumatized—we called it "shell-shocked" back then—and he drinks. Then he finds a nice lady, but it doesn't work because he really hasn't come to terms with the deaths of his buddies or with his own savagery in the war. When he is asked to come and save the life of his sister, he is forced to move across the country.

WACHTEL Frank's sister Ycindra is also struggling with her identity as a poor black girl in 1950s America, and she's unwittingly involved in a near fatal medical experiment by a white doctor, but she recovers thanks to Frank and the women of her home town. What made Ycindra—or Cee, as she's called—so susceptible?

MORRISON Small town, parents working seventeen hours a day, a very hostile grandmother, who really is mad at everybody, but picks on—as short-sighted adults frequently do—the most helpless to exact vengeance on. So Cee is already in a mode that's almost fetal. She needs protection from everything, and she gets it from her brother. And when he leaves, she's out there with no skills. She works. She wants another job. She gets another job. Everything looks wonderful. She has no resources and then she develops many. She grows up enormously towards the end of the book, partly because of what I call the "mean love" of the women in the community. They will take care of you. They will warn you. But they don't want to see you. I think the phrase was, "They looked at tears or crying with resigned contempt." They had these all-seeing eyes. They didn't like the snivel, the whine. They would say, "Shut up. This is going to hurt. Shut up. Drink this. No, do this." And she is healed by them, and then she has to think about those women in a way she's never thought about them before. I remember, as a child myself, that everybody in the neighbourhood felt free to comment: "Take that lipstick off. I'm going to tell your father." My mother would agree. They were all there watching, watching, and it was so very unnerving and confining. It's later on that you understand that this watch is care. That's what she learns, and then she learns how to care for herself.

WACHTEL So gradually Cee develops a sense of identity through what she experiences and, as you say, through the women around her. And she witnesses not just tough love but a remarkable generosity from these older women in her town.

MORRISON They are deep-down Christian women without the sermons and the sermonizing. They just take it in and they help. And she figures out that her lack of education doesn't mean she can't think. That's what they really teach her. "You can think." "Oh, I didn't know he was doing that," she says about the doctor. And they reply, "Misery don't call ahead."

When her brother does arrive, having saved her, and they move back into their parents' home, he comforts her because she's upset that she can't have children anymore. She says, "No. I can cry if I want to. It's miserable. Let it be miserable." But she means, "I don't need that anymore." It's a new sister for Frank, and it helps him come to terms with his own wall of denial, blaming other people for what is in him.

WACHTEL You talked about how your father hated his home town in Georgia, although he went back to visit every year. Why?

MORRISON God knows. He talked about Cartersville, Georgia, and I learned very late that he had seen two men lynched in his home town, businessmen. And they were killed—hanged—in his neighbourhood, so he left when he was fourteen. I think that's part of what made him think Georgia could never be home. But he had relatives there, so he went back every year. My mother, by the way, who was from Alabama and left when she was six years old, thought about it like it was Eden, but she never went back. Oh, the good old days!

WACHTEL You grew up in the town of Lorain, Ohio, in the 1930s and '40s, and you describe your family as having been poor-ish. What did that mean in the context of the times?

MORRISON It meant looking for work for my father, being on what they called in those days "relief." Now they call it welfare or food stamps. I like the word "relief." It sounds like just a pause until you get yourself together. Sometimes we couldn't pay the rent, and we were evicted. I remember my mother tearing the eviction signs off the front door, as though that was going to make a difference, but she was fierce, and we'd move on to another place. But the fact is that "poor" has a really bad name. I understand that to be poor is not necessarily the best place to be, but everybody was poor. The people who were awful were the fat cats. We looked at those people like they were out of their minds. But we shared everything. And mind you, this was a working-class town, a steel town, shipyards, and it was not segregated. People came from Poland and Italy and Mexico. Black people came from Canada. They had escaped the States in the nineteenth century and had come back. So there was a big mix of working-class people, mostly unionized. We had many different churches, but only one high school. So we didn't have time for what seems to be the big divide that people keep talking about in the media these days. The people who lived in the great houses down by the lake were in another world, and we did not envy them. They were just different. We could admire their lawns and their houses. But together we just worked it out. Some Czechs lived next door. They gave my mother beef wrapped in cabbage. They traded recipes. It was sort of like the women in *Home*, except they were of all races and religions.

WACHTEL But your father and your mother had different attitudes towards race. Can you tell me a bit about that?

MORRISON Oh, my father hated white people. He was just, you know, he wouldn't let the insurance agent who came to collect the premiums into the house. My mother, on the other hand, always judged people one by one. Her first inquiry or interest was what kind of human being they were. White, black—it didn't matter to her. But my father had a very firm, hostile relationship with white people. Even though he worked in mills with them, they could not come into his house.

WACHTEL So what did you make of that when you were a child?

MORRISON As a child, nothing. I just thought he was a man, she was a woman. They're different. She talks all the time. He doesn't. That was just a difference. And it was only later that I realized something about his attitude. I was working as a young girl cleaning house after school, and the woman for whom I was working complained bitterly about my work, and she should have because I didn't know what I was doing. I had never seen a vacuum cleaner or a decent stove with an oven. She was trying, I think, to correct me, but at twelve I took it as an affront instead of listening. So I told my mother that the woman was mean to me, and my mother said "Well, quit." But I was getting two dollars a week, I want you to know, one of which went to my mother, and the other I kept, so I didn't want to lose this. When I told my father, he said, "Go to work, get your money and come on home. You don't live there." It was a huge relief to keep the job and know that it was not who I was. "You don't live there. You live here." I haven't had an employment problem since. It wasn't personal. It was just, "That's not who you are."

WACHTEL You once said that you remember things through emotion. What emotional memories stand out for you from that early childhood in Lorain?

298

MORRISON Some scary, because part of my entertainment was telling ghost stories and repeating them and living in houses with gas lamps that make really strange shadows if you're not used to them. There's that sense of alarm: ghosts, demons, something might get you.

But there was also this—I don't know—familiar, understood, taken-for-granted togetherness and affection. I remember walking with my father and my sister with a burlap sack, going out to the railroad tracks to collect coal that fell off the cars. But when we went, there were all sorts of other people out there doing the same thing, bringing home bits of coal for the furnace. This meant we couldn't afford to buy coal, but I didn't think about that part. I just thought about the pleasure of doing it. And, of course, gardens were terribly important. We ate out of the gardens. Yes, we had chickens, and I killed them and we ate them. It was a different kind of existence, one in which I felt very comfortable and very much loved, even though we were very strictly disciplined. The switches when you got in trouble!

WACHTEL What did you do that was so bad?

MORRISON I remember one that stuck with me because it concerned language. When I was about three years old, my sister and I used to write on the sidewalk with pebbles—"c-a-t" and our names, and "I hate you." But there was this big word down the block on the fence in black paint, so we decided to copy it, and we wrote "f," and then "you." My mother came bellowing down the steps, "Go get a broom. Go get a bucket of water. What is the matter with you?" So we cry, and we clean up. And she never says the word; she didn't repeat it, she didn't tell us what it meant. I didn't learn until I was thirteen or so—and then it was about animals. Anyway, two things about the power of language. It could make my mother totally freak out. And at the same time, there was this skill that one had with a pebble on a pavement, you could do something that was just explosive. Now, that's not what I thought at the time, but it stayed with me, and it may account in some way for my being a writer.

WACHTEL You've mentioned that there were a lot of churches. Your mother attended the African Episcopal Methodist Church and sang in the choir, but when you were twelve, you converted to Catholicism. How come?

MORRISON There's a wing of my family who were Catholics. Most of them lived in Cleveland at that time. The architecture was so impressive.

And they went to mass and had all these little holidays. I don't know. I was just impressed. I spoke to my mother about it, and she had no objections. She said, "Any church you want to belong to, so long as it's a church, is fine." So I did. And I was very serious about it. I was a daily communicant for years.

WACHTEL Did that affect your behaviour?

MORRISON I think so. Until I stopped. I'm not sure it was the faith that drew me in as much as it was the art. But I still went to my mother's church when she sang because she had an extraordinary voice.

WACHTEL How would you describe her influence on you?

MORRISON I wonder. There were a lot of years when we didn't get on, when she would come to my house even, and say things like, "Where's your salt?" And I would think, What do you mean? I have salt. Are you accusing me of—The phases one goes through! But she lived to be eighty-six and I don't know if I can articulate how important both of my parents were to me in different ways. I think if I claimed the best of each of them, it would be my version of myself at my best.

WACHTEL When your father died, you said it was an "earthshaking, soul-shaking experience, that the girl he loved,"—you—"died with him."

MORRISON I went away. I didn't go back to town for two years, even though my mother and sister were still there, and lots of family. I thought, What is that town doing? If my father's not in it, it should disappear. I was the girl he loved, the one he was so proud of. He used to carry my letters in his vest pocket when he went to work and show them to people when I was at college. He was there when my first child was born. He drove me to Howard University. He was a quiet man, but he was there. And when he died, I thought, Where is that person that he liked so much? Maybe she'll come back. I don't know.

WACHTEL After high school, you moved from Ohio to Washington, DC, to attend Howard University. Was it always obvious that you'd go to college? Was it hard financially?

MORRISON It was hard financially, but my mother was very encouraging. There had only been one member of our family who had gone to college, an uncle who had gone for, I think, one year at Ohio State. And Howard University was a kind of Harvard in our minds, the best of the black colleges. And I was eager. I had never had an African-American teacher, and I was eager to be in the company of black intellectuals. I could have gone to Oberlin, which is an elegant, excellent college, but

I didn't want to go there because it was seven miles from my home. My mother might call me up and tell me to come and do the dishes or something. So I went as far away as I could. I was glad I did; I was glad I went there. It was an extraordinary experience.

WACHTEL Although Washington, DC, was itself a bit of a shock.

MORRISON Oh, yes. I had never seen what my mother and father had described, which were the signs "Coloured," and "White." As black girls, we could only use a certain restroom—it all seemed very theatrical to me. I didn't really understand. What did I know? I stole one of those signs off the bus and sent it to my mother.

WACHTEL The sign saying what?

MORRISON "Coloured." It never hurt, the physical signs. And also I was on campus with all these really exciting, funny, smart black people. And a lot of people were over there somewhere, hovering and trying to make life difficult, but they weren't the focus, and I didn't see the world through their eyes. I was stunned at the kinds of things I'd heard about, but I guess I just thought that was a story. But there they were. You couldn't try on a hat in a shop because your hair was different. There were just tons of things like that going on in Washington.

But the interesting thing about Washington was that there was a black population within the middle class. They had government jobs. I had a friend whose father worked as a doorman, and when I went back there to teach and I was making—I don't know, $7,000 a year—he was making $20,000. Tips. They had all these jobs that made money. Some of them were government. Some of them were servants. Some of them were doormen. But they were infinitely superior financially than we were in Ohio. So there was that. You could see people who had always been in nice brick houses, always, and their grandfathers had been too. So that was interesting, seeing so many middle-class blacks in Washington.

WACHTEL In a segregated city.

MORRISON Yes, but white people didn't live there. They ran the country there, and they owned the stores, but they lived out in Alexandria. But there was a really elegant, impressive black population in the city then. Now it has changed, very much changed.

WACHTEL But even at Howard, which was an African-American university, I understand that skin colour was still a factor. There was something about the paper bag test. What is that?

MORRISON Apparently, the lighter your skin colour, the better, either because you look better or because whites won't be as mean to you or something. I didn't go to high school there, so I'm not quite sure, but the paper bag test went like this: If your skin was darker than a paper bag, that was bad. If it was the colour of a paper bag or lighter, that was good. More white blood and so on.

WACHTEL Did that actually operate at Howard?

MORRISON I think so. I think I remember my classmates talking about certain sororities as being light skinned versus those that were dark skinned. That's why I wrote *The Bluest Eye*, my first novel. Once you begin to accept the lines of demarcation and the hierarchy of race, even *within* a race, it hurts. You're doomed if you do that. That little girl had no resources when other black people thought she was ugly because she was black. I came face to face with that at Howard.

WACHTEL I was thinking about the distinctions between class and race as a social divide when I was reading your novel *A Mercy*. It's set in the late seventeenth century in what you call a "pre-racial America." What did you want to look at there?

MORRISON The construction of racism in this country. It's a social construct, but it's also a legal one. And it has a function, which is to make sure that poor whites never conspire or associate politically with poor blacks because that would destabilize the upper class. If you have blacks and whites working together for political change, you'll have serious problems. So the deal was to separate them, and they made laws in Virginia: no black man shall ever carry a weapon, and no white man shall ever be arrested or accused or convicted of hurting or killing any black man. So already in Bacon's Rebellion, these were the laws. One group is already privileged, free to kill blacks, and blacks are powerless. That was done for the protection of the elite, and it sifted its way down. Every empire, every nation, has based its profit on slaves, whether it was Greece, Rome, Russia, or England. They called them different names—peons, serfs, whatever—but they were not people who could normally rise. They were owned by the lord. A few of them did manage to rise, but slavery itself was common. What was not ordinary in this country was racism at that level, and it was necessary for slavery to function.

Indentured white servants and black slaves worked together on those plantations, on those farms. The owners could transfer that indentured contract on down through the ages if they wanted to—but the difference was that the indentured white servant could run away, and you couldn't tell who he was because of his skin.

WACHTEL In *A Mercy*, a black slave gives up her daughter to pay a debt that's owed by her owner, and it's a terrible decision for her. She only does it so she can stay with her infant son. You've written about the pain of motherhood before—I'm thinking of *Beloved*—where a mother takes drastic action in the belief that she's saving her child by killing her. What is it that you want to explore in these mother-child relationships?

MORRISON The kinds of decisions that mothers make based on the benefit of the child. Even in *Beloved*, when she kills her daughter and would have killed them all, she's under the impression that they will all be together again in the afterlife. For her as an African, she's not taking anything away. She's just moving them away from what she believes is going to be a terrible life, one that she does not want them to live. And I could not decide whether she was right or wrong when I thought about certain kinds of situations in which I might have to make choices. If you knew your child was being kidnapped in order to satisfy, say, a sex club, might you just—I don't know, I still don't know. So I had to bring in someone who might have a really good opinion about that, the dead child, Beloved.

WACHTEL You had a historical incident concerning a woman called Margaret Garner to go on to get yourself inside that world.

MORRISON Yes. The interesting thing about the newspaper article on Margaret Garner that I read, was that the reporter was so stunned that Garner was not raving mad, that she was so calm when she said she'd do it again. I thought, Wow! But you understand that at the time I wrote this in the 1980s there was all this ferment among feminists, and one of the points of serious feminism was we don't have to have children. We can be free of the responsibilities of motherhood. I was thinking there was a time when having children and being responsible for those children meant freedom. But Margaret Garner had no control over her children. They were like cubs. They could be bought, sold, moved. No one ever asked her what she thought about it. But she said, "These children are mine and I decide." That was a scream of freedom. The question was, when they caught her, whether she should be tried for theft of those children and herself or for murder.

WACHTEL Because the property belonged to the white owner.

MORRISON Yes, that was the thing. And the abolitionists wanted her tried for murder because that way they could claim that she was responsible for the life of these children.

But this was liberation for her. Things differ under different circumstances. In *A Mercy*, this mother, having literally been through those long treks and boat rides into slavery, she had these children, and she knew that her owners were molesters. They molested her and they were looking at her daughter. She figured they wouldn't bother her son. They were looking at her daughter, who insisted on wearing lady's shoes. So when she saw this man look at her daughter as though she was a human, not money, she sent her away. But, of course, she didn't tell the daughter why.

WACHTEL One of the effects of slavery, of course, was this separation of families. What significance has that had for the descendants of American slavery?

MORRISON Big time. They wouldn't allow families to stay together, more often than not. Certainly not if you knew the language. They didn't want everybody speaking Xhosa, for example, so they mixed up language groups so they couldn't organize. You could have families after you got here because they were property, and you were required to reproduce like any other cattle, without knowing where your children were or where their father was. It's devastating, and thus forming a club or church or tribe or community is even more important.

WACHTEL I read that you'd have raised your children differently if you'd been able to anticipate the difficult race relations of the 1980s. In what way?

MORRISON I didn't warn them about things because I didn't think those things were really there. It took me a while to learn that my sons would go into an elevator, and if there was a white woman in there, she would leave. It took me a while to realize why my sons were being stopped by police all the time, particularly the younger one. Luckily they had drivers' licenses and they didn't have drugs and stuff. But just that regular stop. Most of the time, they went to a United Nations school which I thought was a good idea, but it wasn't. I thought the world of the eighties was like the world of the sixties. It wasn't. Things were hardening then, and nothing was breaking down, except verbally sometimes.

WACHTEL You've also written books for children in collaboration with your son Slade. What was it like to work with him on those projects?

MORRISON Oh, that was a delight. I could never think of an idea that was suitable for children. But I remember Slade and I were sitting around thinking about what we hated about Aesop stories, and he said things like, "Why were they mad at the grasshopper? He was playing music all summer." So we rewrote them, poems sometimes or satire—funny stuff.

I thought children's books were so stupid, the language so low: "Run, Jill, run." I remember in one of the old readers the first sentence was, "The wages of sin is death." Now, there's a sentence a six-year-old can get into.

So I wanted to lift the language and make it—I don't know—fly, because children love language. They're always inventing it. They don't necessarily know what you're talking about; they have to listen very carefully for nuance, watch your facial expression, in order to understand language. And they can learn any language. They're very attuned to it. Of course, I had to rely on my son Slade's interpretations of Aesop.

WACHTEL You lost your son Slade to cancer towards the end of 2010. How do you deal with something so impossible?

MORRISON Oh, you don't. On the dedication page of *Home*, I have his name. And they asked me, "What do you want to put after?" And I said, "I just haven't discovered the language to say what I feel. I may never, and I don't care." I'm just so uninterested in the necessity for happiness that we seem to have in the United States. People are sad, so they take a pill. But Slade's death is part of who I am now. My son did not bury me. I buried him. That's it. I'll never, ever be without that. I'm not struggling to be without it. That's part of my life now.

WACHTEL You were working on *Home* when he became ill, and I wasn't surprised to see the book dedicated to him, but there's a kind of hopefulness that you give Frank at the end that made me wonder if you wanted to deliver a happier ending at that time.

MORRISON I didn't know at the time whether I would—I knew there would be reconciliation. What I didn't know is that it would be beautiful. I thought he would make do and maybe even resign, but it was beautiful. And it was like the poem at the beginning of *Home*: "Whose house is this?" And it ends up, "Why does its lock fit my key?" And so for me, it was not just the characters, but a settling-in to what life is.

I was interviewed a couple of weeks ago, and was asked what, at my age—which at eighty-one is advanced—the good things were. I said,

"Work is good." But you know what? I didn't even know I thought this. I said, "The world is so beautiful. It is really beautiful. Not just the colours and the shapes and the seasons." I said, "I'm told it took sixty million years to make a human eye from that little cell in the bottom of the ocean that was responding to light." That is just amazing to me. It's gorgeous, this world. I thought, well, maybe if you live over here on the river, if you live…, but no, no, no. It's all just magnificent. And I think that was part of what I was coming to terms with at the end of *Home*.

May 2012
Original interviews produced by Sandra Rabinovitch and Mary Stinson

MAVIS GALLANT

Mavis Gallant was one of those expatriate Canadians who seemed to disappear from view for about twenty-five years. She was born in Montreal in 1922, an only child, to a British father and American mother, and she had a rather unusual upbringing. At the age of four, she was sent to a French Catholic boarding school, where she was the only Anglophone Protestant. When she was ten, her father died. He was only thirty-one and had gone back to England, where he'd been born. Mavis wasn't told about his death until three years later. She'd been waiting for him to return or to send for her.

She attended some seventeen schools in Canada and the US. She came back to Montreal when she was eighteen and talked her way into a variety of jobs, including writing features—for six years—for *The Montreal Standard*. During that time, she became politically astute, with an openness to the world, and especially Europe. She told me that she found the postwar European refugees and exiles to be the most interesting people she had ever met. "The anti-Hitler wave of refugees was a revelation to me—of culture, of politics. I couldn't get enough of them. They were the first truly cultivated bourgeoisie that had come to Montreal." It formed the seeds of her attraction to Europe.

In 1950, when she was twenty-eight, she quit the paper and moved to Europe, settling in Paris where she lived for the rest of her life. Also around that time, she sold her first short story to *The New Yorker* magazine, continuing to publish there for the next fifty years—well over a hundred stories. As well, Gallant kept journals throughout her life in Paris, and in 1968, her account of the student uprisings in France appeared—first in *The New Yorker* and then in a book, *Paris Notebooks* (1986). (She was editing her journals at the time of her death and I hope these will be published.)

Although Mavis Gallant had been publishing novels and short stories since the early '50s, she was only really "discovered" in Canada in the late '70s, when her story collection, *From the Fifteenth District* (1979) came out. I've always admired Mavis Gallant's writing. There's something almost perfect about it. Every word is right. But for a while, I felt a bit emotionally detached from her characters, often European refugees, intellectuals, adrift in Paris. But when I went back to her books in anticipation of our conversation, I marvelled again at just how good a writer she is, and I also enjoyed the stories enormously. I was impressed by the wit, the range, the depth—in each of her books. (Gallant published ten books of stories, two novels, and a play.)

Mavis Gallant was not only famous for her writing, she was famous for not liking to talk about her writing. Politics, yes; her own work, no. [See my introduction to this book.] But in 2008, when I went to see her in Paris, she was more open to discussing her own unconventional life, dedicated, as it was, to writing. She was expansive, candid, and warm. In some instances, she was so eager that she would scarcely wait for me to finish my question, and she was completely forthcoming about the germ of a story, its opening image, or an actual incident, someone she knew or a story she heard that launched it in her mind. She provided every detail.

Mavis Gallant died six years later, in 2014, aged ninety-one.

WACHTEL When you were young, you've said, you took it for granted that life was tough for children.

GALLANT It was in those days. Not that I was a child who got hit. I had two spankings from my father and they both are seared into my brain. I knew he hated doing it because he would go dead white.

WACHTEL What did you do to cause it?

GALLANT Although he was British, two things in a Canadian education were not to be tolerated: one was outright disobedience and the other insolence. I wasn't really disobedient, but I could be insolent. I had an uncle who I didn't much like, and he would come in the summer to

Canada to stay with my mother's younger brother. I would just look at him at meals—I was a little kid—and he would explode. I would smile. That's insolence. The others didn't see me. Nobody ever saw. I mostly never dared to do that with my parents. Sometimes my mother would fly off the handle, and I'd get a smack on the shoulder or something like that. I'd say, "Hm! My vaccination hurt more than that." That was my rejoinder, which I would never have made to my father because he was a very calm and quiet man.

So you might ask what I did do to earn a spanking from him. Well, we lived on Sherbrooke Street, across from McGill University. I was coming home from school along the opposite side of the street. He had drilled into me only to cross at the corner because there were lights there. I saw him on the other side, and I dashed into traffic. He was making signs to go to the corner, which I pretended I didn't see, and a car braked. I know when people see the cars of the period, which would be about the mid-1920s, they looked comic, but they could kill you, because the chassis was heavier than the motor. So the car braked in time, but he thought I was in for it. When I got to him, his first gesture was a spanking in the street, my dear, in the street, where the whole world could see.

I had all my clothes on. It was winter. I don't know if they still wore the Red River suits, the little girls, when you were young—they'd probably gone to other things by then. But the Red River outfit was worn in Quebec by both French- and English-speaking kids, although it was French to start with. It was very chic. It was a navy-blue coat with brass buttons and a red wool sash. And you had red mittens. I was still at the age where the mittens had strings that went through your sleeves so you didn't lose them every five minutes. And red leggings, all knitted and fireman red. And then we had what we called a toque, which was a knitted hat, with a tassel down to your shoulder, which had to go just this way and not that way. So I had all that on. And the leggings were over your skirt, and then you had two pairs of pants. One was white and meant to be spotless at any hour in case you were taken away in an ambulance. And over them were navy-blue gym bloomers, which went down to the knee. So even if you were being tortured, you had all that on for padding.

But the humiliation of it. The humiliation that people saw this.

And the second one was bad. I was seven or eight, playing on the floor with paper dolls who acted out things that I invented.

WACHTEL They were your characters, in a way.

GALLANT They were my characters, no doubt, yes. Once my parents had visitors, a couple. My father asked me to pick up my things because I was sitting in the way of the visitors, and I pretended not to hear him. That was one of my tricks. He asked two or three times, and I saw that the visitors were actually thinking, Why is that weakling not giving her a clip over the ear to get her out? And he said, "This is the last time I'm going to tell you." And then it was, "Pick up your things," not, "Why don't you..." And I still pretended I didn't hear. He took me by the arm and hauled me outside, and there on the staircase, I had a real spanking without a winter coat to protect me. My father was really upset. He didn't like doing it. I ran upstairs crying and sobbing and put myself to bed, although it was much too early.

But it stays with me: the look on his face. He went white both times.

WACHTEL You seem to identify more with your father than your mother...

GALLANT Admire would be the word. You can't really admire someone who loses her temper every ten minutes. But he was usually totally composed, no matter what happened.

WACHTEL And you had things in common. As I understand, years later people stopped you on the street, and they said you resembled him, you looked like him, you were similar in temperament.

GALLANT When I came back to Canada from the States—I had spent my adolescence in the United States, as I think you know—I was eighteen, and when I was that age the resemblance was striking, except that I was a girl. Once I was on Beaver Hall Hill walking, and a man stopped me and said, "Could you be a sister of...?" And he named him. He was dead by then, and I didn't want to discuss it, so I said, "Oh, yes, but..." as if to say, "Barely heard of him." And I went on. I was very emotional about this.

WACHTEL Certainly, your upbringing was unconventional. You were sent to a French convent school when you were only four.

GALLANT And I was the only Protestant.

WACHTEL And the only English speaker. What was that experience like? Were you homesick? Were you lost in French?

GALLANT I must have been, because I was a boarder there, which was completely ridiculous, and I don't know why that was. The convent was on the same street, on Sherbrooke Street. Really, I can't tell you.

WACHTEL You can't say why. But the feeling?

GALLANT The atmosphere wasn't good. That may have had something to do with it. I don't remember having intense feeling. Children adapt faster than you think, unless they're really being ill treated.

I remember this was a very strict convent, as they were in those days. It was called St-Louis-Gozague, and it had been a Jesuit boys' school, because it has a male name. Normally, a school for girls would have a female saint's name. When I discovered this after I was grown up I thought, That's why it had such a strained atmosphere. There was nothing feminine about anything in the place. It was really wrenching, because all my toys were taken from me. This hasn't left me: there was a point where my father came and got me on weekends, and I noticed my things gradually disappearing.

WACHTEL The toys you had at home were disappearing?

GALLANT Yes, at home. I had real dolls. I was still at an age where I made a train with the dining-room chairs and put the dolls on it, and I blew the whistle—whoo, whoo!—and all that. And all these things were suddenly given away.

WACHTEL And your mother just left you at age four at the convent school. She said she'd be back—

GALLANT She said, "I'll be back in a few minutes."

WACHTEL And that was it!

GALLANT I don't know. She's dead, he's dead, my grandmother's dead—everybody's dead. There's no one I can question.

WACHTEL But even back then, did she ever explain?

GALLANT I never got proper answers, or I got things suitable for children. I gave it up at one point completely. When I knew I wouldn't get answers, I just didn't ask anymore.

I don't want to sound like Little Orphan Annie, because that wasn't the case.

WACHTEL No, it doesn't sound like that. It's just the complexity.

GALLANT Things are complex. Not everybody got answers from their parents in those days.

WACHTEL The disappearance of your father from your life is especially poignant because you weren't told he had died. You were told he went to England when you were ten. And then it wasn't until you were thirteen that you—

GALLANT A woman who's a friend of my mother's said, "Don't you know?" Or "Do you still not know?" or something like that. And I pretended I didn't care. My vaccination hurt more. And then I apparently had a big crying scene.

WACHTEL But why do you suppose your mother didn't tell you?

GALLANT Look, she's dead. R.I.P.

WACHTEL It doesn't work that way. In one sense, yes, she's dead. And in another sense, I think, we still carry these things with us.

GALLANT There was a point where I decided, when I was old enough to do that, that I was not likely to forget it, no. I never have—that's proof. But I also knew that if I dwelt on this, I was unlikely to get on with my life and to be independent, and that I'd be dragging this behind me, like tin cans at the back of a Tin Lizzie. And I did get on. But how many people are completely satisfied with their childhoods?

WACHTEL Where did you find the strength to create your own independent life? Leaving New York at eighteen where your mother was, going back to Montreal alone, embarking on a career as a journalist—

GALLANT I wanted that kind of life. I loved journalism. As I have written, I never looked on it as a waste of time. I loved the experience. Also, I liked the freedom. "Well, I'm just going to do some research." And nobody ever said, "What the hell research do you think you're going to be doing?" "Well, you know that story that so-and-so wants from me," I would say. "Oh, yeah, yeah." And I would get through the work very fast; I had to give myself an alibi. Then I'd go home.

I liked being able to write about things that interested me. But I had to present them in an interesting way to whoever was giving the assignment. I very seldom had an idea turned down. You couldn't write negatively about anything Christian or Jewish—that was out. The royal family was out. You didn't touch the royal family. I was a passionate anti-monarchist. I didn't care if they had it anywhere else, but I thought that it kept Canada trapped in its colonial status.

WACHTEL Two years after you returned to Montreal, you got married. At twenty, you were under-age.

GALLANT I was a minor, yes. It was terrible. He didn't know this.

WACHTEL He, the groom?

GALLANT Yes, he didn't know anything about how strictly this was observed in Quebec. It was still under the Napoleonic Code, and if there were something that you wanted to do that a minor couldn't, and you had no parents—your parents were dead—you had to assemble seven uncles.

WACHTEL Seven uncles—that sounds like something biblical, or a fairytale.

GALLANT I had only two. But this came from a time when people had fourteen children in France, let alone Canada. And I had two uncles on my mother's side, and my father's only brother had been killed in the First World War. I only knew the name Eric. I had one cousin on my mother's side around my age. So I couldn't have assembled three uncles. Or even two. So I got someone to write me a letter, saying "To whom it may concern…" She didn't say she had any power to do this. She just said, "To whom it may concern…" that she absolutely gave complete approval of my marrying John Dominique Gallant. So that was that. I just had to tread carefully. But he didn't know, although when I did tell him, he said, "You could have told me. We could have… done…" I said "Go where?" It was wartime. You couldn't just run across the border and get married in Vermont. But was that a reason? The reason was that I shouldn't be doing it. It was very funny.

WACHTEL What do you think it takes, what inner resources or imagination, to reinvent yourself, as you did when you were twenty-eight and went to Europe? You destroyed all your journals and notebooks before leaving in 1950.

GALLANT I destroyed most. The journals I did destroy, but some had already been converted to fiction. And I kept a lot of things that were dialogue, just dialogue, because I was afraid of adopting another culture and another language and forgetting how people spoke in Canada and New York. A lot of dialogue came from my feature stories. I was afraid of forgetting.

WACHTEL But there is a sense of drawing a line or starting afresh when you left.

GALLANT Oh, yes.

At eighteen, I went back to Montreal because that was where I was from. I had no wish or desire to be anywhere else. This is not nationalism; it is not even patriotism. I was Canadian. *Un point—c'est tout.* I had no desire to become anything else. I thought that speaking two languages was an advantage and I knew I had to work. I had no money.

I had two or three job interviews. I went to the National Film Board. I met someone who was working on a newspaper, and I said, "What's the best newspaper in Montreal?" She said, "*The Standard*, which is a weekly, is probably the best." She worked at a tabloid that came out around noon. "But they don't take people your age there. They take people with lots and lots of experience," and she said, "It's very hard for a girl to get a job." So I went there. I didn't even call. I went and said, "I'm looking for a job on a newspaper, but I don't want to do women's work." So I was interviewed standing in a corridor by someone who I don't think could even have hired me. And he said, "You're too young. Come back when you're twenty-one. In the meantime, get some experience."

As a stepping stone, I worked at the Film Board, which I hated, by the way. They really didn't want women there, except to do mechanical things. Then when I was twenty-one, I went back to the *Montreal Standard*, and they took me on for a three-month trial.

WACHTEL You interviewed Jean-Paul Sartre when he came to Montreal about sixty years ago. What was he like?

GALLANT It was after the war, and he didn't understand what was going on. Quebec isn't like this now—at the time he was considered the Antichrist. He gave a press conference, and the French-speaking press in Montreal was absolutely against him.

We were all standing in a row in the Hotel Mont-Royal, where he was giving his press conference. There were about a dozen French-speaking journalists at the press conference. I was the only woman and the only English-speaking person, but I spoke French. I've spoken it since I was a little kid. I used to always wear either a red coat or a red jacket when I was doing a press conference so that I'd be noticed. I could see that the journalists were very hostile to him. Even if it wasn't personal, they had to show that hostility; if they got fired for having the wrong attitude, where would they go, being French-speaking writers? And so they attacked him. He never came back to Canada, and he didn't really like meeting Canadians after that.

I waited 'til they'd gone. Now, I had read a novel of his—*La Nausée*—and I remember thinking, *Enfin quelque chose de nouveau*, at last something new. It was, completely. It's the one about his character Antoine who sits in a park in Le Havre and looks at a tree until he nearly goes cuckoo, but at that time it was new, and I was thrilled with it.

Sartre was a courteous man, and about the ugliest man I'd ever seen. I was at the age where you still notice how men look. But he was so polite, so well brought up, with an instinctive niceness. I waited 'til everybody had finished insulting him and had gone home, and then I went up. I knew that he had noticed me. He liked girls. He had a wall-eye, but the good one was swivelling. I went up to him and asked him stupid questions about writing because I was already writing fiction, but in secret. He was so patient with this. He must have thought, she looks good but she's dumb. "How much of you is in Antoine?" And he patiently explained that you are in every character you invent. He was what used to be called a "sweet guy." I walked back to my news-paper office because I wanted to think. I knew I had just met someone remarkable, and I thought—I hardly dare tell you because it makes me sound like such a monster of ego—but I actually thought that that is how a really good writer should talk to someone younger. And I thought, well, one day, they will come to me, and I will be nice to the kids. I'll never snub a young person. It was maybe an hour after, I thought, you're crazy. What makes you imagine anyone will even know you're alive by the time you're his age? But that was the effect he had.

WACHTEL You've observed that it's strange to have spent a lifetime describing people who don't exist. In a way, it makes no sense. But in what way do you think it does make sense for you to have devoted yourself to bringing to life characters who are so vivid and complex?

GALLANT I think writers do that. They arrive. It's like a stage, and the curtains part, and there's a phone ringing. And then someone picks up the phone and says, "The madam, she ain't here." You know all about this woman, the one who came in and picked up the phone. You might not even use her, except once or twice. Or more frequently, it's like a movie still, the stills they put outside cinemas, but they come to your mind, and you know all about them. They come with their names. They come with everything. And I always have to keep the name they arrive with, even if I can't ultimately use it, because if I change it in the middle, I can't do the story. Then you get to the end and you go back and change the name, which somehow changes the character a bit.

WACHTEL Do you ever reject characters or choose not to write about them, or is there always something in them that you need to discover?

GALLANT If there are too many characters, one does a winnowing, yes. The whole storyline will change. Because you can't have too many. I don't like to read things that confuse me.

WACHTEL Yes. I was struck by the process of imagining that you reveal in one of your diary excerpts where you're describing seeing a beautiful African woman in a shop in Paris.

GALLANT Yes! That was in a little grocery store, and she came in carrying a baby. It was winter, one of those cold Paris days. She was a very pretty woman, wearing a cotton African dress with a turban.

I spoke to her. We were waiting to be served. I said, "*Vous n'avez pas froid?*" And she burst into the most beautiful smile I think I've ever seen in my life, and she said, "*J'ai la petite.*" And so I made up a whole thing in my mind. I thought, she's married to someone who doesn't care about her really, because no decent man would let her go out in winter with bare feet in sandals. She's married to a swine. And the kindest thing would be to send a posse after him. But that radiant smile. She smelled of coconut oil—I remember that.

WACHTEL Could she inspire a character in one of your stories?

GALLANT She's too mysterious. I couldn't invent for her. And there was the puzzle of her speaking very, very educated French. She didn't have any accent. I couldn't grasp what she was doing in France. But she obviously had no other clothes to wear, or she would have been wearing them. And she had a baby, but it wasn't crying or anything like that. I would not write of someone about whom I had to invent too much.

WACHTEL You've described how some of your stories might begin with something glimpsed. For instance, the story "The Remission."

GALLANT Oh, just glimpsed! Yes.

WACHTEL You saw the characters Barbara, Alec, and their three children getting down from a train in the south of France, and you didn't even use that scene.

GALLANT I didn't need it. But I saw them getting down from the train, and it had rather high steps, because it was soon after the war.

WACHTEL And "The Moslem Wife": You saw the image that became the end of the story, where they're walking in Place Masséna, in Nice. Is it like a puzzle that you have to solve to find out who the character—

GALLANT No, it's solved. It arrives solved. But I don't use all my information. That may come from journalism because when you go to interview people in their home, as soon as you step in, you seize the atmosphere. I remember doing that. You know even the way it can smell of apples in a bowl or of cigarette smoke. You grab that, and you can guess certain things, but you mustn't use them because then you're into fiction.

WACHTEL "The Moslem Wife" began for you with this image from the final scene of the story.

GALLANT She's walking across the Place Masséna with him after the war. She is about to take back the husband she meant to reject. He's said, "I've always loved you," which is probably on the spur of the moment, men are rather like that. Men will say something that hadn't occurred to them for the last six years: "You're the one I love, I've always loved you." And your instinct, the woman's instinct—not necessarily mine—would be to say, "Bugger off."

WACHTEL But actually most women are a soft touch for something like that.

GALLANT Something like that. She really would like to just not have another upheaval in her life.

WACHTEL Like many of the stories, including those in *From the Fifteenth District*, "The Moslem Wife" is set in that milieu that you capture so well: Europe, a seaside hotel in the south of France before, during, and after the war.

GALLANT Before is what was told to me, because I wasn't there during the war. It's from conversations. And also they say things that reveal the kind of life they had before, and they're sorry they can't go on with it.

WACHTEL In "The Moslem Wife," Netta marries her younger cousin Jack, and he offers her freedom of a sort, but that's not what she wants or needs. Jack attracts all kinds of women. He doesn't seem to match Netta's depth and intelligence, but Netta's bound to him painfully and passionately. You write that, whereas—there's this great line—"Jack had settled for the established faith, she had a wilder, more secret God, wanting a prayer a minute, not to speak of unending miracles and revelations." What kind of revelations? What is she looking for?

GALLANT Probably things in herself. Perhaps revelations about herself or about life, which you can certainly acquire from a lover. And if you have twenty lovers, you learn twenty different things. But she wouldn't be likely to do that.

WACHTEL She's such an interesting and unusual character, maybe especially so because you said somewhere that you see a lot of yourself in her.

GALLANT I said that when it was being translated for the first time, and I was reading it very carefully. There's a scene when the doctor comes back after the war, the way all the people are returning, and he asks Netta to marry him, to live with him—anything she wants—

WACHTEL Because Jack is gone now. He's in America.

GALLANT He's in America and he shows no signs of coming back. She says, "Never with a client, never with a customer"—something like that. And she's trying to turn it into a joke really. And he says, "Well, one can't defeat a memory." And alluding to the sexual attraction between her and Jack, he says, "You used to disappear at odd hours," and she says, "Yes, we did." And he says, "Don't be too hard on Jack." And she says, "I am hard on myself." And when I reread that years after having written it, I thought I could have said that.

WACHTEL That you are hard on yourself?

GALLANT Yes, you have to be, if you need discipline in your work. I don't think anybody gets through life in a way that suits them without being a bit hard on themselves. And I am very critical about what I write. That's why I am so slow. Although I can't have been all that slow because there's a lot of—

WACHTEL A fine body of work there. But do you think you're too hard on yourself?

GALLANT No. If you even once say, "I'll just let this go by," the whole thing becomes worthless because you let it go by and didn't change the semicolon into a comma. It's a bit fusspot, yes, but I don't see any other way of doing it.

WACHTEL Netta lives out the hard years of the Second World War in France while Jack is off in America. And at one point, she says, "I've discovered the limit of what you can feel about people. I've discovered something else. It is that sex and love have nothing in common. Only coincidence…" And then, "I suppose this is what men are born knowing and women learn by accident." I've wondered if that was something that you believed.

GALLANT Oh, yes.

WACHTEL She's not bitter about it. She says it's a relief to even realize that sex and love have nothing in common.

GALLANT It gives her freedom.

§

WACHTEL When you left Montreal to live in Paris in those post-war years, did you have any idea of the kind of people you would find there?

GALLANT No, I had no idea because my knowledge came from French emigrés who had come to Montreal during the war, and who were madly patriotic and resented us because we weren't being bombed. I have never liked the idea that Canada had an easy war. It wasn't an easy war. First of all, it's a small population to lose that many people, and it created a deep trench in our lives, one that was hard to get out of. And if you were married, you dreaded every morning because a telegram might come from Ottawa, and if by noon you hadn't had it or nobody had called you on the phone and said, "There's a telegram for you"—but it wasn't done to talk about it. It wasn't even done if you lost someone. It did make a difference because you couldn't get your life started, although I did get going professionally, but I had a singular intention to work all my life.

WACHTEL Coming from Canada, what were you least prepared for in Europe?

GALLANT The attitude to money. We Canadians are supposed to be very uptight about money and very selfish, but I realized that we probably weren't, because I was shocked very often with, "Who's paying for it?" You would hear that, and you would hear a lot about money and a lot about inheritances. I remember my mother saying, "Oh, yes, they're all lovely people, but when it comes to m-o-n-e-y, watch out." I have never forgotten that. And as I got older, I would often think, listening to people, yeah, when it comes to m-o-n-e-y, you know you're not so sweet. It's so hard because Canadians have a reputation for being stingy, as you probably know. And I thought, well, we're not that bad. We had a bad Depression, and then it carried on for two generations, with people so afraid that their children wouldn't make it because another Depression might come along. And there was this madness about people owning property—such nonsense. I didn't want to own anything. And they'd scrimp in their youth, paying off the mortgage and then the second mortgage, and they would start to travel when... You have to do it while it's still fun and while you can travel third and fourth class without feeling it. I travelled fourth class in Spain. It was slats, and if you could get enough room, you'd lie down, because it was easier than sitting.

WACHTEL You had an affinity for Spain because of the Spanish Civil War. It had a certain romance for you.

GALLANT I got to Spain in '52, and it was nothing that I recognized from my reading, especially from fiction. There wasn't anything. Hemingway—*basta*. And I never thought that they would get out of what they were in. The people were passive, and in the afternoon, they would shuffle when it was too hot to go out, and you pulled your shutters shut, and then you'd hear shuffling in the street, which was people going back to work after the siesta. Shuffle, shuffle, shuffle. And I said, "My god, they'll never recover."

WACHTEL You didn't think Spain would ever get over Franco and that kind of oppression?

GALLANT No, I didn't. There was no music, only a Sunday morning concert, I remember, and a few films. They weren't making their masterpieces yet.

WACHTEL You always wanted to live on your own terms and without being told what to do. Do you feel that that's been possible in Paris in a way that wouldn't have been possible in Canada?

GALLANT Yes, if I had given up my job and tried to live on my writing in Canada and been as broke as I was in Europe—and I was really broke a lot of the time—it would not have been possible. To live freelance on writing is very difficult because it's either a feast or a famine, and it's a wonder to me that I managed. I don't know how I did. In Spain I was particularly broke.

WACHTEL I heard you sold your own clothes at one point.

GALLANT I sold my clothes. I had an agent in New York who sold my stories, kept the money and told me nobody wanted to buy them. And I was surprised at *The New Yorker* because they'd taken... By that time, I'd been in Europe almost a year, and they even stopped writing to me. I thought, well, they suddenly don't like my work, but I think they might have told me. I was quite friendly with William Maxwell, the writer and fiction editor of *The New Yorker*, and I thought it's not like him, but I guess I just didn't know him.

In Madrid, I'd sit in the American library and read magazines. So there was *The New Yorker*, and there was a recent story of mine. I couldn't believe it. So I wrote to William Maxwell, and I asked him—not about why didn't they pay me—but why they didn't show me the proofs. Because they'd changed a couple of things, and I wasn't pleased. By return mail, I got, "Thank God I have an address for you. Your agent told us you lived in Capri and that you only gave General Post as your address. So we wrote to General Post and tried to send you the proofs. We sent the cheques to your agent obviously. Did you receive the money for the three stories?" Not just one, but three stories! And my agent knew I was a beginning writer and hard up.

WACHTEL You were saying earlier you were able to live in Paris more easily as a freelancer than you might have been able to in Canada.

GALLANT I could not have done it in Canada with people looking over my shoulder. I knew I'd have a hard time. And to give up your salary—for a girl, as they said, I was getting well paid. When I pulled out, they had just raised my pay to $75 a week, which was huge for a girl, as they kept telling me. I had started at $30 a week, and it had gone up gradually. They raised it to $75 because they didn't want me to go. They felt they'd trained me. I gave them six months' notice, which was pretty good.

And I felt very free. I remember the flight over the Atlantic. Sixteen hours it was. A noisy propeller plane. You'd burst your ears with it. And the feeling of freedom I had going to a city where I knew no one was absolutely wonderful.

December 2007
Original interview produced by Sandra Rabinovitch

ZADIE SMITH

Z adie Smith started writing *White Teeth* (2000) while she was still a student at Cambridge. She graduated with a First and a reported half-million-dollar advance. The novel was published when she was only twenty-four years old. A big, vibrant story of cross-cultural, cross-generational, modern, ethnically diverse London, *White Teeth* won three first-novel awards: the Whitbread, the Commonwealth, and the Guardian. It was made into a television mini-series, translated into more than twenty languages, and sold over a million copies. Some way to launch a career.

Zadie Smith was born in North London in 1975, the oldest of three children, to an English father and a much younger Jamaican mother. She was a bookish kid and in 2003–4, spent a year as a Fellow of the Radcliffe Institute for Advanced Study at Harvard University.

I first met her just before her thirtieth birthday, when she published her third novel, *On Beauty* (2005), another big multi-cultural, multi-generational story, this time set mostly in New England, in the Boston area, in part a campus novel in that the main character, Howard Belsey, is a professor of art history. Zadie Smith is a generous writer, moving easily between sensibilities, ages, intellect. *On Beauty* was shortlisted for the Man Booker Prize and won the Orange Prize. For someone who made it so big, so young, she was remarkably modest, interested, and thoughtful. I think I realized right then that this would be someone I'd want to talk to with every subsequent title. In fact, when *Writers & Company* was celebrating its twenty-fifth anniversary last fall at the International Festival of Authors in Toronto, I was thrilled when she agreed to participate.

Smith is a brilliant essayist and the next time we spoke it was about *Changing My Mind* (2010), her book about writing, her addiction to reading, and her family. In our conversation, she was already expressing some unease about "the big, almost nineteenth-century-style" novels she'd been writing—she didn't exactly disown her early books, but she sometimes referred to them as embarrassing, the work of someone she only slightly knew—so the unusualness of her next novel, *NW* (2012), didn't come as a surprise. About four Londoners who spent their childhoods on a council estate in the northwest corner of the city, *NW* is about time, race, class, and friendship. Almost half the story is revealed in numbered fragments. It's a book that requires a little more attention, but—as the cliché goes—richly rewards it.

First, our conversation about the essays.

WACHTEL The opening essay in your collection, *Changing My Mind*, describes your first encounter with the novel *Their Eyes Were Watching God* by early twentieth-century African American writer Zora Neale Hurston. Can you tell me about that?

SMITH In my early teens, my mom was always pushing black American fiction my way with absolutely the best intentions, and I had some of my best reading experiences through early Toni Morrison, early Alice Walker. But I suppose after a while I became suspicious about why she was continually pushing only black American fiction. So when she gave me Zora Neale Hurston I was reluctant to read her, but the book got around that.

It's really just a simple love story about a woman looking for the right man in her life, and she goes through three of them before she finds him. But it's also obviously a story about what it was like to be a black woman in America in the late 1920s, early 1930s. It's the story of a consciousness coming to life—from an oppressed consciousness to one that is genuinely free.

WACHTEL You say it took you only three hours to read but it left you in tears. Why did it have such an impact?

SMITH I've read it so many times now, and taught it and studied it, that it's difficult to remember exactly because it's become such an artifact to me. I think my initial response was a personal one. Not that the character was like me in practical terms—we were from different universes—but her genetic inheritance and mine were similar, her hair and my hair, her eyes and my eyes, and her skin and my skin. These were reading experiences that I didn't normally have and I didn't realize how much I wanted them. So I think it was a sense of relief.

WACHTEL You were fourteen when you read *Their Eyes Were Watching God*. But what else had you been reading around that time? What kind of writing interested you?

SMITH Actually, I just left my husband this morning reading *Jane Eyre* for the first time, which reminded me that a) he should have read *Jane Eyre* before, and b) I read *Jane Eyre* when I was about fourteen. There's a thing that Nabokov said once that I completely agree with: you will never read as many books as you did between the ages of eleven and fifteen. So it's almost impossible for me to answer that question because when I think back over what I have read, almost everything was in that period. It was an extraordinarily fruitful time.

Off the top of my head, I was reading a lot of Victorian fiction and everything on my mother's shelves. I was reading a lot of inappropriate books like *Our Bodies, Ourselves* and various kinds of feminist fiction that she had. My mom had this very eclectic bookshelf, partly because she wasn't particularly educated herself—neither was my father—but they had an idea that if they bought books with penguins on the spine this was a sign of quality, so they would go to car-boot sales, et cetera, and buy these books. Of course in that period, the mid-1970s and early 1980s, this was absolutely a sign of quality. So we had the green Penguins and the blue Penguins and the orange Penguins, and I made my way through them and it was quite a good early education.

WACHTEL One of the terms you use to describe *Their Eyes Were Watching God* is *soulful*, and you admit that it's a hard word to define. What is it about Hurston's novel that gives it soul?

SMITH Soulfulness to me means authenticity and naturalness; obviously both of these things are very awkward in literature. There is no such thing as "natural" in art—there is only the artifice of looking natural. But Hurston does it incredibly well. It was a language she had in her ear, the language of Eatonville, which is the town in Florida where she grew up. It's not patronizing, though I know a lot of black readers at that time did find it painful, maybe because it was so accurate and they felt that their language was being exposed to an audience that might not appreciate or understand it. But reading it now, there's no doubt that that language is rendered with love and affection and respect. It's so full of imagery, so immediate. There aren't many people who write dialogue that apparently natural; Salinger was another one, but in terms of "black speech," if you can say that, I don't think anyone can touch Zora Neale Hurston.

WACHTEL Did you ever talk with your mother about the book afterwards?

SMITH Yes, I think she was pleased I became such a fan. I know when she read that essay she was pleased because she tends to think that her children have sprung from nowhere. She finds it hard to comprehend how they are the way they are. So it was nice for her to know she had a great influence on the way we are.

WACHTEL Did reading *Their Eyes Were Watching God* make you see your mother or her life any differently?

SMITH It did. I don't think it had really dawned on me what it was like to be a black woman—black as my mother is, not mixed as I am—in a white culture. She told me stories about her honeymoon. My parents went to two places, Morocco and Paris, and in Paris they couldn't get a hotel room—they had to come home. Everywhere they went, they were turned away. And even in the early days when they were trying to rent apartments, she said she would phone and ask for a room and be told it was free, and then turn up and be told it *wasn't* free. She kept experimenting and making the distance between those two events as short as possible, so she would phone from the end of the road and turn up two minutes later and it would never change: she was always told the room wasn't free.

I didn't grow up in an England *that* overtly racist so it was a surprise for me to hear those stories. And it made me better understand the connection she felt with black American writers. It seemed to me that we're English and they're American—the history of our communities is so diverse. But there was a connection for my mother in terms of history and, I suppose, humiliation.

WACHTEL It's astonishing to think we are talking about, what—the early 1970s? In Paris and London?

SMITH Yes, isn't it? Mid-1970s, just before I was born. But I was recently turned away from a club in Paris with my brother for similar reasons: they thought my brother was a thug from the suburbs. So it's not that unusual. Certainly in the areas my parents lived in, in the 1970s, there were still posters in the windows that said, "No Irish, no blacks, and no dogs," which people in Britain do remember. It was extraordinary!

WACHTEL You had been reading Toni Morrison and Alice Walker. Did Zora Neale Hurston's book hit you in a different way? Was there something about this book, especially, that got you?

SMITH It's not all racial; it's partly stylistic. I was used to a kind of English fiction that was very formal in its effects and had a third-person voice—almost stuffy, at least very fixed. What is unusual about Hurston is this thing she does between a very close first-person voice and a third-person voice. There isn't much of that in English fiction.

And then, at a much more basic level, I think if you're a kid and you want to do something and you don't see many people like you doing what you want to do, it's a great joy to find out that it has been done, not just competently but brilliantly, so that meant a lot to me at the time.

WACHTEL In contrast, your essay on Kafka shows someone who didn't identify with his own community or with any sense of community, or even, sometimes, with human beings. Did that sense of alienation strike a chord with you?

SMITH In fact, Zora was quite like that, too. Her natural instincts were to be a loner, and in her autobiography, which many of her fans don't like to read, she really is quite conservative. A lot of her opinions vary from what you would think the black community of her time might have felt, so she struck out alone and was really determined to write what she liked, not write on behalf of a community. One book she wrote, *Seraph on the Suwanee*, for example, is entirely populated by white people, which was an enormous shock to her black readers. But she had decided, I feel, that the whole of humanity was going to be her province, not just the black part of it, so I think she has a connection with Kafka there.

But Kafka was a more extreme case, you're right. He really didn't feel he had much in common with humanity as a whole. I mean, I like Kafka, like everybody, because the prose is extraordinary and that is the thing: before any politics of identity or discussion of community. It's just about how you make a sentence. Zora Neale Hurston makes an extraordinary sentence that is all *hers,* and Kafka makes a different kind of sentence that is all *his*. I think that's what matters to me first, above everything else.

WACHTEL You see Kafka as a kind of existential prophet whose alienation is a twenty-first-century concern.

SMITH I wanted that essay to question the idea that he is *only* an existential prophet. I really wanted to return Kafka to the banality of his everyday life because it's very easy to think of him as somebody who stands outside of literature altogether, who isn't a writer in a way that we are writers, or human in the way that we are human. I think that is a mistake and a romanticization—which is not to take away from the work what *is* extraordinary and transcendent. But I think what is fascinating with Kafka is to try to hold the two ideas in your head at the same time. He was this quite dull, quite tall, quite elegant, quite handsome man—all things we block out when we're thinking of Kafka. We would rather think of him as a peculiar outcast, but in fact he was dashing.

WACHTEL Going back to the existential prophet idea, it also had to do with the way he captured the modern sense of alienation from oneself, that conflicted assimilation of immigrants where you lose one place but don't completely gain another.

SMITH Absolutely. In that sense, he *is* a prophet. He predicted what was clearly inevitable by that point: people were going to start living in places where they hadn't been born, and start attaching themselves to cultures from which they didn't come, and experience the kind of anxiety this would cause. He came from a community that had been doing that for more than a thousand years, so he knew about it. I think that's a lesson Judaism teaches us about religion becoming culture, and about community having an almost sacred content. That is something we have all learned retrospectively.

WACHTEL I read somewhere that you and your husband, Nick Laird, have been working on a musical about Kafka?

SMITH This is the bane of my life. I think I had this half-thought once and mentioned it somewhere, maybe ten years ago, and now it follows me around, this imaginary musical. I would love it to be true; I don't have the time right now, I have so many things I haven't finished. What I was thinking about was an operetta—before anyone starts fearing a glistening Kafka musical.

WACHTEL Did you fantasize about an approach to take?

SMITH I have a great deal of love for things like *The Threepenny Opera*. I love the musical as a form anyway. It's one of my favourite things—not present-day stage musicals, I suppose, but 1930s and 1940s film musicals. I thought the operetta would be an interesting way to tell Kafka's life and incorporate his fiction. So we'll see, maybe it will happen.

WACHTEL Another novel that has made a lasting impression on you is *Middlemarch* by George Eliot. You point out that it gets better as you get older. You quote Virginia Woolf's famous remark that it was "one of the few English novels written for grown-up people." What makes *Middlemarch* part of that select group?

SMITH When I was writing this book, I really wanted to convey the books of my adolescence and early adulthood, and *Middlemarch* was one of those books. It's just an extraordinary achievement in a novel. It's so diverse and gigantic—its concentration is so diffuse. It's a social novel, which England has always aspired to; at the same time, it's a great philosophical novel, like its continental cousins. It seems to do almost everything, and it was written in circumstances that are incredible to me. I've read several biographies of Eliot recently, and I'm always amazed that she made it out of her terribly difficult adolescence and very difficult adulthood to get to that book. At every point of her life it seemed completely improbable that she would have the freedom or time or mental peace to write something like that, and yet she managed it. This was not a woman who got to go to Oxford or Cambridge or be educated like her male peers. Everything that she learned she learned by herself and by dint of useful friendships. She sat around translating Spinoza by herself. She just amazes me.

WACHTEL She was living with George Henry Lewes, who was also translating Spinoza. Who started it?

SMITH I think she was first. They met each other late and were each other's saviours, to a certain degree. But also each other's curses, socially, because once they met, no one would visit them at the house. They were the shame of London.

WACHTEL Because he was married?

SMITH Yes. She had a very, very difficult life, but the book doesn't bear any sign of that struggle. I always think how Virginia Woolf's wonderful extended essay *A Room of One's Own* says that the reason why so many female writers' books either don't exist or tend to be bad is that they're so deformed by the struggle of just getting to write that it shows on the page, that they can't repress their anger or disappointment or fury. What is so remarkable about people like Eliot and Austen is that they did manage somehow to process all the oppression that they experienced and still create art of the highest order.

So *Middlemarch* means a lot to me for that reason. It's so witty, so expansive, so full of character and well balanced, and yes, because it changes the older you get and the more you read it. I was fifteen when I first read it and I've noticed, particularly for young women, that Dorothea is a kind of heroic figure. When you come back to it in your late twenties or early thirties and beyond, Dorothea becomes increasingly ridiculous, and you realize how much of it was a satirical portrait of George Eliot as a younger version of herself—so religiously serious, so completely lacking in a sense of humour, so devoted to the wrong things. When I was fifteen, I took all of that straight and I didn't realize the satire in there.

WACHTEL You just think she's making a bad marital choice.

SMITH You think she is making a bad marital choice, but you think she's incredibly noble and committed and terrific. And she is all those things, but she's also extremely dogmatic, doesn't understand compromise, has no respect for other people's weaknesses—and that is something the book is interested in: people aren't perfect, they are flawed, and it is still possible to comprehend and love them. Dorothea does learn that at the very end. But when I was fifteen, she was the model of behaviour and I wanted to be exactly like her.

WACHTEL George Eliot believed that ideas can't be separated from life if they are to have any meaning and, as you said, she was translating the seventeenth-century philosopher Spinoza. How did she apply his work to her own writing, or how did he influence her writing?

SMITH She was interested in natural science anyway, and I think he made it possible for her to think of nature as an illuminated thing. She had come from an extremely religious Methodist family and turned her back on that religion, which was very difficult and isolating.

Spinoza gave her the opportunity to see the world as illuminated, as fraught with something holy that wasn't to do with a monotheistic God or obeying certain religious rules. That's the way she chose to interpret it, and the world she offers you in *Middlemarch* is holy in and of itself. It has a great kind of humanistic spirit that pushes through it: that people are holy, even in their flaws, even in their sinfulness. I think that really mattered to her and was the engine of her art. It's something that even for me is completely nostalgic. I can't imagine feeling that positively about the world. I don't think that any writer my age could have that feeling for the world that Eliot has. It's particular to her moment and her experience, and it is a joy to read because it reminds you that it was once a possible position to take.

WACHTEL There is a short passage from *Middlemarch* that is among its most famous lines: "If we had a keen vision and feeling of all ordinary human life, it would be like hearing the grass grow and the squirrel's heart beat, and we should die of that roar which lies on the other side of silence." Why did this line stay with you?

SMITH Honestly, I think it's a kind of philosophical nostalgia because what those lines suggest is that if we had complete empathy, if we could understand how people are from the inside, we would be capable of loving them as God loved them. That's what this great nineteenth-century novel is trying to show you: to force you into empathy with people unlike yourself, people of great diversity, unlike each other.

I think contemporary fiction, and certainly fiction since the 1960s, has questioned the assumption that knowing what lies in somebody's heart would allow you to empathize with them totally, would allow you to become them. I don't think that's necessarily true myself. I think it's a wonderful thought, and I think Eliot believed it and it gives those nineteenth-century novels that we all have affection for their incredible power. But I think for people in the postmodern age, for lack of a better word, the idea that empathy naturally leads to "right" action is harder to believe because we have an enormous amount of information about people's lives, an almost constant flow of information, and it doesn't seem to make us behave any better towards them.

So I guess when I write about Eliot it's not that I wish that people wrote novels like Eliot anymore, because I don't think it's possible, but I'm saying that this path she walked down is so engaging and works so well, how can we find a path as contemporary writers to strike off in different directions but move toward the same need to engage people in that way.

WACHTEL You say these aren't particularly healthy times for the novel.

SMITH You know, it depends. Sometimes I am incredibly hopeful, but then sometimes I think we might have to stop thinking that the novel will keep coming to us in the same form. I spent this morning reading graphic novels, which I love, and it struck me that within thirty pages there were more vibrant ideas than I had read in twenty novels this month. So sometimes the exciting narrative forms are not the ones you think they are going to be, to me anyway. American graphic novels are extraordinary at the moment.

WACHTEL I agree. There seems to be the deepest, baldest honesty coming out of them.

SMITH Absolutely! I just read one by Adrian Tomine, an old one I hadn't read. It's a collection of ten stories, and every story has such life in it. I would kill to be able to come up with a book of ten short stories of such vibrancy, of such interest.

WACHTEL It seems like the polar opposite of a nineteenth-century novel like *Middlemarch*, although you say there is nostalgia for that kind of book as well.

SMITH It's funny, part of the exercise of writing this book of essays is not exactly that it is the end of my interest in these things, but it is certainly a record of a past interest. I wanted to try to pay tribute to the books that had made me, but the books that I hope for in the future, the books I want to read, will be quite different, I think.

WACHTEL You have written about the disappointment a writer feels in his or her own work, and much of it seems to come down to self-betrayal. Can you tell me about that?

SMITH It's strange for me because when I first started writing, I was very young, and I thought everybody felt the way that I did, as you do when you are young. As I met writers (I had never met any writers before in my life), you realize there are plenty of writers who just adore their work and think every word they write is absolutely fantastic and will defend it to their dying day. Some writers feel that way; I just can't find that con-fidence in myself. At the same time, there is not much point in talking about it all the time because people think you are being falsely modest. But to me, writing is a very painful experience. I hope it will stop being so painful as I get older, but it doesn't seem to be getting any better.

WACHTEL You describe when you tried to reread your first novel, *White Teeth*, you literally felt sick. What do think that was about?

SMITH I think anybody out there forced to read something they wrote when they were twenty-one would have a problem with that—it's hard. You don't go back and read your college essays with delight, and it just so happens that my college essay was a novel. The important thing is to respect the fact that other people appreciate the book you wrote. You shouldn't dismiss it for them.

WACHTEL Although you said your experience was a bit better when you picked up your novel *On Beauty*.

SMITH It's always a bit better the closer to the time you are reading it. But the only thing that really gives me pleasure is reading some of the very short non-fiction, because non-fiction is an area I can control. At least you can "be right," which I find a nice sensation. Whereas with novels, it's impossible to be right. You are always wrong to most people, or half the people. I just find it very painful.

WACHTEL You talk about the connection between style and the author and how there is almost a connection between aesthetic choices and ethics. How is a writer's style a way of telling the truth?

SMITH In talking to younger students when I am teaching, it seems they're very concerned about having a voice. But to me, a style is something you can't *help* but have. It's like your skin. It's not something you can go out and buy; it's just the way you express yourself. It is implicit in everything you do. Ten years ago, when I was starting and I began to meet writers for the first time, it struck me very forcibly that they were *like* their books. And I thought that this was something I hadn't been allowed to even consider as a university student, where we really divorced the author from the work in order to take the work to ourselves more intimately. We just weren't interested in authors, we never saw them. I had never even considered them. I just considered the "text," as we went about calling it at the time.

And then when I met authors, the similarity between what you'd call their personality and the sensibility of their work on the page amused me, I was just so surprised by them. It might sound stupid and obvious to general readers who assume that anyway, but I think I had disappeared so far into an academic funnel I'd forgotten that there is a relation, an intimate relation, between the human being and the book. It doesn't mean that the book is autobiographical— in fact entirely the opposite is usually the case—but something in the voice of the person, something in the sensibility, is inextricably tied to the way they write, and once I could admit that to myself, I found writing criticism a completely different experience. In college, I had been writing these very academic, very jargon-heavy— very pleasure-free, to be honest—essays about books that I loved. It was such a liberation to be able to write about books I love in a way that I love writing and to say, Look, there is a relation here. The author and the text, they go together and the relation between them really matters.

WACHTEL It almost seems to be a question of personality rather than ethics, because there are writers we would find ethically objectionable. Like T.S. Eliot's anti-Semitism, for instance, or Philip Larkin's misogyny…

SMITH To me, those things are superficial—I agree with you, but they are not really about style. Larkin's style is one of the most ethical styles that exists. What Larkin said in his letters or what he might have said to so-and-so at his dinner parties is something separate, but the way his sentences are formed, the things his poems believe in, are incredibly important to me and it is sometimes very hard to make that distinction. Larkin could be racist, could be misogynist, was frequently offensive, but the things that matter about Larkin to me—his poems about death, his poems about time—those seem to me extraordinarily… *ethical* is the wrong word because it sounds as if someone is pushing a point and that's not what I mean. I mean ethics in the largest sense, that certain poems of Larkin's have a way of showing me how to be alive and that is the most important thing a piece of writing can do.

WACHTEL I don't disagree. It's the idea of the work or style as an expression of personality, of the writer's way of being in the world.

SMITH Wouldn't you say that a great style represents the best of a writer's person? I know that if something I write works, if it is done well, that what is expressed in that essay or piece of fiction is really the best of me, to the extent that if you then ask me about it, I feel stupider than the essay. I can't remember half the things I put in it. The essay is smarter than me in every way because in those four pages I was able to organize everything just the way I wanted and express the best side of myself. The rest of me, the real human side, kind of drags around behind the work. I think that's also why people are disappointed when they meet writers because they seem less than their work in some way. I think it's probably true, but they *are* connected.

WACHTEL What does writing do for you? Can you say why you write?

SMITH I don't write that much. There are people who write every day, and it's part of their life, but I go for months, and recently years, without writing fiction, for example. For me, it is not a matter of daily survival. I've heard writers speak of something that they can't help but do. The only thing I can't help but do is read. If I don't read every day

I'm just completely doomed. I think the more effective question for me is what does reading do for you because it's reading that I am really addicted to. Writing is a kind of outgrowth of that passion.

WACHTEL Okay, what *does* reading do for you?

SMITH I'm just completely addicted to it. Nothing will stop me doing it. I realize now with my baby, I'm breast-feeding her and all I do is read all the time. My husband reminded me, "You know you have to *speak* to the child occasionally"—because otherwise, she might never learn to speak! She's used to just sitting on my lap and then when I turn a page, she jerks. That will be her childhood memory: this page-turning noise. So I don't know, it's something that allows me not to be myself, or allows me to be in other places among other people, and I get great joy out of good sentence making. Nothing makes me happier. I usually spend the mornings reading and then I do my best to try to write something in the afternoon. The afternoon thing almost never happens, whereas the morning thing *always* happens.

WACHTEL *Changing My Mind* is dedicated to your father's memory, and you write about him with such unsentimental tenderness. Can you tell me a bit about him?

SMITH Well, I guess I don't know that much about him, which is the reason I'm always writing about him, trying to work it out a little. He was an unusual father in that he was much older than he should have been to have a daughter my age. He was fifty when I was born, so he was always "old."

And the stories he had to tell were somewhat unusual: he had heard Ella Fitzgerald sing on the Kilburn High Road, he went to see *Casablanca* in the movie house, he was in the Second World War, slightly younger than he should have been. So to me he was already a bit of a fictional character. I couldn't understand how someone that old was my father, and I was always very concerned about him dying. On the one hand, that kind of thought is a negative thing, but it's also just an interesting idea to have in your mind as a very young child. The idea of him disappearing or being part of this distant generation was very preoccupying to me, and it also gifted me a lot of my slightly anachronistic tastes. The films that he loved are the films I love, but of course they're the films of the 1930s and 1940s, and I know all the popular songs that he loved, which I probably shouldn't know, because they are the songs of the 1920s.

He was a very disappointed man—he'd left school at the age of twelve and was never properly educated. I think he was smart and would have liked to have had more of an education, so as the years went by we were sort of at odds with each other. He was a man in his late seventies, white, English, uneducated, with a black daughter. We made a funny pair walking down the street. So he was always a bit mysterious to me, and I think in him is the seed of my interest in writing—wanting to figure out who this man was who lived in our house. And a lot came from that, I think.

WACHTEL And when you say "at odds," do you mean you were argumentative?

SMITH I think we had a hard time in my teenage years because he was such an anomaly compared to my friends' fathers that I just started pretending he didn't exist. And as I got older and particularly once he got older and more vulnerable, as is common for children with older parents, it all turned around when I realized there was no point in being angry or upset with him because all the responsibility of caring for him was on my side now. So, no, we were at odds because our lives were so different. He made this effort to make sure that all his children were educated, but once you do that in a family, it was just odd, you know. He had a working-class accent, I don't anymore. He hadn't read that much and I became well read. I think a lot of working-class or immigrant parents who put their children through school hope that they will have different lives—you get what you hope for, but what you hope for isn't something you can always recognize, so it's a strange relationship.

WACHTEL Did that accent shift just happen overnight when you went to Cambridge?

SMITH No, it's impossible for me now to remember. I have two brothers and we all speak differently and it's partly who we were hanging out with as children. Parents think they are the biggest influence on their children. Parents have almost no influence on their children. What influences children are their friends and where they go and what they do. So my youngest brother was much more a kid of the street than I was and he sounds like a "street kid," and my middle brother was less so and he is somewhere in the middle, and I was at home reading George Eliot—I don't know what happened to me. We were all from the same family, but you would say we were three different "classes."

This interests me, because people assume that when you are from one place, you are one people. But we are all very different. We dress differently, we think differently, we have different politics, and we're all from one household.

WACHTEL As an adult, you asked your father to tell you about his time in the military during the Second World War because it was something he hadn't really talked about before. Do you know why not?

SMITH I don't know. People often say that about war veterans, that they don't talk about it. I can't really imagine what it was like, landing in Normandy. I've seen the movies, but it's impossible for me to conceive of my father in that situation. I don't know how he survived it; it's amazing to me. But he just never mentioned it. He had a young wife, young children, it was the 1980s. The Second World War seemed a long way away to us. I don't know if he could ever have made us understand it, really.

But when I was an adult I did want to know, and he was really interesting and eloquent about it, although very resistant to my attempts to turn it into a more interesting story. For him it was a very banal story, I think, for the most part. I didn't think it was banal when he told it to me, but it certainly wasn't full of glamorous heroics or anything.

WACHTEL As you describe it in your book, he would focus on what seemed like small details.

SMITH There was a ridiculous moment when I was trying to get him tell me what happened just after they had landed on the beach, and then he decided to tell me he went to buy a pen—but that was like my father, he was quite fixated on the small details. I mean, he helped liberate Belsen. I thought that was more interesting than buying a pen. But it was much more like my father to get into the pen. It was good to hear it, good in a very simple way to have it recorded, and now it's there always and I can show it to my daughter and I know what he did. And I am very proud of him because it seems like such an unlikely thing for him to do.

WACHTEL Do you think he focussed on the pen because of the incident after that?

SMITH Yes, he made this rookie mistake. He was making a small fire to make some tea and it was spotted by the Germans, and they shelled, and people died. My father was injured. It was his fault. Try to think about a young man having that kind of responsibility. For my generation, yes, things can go wrong when you do something stupid, but the consequences are so minute compared to that. He was so ill-equipped for it. He was seventeen, and having an experience like that... I had no idea, he'd never told me. I never knew why he had shrapnel in his leg. I still don't know how to feel about it. I mean, he was responsible for this terrible thing, but it depends what you think of the nature of responsibility—it's also a terrible accident. But he did cry when he told me, so it must have been on his mind all those years. I had no idea.

WACHTEL How did hearing about his experiences affect how you saw him?

SMITH I was saying to my brothers that when we were kids, we were desperately looking for a way to be proud of our father and also to be interested in him. He just seemed to us the dullest man in the world. Please forgive me for saying that, but he has passed—he just seemed to have no interests, he didn't *like* anything. The only thing he seemed to like were old movies, and I fixated on that because I wanted to share an interest with him. I had this preoccupation with the idea that there were these middle-class families out there who had *interests*—who loved books and had conversations at the dining table about interesting things. And I wanted to be in one of those families. I think *On Beauty* was an expression of a fantasy I had of being in this kind of family. Then realizing, growing up, that those families have plenty of their own problems.

So I wanted him to be a different kind of man. And then asking those questions of him in later life, finding out this amazing stuff, I realized I'd actually been living with a very interesting man all my life and I had been too stupid to recognize it.

WACHTEL Your father shows up in your work in a number of ways, not just in *White Teeth* and the fantasy levels of *On Beauty*. You wrote some short stories about a man named Hanwell who was about the same age as your father. Does he share some of his background?

SMITH Those are stories inspired by my father and inspired by generations of my father's family. He had a strange relationship with his father—his father was another kind of unknowable man, and when he died, my father never went to his deathbed, which interested me. So I wrote a story about that, too.

Hanwell became a series of linked lives and stories of my father. Of everything that I've written, I found them the easiest to write and the most fulfilling in terms of fiction. They are the only fiction I have written that I uncomplicatedly appreciate.

WACHTEL It's interesting because these stories also incorporate the sense of disappointment and sadness in his life.

SMITH Yes. I'm very inclined when things get tricky to tell a joke instead, and my fiction is like that. I think it relies a lot on humour, like a lot of English fiction, to avoid difficult things. But when I was writing those Hanwell stories, I found that I didn't want to do that—I didn't feel the need to do it—and that was a good thing. I am so early in my writing life, I have no idea, but maybe those stories will prove to be transitional. To me, they seem like a different kind of writing, a different kind of thing I wanted to do.

WACHTEL But a love of comedy was one of the things that you shared with your father?

SMITH Yes, absolutely. He did have a good sense of humour, which I really appreciated. And we found the same things funny. He liked absurdist things; he liked the Goons a lot. *The Goon Show* is very intellectual comedy, you know, but at the same time it is slapstick and ridiculous. I love that. He was also a massive Monty Python fan, which meant a great deal to me because I felt they were extraordinary.

When I sat down to write *White Teeth*, believe it or not, I was a very serious young woman. I thought I was writing a very serious book, and when it turned out all comic I was so surprised. I didn't realize that that was the kind of writer I was going to be—but I think I must be under the influence of all that comedic stuff from my childhood.

When I finished *White Teeth* I went on holiday. A lot of college friends were there and they did me the favour of reading the manuscript. I know there are still historical mistakes and all kinds of nonsense in it, but they were all smart kids and they checked spelling mistakes and bad facts. One girl there said to me, when she finished the book, "You know, I think you are fatally out of step with your generation"—which made me laugh, and I think it's profoundly true! I think that now I am getting a bit closer to them and my tastes have changed, but definitely when I was twenty-one I was just completely at the wrong end of everything. Of every trend and of every possible idea in the arts and fiction and the rest of it, and that is partly my father's influence as well.

WACHTEL So much of British comedy is based on class. Did your father see his own foreshortened possibilities in relation to his class?

SMITH Yes he did, and I think he was right to. I am constantly amazed now in England that class has stopped being a conversation. One thing that Thatcher did which was so brilliant was to suggest that we are all democratic now, and that even to talk about class is a kind of snobbery. It's the most extraordinary piece of doublethink I have ever heard. Recently I was watching a news show on TV and somebody dared to bring up the fact that what will probably be the incoming Tory government are almost all Eton-educated. The working-class people in the audience stood up, enraged, saying we don't talk about that, it doesn't matter, we're all equal now. It is so unbelievably perverse. But my father's generation *was* politicized and *did* feel that class mattered. Class matters when it foreshortens what you can possibly do in your life. And the fact is that the boy who is Eton-educated and the boys in that TV audience who are educated in schools that politicians wouldn't deign to put their own children in have different possibilities in front of them and that does matter.

It mattered enormously to my father that he couldn't afford to go to the school that he got in to at thirteen. He couldn't afford the uniform, which must have cost, whatever, two and six. And for two and six he lost a life—if that is not a matter of class, I just don't know what to call it. It is a tragedy, and a lot of men in my father's generation suffered it.

WACHTEL It certainly wasn't ability because, as you say, he got in to the school.

SMITH I sometimes feel, but I hope it isn't true, that my generation are the very last generation of the British meritocracy. I went to Cambridge and I didn't pay a penny. And that is just not possible anymore. I think the fees are already three- to four-thousand pounds plus the loan. And you hear people say, "Well, if you care about your education you will pay for it." People who say that don't understand what it is like to not have money. When you don't have money, *you don't have money*. And you don't borrow either, because you're scared to borrow that amount of money. If those fees had existed in 1993, I wouldn't have gone to Cambridge because I never would have thought to borrow the money. We would have just thought, Well, that's not for us, end of story. What is happening now in British education breaks my heart because it means that the meritocracy that created, for instance, people like Alan Bennett—it's gone. It can't happen anymore. You can't be a working-class boy from Yorkshire and go to the best university in the country. You can't afford to. It's tragic, really.

WACHTEL So it was just that slice of time when access and scholarship were available?

SMITH Yes. It's sad and it is a question of class, but if you ask me, most British people these days have come to accept it. We're going towards an American model, and I don't think there is much that can be done to stop it anymore.

WACHTEL When we talked last time, you said that families were a messy business. Now you recently had a baby, your first. Has being a parent changed anything in the way you see or feel about family?

SMITH You know, in all the usual ways: I do have more sympathy for my mother, which I guess recently I have been lacking. We have a pretty fiery relationship, and my mother and her mother have a pretty fiery relationship. Now I have a daughter and I'm almost thirty-five, and I realize it is not so easy to have a kid. Mother was twenty and so young and innocent, married to a man thirty years older.

You start to appreciate what somebody else went through, so it makes you more sympathetic, I suppose. The thing that really strikes me is how much arrant nonsense is spoken about family life and family emotion. I kept on hearing that once you have a baby you just become a different and more wonderful person, so full of sympathy, your ego disappears—all complete nonsense. It seems to me that having children is a massive act of egotism in the first place. I am as egotistical and unpleasant as I've always been, but now "with child," so the selflessness I was hoping for hasn't happened. Maybe it's different for people who have "proper jobs," but for me there's been a strange feeling of continuity. My life has always been about sitting in a chair, reading a book, occasionally typing, and it's the same now, but I've got drool on me.

WACHTEL We talked about how the understanding of life experience can inform or affect a work. Do you think the experience of having a child will affect your writing?

SMITH My writing is all about making the future safe. So I get married and I write a book about a marriage of thirty years, still standing. I've always tried to write things out before I've done them as a way of pre-experiencing them, or a way of *not* experiencing them, a way of phonily getting through life. I guess I imagined that childbirth and having a child would be that one experience that would be impossible to mediate, the real thing, the genuine thing—here's life coming at you. But again that isn't true. It's possible to mediate almost everything, or at least it's possible for me to mediate everything, sadly. So I don't know if it will be a big transformation. I feel like in print, I already had children.

WACHTEL One of your non-literary models is Katharine Hepburn, and the title of your book of essays, *Changing My Mind*, is loosely based on a line that one of Hepburn's characters, Tracy Lord, says in *The Philadelphia Story*. What is it that inspires you about Katharine Hepburn?

SMITH When I was a kid, I was what people called a "tomboyish girl," whatever that means, and I suppose I still am. I wasn't that interested in feminine things, I was just looking for women who were interesting to me. A way of being alive that didn't involve princesses or pink or any of that scenario. Katharine Hepburn seemed to be one of those women. She was very attractive, bold, intelligent. She was—*womanly* is the word I would use.

And when I was very young and reading books I shouldn't have been reading, I remember reading an Alice Walker essay where she defined *womanist* and *womanly* and those concepts interested me. I really didn't want to be a girl, ever. If I *had* to be female—that's how I conceived of it when I was young—I wanted to be a *woman*, and Katharine Hepburn was definitely a woman, in that sense: an adult person of her own mind. I loved her movies for that reason.

As an adult now, looking around at the contemporary scene, I am really grateful that I am not eight years old in 2010 and a girl, because it is a nightmare, really, a nightmare compared to the landscape when I was ten, in which extreme femininity was an option but you could easily ignore it. Now it's the only option. Every magazine, every TV show has these painted dolls everywhere with fake bodies and fake chests and redone faces. I don't think I could have survived that; I would have been completely defeated by it. Whereas thirty years ago, it was a little easier and I had those great old movies and great role models, and Hepburn was one of them. She just seemed so much of a *person*, and that's what I wanted to know that women could be.

WACHTEL You call Hepburn the last of the great stars—the very last. Not that she wasn't unique even in her own time, but why do you think we haven't had stars like her since?

SMITH It's not the actresses. I constantly see actresses and think, You would be so great if somebody would write you a movie that is not complete and utter nonsense from beginning to end. I don't go to movies that much, but when I do there are only a few options, plot-wise, for women. Most of them involve whether you're going to get married, whether you're beautiful, or whether you're going to have a baby. There doesn't seem to be much else going on for girls these days.

WACHTEL It strikes me that the revelation of the Katharine Hepburn character in *The Philadelphia Story* is precisely what you articulated about *Middlemarch*, which is respect for the weakness of other people.

SMITH Absolutely. The thing about Tracy Lord is that she has this enormous will to power, and I guess when I first watched that film I was really young, and I felt almost personally offended or shocked by it. Not that I was anywhere near as glamorous or wonderful as Tracy Lord, but I did think I could organize myself in a certain way and I was very set upon it. I thought that having a strong will was everything you needed in life—that is certainly what Tracy thinks. I was absolutely outraged by that scene where her father, who is a hypocrite and a great sinner and has cheated on his wife, gives her a lecture and says something like, "You may have a fine body and an intelligent mind, but you need more than that in life." And I thought, Who the hell are you? Get out. Go away.

It is very hard in that movie to appreciate the fact that (a) the man is a hypocrite and a waste of space and (b) he is also right. That is the crux of the movie. Two things can happen: you can be a complete ass and you can also, on this occasion, be correct. Tracy does need to have some sympathy, she does need to open up, and it is not enough to be talented and wondrous and beautiful, you also need to be kind. When I was a kid and watched that movie, I just didn't know how to settle those two things in my mind. I thought he was being some kind of misogynist in trying to put down this great woman who was so full of life. And now when I watch it, I just see it as a comedy of errors. Everybody is at fault. Everybody has their flaws. The movie is an appreciation of that.

WACHTEL Hepburn may not have been a literary model, but you say that famous line from *The Philadelphia Story*, "The time to make up your mind about people is never," is your lodestar every time you pick up a pen to write anything. How does that line inspire you?

SMITH I think of it as something I aspire to. It is incredibly difficult in life. I really feel that once you have a child, once other people have children, every moment is about judging each other, you almost can't help it. It is disgusting and self-serving: you decide that the way you will bring up your child is somehow superior to the way your friend is going to, or your neighbour. That invidious comparison in which you are always "the winner" is kind of sickening, but really, I just keep finding myself walking into it.

And in writing, particularly, that way of being in the world—in which you're always the hero of your own story—is a disaster. The caricature of other people is a disaster, but also trying to convey people in their unknowability is very, very difficult in fiction, yet I think it's what all fiction writers, good fiction writers anyway, aspire to. Not to pin down people, like a bad comedian: "She's just like this" or "She's just like that" because we can all do that, and that's the business of everyday stupidity. The difficult thing is to confront the fact that the person you've lived with for twenty years is in some way, in the very centre, not your possession, not yours to know. And mysterious. That is the thing that interests me. And it does not only have to be expressed as alienation.

I always think of French fiction as incredibly brilliant at suggesting that the person who you walked down the aisle with is as strange to you as the person you see passing on a tube platform. It can be terrifying, that realization. But to me it's also—I can't believe I'm going to use the word *nourishing*, but I am!—nourishing to know that you can't pin somebody down, that they are constantly going to surprise you, and that your knowledge of the world is continually limited and limiting. You have to keep on confessing your ignorance, keep on recognizing your ignorance, confronting it *every day*. The people who have done it most purely are our greatest philosophers who we celebrate two thousand years later. Most of us can't get anywhere near that kind of purity, but it's a healthy reminder to say, Maybe I don't know this guy. Maybe there are things I can't caricature or pin down. And maybe this person has an inviolability that's not mine to mess with.

February 2010

§

WACHTEL Most of your 2012 novel *NW* takes place around a neighbourhood called Willesden in the northwest part of London, where you grew up. What's your earliest memory of your neighbourhood?

SMITH I was embedded in it from quite early on. My mother was a social worker in the area for most of my childhood, so I think my earliest memory is of going to her youth groups and hanging about. I had to hang about a lot because she was always working, and there was nowhere else for me to go. I have quite early memories of hanging out with enormous, strapping, troubled teenagers.

WACHTEL You started off in council estate housing and said it was very nice. How would you describe the neighbourhood?

SMITH Yes, I started off in a very nice council estate, I think, as far as these things go, and then we moved to a flat up the road, which is where my mother still lives.

I recently watched a great English documentary about the nature of council estate planning, and it turns out that lots of very small differences can be very important, like whether or not a stairwell is enclosed or see-through, for example. It turns out to have massive social results in the life of the estate, and in my case it was see-through, which is better apparently—everyone can see what's happening—than the enclosed, dangerous stairwells. And also it was low rise, which makes a difference. The opposite estate was twenty-five storeys high. So it was an interesting place. When I was growing up, it was very Jamaican and Irish. Now it's far more mixed.

WACHTEL Was that a good mix?

SMITH It resulted in a lot of children who look like me. That was a very common result of the mixing. It was a good mix. My parents are both quite tempermental people. A lot of the Jamaican women in my family ended up marrying Irishmen. I ended up marrying an Irishman, so it's somewhere deep in my DNA, that combination.

WACHTEL Kilburn is another northwest London neighbourhood that you feature in your novel. You write about an optimistic vision for this neighbourhood. What went wrong?

SMITH I don't think anything went wrong. I just think one of the consistent things about London is constant change. So if you hoped, in the 1880s, to have a lovely suburban villa with property, well, it was like that for about twenty years. And then it shifted; the railways came, the subway came. Things changed constantly in Kilburn. In that period, you could literally take sheep from Kilburn and drive them all the way up to Oxford Street. So it was a vision based on a completely different life, but I don't see it as a tragic failure. That's what I like about London: it's always changeable.

WACHTEL I guess it's the people coming from these other countries who are disappointed.

SMITH My mother was often like that—there were always a lot of complaints. And yet if you said to her, "Well, how about we go back to Jamaica?" she would react in horror. My mother couldn't be more English; she has a voice like the Queen, the whole nine yards. There's a kind of halfway space, I think, where people think the grass is always greener somewhere else.

WACHTEL Some of the characters in your novel *NW* have ambivalent relationships with their neighbourhood. I'm thinking, for instance, of Keisha, who later goes by the name Natalie. From an early age, she's aware that she wants something else. Where does her ambition come from?

SMITH What interested me in Keisha was the idea of talent, the idea of being good at something and what, if anything, that entitles you to. The thing that worries Keisha is that she's smart. Everybody keeps on telling her she's smart, and the assumption is that, because she's smart, certain things are her right, which is an interesting but problematic idea because does it mean that people who don't have this ability don't have the right or shouldn't have the opportunity? So I think that's what concerns her. But where does anybody's willpower or talent or ability come from? It's a complete accident. It's a kind of gift. But the question is, what do you take from that fact? Clearly, a lot of people believe that they deserve everything that's coming to them. They've been somehow especially blessed. I don't know if I would feel that way.

WACHTEL Keisha, or Natalie as she becomes, is a very bright student and eventually becomes a lawyer, but she isn't comfortable in her own skin. She wonders at times who she is. Why is her own sense of self so elusive?

SMITH When I researched barristers, I talked to a young black male barrister about whom I was curious. He described how he'd got there. It was the usual. He was also from northwest London, and he had passed the exams, and he had struggled, and he'd got into Oxford and found it very, very difficult to be there. When he started working at a law firm, I wanted him to describe to me what the difficulty was, because it's sometimes hard to figure out. He was the one who gave me the idea in the book about having to be neutral, because it was something he found. When he went to court, the first few times, he realized that the judge would reprimand him, or he couldn't get very far, and that his normal way of speaking, his normal way of being, his blackness, registered to the judge as aggressive. It was such a shock to him. You realize how you are seen by other people, and he had to consciously find another way to be in this courtroom. That small example was multiplied in various ways.

The English barrister system is fascinating because it's not just a matter of knowing the information and passing the exams and going to court. You also have to attend these elaborate dinners. There's a whole social world around it. So you effectively have to become the type of person who is allowed to be an English barrister, which turns out to be a very narrow kind of person. And so this young barrister had had to distort himself in order to become, as he ended up being, very successful. He said he had suffered from depression and felt he was not the person he'd started out as. That's what interested me: people who are outside of the mainstream have to sometimes compress themselves, to adapt, in order to survive. But it's also, I think in his case anyway, a kind of gift, because he was so adept at adapting that it became an advantage. That's a useful thing in a lawyer, so I gave some of those qualities to Natalie/Keisha.

From the very beginning, I had the idea of writing a black existential novel. Quite often when you read black novels, everybody has this very firm sense of identity. There are always incredibly confident black women who are always full of wisdom, throwing wisdom everywhere. Well, yes, we have some, but we're not constantly full of wisdom. In every movie, the black woman is this fount of spiritual wisdom. So I wanted to try and reflect the fact that people of colour also have existential crises, also have dubious senses of self, like everybody else. I was interested in the idea of writing a novel of identity in which identity was a problematic thing.

WACHTEL It's very elusive and it's not just professional. In the rest of her life, the idea of who she is, or if there is a self there, is one she refers back to. So, yes, in existential terms, it would fit.

From the outside, Natalie seems to have an enviable life. She has a very good job. She has an attractive husband. She has two children. But she becomes involved in a kind of obsession, which I won't give away, but it puts everything at risk. Why would she do this?

SMITH I guess the other thing I was interested in is the idea of a certain kind of success, the thing which everybody is supposedly pursuing, being in fact, in some ways, quite isolating. Just from my own experience, I grew up with a lot of people, and then I went to college and was surrounded by people. And then adult life becomes a continual process of isolation. You get the house in which only you and maybe two other people will live, hopefully far away from any other people, and with a car that locks down so nobody can get in. You extend this to private holidays and private schools and restaurants in which only twelve people can fit and so on. That's meant to be what we're all ambitious for. I wondered whether that was truly the case, because if you ever spent time with the super rich, if you go to Capri or to the Venice Biennale, what you see are people who seem intensely lonely and bored and depressed—or that's how it seemed to me—who fought for so long for this holy isolation of privacy. And then when you get there, you're just stuck, looking at your wife as she looks at you, and the years go on and on. It seems to me a part of middle-class, probably straight, life that your circle gets smaller and smaller, gets incredibly tiny, until it's just you and your partner and perhaps your child, a dog. The whole system is built to make sure that you are this kind of solid, isolated economic unit, and I think people are lonely inside it.

WACHTEL Is some of her sense of alienation feeling guilt at escaping from the council estate?

SMITH I think that's certainly a part of it, always. If you have success and you leave people behind you, I think that's a stressful thing to have on your mind or on your conscience, and you end up with different relationships. Nobody wants to feel that, by moving ahead, you lose the things you came from, but that's one of the binds of a meritocratic rise.

WACHTEL Natalie's best friend, Leah, is one of the characters who stays closer to her roots. She's happy to stay in the neighbourhood, even though her husband would prefer to move to a different part of town.

SMITH I think for Leah that's where her whole sense of self is determined. She can't really imagine herself in any other environment. I wanted to depict what my younger brother would call a frenemy relationship, this relationship which is both close and extremely antagonistic. It does happen between women, and it happens between men as well, but I'm a woman so I'm more familiar with the female version of it. I found this Nietzsche quote, which ended up in the book: "We live in the age of comparison." It seemed to me so true that there's this insane need to know how other people are living their lives so one can decide whether one is living one's life well or better or better than them, at least. It seems impossible for people to just live without this total concern about what's going on next door or what their friends are doing and when they did it. And it really becomes poisonous between the two of them; they can't just live their own lives. But that's the thing: it turns out they don't seem to have lives without this contrast. Part of Natalie's whole sense of herself is, well, at least I'm not Leah, and part of Leah's sense of herself is, well, at least I'm not Natalie. I don't think that's an unusual dynamic, unfortunately, amongst friends or supposed friends.

WACHTEL Although some corner of Leah seems to envy Natalie. They seem to get it so wrong, too. I know that everyone's exterior is utterly misleading, and inside is a quivering mass of jelly.

SMITH Yes, but I think that's another thing about friendship which you learn as you get older. It's incredibly complicated, and it takes a lot of work and art. I know if I have an argument with my husband, if he says to me that I'm a terrible person, I'm, like, "Yeah. Whatever." But if my friend says I'm a terrible person, it's the worst thing in the world. To say, "You've really disappointed..." There's something about that relationship, perhaps because it's not sexual, and it's not got the advantage of, for example, kinship. It's the worst thing for your friend to condemn you. It's unspeakable to argue with a friend and then spend two weeks not talking or wondering whether you should call.

So I've always been interested in family relationships and friendships because of that. They seem to get to the heart of something. In some sense, they're very pure, and they're also so personal to me, much more than romantic relationships in some ways.

WACHTEL Race differences are part of the fabric of *NW*, but you say, "Most human problems are about class or money." Has the importance of race shifted in recent years?

SMITH No. It's always tempting to make that conclusion. When I was asked to write about the anniversary of 9/11 a while ago, I spent a long time thinking about what I was going to write. I had been reading about the impossibility of people of different cultures ever truly understanding each other, which has become a great fashion in the past few years. I was downstairs in my apartment building; it was near Christmas. And on the walls, the mixture of Stars of David and crosses and Christmas trees in the lobby of our apartment building—I thought, well, what two religions could have more of a fundamental difference than these two religions? What more fundamentally opposed at the level of the text than the Jewish people and the Christian people? This is supposedly the kind of fundamental cultural difference above which we cannot ever rise, nor can we live with it. And it's not that everyone in my building is secular. That's not that point. There are seriously religious people of both kinds, but they're at an economic level in which these differences don't grate in the same way. People are able to live intimately, separately and also together in many ways without there being a textual argument every day. They're not arguing about the Torah in the playground every day. But this sense of equilibrium takes hundreds of years. It takes time and the right circumstances and the right kind of economic environment. It implies aspiration for everybody involved. So that's what I would put the emphasis on. I don't believe in this idea that in one book Abraham does this, and in another book Abraham does that, and in a third book he does another thing—suggesting we can never live together. I think it's complete nonsense and it's shown to be nonsense over and over again. But it's a tempting and easy solution when you don't want to deal with underlying economic issues.

WACHTEL One of your strategies in this book is not to necessarily mention what shade or colour a character is, except when they're white.

SMITH It really wasn't a strategy in the beginning. It just happened halfway through. It amused me. I thought it was funny, and so I decided to stick with it.

I don't walk into my family home and think, oh, look, there's my black mother with her extraordinary multicultural family. That's not how I think, so I don't see the point of doing that in fiction.

WACHTEL It reminds me of Jamaica Kincaid, who once said to me that when she wakes up in the morning, the real struggle, she says, is how to face the day, how to get out of bed. She doesn't think, oh, I'm a black person.

SMITH No. It's not a matter of racism; it's just a matter of familiarity. There have been thousands of years with white people thinking of themselves as the central subject. So it takes a long time to get used to the fact that you are not the centre of the universe. It's taken us a long time to realize that, as a planet, we are not the centre of the universe. So these are lessons which take time, as we try to decentralize ourselves and realize that other people also consider themselves central, not on the margins.

WACHTEL Is it significant that Natalie, the black character, is the one who does escape from the council estates, who is vertically mobile, and Leah, who is white, stays behind?

SMITH No. I think, in Natalie's case, she's lucky. The question is, what does luck accrue to it? What does luck have to say for itself? Because if you think of it as luck, that's one thing. If you think of it as some kind of innate superiority, that's another thing. And even if it was innate superiority, does that mean that it shouldn't be a quality of aspiration for other people in that council estate? It doesn't mean that everybody can end up like Natalie. That's probably not possible or even desirable. Everyone should have the opportunity, the access. Leah has the access, but she just isn't concerned with the same things Natalie is. But some of the other people in that book, particularly the boys, do not have the same access, do not have the same possibilities offered to them, and that is a matter of concern, I think.

WACHTEL The boys who become the men from the council estate are much worse off than the women. Is that to do with the fact that they're men? At one point, one of the characters says, "I was fine 'til I was ten... Your family would accept me up to the age of ten. At fourteen, your mother would cross the street." So he felt rejected by both black and white communities.

SMITH I think a lot of black men feel that. I have two brothers, and it's very clear to me, as we were growing up in England, that, once they became teenagers, they were in a different situation than I was. It's obvious. I was never stopped by the police in my entire life. My brothers have been stopped continually. So immediately something changes for young black men, and it's incredibly painful, of course, and completely unfair. Things which are really the most superficial kind of accidents— the fact that I'm slightly paler than my brothers, that my nose is more aquiline—makes it a different life, one way or another. It shouldn't be, but it is. And at a very simple level, once the black boys get to a certain age, their teachers are in some way nervous around them. There's a different relationship with those boys than with the girls in the class-room, and that's another problem. So I do feel that they have different opportunities, fewer opportunities often. When I was writing, I was just trying to write about life as I see it—the numbers, I think, will back me up—that in British life anyway, black women have been pro-fessionally much more successful than their male counterparts.

WACHTEL Leah's story opens the book, and it's written almost as a stream of consciousness in contrast to Keisha's, which is more fragmented. When did you first become aware of language as a thing in itself and not just something to convey plot or description?

SMITH You mean in my life or in this novel?

WACHTEL In your life.

SMITH It's a family habit. My brother was a rapper and is now a come-dian. My other brother is still a rapper. There was a lot of wordplay in my house, one way or another, a lot of interest in words. To me, the story is always language. That's always what interests me, a different kind of sentence. To me the sentences of *White Teeth* are very different from *The Autograph Man* and *On Beauty* and the sentences in *NW* are different again. You have to interest yourself in that basic building block of the form; you have to make it interesting to yourself. *NW* was a joy to write because I had so many different ways to construct a sentence. It was a pleasure to realize that different sentences make people feel different ways. Some of them literally repulse people. I find it amazing how angry people can get about a certain form of sentence. They're outraged. A sentence without a speech mark—ahh, they go mad! So I like the idea that language still has that power.

WACHTEL We're also more aware of how time moves in *NW*. When Leah goes through her days, it's almost as if we're in real time. What did you want to do with that?

SMITH All the way through, it struck me again how so much of this book comes from hanging around people and family. On the one hand, I spent a lot of time by myself reading. On the other hand, I spent a lot of time with people. A lot of girlfriends would say to me—and it's ended up in the book—"I feel like I'm getting older quicker. I was twelve for ages and ages, and then I was thirty-four for five seconds. And now I'm thirty-five. I'm going to be thirty-six in twelve seconds. I can't stand it. It's going faster and faster." I wanted to take that idea seri-ously—a book that genuinely did speed up towards the end—because I think that is a feeling people have in their thirties and forties, that time is racing in a way that's quite frightening and suffocating. And at other times—maybe it's particularly true of writers—your childhood feels infinite, a space that went on forever. So perhaps because you had no control of time, when your parents said it's summer holiday, you had no idea when that was going to end, so it felt like an infinite amount of time. I wanted to recreate some of those sensations of time coming, running out of time, sometimes slowing down, time sometimes speeding up, because those are real experiences.

WACHTEL Have you ever had an experience where you felt yourself to be outside of time?

SMITH Yes, actually, yes. It's a very boring reason, probably a neurological one. I had an almost fatal accident once, and I had that experience—I think Ian McEwan describes it in *The Child in Time*—of time slowing down or almost stepping entirely outside of the normal run of things. There's probably a perfectly reasonable scientific explanation for it, but it always struck me as curious.

WACHTEL You've said that the life you lived up 'til age fifteen is more vivid than anything you've lived since. That's not the same as the slowing down of time, but why do you think that is?

SMITH I think it might be a constitutional aspect of writers. I think it's extremely common. If you talk to writers, they will not only return to that period in their work, but they seem to fixate on it, even maybe more extremely if they are graphic novelists and cartoonists. I don't know why that is. Writers seem to feel the injustices of their childhood very keenly. Most people get over it or move on, but they never forget. Unusual perhaps, though I know there are a few other cases, such as Emerson, who also felt like this: I found my childhood to be very beautiful and illuminated, which is an embarrassment to confess because you're meant to say how miserable your childhood was. But my memories are of a very intense, joyful time. So it's useful for me, when I'm trying to write about joy, that I have that access.

WACHTEL *NW* is, among other things, about where we are in time, the hold that the past has on us, inhabiting the present and trying to move ahead. How do you see that balance, if it is a balance, in your own life? Which tense is in the ascendant?

SMITH I feel quite estranged from what I wrote in the past. I feel alienated from it and surprised by it all the time, but, like most people, utterly terrified of the future. So I suppose I'm stuck somewhere in the present time. For me, I guess, redemption lies in my current work, in writing and reading. That seems to keep me grounded.

October 2012
Original interviews produced by Mary Stinson

ACKNOWLEDGMENTS

It was Dan Wells who had the idea for this book. He approached me before Biblioasis was hailed as the Canadian publishing good news story of 2015. When we met, I was impressed by his commitment to publishing an English poetry line in Montreal; his ending up at Rideau Hall when one of his titles won a Governor General's Award, and at the Scotiabank Giller gala when two of his books were finalists, are just signs of divine justice.

As proud as I am of the extraordinary writers I've had the privilege to interview, I'm especially proud of the small team behind *Writers & Company* who've worked on the show for twenty-plus years: co-founding producer Sandra Rabinovitch, 25 years; associate producer Nancy McIlveen, 22 years; and producer Mary Stinson, 20 years. An amazing gift. Not only would there be no book without them, there would be no program. Late last year, Nancy retired and Katy Swailes took over with enthusiasm.

Since this collection looks back over 25 years, I'd like to acknowledge the program's executive producers: Anne Gibson, Susan Feldman, Bernie Lucht, and Tara Mora.

A book wouldn't have been possible without the astuteness and friendship of my editor, Carroll Klein. On this, our third collaboration, she continues to dazzle with her capacity to ferret out meaning from mumble. I'm also thankful for the encouragement of Michael Ondaatje, Nadia Szilvassy and the editors of *Brick* magazine, my agent Jackie Kaiser, CBC's Heather Conway, Geoffrey Taylor and Christine Saratsiotis of the International Festival of Authors. And I appreciate the help of Ian Godfrey, Chris Andrechek, Allana Amlin and Jennifer Warren in the preparation of the manuscript.

It's not often that one has the opportunity to publicly recognize the love and support of family and friends. The Oscars are the prototype, though perhaps not the best model. Still, I am very grateful to Marlene & Frank Cashman, Avivah & Eric Zornberg, Jeannie Wexler, Bernice Eisenstein, Margie Mendell, Marta Braun, Trish Wilson, Lynn Smith, Beth Haddon, Gayla Reid, Andy Wachtel, Barbara Nichol and the unstinting Sherry Simon.

This collection is in some ways retrospective but also, I hope, a gesture towards the future. I feel fortunate to live in a country that believes in public broadcasting and I continue to be honoured by the responses of listeners.

ABOUT THE AUTHOR

Award-winning writer and broadcaster Eleanor Wachtel has earned a reputation for being one of the world's best interviewers. Over 25 years as host of CBC Radio's *Writers & Company*, Eleanor's unique blend of integrity, warmth and intelligence consistently wins the trust of international and high-profile writers. At the end of their conversation in 2013, John le Carré told her, "You do it better than anyone I know." Booker Prize-winning novelist Kazuo Ishiguro stated, "Eleanor Wachtel is one of the very finest interviewers of authors I've come across anywhere in the world."

She also co-founded and hosts CBC Radio's *Wachtel on the Arts*, which features conversations with filmmakers, composers, architects, artists, etc, and for 12 years, she hosted *The Arts Tonight*.

Knopf Canada has published two selections of interviews: *Writers & Company* (1993) and *More Writers & Company* (1996). *Original Minds* (2003, HarperCollins) was inspired by a series devoted to women and men who have made a difference in the way we understand the world—extraordinary writers from the fields of art, science, economics, anthropology and social policy. And in 2007, she published *Random Illuminations* (Goose Lane Editions), a book of reflections, correspondence and conversations with Carol Shields; it won the Independent Publisher Book Award.

Wachtel has received many honours for her contributions to Canadian cultural life: the Jack Award for the promotion of Canadian books and authors, eight honorary degrees (most recently from Concordia, Dalhousie, Simon Fraser, and her alma mater, McGill University), as well as Officer of the Order of Canada.